Pentecostal Theology and
Jonathan Edwards

Systematic Pentecostal and Charismatic Theology

Series editors
Wolfgang Vondey
Daniela C. Augustine

Pentecostal Theology and Jonathan Edwards

Edited by
Steven M. Studebaker and Amos Yong

LONDON • NEW YORK • OXFORD • NEW DELHI • SYDNEY

T&T CLARK
Bloomsbury Publishing Plc
50 Bedford Square, London, WC1B 3DP, UK
1385 Broadway, New York, NY 10018, USA
29 Earlsfort Terrace, Dublin 2, Ireland

BLOOMSBURY, T&T CLARK and the T&T Clark logo are trademarks
of Bloomsbury Publishing Plc

First published in Great Britain 2020
This paperback edition published in 2021

Copyright © Steven M. Studebaker and Amos Yong and contributors, 2020

Steven M. Studebaker and Amos Yong have asserted their rights under the Copyright,
Designs and Patents Act, 1988, to be identified as Editors of this work.

Cover design by Anna Berzovan
Cover image © naqiewei / GettyImages

All rights reserved. No part of this publication may be reproduced or transmitted
in any form or by any means, electronic or mechanical, including photocopying,
recording, or any information storage or retrieval system, without prior permission
in writing from the publishers.

Bloomsbury Publishing Plc does not have any control over, or responsibility for, any
third-party websites referred to or in this book. All Internet addresses given in this
book were correct at the time of going to press. The author and publisher regret any
inconvenience caused if addresses have changed or sites have ceased to exist, but
can accept no responsibility for any such changes.

A catalogue record for this book is available from the British Library.

Library of Congress Cataloging-in-Publication Data
Names: Yong, Amos, editor. | Studebaker, Steven M., 1968- editor.
Title: Pentecostal theology and Jonathan Edwards / edited by Amos Yong and
Steven M. Studebaker.
Description: London; New York: T&T Clark, [2019] | Includes
bibliographical references and index.
Identifiers: LCCN 2019021444 (print) | LCCN 2019981363 (ebook) | ISBN 9780567687876
(hardback) | ISBN 9780567687890 (epub) | ISBN 9780567687883 (pdf)
Subjects: LCSH: Edwards, Jonathan, 1703-1758–Influence. | Pentecostalism–North
America–History. | Pentecostal churches–Doctrines. | Theology, Doctrinal.
Classification: LCC BX7260.E3 P46 2019 (print) | LCC BX7260.E3 (ebook) |
DDC 230/.994–dc23
LC record available at https://lccn.loc.gov/2019021444
LC ebook record available at https://lccn.loc.gov/2019981363

ISBN: HB: 978-0-5676-8787-6
PB: 978-0-5676-9890-2
ePDF: 978-0-5676-8788-3
ePUB: 978-0-5676-8789-0

Typeset by Deanta Global Publishing Services, Chennai, India

To find out more about our authors and books visit www.bloomsbury.com
and sign up for our newsletters.

Contents

Preface	vii
Introduction: Tongues of Pentecost—The Pneumatological Nexus of Pentecostal and Edwardsean Theology *Steven M. Studebaker*	1

Part One Affections and the Spirit

1 "True Religion, in Great Part, Consists of Holy Affections": A Critical Comparison of the Biblical Hermeneutics of Jonathan Edwards and Pentecostals *L. William Oliverio, Jr.*	23
2 Speculative Theology and Spiritual Practice: A Reformed, Catholic, and Pentecostal Conversation on an Aspect of Theological Method *Christopher A. Stephenson*	40
3 Divine Action and Divine Affections: Jonathan Edwards, the Pentecostal and Process Theologian *Joshua D. Reichard*	51
4 Discerning the Signs of the Spirit: Pentecostal Experience Engages Edwardsean Religious Affections *David J. Courey*	68

Part Two God and Salvation

5 The Holy Spirit and the Trinity: A Pentecostal Improvement on Edwards *Steven M. Studebaker*	85
6 Divine and Human Excellencies: Jonathan Edwards and the Challenge of Spirit Christology *Gerald R. McDermott*	102
7 The Spirit of Power and Love: Edwards and Pentecostals on Constructive Pneumatology *Andrew K. Gabriel*	115
8 Transformation by the Spirit in Justification and Sanctification *James M. Henderson*	127

Part Three Church and Culture

9 Edwardsean Charismatic Ecclesiology: The Spirit as Gift *Lisa P. Stephenson*	151
10 Edwards against Himself? Conflicting Appeals to the Writings of Jonathan Edwards during the 1990s Pentecostal-Charismatic Revivals in Toronto and Pensacola *Michael J. McClymond*	163
11 Edwards and Aesthetics: A Critical and Constructive Pentecostal Appropriation *Edmund J. Rybarczyk*	180

Part Four Mission and Witness

12 Jonathan Edwards, Pentecostals, and the Missionary Encounter with
    Native Americans   *Angela Tarango*   197
13 "The Grand Design of God in All Divine Operations": Pentecostal
    Retrieval of Jonathan Edwards' Distinctive Contribution to the Positive
    Significance of Non-Christian Religions   *Tony Richie*   210
14 Voices Crying Out in the Wilderness and the Public Square:
    Redirecting Jonathan Edwards' Teleology of the Political after
    Pentecost   *Amos Yong*   227

Part Five Responses

15 The Promise of Edwardsean Theology   *Oliver D. Crisp*   249
16 The Surprising Work of God Continues   *Amy Plantinga Pauw*   254
17 "Some Thoughts" on the Retrieval of Jonathan Edwards by Pentecostals
    Robert W. Caldwell III   262

Notes on Contributors   271
Index   274

Preface

Due to unforeseen circumstances, the production of this book has undergone a long and arduous six-year process. Our gratitude extends to our graduate assistants who have helped variously in our work: Taylor Murray, Bonghyun Yoo, and Gerhard Mielke from McMaster Divinity College, and Nok Kam and Jeremy Bone of Fuller Seminary. Thanks also to our deans and other administrative heads of our respective institutions, located on almost opposite ends of the North American hemisphere, for supporting our work and scholarship. Last but not least, to our spouses—Sheila Studebaker and Alma Yong—who are patient and forbearing, and always give us the encouragement and strength to be faithful in our vocations. As the book goes to press, we can only marvel at how sagely has been the thought of our Northampton minister and missionary for anticipating and fueling the theological considerations of a revivalist movement that is at the vanguard of a worldwide Christianity almost three centuries later.

For references to Edwards' writings, we use an abbreviated format throughout the text when the reference is to the *Works of Jonathan Edwards Online* provided by the Jonathan Edwards Center (JEC) at Yale University (edwards.yale.edu). The JEC at Yale provides seventy-three volumes of Edwards' work in digital format. The pagination, moreover, of the digital format corresponds with the print copies of the Yale editions of *The Works of Jonathan Edwards*. So, page references in footnotes correspond to the print and digital versions of the Edwards' *Works*. The citations include the following information: Edwards as author, title of the source, reference to *The Works of Jonathan Edwards*, volume number, and page number/s. Thus, a reference to an Edwards writing has this format: Edwards, *Charity and Its Fruits*, WJE 8:125 and Edwards, "Miscellany 614," WJE 18:146–47. In cases where the online edition does not give page numbers, we include the information that will facilitate identifying the reference—for example, Edwards, *Sermon Series II*, 51: no. 412. Rev. 14:14. On several occasions, authors reference other editions of Edwards' works. In those instances, we include the full bibliographic information in the footnote. We also list the bibliographic information in the Yale edition when the editor of a Yale volume's scholarship is the subject of discussion—but not in references to the "Editor's Introduction" in the Yale volumes.

Introduction: Tongues of Pentecost— The Pneumatological Nexus of Pentecostal and Edwardsean Theology

Steven M. Studebaker

Introduction

Though Northampton and Azusa Street seem worlds apart, they are not. Jonathan Edwards may rise as a specter of stern and colorless Calvinism in the minds of many Pentecostals. Unhinged, wild-eyed charis-maniacs are still the view of Pentecostals held by some Evangelicals. Both views are misleading caricatures. Edwards and Pentecostals share common theological interests and heritage in the evangelical tradition.

Jonathan Edwards (1703–58) is one of America's premier theologians that continue to inspire Christians across the theological spectrum and around the world. He set forth rigorous and sophisticated defenses of Calvinism (e.g., sermons like *God Glorified in Man's Dependence* and the treatise *Freedom of the Will*). He was a key leader in the First Great Awakening. Despite lacking the stage presence of George Whitefield, his treatises on revival (e.g., *A Faithful Narrative of the Surprising Work of God* and *Distinguishing Marks of the Work of the Spirit of God*) and spirituality (e.g., *Religious Affections* and *The Nature of True Virtue*) shaped central theological ideas of American Evangelicalism— revivalism, conversionism, and evangelism. Edwards was and remains a formative figure in American theology.[1]

The rise and global expansion of Pentecostalism is one of the leading stories of modern Christian history. Little more than upstart and disparate revivalist groups a century ago, today more than one in four Christians worldwide is a Pentecostal (over 500 million).[2] Pentecostals have established over seven hundred denominations and have members in every traditional Christian church. Initially mostly white and North American, the face of Pentecostalism now is Asian, Latino, and African. Indeed, the influence of Pentecostalism has become so widespread that the Institute for the

---

[1] Douglas A. Sweeney, "Evangelical Tradition in America," in *The Cambridge Companion to Jonathan Edwards*, ed. Stephen J. Stein (New York: Cambridge University Press, 2007), 217.
[2] "Global Christianity: A Report on the Size and Distribution of the World's Christian Population," *Pew Research Center: Religion and Public Life*, December 19, 2011; http://www.pewforum.org/2011/12/19/global-christianity-exec/ (accessed February 27, 2015).

Study of American Evangelicals at Wheaton College indicated that Pentecostalism is becoming the face of "world evangelicalism."[3]

This volume brings "America's theologian" and one of the fastest growing forms of Christianity into dialogue.[4] The primary purposes are theological: Mining Edwards for constructive pentecostal theology, critically evaluating his theology from the perspective of pentecostal theology, and engaging in and contributing to dialogue with Edwards and the issues shaping the wider field of contemporary theology are the goals. Before outlining how each chapter interfaces with these purposes, sketching the trajectories of Edwardsean and pentecostal theological studies and highlighting points of common theological interest establish the basis for this Edwards-pentecostal dialogue.

Edwardsean trajectories

Edwards is one of the foremost figures in American theology. From his day to the end of the nineteenth century, Edwards was a leading figure in American theology. For a time though, during the late nineteenth and first decades of the twentieth century, Edwards fell out of favor among theologians. The popular narrative is that with the advance of modernism and progressive politics in the late nineteenth and early twentieth centuries, Edwards, regarded as little more than a cranky and retrograde "Puritan" preacher, fell out of favor. Vernon Louis Parrington's negative account in "The Anachronism of Jonathan Edwards" often stands as scholarly consensus for the period.[5] Stephen D. Crocco, however, argues that a wider survey of scholarship challenges the decline-renaissance narrative or at least makes it less dramatic. Crocco shows that Edwards remained a sustained subject of critical engagement, including both negative and positive assessments, by scholars of religion and intellectual currents in American history.[6] Although interest in Edwards fell off in erstwhile traditional theological and ecclesial contexts, he became a focus for scholars in religious and philosophical studies.

In the mid-twentieth century, interaction with Edwards' legacy became more widespread and visible. H. Richard Niebuhr's positive discussion of Edwards in *The Kingdom of God in America* (1937) and Ola Winslow's biography of Edwards (1940) were key in this period.[7] Perry Miller's biography of Edwards (1949) and launch of the

---

[3] The institute is now closed, but made this comment in a piece titled "Pentecostalism and the Charismatic Movement," *Wheaton College*: http://www.wheaton.edu/ISAE/Defining-Evangelicalism/Pentecostalism (accessed March 4, 2015).

[4] Robert Jenson titled his book on Edwards, *America's Theologian: A Recommendation of Jonathan Edwards* (New York: Oxford University Press, 1988).

[5] For example, Michael J. McClymond and Gerald R. McDermott, *Theology of Jonathan Edwards* (New York: Oxford University Press, 2012), 637. For Parrington's essay, see Vernon Louis Parrington, *Main Currents in American Thought*, 2 vols. (New York: Harcourt, Brace, and Co., 1927), 1:148–63.

[6] Stephen D. Crocco, "Edwards' Intellectual Legacy," in *The Cambridge Companion to Jonathan Edwards*, ed. Stephen J. Stein (New York: Cambridge University Press, 2007), 301 and 305–9.

[7] H. Richard Niebuhr, *The Kingdom of God in America* (Chicago, IL: Willett, Clark, and Co., 1937) and Ola Winslow, *Jonathan Edwards, 1703–1758: A Biography* (New York: Macmillan, 1940).

publication of *The Works of Jonathan Edwards* by Yale University, however, sparked the renewal in Edwards studies that continues today.[8] Miller argued that Edwards was not a narrow-minded provincial, but a cosmopolitan and avant-garde philosopher and theologian. Today, Edwards is probably the most studied American religious thinker.[9] But why did Edwards draw the attention of scholars like Niebuhr and Miller during the mid-twentieth century? Part of the answer is the tarnish political and theological liberalism received in the first half of the twentieth century. Two world wars undermined the self-confidence of secular and religious liberalism. Figures like Edwards, who recognized the unsavory aspects of human nature and a source of redemption arising, not in itself but only in and from God, returned to credibility.[10]

Although Edwards never disappeared from academic discourse and Miller initiated a genuine renewal in Edwards studies, tracing trajectories of scholarship is difficult because they are so varied. From Perry Miller's promotion of Edwards as a substantial American thinker and publication of *Freedom of the Will* (1957), the first volume of Yale's *The Works of Jonathan Edwards*, through the 1980s scholarship on Edwards was sporadic and focused on issues related to philosophy, aesthetics, ethics, and religious psychology and experience.[11] Works on Edwards' view and appreciation of nature extended this stream of research, though also took it in new directions.[12] The publications during this period more or less reflect the subject matter of the new Yale volumes and the research orientations initiated by Miller. Edwards' *Religious Affections* correspond with Terrence Erdt's and Harold P. Simonson's work on the sense of the heart.[13] Allen C. Guelzo's critical appraisal and history of influence of Edwards' view of the human will correlates with Yale's *Freedom of the Will*.[14] Edwards' contribution to areas of religious psychology and practices (aesthetics and ethics) and his relationship to the emergence of modernism in eighteenth-century New England were the most

---

[8] Miller's biography was a prime catalyst for the Edwards renaissance, *Jonathan Edwards* (1949; reprint, New York: Delta, 1967).

[9] Kenneth P. Minkema, "Jonathan Edwards in the Twentieth Century," *Journal of the Evangelical Theological Society* 47, no. 4 (2004): 659–87.

[10] Crocco, "Edwards' Intellectual Legacy," 315–16.

[11] For example, Douglas J. Elwood, *The Philosophical Theology of Jonathan Edwards* (New York: Columbia University Press, 1960); Roland André Delattre, *Beauty and Sensibility in the Thought of Jonathan Edwards: A Essay in Aesthetics and Theological Ethics* (New Haven, CT: Yale University Press, 1968); Clyde A. Holbrook, *The Ethics of Jonathan Edwards: Morality and Aesthetics* (Ann Arbor: University of Michigan Press, 1973); and Norman S. Fiering, *Jonathan Edwards' Moral Thought and Its British Context* (Chapel Hill: The University of North Carolina Press, 1981).

[12] Paula Cooey, *Jonathan Edwards on Nature and Destiny: A Systematic Analysis* (Lewiston, NY: Edwin Mellen, 1985); Clyde A. Holbrook, *Jonathan Edwards, the Valley and Nature: An Interpretive Essay* (Lewisburg, PA: Bucknell University Press, 1987), and more recently, Avihu Zakai, "Jonathan Edwards and the Language of Nature: The Re-Enchantment of the World in the Age of Scientific Reasoning," *The Journal of Religious History* 26, no. 1 (2002): 15–41 and "The Theological Origins of Jonathan Edwards' Philosophy of Nature," *Journal of Ecclesiastical History* 60, no. 4 (2009): 708–24.

[13] Terrence Erdt, *Jonathan Edwards: Art and the Sense of the Heart* (Amherst: University of Massachusetts Press, 1980) and Harold P. Simonson, *Jonathan Edwards: Theologian of the Heart* (Macon, GA: Mercer University Press, 1982).

[14] Allen C. Guelzo, *Edwards on the Will: A Century of American Debate* (Middletown, CT: Wesleyan University Press, 1989).

common topics of this period of Edwards studies. These studies tended to fall within the genre of intellectual history and religious studies.

The renewal in Edwards studies gained major momentum in the late 1980s. The years 1988 and 1989 saw the publication of important monographs by Allen C. Guelzo, Robert W. Jenson, Sang Hyun Lee, and Nathan O. Hatch and Harry S. Stout's edited volume.[15] Paul Ramsey was pivotal moreover. A widely influential Christian ethicist at Princeton University, his editorial work on and introduction to Edwards' *Ethical Writings* (1989), volume eight of Yale's *The Works of Jonathan Edwards*, provided a modern critical edition of one of the richest theological resources in Edwards' writings. The late 1980s and especially the decade of the 1990s also saw the rise of Yale and Princeton as centers of Edwards studies. Interest in Edwards radiated from Yale and Princeton into graduate programs in universities and seminaries. Within a decade, it yielded a rich harvest of new historical, theological, and literary scholarship on Edwards. The critical concentration of this scholarly activity and interest in Edwards at Yale and Princeton catalyzed the productivity in Edwards studies that took place during the 1990s.

These scholars and their work also marked a renewal of theological interest in Edwards. In the decades after Miller, the majority of research considered Edwards' relationship to modern and enlightenment intellectual trends and from literary and cultural perspectives.[16] Conrad Cherry's and Bruce M. Stephens' monographs are important, but isolated, theological investigations of Edwards during this period. Jenson's *America's Theologian* and Lee's *The Philosophical Theology of Jonathan Edwards* (both appearing in 1988) re-invigorated philosophical and theological investigations of Edwards' thought. Stephen R. Holmes and Oliver Crisp, for example, though challenging Lee's account of Edwards' dispositional ontology, build on the trajectory of research initiated by Lee's work.[17] Anri Morimoto's ecumenical theology of Edwards and Amy Plantinga Pauw' and William J. Danaher, Jr.'s projects in Edwards' trinitarian theology represent Yale's and Princeton's, as well as Lee's, formative influence.[18]

---

[15] Ibid.; Jenson, *America's Theologian*; Sang Hyun Lee, *The Philosophical Theology of Jonathan Edwards*, rev. ed. (Princeton, NJ: Princeton University Press, 2000); and Nathan O. Hatch and Harry S. Stout, *Jonathan Edwards and the American Experience* (New York: Oxford University Press, 1988).

[16] Examples of literary scholarship on Edwards are Sacvan Bercovitch, *Typology and Early American Literature* (Amherst: University of Massachusetts Press, 1972) and Jennifer Leader, *Knowing, Seeing, Being: Jonathan Edwards, Emily Dickinson, Marianne Moore and the American Typological Tradition* (Amherst: University of Massachusetts Press, 2016).

[17] Stephen R. Holmes, *God of Grace and God of Glory: An Account of the Theology of Jonathan Edwards* (Grand Rapids, MI: Eerdmans, 2001) and Oliver D. Crisp, *Jonathan Edwards and Creation* (New York: Oxford University Press, 2012). Lee can also be seen as building on the work of Douglas Elwood's panentheistic interpretation of Edwards—*The Philosophical Theology of Jonathan Edwards*.

[18] Anri Morimoto, *Jonathan Edwards and the Catholic Vision of Salvation* (University Park: The Pennsylvania State University Press, 1995); Amy Plantinga Pauw, *"The Supreme Harmony of All": The Trinitarian Theology of Jonathan Edwards* (Grand Rapids, MI: Eerdmans, 2002); and William J. Danaher, Jr., *The Trinitarian Ethics of Jonathan Edwards* (Louisville: Westminster John Knox, 2004). Although studying at Marquette University, Lee's work, along with Plantinga Pauw's, was also inspirational and foundational to my dissertation on Edwards' trinitarian theology. Following in Morimoto's ecumenical style, my book *The Trinitarian Vision of Jonathan Edwards and David Coffey* (Amherst: Cambria, 2011) shows the strong continuities between Reformed Protestant Edwards and Rahnerian Coffey on the Trinity, pneumatology, and grace.

Phil C. Zylla's pastoral theology of Edwards' virtue ethics shows both the continuation of the earlier aesthetics and ethics trajectory of scholarship and the ongoing influence of Princeton and Lee in the field of Edwards studies.[19] Gerard R. McDermott's case for Edwards as a public theologian who frequently commented on social, economic, and political issues was also a seminal contribution to this generative period of Edwardsean scholarship.[20] McDermott's ongoing work includes Edwards' theology of religion, an edited volume that brings eastern European (principally Hungarian) theologians into dialogue with Edwards, co-production with Michael McClymond of the exceptional *Theology of Jonathan Edwards*, and additional work with Ronald Story on Edwards' public theology and view of social justice.[21]

The emergence of theological work on Edwards did not mean the abandonment of research on Edwards' relationship to modern philosophical movements. Indeed, it was even extended in postmodern directions. Leon Chai explored Edwards' relationship to the Enlightenment's quest for epistemic certainty (1998).[22] In the same year as Chai, Michael McClymond argued that Edwards' theology of spiritual perception grounded Christian faith on foundations that synthesize the two epistemological trajectories of the Enlightenment—rationalism and subjectivism—and thereby provided an apologetic for the Christian faith that retained its theological basis but was also credible in the emerging intellectual context of the Enlightenment.[23] Like McClymond, Gerald McDermott shows that Edwards developed a theology of religion in conversation with Enlightenment critiques of Christianity.[24] Steven H. Daniel dialogues with Edwards' philosophy and postmodern, poststructuralist, semiotics.[25] On the basis of analytic philosophy and theology, Oliver Crisp challenges Lee's dispositional ontology and

---

[19] Phil C. Zylla, *Virtue as Consent to Being: A Pastoral-Theological Perspective on Jonathan Edwards' Construct of Virtue* (Eugene: Pickwick, 2011).

[20] Gerald R. McDermott, *One Holy and Happy Society: The Public Theology of Jonathan Edwards* (University Park: Pennsylvania State University Press, 1992).

[21] For Edwards and theology of religions, see Gerald R. McDermott, *Jonathan Edwards Confronts the Gods: Christian Theology, Enlightenment Religion, and Non-Christian Faiths* (New York: Oxford University Press, 2000). For the edited volume with eastern European theologians dialoguing with Edwards, see Gerald R. McDermott, ed., *Understanding Jonathan Edwards: An Introduction to America's Theologian* (New York: Oxford University Press, 2009); and for Edwards and social justice see Gerald R. McDermott with Ronald Story, *The Other Jonathan Edwards: Selected Writings on Society, Love, and Justice* (Amherst: University of Massachusetts Press, 2015).

[22] Leon Chai, *Jonathan Edwards and the Limits of Enlightenment Philosophy* (New York: Oxford University Press, 1998).

[23] Michael J. McClymond, *Encounters with God: An Approach to the Theology of Jonathan Edwards* (New York: Oxford University Press, 1998).

[24] McDermott, *Jonathan Edwards Confronts the Gods*. Their work inspired my research on Edwards that highlights the way Enlightenment challenges to the Trinity as well as broader philosophical movements provided the context for his trinitarian theology: Studebaker, *Jonathan Edwards' Social Augustinian Trinitarianism in Historical and Contemporary Perspective* (Piscataway, NJ: Gorgias, 2008).

[25] Steven H. Daniel, *The Philosophy of Jonathan Edwards: A Study in Divine Semiotics* (Bloomington: Indiana University Press, 1994). Appearing earlier, R. C. DeProspo challenged modern reading of Edwards promoted by Perry Miller and suggested that a theistic dualism is fundamental to Edwards rather than Enlightenment intellectual issues. See R. C. DeProspo, *Theism in the Discourse of Jonathan Edwards* (Cranbury, NJ: University of Delaware Press, 1985).

argues that Edwards embraces a type of Neoplatonic panentheism.[26] This scholarship carries on the line of historical and contextual research led by Miller.

The beginning of the new millennium brought expanding interest and publications on Edwards. The year 2003, the tercentenary of Edwards' birth, saw George M. Marsden's biography of Edwards. Marsden's *Jonathan Edwards* was not only a crowning achievement for the more or less decade of the late 1980s and 1990s expansion of Edwards' studies but also the new benchmark for an entryway to Edwards' life, thought, and background.[27] McClymond and McDermott's *Theology of Jonathan Edwards* (2012) joins with Marsden's biography as the starting point for research on Edwards' theology.

Edwards also draws international attention. Although known as "America's theologian," Edwards was never only that. He was first a Briton. His writings gained wide readership and influence in England, Wales, and Scotland as well as in Holland during his own lifetime and afterward.[28] The United Kingdom has been particularly fertile for Edwards studies, yielding scholars like Paul Helm, Oliver Crisp, Stephen R. Holmes, W. Ross Hastings, and Josh Moody. Interest in Edwards is part of the rise of global Christianity as well. Centers for Edwards studies can be found in Africa, Germany, Belgium, Poland, Hungary, Japan, Australia, Brazil, as well as two in the United States (the Jonathan Edwards Center at Yale University and the Jonathan Edwards Center at Trinity Evangelical Divinity School).[29] Edwards also engenders significant interest among Korean and Chinese scholars and students.[30] In recent years, moreover, significant numbers of Edwards' writings and works on Edwards have been translated into Portuguese.[31]

The first decade of the twenty-first century, moreover, saw Edwards become a favorite of the re-invigorated and even militant Calvinism popular among younger Evangelicals. Colin Hansen describes this movement in *Young, Restless, and Reformed: A Journalist's Journey with the New Calvinists* (Wheaton: Crossway, 2008), which has on its cover a T-Shirt declaring "Jonathan Edwards is My Homeboy."[32] But the return

---

[26] Crisp, *Jonathan Edwards and Creation*.

[27] George M. Marsden, *Jonathan Edwards: A Life* (New Haven, CT: Yale University Press, 2003).

[28] Kelly Van Andel, Adriaan C. Neele, and Kenneth P. Minkema, eds., *Jonathan Edwards and Scotland* (Edinburgh: Dunedin Academic, 2011) and D. W. Bebbington, "The Reputation of Edwards Abroad," in *The Cambridge Companion to Jonathan Edwards*, ed. Stephen J. Stein (New York: Cambridge University Press, 2007), 243–44.

[29] "Global Centers," http://edwards.yale.edu/Global+centers, Jonathan Edwards Center at Yale University (accessed March 5, 2015).

[30] Korean translation of primary Edwards' texts as well as secondary scholarship is massive. Korean scholars have produced significant numbers of monographs on Edwards—for example, Seng-Kong Tan, *Fullness Received and Returned: Trinity and Participation in Jonathan Edwards* (Minneapolis: Fortress, 2014). For an account of Edwards among Asian theologians, see Anri Morimoto, "An Edwardsean Lost and Found: The Legacy of Jonathan Edwards in Asia," in *After Jonathan Edwards: The Course of the New England Theology*, ed. Oliver D. Crisp and Douglas A. Sweeney (New York: Oxford University Press, 2012), 225–36.

[31] Ken Minkema and Adriaan Neele, "Recent Publications," *Jonathan Edwards Studies* 4, no. 1 (2014): 147–48.

[32] For a discussion of the rise of Edwards among more or less conservative evangelical Calvinists, see D. G. Hart, "Before the Young, Restless, and Reformed: Edwards' Appeal to Post-World War II Evangelicals," in *After Jonathan Edwards: The Course of the New England Theology*, ed. Oliver D. Crisp and Douglas A. Sweeney (New York: Oxford University Press, 2012), 237–53.

to Edwards among evangelical scholars has been slower than among their mainline counterparts. The irony is that "Evangelicals often consider Jonathan Edwards . . . to be 'their' theologian, the one thinker in the history of Christian thought who probably 'got it right,'" notes Gerald R. McDermott.[33] The renewal in Edwards studies, however, did not begin with Evangelicals, but with an agnostic professor at Harvard University—Perry Miller.

Evangelicals championing Edwards like his emphasis on divine providence, hard-nosed apologetic toward Arminianism, fidelity to orthodox Christian doctrines during a time of perceived doctrinal decay, zeal for converting souls to Christ, and spiritual vigor. John Gerstner's *Steps to Salvation: The Evangelistic Message of Jonathan Edwards* (Philadelphia: Westminster, 1959) was an early and important work in the recovery of Edwards for the evangelical community. Richard Lovelace, professor at Gordon-Conwell Theological Seminary, made Edwards an important resource for church renewal/revival and Christian spirituality in *Dynamics of Spiritual Life: An Evangelical Theology of Renewal* (Downers Grove: InterVarsity Press, 1979). More recently, church leaders such as John Piper and Sam Storms have become strong proponents of Edwards' theology and vision of Christian spirituality for church renewal. Piper became the influential pastor of Bethlehem Baptist Church in Minneapolis. A promoter of Edwards for his evangelical orthodoxy, he also emphasizes his theology of divine happiness as the chief end of human life. This Edwardsean theology of happiness is the basis of Piper's "Desiring God Ministries" and Sam Storms' endorsement of "Christian hedonism" on his "Enjoying God Blog."[34]

The evangelical trajectory also includes notable scholars such as Robert W. Caldwell III, D. G. Hart, W. Ross Hastings, Paul Helm, Josh Moody, and Kyle Strobel, as well as thoughtful and popular presentations of Edwards' theology for ministry leaders by theologians such as Michael A. G. Haykin and Stephen J. Nichols.[35] These scholars not only produce critical and constructive work in Edwards' theology but also present it in a way useful for ministry leaders. Douglas A. Sweeney's academic work on Edwards and the wider evangelical tradition as well as leadership of the Jonathan Edwards

---

[33] Gerald R. McDermott, "Jonathan Edwards on Justification by Faith—More Protestant or Catholic?" *Pro Ecclesia* 17, no. 1 (2008): 92.

[34] See http://www.desiringgod.org/ and http://www.samstorms.com/enjoying-god-blog. Also see John Piper and Justin Taylor, *A God-Entranced Vision of All Things: The Legacy of Jonathan Edwards* (Wheaton, IL: Crossway, 2004) and C. Samuel Storms, *Signs of the Spirit: An Interpretation of Jonathan Edwards' "Religious Affections"* (Wheaton, IL: Crossway, 2007).

[35] Robert W. Caldwell III, *Communion in the Spirit: The Holy Spirit as Bond of Union in the Theology of Jonathan Edwards* (Milton Keynes: Paternoster, 2006); D. G. Hart, Sean Michael Lucas, and Stephen J. Nichols, eds., *The Legacy of Jonathan Edwards: American Religion and the Evangelical Tradition* (Grand Rapids, MI: Baker, Academic, 2003); W. Ross Hastings, *Jonathan Edwards and the Life of God: Toward an Evangelical Theology of Participation* (Minneapolis, MN: Fortress, 2015); Paul Helm and Oliver D. Crisp, eds., *Jonathan Edwards: Philosophical Theologian* (Burlington, VT: Ashgate, 2003); Josh Moody, ed., *Jonathan Edwards and Justification* (Wheaton, IL: Crossway, 2012) and *Jonathan Edwards and the Enlightenment: Knowing the Presence of God* (Lanham, MD: University Press of America, 2005); Kyle Strobel, *Jonathan Edwards' Theology: A Reinterpretation* (London: Bloomsbury, 2013) and *Formed for the Glory of God: Learning from the Spiritual Practices of Jonathan Edwards* (Downers Grove: IVP, 2013); Michael A. G. Haykin, *Jonathan Edwards: The Holy Spirit in Revival* (Darlington: Evangelical, 2005); and Stephen J. Nichols, *Heaven on Earth: Capturing Jonathan Edwards' Vision of Living in Between* (Wheaton, IL: Crossway, 2006).

Center at Trinity Evangelical Divinity School exemplifies evangelical scholarship that serves the church.[36]

The Jonathan Edwards Center at Yale University describes Edwards as "America's premier theologian" and further remarks that "Edwards has proven to be the most influential religious thinker in American history."[37] Yale University's *The Works of Jonathan Edwards Online* (1957–2008) makes available in digital online format seventy-three volumes of Edwards' writings. This project alone fortifies the claim that Edwards was and remains an important figure in North American theology. Moreover, books, articles, and conferences on Edwards have blossomed in the past thirty years and the Jonathan Edwards Center at Yale University launched the online journal *Jonathan Edwards Studies* in 2011.[38] Although Edwards does not embody the totality of American or even of evangelical theology, his status as one of their most prominent representatives is firm.

Pentecostal trajectories

Although a relatively young movement in the sweep of Christian history, Pentecostalism has three major historical forms that now more or less coexist—Classical Pentecostalism, the Charismatic movement, and the Third Wave or Neo-charismatic movement. The Azusa Street Revivals of 1906–09 and 1911–12 led by William J. Seymour effectively launched Classical Pentecostalism as a worldwide movement. The distinguishing belief of Classical Pentecostalism is that Spirit baptism is a post-conversion experience for empowered ministry evidenced by speaking in tongues. Representative denominations include the International Pentecostal Holiness Church, Church of God in Christ, the Church of God (Cleveland), the Assemblies of God, the Pentecostal Assemblies of Canada, and the International Church of the Foursquare Gospel.

The Charismatic movement was the first major development in Pentecostalism. The movement arose in the 1950s and remained strong through the 1970s. Sharing much

---

[36] Douglas A. Sweeney, ed., *The "Miscellanies" (Entry nos. 1153–1360), The Works of Jonathan Edwards*, vol. 23 (New Haven, CT: Yale University Press, 2004), and his published books such as *Nathaniel Taylor, New Haven Theology, and the Legacy of Jonathan Edwards* (New York: Oxford University Press, 2003), *Jonathan Edwards and the Ministry of the Word: A Model of Faith and Thought* (Downers Grove: IVP Academic, 2009), *Edwards the Exegete: Biblical Interpretation and Anglo-Protestant Culture on the Edge of the Enlightenment* (New York: Oxford University Press, 2015), and, edited with Oliver D. Crisp, *After Jonathan Edwards: The Courses of the New England Theology* (New York: Oxford University Press, 2012).

[37] Douglas Sweeney, "'Jonathan Edwards' Legacy," *Jonathan Edwards Center at Yale University*, http://edwards.yale.edu/research/about-edwards/legacy (accessed March 6, 2015).

[38] See the article and book bibliographies available on the Jonathan Edwards Center at Yale University, which lists over 900 and 600, respectively (http://edwards.yale.edu/node/100). In addition to providing access to the digitized writings of Edwards, the Edwards Center at Yale sponsors a journal dedicated to Edwards—*Jonathan Edwards Studies*. For a more thorough source through 2005, see Max X. Lesser, *Reading Jonathan Edwards: An Annotated Bibliography in Three Parts, 1729–2005* (Grand Rapids, MI: Eerdmans, 2008). For the online journal, *Jonathan Edwards Studies*, see http://jestudies.yale.edu/index.php/journal/index

in common with Classical Pentecostals, Charismatics, however, came from mainline Protestant denominations and the Catholic Church rather than evangelical churches. They embraced the experience of Spirit baptism, but were less tied to the doctrine of subsequence and speaking in tongues as its initial evidence. Rather than leaving their traditional churches and joining pentecostal ones, as did the earlier Pentecostals, Charismatics tended to remain within their denominations.

The early 1980s saw the emergence of the Neo-charismatic movement or "Third Wave" (the first and second waves being Classical Pentecostalism and the Charismatic Renewal). Key leaders are C. Peter Wagner (1930–), who coined the term "Third Wave" to refer to the spread of charismatic experience and spirituality in evangelical churches, and John Wimber (1934–97), who founded the Vineyard Christian Fellowship in Anaheim, California, the movement's most visible organization. The emphasis on spiritual renewal through the Holy Spirit without the traditional pentecostal doctrine of Spirit baptism appealed to Christians within evangelical churches in North America and Britain. Third Wavers often have no clear connection with traditional pentecostal and Charismatic Renewal churches, but nevertheless embrace charismatic forms of spiritual experience and worship.

The three-stage story of—Classical Pentecostalism, Charismatic Movement, and the Third Wave—is mainly a North American narrative of Pentecostalism. This project arose for the most part from this particular pentecostal history. Similar trends and characteristics, nevertheless, shape Pentecostalism worldwide because pentecostal missionaries exported Pentecostalism around the world during the twentieth century. The themes explored here, even if initially informed by the North American narrative, therefore, have value to the global field of pentecostal studies and contemporary theology. The theological vision of Pentecostalism of this volume, moreover, transcends the North American narrative. Pentecostalism has a global narrative with at least two major plot lines.

First, Pentecostalism both emerged and spread around the globe. Azusa may have been the epicenter and clearinghouse of early Pentecostalism, but it was not the only center and exclusive source of the movement. Pentecostal revivals took place in Korea (1903), China (1908), and India (in Tamil Nadu in 1860–65, in Travancore in 1873–81, and with Pandita Ramabai Mukti's Mission in 1905–07) prior to and independent of the Azusa Street Revival.[39] Canadian Pentecostalism also developed centers of revival independent and distinct from its American counterpart.[40]

Second, the history of contemporary Pentecostalism parallels and indeed plays a key role in the macro-trends shaping global Christianity. While God was "dying" in Europe and North America and the march of secularization marginalizing the church, the worldwide church underwent "its greatest period of expansion ever."[41] More and

---

[39] Allan Anderson, "Revising Pentecostal History in Global Perspective," in *Asian and Pentecostal: The Charismatic Face of Christianity in Asia*, ed. Allan Anderson and Edmond Tang (Baguio City: Regnum, 2005), 152–56.

[40] Michael Wilkinson and Peter Althouse, eds., *Winds from the North: Canadian Contributions to the Pentecostal Movement* (Leiden: Brill, 2010).

[41] Kenneth Hylson-Smith, *To the Ends of the Earth: The Globalization of Christianity* (London: Paternoster, 2007), xxv.

more Christianity is no longer a religion of Western Europeans and North Americans but the faith of the Global South.[42] Philip Jenkins forecasts that the Global church will undergo (and is already undergoing) a massive geographical shift by 2050.[43] Given declining or low-growth population trends and declining numbers of Christians in the West and increasing populations and numbers of Christians in Latin America, sub-Saharan Africa, and parts of Asia, the center of the Christian faith (at least numerically) has shifted to the Global South.[44] Already more Catholic baptisms occur each year in the Philippines than in France, Spain, Italy, and Poland together, and by the middle of the twenty-first century, one African country, Uganda, could have "more active church members than the four or five largest European nations combined."[45] The percentage of the world's population who are Christians has never been higher.[46] What is more, as the face of Christianity became global it also became more pentecostal.

A key factor in the globalization of Christianity, pentecostal theology has also become a global conversation. Consequently, local and indigenous voices outside the Western theological tradition increasingly shape its agenda and content.[47] Pentecostal thinkers, especially ones shaped by North American pentecostal traditions, should endeavor to engage the wider global conversation. At the same time, however, engaging their local and indigenous theological traditions, which includes Edwards, remains vital. Interest in Edwards is part of the rise of global Christianity as well, as already noted in the proliferation of research centers and scholarship around the world.

Along with the pentecostal movement, pentecostal scholarship passed through several evolutions from the middle decades of the twentieth century to the early twenty-first century.[48] The early Pentecostals embodied the trajectory of American Evangelicalism that emphasized spiritual experience and piety. By the time they needed to formulate doctrine and theology, two options—Liberalism and Fundamentalism—were available. The first formal pentecostal theologies readily adopted the Bible doctrines method of theology popular among the Fundamentalists and later the

---

[42] Philip Jenkins, *The Next Christendom: The Coming of Global Christianity*, revised and expanded edition (New York: Oxford University Press, 2007), 91–105.
[43] Ibid., 79–105. Jenkins is acutely aware of the difficulties associated with statistics and extrapolation (especially in the area of determining religious affiliation), but is convinced that the major trends should hold (ibid., 85–89).
[44] In the United States, however, population is expected to grow steadily and Christian adherence to remain stable (buoyed in part by the massive immigration of people from Latin America). Ibid., 99–105.
[45] Ibid., 91–92. The latter claim obviously assumes continuing trends and the absence of a Christian revival in Europe.
[46] Hylson-Smith, *To the Ends of the Earth*, 165–66.
[47] Simon Chan, *Liturgical Theology: The Church as Worshiping Community* (Downers Grove: IVP, 2006) and *Grassroots Asian Theology: Thinking the Faith from the Ground Up* (Downers Grove: IVP, 2014); Clifton R. Clarke, *African Christology: Jesus in Post-Missionary African Christianity* (Eugene: Pickwick, 2011); and Clifton R. Clarke, ed., *Pentecostal Theology in Africa* (Eugene: Pickwick, 2014).
[48] This discussion of the development of pentecostal scholarship derives from L. William Oliverio, Jr., *Theological Hermeneutics in the Classical Pentecostal Tradition*, Global Pentecostal and Charismatic Studies 12 (2012; reprint, Boston: Brill, 2015), chapters 2–6, and Steven M. Studebaker, *From Pentecost to the Triune God: A Pentecostal Trinitarian Theology* (Grand Rapids, MI: Eerdmans, 2012), 19–26.

Neo-Evangelicals, which followed in the tradition of Protestant scholasticism developed at Princeton by Charles Hodge.[49]

The genesis of critical pentecostal scholarship was the 1970s. Developing in relationship with evangelical theology of the time gave pentecostal theology an apologetic edge. Pentecostal scholarship through the late 1980s was occupied with defending the classical pentecostal doctrine that Spirit baptism is subsequent to conversion, evidenced by speaking in tongues, and for the purpose of charismatic empowerment vis-à-vis criticisms from evangelical theologians.[50] Apologetics for this doctrine raised two hermeneutical issues: the legitimacy of basing doctrine on historical narratives and the role of experience in theology.[51] The latter topic in particular connects with Edwards' theology of religious affections.

As for Edwards studies, the 1980s and 1990s were formative for pentecostal scholarship. Pentecostal scholars began to move beyond the confines of evangelical approaches to theology and the biblical-theological issues related to the pentecostal interpretation of Luke-Acts and doctrines of Spirit baptism and speaking in tongues. Increasing numbers of Pentecostals, moreover, pursued doctoral degrees in non-evangelical institutions. Doing so facilitated their interaction with theological issues that differed from those that drove the pentecostal-evangelical debates. Pentecostal theologians engaged major figures in the Protestant, Catholic, and Orthodox traditions.[52] They made contributions to biblical studies, historical theology, systematic theology, contemporary theology, theological hermeneutics, and philosophy.[53]

---

[49] An excellent example and widely popular text was Myer Pearlman, *Knowing the Doctrines of the Bible* (1937; reprint, Springfield, MO: GPH, 1981). For an account of this period of pentecostal theology, see Oliverio, *Theological Hermeneutics in the Classical Pentecostal Tradition*, 83–131. Earlier Pentecostals pursued theological self-understanding, but the first more or less formal efforts to outline a pentecostal systematic theology began to appear mid-century. For earlier pentecostal theological reflection, see Douglas G. Jacobsen, *Thinking in the Spirit: Theologies of the Early Pentecostal Movement* (Bloomington: Indiana University Press, 2003) and Oliverio, *Theological Hermeneutics*, 31–82.

[50] For example, Roger Stronstad used redaction criticism to support the classical pentecostal interpretation of Luke-Acts and theology of Spirit baptism in *The Charismatic Theology of St. Luke* (Peabody, MA: Hendrickson, 1984). A good starting point for entering this discussion is Chad Owen Brand, ed., *Perspectives on Spirit Baptism: Five Views* (Nashville, TN: Broadman & Holman, 2004).

[51] For example, Robert P. Menzies, *The Development of Early Christian Pneumatology with Special Reference to Luke-Acts*, Journal for the Study of the New Testament Supplement Series 54 (Sheffield: Sheffield Academic Press, 1991) and Howard M. Ervin, "Hermeneutics: A Pentecostal Option," *Pneuma: The Journal of the Society for Pentecostal Studies* 3, no. 2 (1981): 11–25.

[52] See Terry L. Cross, *Dialectic in Karl Barth's Doctrine of God* (New York: Peter Lang, 2001); Peter Althouse, *Spirit of the Last Days: Pentecostal Eschatology in Conversation with Jürgen Moltmann* (London: Sheffield Academic Press, 2003); Wolfgang Vondey, *Heribert Mühlen: His Theology and Praxis. A New Profile for the Church* (Lanham, MD: University of America Press, 2004); and Edmund J. Rybarczyk, *Beyond Salvation: Eastern Orthodoxy and Classical Pentecostalism on Becoming Like Christ* (Waynesboro, GA: Paternoster, 2004). Amos Yong engaged Catholic theologian Donald Gelpi as well as American philosopher Charles S. Pierce and philosopher-theologian Robert Cummings Neville in *Discerning the Spirit(s): A Pentecostal-Charismatic Contribution to Christian Theology of Religions* (Sheffield: Sheffield Academic Press, 2000).

[53] Select examples are in order of field listed above: Jerry Camery-Hoggatt, *Irony in Mark's Gospel: Text and Subtext* (New York: Cambridge University Press, 1992); John Christopher Thomas, *Pentecostal Commentary on 1 John, 2 John, 3 John* (New York: T & T Clark, 2004);

Pentecostal scholars also took up historical, political, and sociological projects.[54] Dialoguing with and contributing to wider fields of theological discourse from the perspective of pentecostal convictions, moreover, marks an important development in pentecostal theology.

This volume advances the maturation of critical, constructive, and ecumenical-pentecostal theology. Jonathan Edwards, as a Calvinist Puritan, is perhaps not the most likely figure for pentecostal engagement. Edwards is, however, part of the North American evangelical tradition. Although contemporary pentecostal theologians maintain that pentecostal theology is distinct from the evangelical tradition, Pentecostalism, at least its North American varieties, emerged from within and often out of evangelical revival groups. These latter movements, both in their Wesleyan-Holiness and Reformed forms, were heirs to Edwards' contribution to the revival tradition of North America. Thus, an irony characterizes the relationship between Edwards and pentecostal theology today. On the one hand, Edwards and Pentecostals share a historical nexus. Edwards was a formative figure in the genesis of North American revivalism. Pentecostalism emerged within the historical and theological context of North American revivalism. But, on the other hand, a contemporary disparity characterizes Edwards and contemporary pentecostal theologians. Few contemporary pentecostal theologians want to be lumped together with the conservative evangelical theology that counts Edwards as one of its chief forerunners. Given that Edwards' primary influence was in the North American evangelical tradition and that the forms of Pentecostalism that share the most historical and theological affinity with him are North American, the pentecostal dialogue partners in this volume derive from North American pentecostal traditions—for example, Church of God, Assemblies of God, and Pentecostal Assemblies of Canada. The North American context of this dialogue (subject and interlocutors) is, therefore, unavoidable.

Though short of a mature tradition, Pentecostalism can no longer be considered a theological upstart or only a movement concerned with charismatic experience. Pentecostal theology today is ecumenical, constructive, and global.[55] This project

---

Graham H. Twelftree, *People of the Spirit: Exploring Luke's View of the Church* (Grand Rapids, MI: Baker Academic, 2009); Dale M. Coulter, *Per visibilia ad invisibilia: Theological Method in Richard of St. Victor (d. 1173)*, Bibliotheca Victorina 19 (Turnhout: Brepols, 2006); Andrew K. Gabriel, *The Lord Is the Spirit: The Holy Spirit and the Divine Attributes* (Eugene, OR: Pickwick, 2011); Néstor Medina, *Mestizaje: (Re)Mapping Race, Culture, and Faith in Latina/o Catholicism* (Maryknoll: Orbis, 2009); Kenneth J. Archer, *A Pentecostal Hermeneutic: Spirit, Scripture, and Community* (Cleveland, TN: CPT, 2009); James K. A. Smith, *Thinking in Tongues: Pentecostal Contributions to Christian Philosophy*, Pentecostal Manifestos (Grand Rapids, MI: Eerdmans, 2010); and Amos Yong, *Spirit-Word-Community: Theological Hermeneutics in Trinitarian Perspective* (Eugene, OR: Wipf & Stock, 2002).

54 Daniela C. Augustine, *Pentecost, Hospitality, and Transfiguration: Toward a Spirit-inspired Vision of Social Transformation* (Cleveland, TN: CPT, 2012); Nimi Wariboko, *The Pentecostal Principle: Ethical Methodology in New Spirit* (Grand Rapids, MI: Eerdmans, 2011); and Michael Wilkinson and Peter F. Althouse, *Catch the Fire: Soaking Prayer and Charismatic Renewal* (Dekalb: Northern Illinois University Press, 2014).

55 The Society for Pentecostal Studies, for example, promotes diverse, creative, and constructive approaches to the study of the pentecostal movement and its theology through the papers and events of its annual conference and its journal *Pneuma*. The Pentecostal Manifestos series coedited by James K. A. Smith and Amos Yong and published by Eerdmans as well as this series, Systematic

advances these trajectories in pentecostal theology by engaging a major historical figure in the American theological tradition for both critical assessment of pentecostal theological habits and constructive contribution to the broader theological communities. But how do the Edwardsean and pentecostal theological traditions connect?

Edwardsean and pentecostal connections

Edwards was an eighteenth-century New England Calvinist. But his theological interests and, in many cases, innovative insights transcend his time and tradition and align with significant areas of pentecostal theology. Edwards was a promoter of the First Great Awakening. Pentecostalism began as and remains a renewal movement. Edwards explored the nature of religious experience and its correlation with the grace of the Holy Spirit. Probing the relationship between charismatic experience and pneumatology is a perennial project within pentecostal theology. Pneumatology was the arena of some of Edwards' most innovative work, and it is a staple of pentecostal theology. Strong historical-theological ties, therefore, exist for a dialogue between Edwards and pentecostal theologians. Engaging Edwards expands the historical and theological horizon of pentecostal dialogue partners and connects Pentecostals with an important historical forerunner. The following section outlines several points where Edwards' and pentecostal theological interests intersect.

Edwards endeavored to identify the nature of authentic Christian spirituality in *Religious Affections*. Neither visible manifestations nor orthodox professions alone denote genuine piety, according to Edwards. Authentic religious affections arise from a heart (the "disposition of the soul") transformed by grace and fired with love for God. The fundamental alteration of the heart enables the person to know and delight in the things of God. Pentecostal scholar Steven Land's *Passion for the Kingdom* drew on Edwards' theology of religious affections to explore the fundamental nature of Pentecostalism.[56] In a way similar to Edwards, Land maintains that not mere emotion and charismatic experience but the synergy of orthodoxy and orthopraxy is the nature of the pentecostal passion for the kingdom.

The term "Spirit baptism" was not central to Edwards' theology, but the Holy Spirit was. Breaking with traditional Protestant pneumatology Edwards argued that the

---

Pentecostal and Charismatic Theology edited by Wolfgang Vondey and Daniela C. Augustine published by Bloomsbury, showcases examples of the diversity of contemporary pentecostal theology.

[56] Steven J. Land, *Pentecostal Spirituality: A Passion for the Kingdom* (Sheffield: Sheffield Academic Press, 1993). For the ongoing importance of religious affections for pentecostal scholarship, which includes historical and contemporary investigations of pneumatology and religious affections, see Dale M. Coulter and Amos Yong, eds., *The Spirit, the Affections, and the Christian Tradition* (Notre Dame: University of Notre Dame Press, 2016), including, as especially relevant to this discussion of Edwards and pentecostal theology, chapter 12 by Gerald R. McDermott, "Jonathan Edwards on the Affections and the Spirit," in *The Spirit, the Affections, and the Christian Tradition*, ed. Dale M. Coulter and Amos Yong (Notre Dame, IN: University of Notre Dame Press, 2016).

Holy Spirit does not merely apply the benefits of Christ's redemption, but is the gift, indeed the purchase, of redemption. Although Spirit baptism has been the distinctive doctrine of Pentecostalism, some contemporary pentecostal theologians challenge it. Charismatic experience of the Spirit rather than a theology of the Spirit has become the preferred mark of Pentecostalism for many pentecostal scholars. The diversity of pentecostal theology mitigates a doctrinal or theological essence, even if that essence is pneumatological, according to this view.[57] A contrarian to this trend, Frank D. Macchia argues that a theology of Spirit baptism is at the heart of Pentecostalism. He frames Spirit baptism in the wider context of trinitarian theology than the traditional classical pentecostal account of the doctrine. He proposes this renewal of the pentecostal theology of Spirit baptism first in *Baptized in the Spirit: A Global Pentecostal Theology* (Grand Rapids: Zondervan, 2006) and later used it to develop a pentecostal theology of justification in *Justified in the Spirit: Creation, Redemption, and the Triune God* (Grand Rapids: Eerdmans, 2010). Amos Yong has also championed, in various ways, a pneumatological approach to pentecostal theology.[58]

A personal and life-changing encounter with God's grace is central to Edwards' vision of redemption. Here Edwards and Pentecostals share common cause. Although they may differ on the nature of divine election and the role of free will in the process of conversion and sanctification, Edwards being a Calvinist and Pentecostals tending toward Arminianism, the essential vision of redemption as a life transformed by the work of the Spirit and shaped to the image of Christ is mutual. Edwards called the Holy Spirit a "principle of grace" that transforms the fundamental orientation of the soul from self-regard to God.[59] The Spirit transformed life is elemental to pentecostal theology and practice.[60]

Edwards was a promoter of revivals. Pentecostalism began in revivals. Edwards believed that the church and faithful believers should prepare for revival through diligent pursuit of the Christian life. God would, at the appointed time, shower the blessing of a revived faith on the church. For Edwards, revival was the product of providence, not the result of human religious means. Pursuing spiritual disciplines can cultivate fertile soil for the showers of revival, but God alone dispenses the grace of renewal. Pentecostals have inherited the strong providential sense of Edwards as well as the Arminian methods pioneered by Charles G. Finney in the nineteenth-century revival movements. Pentecostals believe that God can and will send revival, Jesus Christ saves, and the Holy Spirit sanctifies and renews lives. They also, however,

---

[57] Allan Anderson, *An Introduction to Pentecostalism: Global Charismatic Christianity* (2004; reprint, New York: Cambridge University Press, 2006), 1–15 and Keith Warrington, *Pentecostal Theology: A Theology of Encounter* (New York: T & T Clark, 2008).

[58] The scope and volume of Yong's work is unprecedented, developing pentecostal approaches to theology of religions (*Discerning the Spirit(s)*; *Hospitality*), theological method (*Word-Spirit-Community*), theology of the Holy Spirit (*The Spirit Poured Out on All Flesh: Pentecostalism and the Possibility of Global Theology* [Grand Rapids, MI: Baker Academic, 2005]), as well as a comprehensive pentecostal systematic theology: *Renewing Christian Theology: Systematics for a Global Christianity* (Waco, TX: Baylor University Press, 2014).

[59] Edwards, *Treatise on Grace*, WJE 21:176.

[60] Amos Yong, *The Spirit of Love: A Trinitarian Theology of Grace* (Waco, TX: Baylor University Press, 2012).

believe that the work of God is a response to fervent faith and seeking God for fresh outpourings of the Holy Spirit. Pentecostals consequently find no tension between, on the one hand, scheduling a revival service on the church calendar and attending it with the expectation of a revival taking place because they have earnestly prayed in the run-up time to the event and, on the other hand, maintaining that it is the sovereign work of God's Spirit.

The term "revivalism" has fallen out of favor, but the missional nature of the Christian life and church has become more pronounced in recent theology. Edwards and Pentecostals can contribute to missional theology. Edwards' theological vision of God's communication of grace to the world inspired his Christian mission. Edwards' account of David Brainerd's mission efforts among the Indians on the frontiers of New Jersey, New York, and Pennsylvania made Brainerd's life an icon and the book itself, *The Life of David Brainerd* (1749), a manual of dedicated and sacrificial evangelical missions. Edwards, moreover, ended his pastoral ministry on the Massachusetts frontier, the edge of the colonial mission field. Revival and mission are also in the DNA of Pentecostalism. The early Pentecostals believed that the gift of tongues, a sign of revival and the baptism in the Spirit, gave them the ability to speak foreign languages. Experience on the mission field disappointed this expectation, but it did not dampen their zeal for evangelism and mission. Edwards and Pentecostals share the activism intrinsic to revival and renewal movements.

Edwards is also a model for progressive theological efforts. He sits squarely within the tradition of North American evangelical theology and was a committed Calvinist but he was critical of that tradition as well. Edwards was a creative theologian. Pneumatology, Trinity, and the experience of grace were key areas of his generative theological work. In significant ways his theology does not share the same concerns that have dominated modern evangelical theology—for example, biblical inerrancy and gender relations. Edwards was a post-Puritan, eighteenth-century, New England Calvinist. But his theological pursuits intersect with important areas of pentecostal and contemporary theology. He, therefore, provides a resource for the conservative and progressive movements within contemporary theology. The chapters in this volume assess his theological convictions along with his innovations with the goal of furthering the contribution of his theology to contemporary theology.

Pentecostal theology has become more self-critical and creative over the past two decades. Some may regard this trend negatively and consider innovation as falling away from the pentecostal distinctive doctrine—for example, Spirit baptism with the evidence of speaking in tongues. Yet pentecostal theology began as a renewal movement. It rejected received assumptions about the nature of the Christian life. Pentecostalism was a movement defined by an effort both to recover an apostolic experience of the Spirit, something they believed the church had lost, and by doing so to renew Christian theology and ministry.

Contemporary theology has similar tensions. Some want to remain true to the timeless truths of Christian orthodoxy. Others regard elements of theology, not as timeless, but time-bound doctrines that emerged within the cultural world of modernism and now react to the rise of postmodern culture and the pressures it places on conservative social values. Confronted with the reality and prospect of change, the easy options are to either reclaim the doctrine and practice of tradition (e.g., The Westminster Confession or the Sixteen Fundamental Truths) or abandon them and move on to something new and "relevant." Both options alone are misguided. The best way to address the challenges and opportunities confronting ministry and theology in today's world involves a synthesis of both concerns—remembering and resourcing the past to engage the demands facing contemporary Christian thought and life. The chapters in this volume embrace the latter view. In doing so, they share the dynamic theological orientation of Edwards and the pentecostal movement. Pentecostal theology is "radically open to the continued operations of the Spirit."[61] Engaging Edwards with an eye on the contemporary issues facing theology is an effort to "keep in step with the Spirit" (Gal. 5:25).

The Edwards-pentecostal dialogue

Though sharing core theological concerns, no critical conversation between pentecostal theology and Edwards, his legacy, and Edwards scholars has occurred. This volume is the first step in resolving this shortcoming. It provides pentecostal readings of Edwards' theology that contribute to contemporary pentecostal theology and Edwards' scholarship. The volume's chapters address four topic areas: (1) affections and the Spirit; (2) God and salvation; (3) church and culture; and (4) mission and witness. Parts One and Two each include four chapters, and Parts Three and Four each have three chapters. They discuss key issues in Edwards' work and contemporary theology. Each chapter offers creative and critical consideration of Edwards' thought by a pentecostal theologian. The book concludes with chapters by three contemporary Edwards scholars—Oliver Crisp, Amy Plantinga Pauw, and Robert Caldwell. Crisp, Plantinga Pauw, and Caldwell provide a dialogical contribution from the Edwardsean trajectory of this theological conversation.

Before describing the individual chapters, we want to give the rationale for the overall organization of the topics covered in Parts One through Four. Part One treats affections and the Spirit because they are the point of most explicit common concern between Edwards and Pentecostals. Starting with the broadest bridge seems sensible. This part also addresses issues of theological method and hermeneutics, which have been an area of important contemporary pentecostal scholarship and the starting point of theological reflection more generally. Having erected this methodological frame, Parts Two, Three, and Four continue the progression of topic areas found more or less in Protestant systematic theology. Part Two covers God and salvation, Part Three turns to the church and its relationship to culture, and Part Four concludes with consideration of pentecostal mission and public witness in the context of post-Christendom and pluralism. Since one of the main purposes of this book is to engage with contemporary Edwardsean scholarship, within each part we follow more or less the classical order of the loci, with minor adjustments (as shall be clarified).

---

[61] Smith, *Thinking in Tongues*, xvii.

Yet, although adopting the topical trajectory of systematic theology, the respective chapters operate from a pentecostal orientation in respect to both the particular dialogue with Edwards and the approach to the broader theological categories. This project is not an exercise in showing that pentecostal theologians agree with Edwards and speak in the same categories of their Protestant counterparts. Using the familiar structure of systematic theology, nevertheless, provides common ground in subject areas for what the authors hope will be an ecumenical audience for the book. The content developed in critical dialogue with Edwards and addressing the common areas of systematic theology carries a pentecostal register however.

Part One on affections and the Spirit has four chapters that show the vital place of the affections in Edwards' understanding of Scripture, theological method, and religious experience and how these connect to discussions at the vanguard of pentecostal theology. It begins with L. William Oliverio's investigation of Edwards' and pentecostal approaches to biblical hermeneutics. He shows the characteristics and correspondences between Edwardsean and pentecostal hermeneutics, addressing patterns of scriptural interpretation and use, with a special focus on the roles of the affections in the hermeneutics of Edwards and Daniel Warren Kerr, an early influential pentecostal theologian. He also frames the more particular comparison between Edwards and Kerr within his wider typology of pentecostal hermeneutics. The next chapter by Christopher A. Stephenson on theological method has two goals: it highlights an important similarity between Edwards' and early pentecostal theology and it explores the possible intersections between a central aspect of Edwards' theological method and future pentecostal theological method. He argues that Edwards' refusal to bifurcate theological knowledge and affectivity could assist Pentecostals in overcoming their perennial reluctance to engage in speculative theology. If the first two chapters of this part operate more at the theoretical level, the next two engage more with contemporary voices or with practical concerns. Joshua D. Reichard's chapter mines the works of Jonathan Edwards to develop a unique theology of divine action in the context of divine affections. The theology of Jonathan Edwards has deep roots in the affections and religious experience, which makes his theology highly compatible with, if not prototypical of, pentecostal-charismatic theology. This diversity in Edwards' thought enables him to be cast as a process-relational theist in terms of divine action and a pentecostal-charismatic theist in terms of religious affections. David J. Courey explores the way by which Edwards develops his view of the affections and the Spirit's work in transforming the soul toward authentic religiosity, as well as the signs Edwards believes point toward this reality. It also surveys key elements of pentecostal spirituality, the overall goal being to place Edwards and Pentecostalism in conversation. Edwards' theology of the affections can help Pentecostals better understand their experience of God and strengthen their theology and spirituality. At the same time, Pentecostalism's holistic and pragmatic spirituality may also help supplement Edwards' theology of the affections.

The four chapters in Part Two, "God and Salvation," investigate the theological areas of the Trinity, Christology, pneumatology, and grace in Edwardsean and pentecostal theology, in effect an intra- to extra-trinitarian arc. Steven M. Studebaker outlines Edwards' trinitarian vision of God, highlighting its communitarian and pneumatological emphases in Chapter 4. He shows that Edwards can contribute to pentecostal theology and that a pentecostal trinitarian insights help resolve and advance areas of Edwards' trinitarian theology. Chapter 6 by Gerald R. McDermott proposes that the Holy Spirit is integral to Jonathan Edwards' Christology. He shows that Christ's beauty is from the Spirit, the love of the messiah *is* the Spirit, and the Incarnation was (and is) made possible by the Spirit. The Holy Spirit, moreover, is an equal partner with Christ in the ongoing history of the work of redemption, which for Edwards is the secret to all of history, both sacred and secular. He also suggests four ways that Edwards' pneumatological Christology might be useful to pentecostal theology: its theology of revival, discernment, missions, and aesthetics. Pentecostal theologian, Andrew K. Gabriel's chapter shows that Edwards' doctrine of God, with its emphasis on the Holy Spirit as the mutual love of the Father and the Son, offers a dialogue point with pentecostal theology. Although some Pentecostals might be concerned that viewing the Spirit as the bond of love (in an Augustinian manner) could lead to a subordination of pneumatology to Christology or to a depersonalized portrayal of the Spirit, Edwards' emphasis complements a recurring theme that is emerging among Pentecostals (especially Amos Yong and Frank Macchia) of relating the Spirit to the love of God. The pneumatologies of Pentecostals and Edwards, then, can support one another to present the Holy Spirit as the Spirit of love and power. James M. Henderson completes this section by exploring Edwards' views on justification and sanctification and their relationship to twentieth- and twenty-first-century pentecostal thinkers. Although Edwards maintains the language of a forensic declaration, he grounds justification primarily in the Holy Spirit uniting the soul with Christ. On this basis, he argues for significant and mutually illuminating agreement between Edwards and Pentecostal Holiness and Finished Work schools of thought.

Part Three turns to the topics of the church and culture, moving from ecclesiology proper to the margins where the church meets the world and then into the beyond of the cultural domain. Lisa P. Stephenson engages the nascent ecclesiologies of Edwards and Pentecostalism. Notwithstanding their differing ecclesial and confessional backgrounds, Stephenson shows that both Edwards and Pentecostals share a common interest in a pneumatology of love that, though expressed in different ecclesiological ways, provides a rich opportunity for dialogue. Edwards' vision of the Holy Spirit as love fortifies the theological basis of pentecostal praxis-oriented ecclesiology. Pentecostal ecclesiology, however, affirms the interrelationship of the love and gifts of the Spirit's in place of Edwards' tendency to distinguish them. Michael J. McClymond's chapter profiles the prominent place of Edwards in the arguments by promoters and critics of the 1990s Christian revival known as the Toronto Blessing. McClymond maintains that this disparate use arises from Edwards' evolving perspective on revival and the manifestations that often attend them. McClymond presents Edwards' evolving views on revivals and principles of spiritual discernment and considers the Toronto Blessing in light of them. Edmund J. Rybarczyk's chapter examines Edwards on God as beauty and the Holy Spirit as beauty. Recognizing that Pentecostals have been more about missions and spiritual gifts, than aesthetics and the arts, Rybarczyk argues that a conversation between pentecostal pneumatology and Edwardsean aesthetics can enable Pentecostals to develop theology of aesthetics and practice of the arts that serve the church and the world.

Part Four builds off the preceding trek and completes the dialogue with three chapters on ways that Edwardsean and pentecostal theologies contribute to Christian mission and witness, starting with Edwards' mission to the Indians, extrapolating then from his implicit theological understanding of the religions, and concluding with his eschatological perspectives as applied to his views regarding the public square. Angela Tarango's lead chapter in this part investigates Edwards' ministry among the Stockbridge Indians and pentecostal ministry among Native Americans. She compares Edwards' theology and mission to the Stockbridge Indians and pentecostal missionary work to highlight the multiple and complex issues that emerge when studying Christian missionary work to Native peoples. That missionary work to Native peoples, moreover, challenged Edwards' and Pentecostals' notions of revival and theology, styles of preaching, and understandings of Native Americans' capacity to become Christians. Tony Richie's chapter on theology religion proposes that Edwards' efforts to understand all history from the standpoint of God's universal work of redemption suggest that the world's religions have a place in God's particular work of redemption in Jesus Christ. Richie argues that Edwards' theology of religion reveals an honest, consistent, dynamic, developmental, and, ultimately, progressive attitude toward non-Christian religions rooted in a thoroughly Christian theology of redemption. Remaining faithful to his Calvinist tradition, Edwards' reflection on world religions, nonetheless, is a critical if not infallible resource for contemporary Christian interreligious dialogue and theology. Amos Yong brings the political theologies of Edwards and Pentecostals into dialogue. Although neither Edwards nor Pentecostals are known for their contributions to political theology, Yong maintains, nonetheless, that together they provide resources for one. He argues that pentecostal perspectives can provide the pneumatological credentials for securing Edwards' stature as a political theologian even as the latter's dynamic millennial ruminations can also expand pentecostal eschatology toward a more potent political theology.

The volume concludes with three response chapters from Edwards' scholars: Oliver D. Crisp, Amy Plantinga Pauw, and Robert W. Caldwell III. The response chapters are important for the dialogical character of this book. They provide an Edwardsean interaction with the pentecostal forays into Edwards' thought and life. Crisp begins noting that Edwards has become a historical resource for diverse groups and movements within contemporary Christianity; Pentecostals now counted among them. Crisp engages the chapters in an analytical and critical manner. He not only highlights areas of correspondence that chapter authors draw between pentecostal theology and spirituality but also questions both the appropriateness of Edwards theology at points and the limits to the connections that can be drawn between Edwards and contemporary Pentecostalism. Plantinga Pauw's chapter highlights the positive conversation between the chapter authors and Edwards. Pauw suggests that extending interaction with Edwards beyond an "intramural Reformed exercise" testifies not only to the depth and breadth of Edwards' theology but also to the inquisitive and creative nature of the pentecostal movement. Making prominent areas of Edwards' thought and life often overlooked by scholars from other theological backgrounds is a major benefit of this Pentecostal and Edwards' dialogue. Caldwell regards Edwards' and Pentecostals as fitting dialogue partners. He welcomes this conversation between Edward and pentecostal theologians, but hopes that it is just the beginning. He recommends that Pentecostals can mine deeper into Edwards' theology of the Trinity and spirituality and religious experience as well as the historical context of Edwards' thought, which he suggests will likely show more continuity with his Puritan-Reformed tradition even if not with some forms of contemporary Evangelicalism. He, moreover, provides specific and detailed assessment of the chapter and directions for further dialogue between pentecostal theologians and Edwards' thought.

This volume opens the conversation between Edwards' and pentecostal theology. Accordingly, although the scope of the volume is comprehensive, it is not exhaustive. This project is the beginning, not the end, of the fruitful theological investigation of Edwards' theology by pentecostal scholars and, hopefully, engagement and collaboration among pentecostal and Edwards' scholars.

Part One

Affections and the Spirit

1

"True Religion, in Great Part, Consists of Holy Affections": A Critical Comparison of the Biblical Hermeneutics of Jonathan Edwards and Pentecostals

L. William Oliverio, Jr.

Introduction

In the midst of the formative years of his young adulthood, while pastoring in New York City, summering in East Windsor, then pastoring in Bolton, Connecticut, and into his years tutoring at Yale, Jonathan Edwards kept a book of resolutions.[1] The full list of seventy resolutions is a revealing instance of what Michael McClymond and Gerald McDermott have described as Edwards' understanding of creaturely participation in God as these meet the dispositions, loves, and habits that govern a person—both key components of the great "symphony" found in Edwards' life and corpus.[2] Among these stands Resolution 28: "Resolved, to study the Scriptures so steadily, constantly and frequently, as that I may find, and plainly perceive myself to grow in the knowledge of the same."[3] To judge from the vast proliferation of the use of the Bible in his written

---

[1] Edwards, "Resolutions," *WJE* 16:753–59.
[2] Michael J. McClymond and Gerald R. McDermott, *Theology of Jonathan Edwards* (New York: Oxford University Press, 2012), 3–9. In the opening of *Theology of Jonathan Edwards*, McClymond and McDermott compare the work of Jonathan Edwards (1703–58) to a symphony played by five instrument sections. The first constituent of the symphony, the violins in their image, is the self-communication of the beauty of the trinitarian God. The second, the other strings, is creaturely participation in God, as divine beauty confers spiritual beauty upon others. The horns, the third constituent, represent Edwards' necessitarian dispositionalism where all beings, including God, have at their essence dispositions or habits, those human loves and affections that most truly reveal personal identities. Fourth, as the woodwinds, Edwards' Calvinism sounds forth in its theocentric voluntarism, as God continually sustains all reality. As the percussion section, the fifth section of the symphony is Edwards' harmonious constitutionalism in which he found harmony in the entire course of redemptive history. McClymond and McDermott suggest that the totality of Edwards' works produces this symphony, even as some interpretations of Edwards "capture one or another part of the symphony, yet fail to construe the sound and flow of the whole" (ibid., 8).
[3] Edwards, "Resolutions," *WJE* 16:755.

works, the conclusion is compelling that Edwards missed little opportunity to steadily, constantly, and frequently study the Bible.

For Edwards, biblical interpretation was no dispassionate or technical exercise. He came to the important doctrinal conclusion that "true religion, in great part, consists in holy affections," the central thesis of his *Religious Affections* (1746).[4] Yet Edwards was also a remarkable philosophical theologian who utilized innovative and complex philosophical convictions as he theologically interpreted Scripture. Standing among those who turned away from the idea that human reason could serve as the arbiter of all things during the period of the Enlightenment, Edwards came to understand the affections and the intellect as fused together because he considered that "the affections are no other, than the more vigorous and sensible exercises of the inclination and will of the soul."[5] His biblical hermeneutics can thus not be properly described in merely technical terms, but they must account for the primacy of the spiritual in his interpretation of Scripture.[6]

Pentecostals have likewise operated with a strong affirmation of the role of the affections in an authentic Christian life. Like Edwards, pentecostal hermeneutics have stood against rationalisms and merely academic or technical hermeneutics of the Bible. They, too, though not as often recognized, have come to the biblical texts with important philosophical, ontological, and theological assumptions as they have interpreted Scripture for its spiritual content.[7] Nevertheless, the affections or feelings have been central to all major pentecostal hermeneutical types. Steven J. Land's thesis that pentecostal theology is found in its spirituality, and that pentecostal theology is not just about right belief or right practices but centered on right feelings, concluded that pentecostal spirituality and theology are about affections shaped by a longing for the kingdom of God.[8] Pentecostal biblical hermeneutics have likewise placed significant emphasis on the affective and the role of the Spirit.[9]

Pentecostal hermeneutics is a broad and general category to compare to the hermeneutics found in the work of a particular person, even that of a theological and philosophical giant like Edwards. Pentecostalism is itself a category that is complicated and contested, as Pentecostalism includes the Classical Pentecostals who find their roots in the early movement, of which the Azusa Street Revival was its exemplary original manifestation, through to the vast varieties of the 500 million plus Pentecostals

---

[4] Edwards, *Religious Affections*, WJE 2:95.
[5] Ibid., 96.
[6] Conrad Cherry, "Symbols of Spiritual Truth: Jonathan Edwards as Biblical Interpreter," *Interpretation* 39, no. 3 (1985): 263–71 and Stephen J. Stein, "The Quest for the Spiritual Sense: The Biblical Hermeneutics of Jonathan Edwards," *Harvard Theological Review* 70, nos. 1–2 (1977): 99–113.
[7] Identifying these was a key task of mine throughout *Theological Hermeneutics in the Classical Pentecostal Tradition*, Global Pentecostal and Charismatic Studies 12 (Leiden: Brill, 2012).
[8] Steven J. Land, *Pentecostal Spirituality: A Passion for the Kingdom* (Sheffield: Sheffield Academic Press, 1993), especially 125–64.
[9] Kenneth J. Archer, *A Pentecostal Hermeneutic for the Twenty-First Century: Spirit, Scripture and Community* (Cleveland, TN: CPT, 2005); Lee Roy Martin, ed., *Pentecostal Hermeneutics, A Reader* (Leiden: Brill, 2013); and Lee Roy Martin, "Longing for God: Psalm 63 and Pentecostal Spirituality," *Journal of Pentecostal Theology* 22, no. 1 (2013): 54–76. Craig S. Keener has significantly developed contemporary pentecostal hermeneutics in *Spirit Hermeneutics: Reading Scripture in Light of Pentecost* (Grand Rapids, MI: Eerdmans, 2016).

worldwide today, and their relation to broader charismatic and renewal movements.[10] Pentecostalism is itself best understood when accounted for as simultaneously local and global, particular and general.[11] Further, both pentecostal hermeneutics and Edwards diverged from the hermeneutical canons of Enlightenment modernism, and so certain assumptions common in modern thought have been brought into question. The hermeneutics at Azusa Street, 1906–09, and the hermeneutics of Edwards, who pastored in Northampton from 1726 to 1750, continued and further initiated alternatives to standard forms of Enlightenment modernism and their approaches to Scripture.

This chapter, while focusing on biblical hermeneutics, operates with an approach to hermeneutics that also stands, with Edwards in particular and Pentecostals in general, in contrast to the Enlightenment's attempts to elevate its naturalistic and foundationalist epistemic canons as the proper ones for human knowing. Along with some forms of Christian thought, much of late modern or so-called postmodern thought has concurred so that the result has been that hermeneutical understanding has superseded the foundationalist epistemologies established during the Enlightenment, for what are, at least in my estimation, some compelling reasons.[12] Most importantly, the hermeneutical approach has trumped Enlightenment epistemic conceptions because the ontological, metaphysical, anthropological, theological, epistemic, and other assumptions built into foundationalist approaches are themselves contested. Those conclusions are built into the epistemologies which serve as arbiters of further ontic affirmations. Reductive materialism, for example, cannot simply beg the question of its truth. Declaring a particular epistemology the indubitable foundation for human knowledge is either to assume the triumph of or to beg the question of all these assumptions.

As Merold Westphal has efficiently formulated it, the late modern or postmodern turn contends that, instead, "hermeneutics is epistemology."[13] What this hermeneutical approach means for comparing the biblical hermeneutics of Edwards and Pentecostals is that the biblical hermeneutics of both, while a critical center and source for their theologies, are interdependent in relation to their entire paradigms of understanding life and reality, and thus the funding of conceptions is multidirectional.[14] In a paradigm

---

[10] See Allan Anderson, *An Introduction to Pentecostalism: Global Charismatic Christianity*, 2nd ed. (Cambridge: Cambridge University Press, 2014); Douglas G. Jacobsen, *Thinking in the Spirit: Theologies of the Early Pentecostal Movement* (Bloomington: Indiana University Press, 2003), 1–15; Douglas G. Jacobsen, *Global Gospel: An Introduction to Christianity on Five Continents* (Grand Rapids, MI: Baker Academic, 2015), 34–39; and Amos Yong, *The Spirit Poured Out on All Flesh: Pentecostalism and the Possibility of Global Theology* (Grand Rapids: Baker Academic, 2005), 17–30.

[11] Wolfgang Vondey, *Pentecostalism: A Guide for the Perplexed* (London: Bloomsbury, 2013), 25–26.

[12] For some narrations of the supersession of epistemology by hermeneutics, see Charles Taylor, "Overcoming Epistemology," in his *Philosophical Arguments* (Cambridge: Harvard University Press, 1995), 1–19 and Merold Westphal, "Hermeneutics as Epistemology," in his *Overcoming Onto-Theology: Toward a Postmodern Christian Faith* (New York: Fordham University Press, 2001), 47–74.

[13] Westphal, "Hermeneutics as Epistemology," 50.

[14] I describe this paradigmatic approach to hermeneutics in more detail in my *Theological Hermeneutics in the Classical Pentecostal Tradition*, 319–54.

as bountiful and as ingenious as that of Edwards, a rich biblical hermeneutic both funded and emerged from his theology and philosophy. This chapter, as with this entire volume, might only begin to put Edwards into dialogue with Pentecostalism.

Elements of Edwards' biblical hermeneutics

McClymond and McDermott estimate that the combined exegetical elements found in Edwards' written works, from his sermons to the primarily exegetical material found in his other works, run around 5,000 printed pages. Edwards' dedication to scriptural knowledge and interpretation came from his theological conviction that any true knowledge of God comes from divine revelation as well as his resolution to study such.[15] The mid-twentieth-century resurgence of interest in Edwards focused on his metaphysical genius and often underestimated the place of Scripture in his thought.[16] Recent decades have seen a surge in interest in the biblical interpretation that played a crucial role in Edwards' thought.[17]

Edwards' biblical interpretation might be well understood, though, from today's vantage point, as primarily theological interpretation of Scripture.[18] For theological reasons, he rejected the emerging modern canons of historical-critical scholarship, themselves still young in development and far away from Edwards' own context on the American frontier. Edwards' biblical interpretation was deeply informed by his core theological affirmations. These core theological affirmations were deeply informed by his reading of Scripture, though it seems that the whole tended to have more noetic authority than the part in Edwards' hermeneutical circle. Edwards' sermons typically exposited a verse of Scripture in the Puritan style of proclaiming a doctrine abstracted from the text to be followed by application or improvement for the hearers.

Commonly seen as one of his most revealing sermons, "A Divine and Supernatural Light," originally delivered in Northampton in August 1733, is an exposition of Jesus' affirmation of Peter's confession that he is the Christ, the Son of the living God in Matthew's gospel. In the Authorized (King James) Version used by Edwards, it reads, "And Jesus answered and said unto him, Blessed art thou, Simon Barjona: for

---

[15] McClymond and McDermott, *Theology of Jonathan Edwards*, 167–69.
[16] Stein, "Quest for the Spiritual Sense," 99–101. The appreciation of his metaphysical genius and depreciation of his love of Scripture follows the lead of Perry Miller, *Jonathan Edwards*, American Men of Letters Series (New York: William Sloane, 1949).
[17] Among these are Robert E. Brown, *Jonathan Edwards and the Bible* (Bloomington: Indiana University Press, 2002); Cherry, "Symbols of Spiritual Truth," 263–71; McClymond and McDermott, *Theology of Jonathan Edwards*, 167–80; Douglas A. Sweeney, *Edwards the Exegete: Biblical Interpretation and Anglo-Protestant Culture on the Edge of the Enlightenment* (New York: Oxford University Press, 2015); Stephen J. Stein, "Editor's Introduction," in *The Works of Jonathan Edwards*, gen. ed. Harry S. Stout, vol. 15, *Notes on Scripture*, ed. Stephen J. Stein (New Haven, CT: Yale University Press, 1998), 1–46; and Stephen J. Stein, "Editor's Introduction," in *The Works of Jonathan Edwards*, gen. ed. Harry S. Stout, vol. 24, *The Blank Bible*, ed. Stephen J. Stein (New Haven, CT: Yale University Press, 2006), 1–4. Further, George M. Marsden's *Jonathan Edwards: A Life* (New Haven, CT: Yale University Press, 2003) provides regular attention to Edwards' hermeneutics.
[18] See, for example, *The Journal of Theological Interpretation*, for contemporary discussions regarding theological interpretation of Scripture

flesh and blood hath not revealed it unto thee, but my Father which is in heaven" (Mt. 16:17).[19] In the sermon, Edwards exposits the doctrine that "there is such a thing, as a spiritual and divine light, immediately imparted to the soul by God, of a different nature from any that is obtained by natural means."[20] All knowledge, for Edwards, is, of course, imparted by God. Material things operate as mediate or secondary causes of knowledge. But the special divine and supernatural knowledge that he speaks of here is immediately imparted by God.[21] That is what appears in this passage in the Gospel of Matthew, according to Edwards, as this light of a different nature has been imparted to Peter. He uses the theological distinction between common grace and special grace to explain what has happened to Peter's understanding. If it was merely a sense of his own sinfulness and misery or the anger of God that Peter had sensed, men in their natural condition may experience that, for "common grace only assists the faculties of the soul to do that more fully, which they do by nature."[22] But here Edwards sees the Spirit of God acting upon Peter in special and regenerative grace where the Spirit "acts in the mind of a saint as an indwelling vital principle."[23]

Edwards' sermon and interpretation of Mt. 16:17 is a theological and philosophical exposition that seems to burst forth spiritual meaning from the statement found in the text. He explains how the divine light does not spring from the human imagination but affects it, that it suggests no truths not revealed in the Word of God, and that not every lofty affection is a movement of the divine light. He teaches that the light is an apprehension of the divine excellency of what the Word of God reveals. The light removes the hindrances placed by man's reasoning, and moves attention to a clearer view of the truth of the objects of reason and their mutual relations. The divine excellency is perceived, and it removes all doubt that it is from God, not man. He defends the rationality of his doctrine of the divine light as well. He argues that if transcendent things do exist, they should be exceedingly different from other things, that it is not irrational to then see such things, and that it is logical that God should give them immediately and not by natural means.[24] But he also justified the doctrine as scriptural on the basis of other texts. He cites other texts as describing this supernatural knowledge as a seeing or knowing. Still other biblical texts portray this light and knowledge as always only immediately given from God. This kind of knowledge distinguishes the saved from the unregenerate, according to the witness of Scripture.[25] Edwards' use of other biblical texts in reference, here, as in his other works, could be characterized as encyclopedic.

There is little doubt that the whole works strongly on the part in Edwards' hermeneutics, but also that, as in this exposition of this biblical text, we find a part that contributes to and integrates itself with that intricate whole. Edwards' whole was robust in content and influence. Against the fragmentation of modern approaches to

---

[19] Edwards, "A Divine and Supernatural Light," *WJE* 17:408-26.
[20] Ibid., 410.
[21] Ibid., 409.
[22] Ibid., 410.
[23] Ibid., 411.
[24] Ibid., 411-15, 420-23.
[25] Ibid., 416-19.

the Bible, Edwards prioritized the whole, which, in his case, led to a prioritization of the spiritual sense. McClymond and McDermott aptly explain how this operates, and its implications for interpreting the larger story of Scripture:

> In Edwards' biblical hermeneutics the whole has epistemological priority over the parts. This is one reason the spiritual sense is so crucial. The spiritual interpretation of Scripture allows the interpreter to put the pieces together into a coherent whole. Without the spiritual sense, the events of the Old Testament might seem like a set of random and disconnected events, having little relationship to one another and even less connection with the New Testament.[26]

The theologically formed historical narrative Edwards operated with oriented his reading of Scripture and his understanding of what Scripture meant for himself and his audience.

Yet cultural elements were also factors. George Marsden, as one of his leading biographers, found Edwards continually interpreting the Bible in relationship to contemporary events "through the lenses of his millennialist categories and Constantinian assumptions."[27] Edwards interpreted the parts of Scripture, along with current events, through his larger affirmations of postmillennialism and what he saw as God's hand at work in furthering the gospel through Protestant political governments. Much of what governed his narrative, by which he interpreted Scripture and the world, was his theological narrative of history. It was his plan to complete two works articulating that narrative when he arrived at Princeton in early 1758, and which were left uncompleted at his death. One was supposed to be his master work, to be entitled *A History of the Work of Redemption*, to be a theology in the form of a history.[28] In it, "history, prophecy, types, and doctrine would center in Christ's redemptive work," providing a cosmic history that was playing out in Edwards' periodization of history.[29] The other plan was to write a text harmonizing the Old and New Testaments with a focus on the relationship between Christology and typology.[30]

Edwards' Puritanism, of course, also loomed large. His reading of the Bible drew on favored commentators and theologians, while his arguments regularly contested with Arminians (though occasionally siding with them in issues of Christian apologetics), deists, and skeptics.[31] He predominantly read the Bible as an orthodox Calvinist who, in Marsden's words, was "an apologist for 'Calvinistic' theology versus

---

[26] McClymond and McDermott, *Theology of Jonathan Edwards*, 174.
[27] Marsden, *Jonathan Edwards*, 424–25.
[28] Edwards, *"History of Redemption" Notebooks*, WJE 31: n.p. 3 books.
[29] Marsden, *Jonathan Edwards*, 481–89, esp. see 482.
[30] Edwards, *"Harmony of the Scriptures,"* WJE 29: n.p.
[31] Marsden, *Jonathan Edwards*, 474, regards Matthew Poole, Matthew Henry, Moses Lowman, and Philip Doddridge as among his favored sources; E. Brooks Holifield, *Theology in America: Christian Thought from the Age of the Puritans to the Civil War* (New Haven, CT: Yale University Press, 2003), 103–4, notes the theological influence of Petrus van Mastricht, along with Poole and Henry; Stein, "Introduction," 6–9, considers Poole and Henry foremost as his trusted sources, while Edwards sought out interesting exegetical ideas from a variety of sources.

'the modern writers.'"[32] Still, he drew on Enlightenment ideas, and especially Locke, though primarily with the motivation of using the new learning in defense of Christian theology, even as he adopted aspects of Locke's system of ideas and empiricism. Edwards had investigated Enlightenment philosophy since his teenage years, and had found a continual theological and philosophical enemy in what he considered the pernicious philosophies that sought to elevate the human in judgment over God and to reject and ridicule Christian doctrines like that of original sin and its epistemic and moral ramifications. While Edwards appreciated the emphasis on observation and the scientific interest of the day, as the book of nature is the self-communication of God, and having written a scientific paper on spiders as a young man (1714), he found the optimistic anthropologies and epistemologies produced by Enlightenment thinkers to be enemies of true religion.[33]

The doubt of the proper spiritual condition of the human mind led such a brilliant mind as Edwards' to consider proper spiritual understanding of the Scriptures as necessitating a regenerated heart and mind. This was, of course, standard Calvinist doctrine, but Edwards' idealism, as can be seen in "A Divine and Supernatural Light," took this to new heights. And Edwards' sophisticated defense of Calvinistic determinism and criticism of the supposed freedom of the will also provided an important theological tenet that informed his interpretation of Scripture.[34] As Marsden explains, "Edwards' philosophy started with his theology. While his opponents were starting with principles of human morality and psychology and from those inferring what God's moral government of the universe must be like, Edwards was starting with what God must be like and then examining the human condition in that light."[35] Robert Brown concluded similarly that "the great task of Edwards' theological career was to reconstruct and reinterpret the rationality or cogency of Christian belief with reference to the intellectual assumptions of the age."[36] Brown characterizes the approach of Edwards to the Enlightenment and to deist attacks on Scripture as a "modernizing traditionalism" that held to the basic historical outlines of the Bible by arguing for their truth.[37]

Edwards' biblical interpretation operated with this "modernizing traditionalist" approach. This can be seen in the longest of the notes found in his notebook, "Notes on Scripture," No. 416, essentially an apologetic treatise defending the Mosaic authorship of the Pentateuch.[38] In it, Edwards argued by producing lengthy scriptural demonstrations. He pieced together the evidence of Mosaic authorship by, first, cataloguing and often quoting in full the places in the Pentateuch and elsewhere in the Old Testament where it was stated or remembered or referred to that it was Moses who had been tasked with writing the covenantal history. In the Yale *Works* edition, this goes on for twenty pages, as Edwards moves into connecting the covenantal law and

---

[32] Marsden, *Jonathan Edwards*, 437.
[33] Edwards, "Of Insects," *WJE* 6:154–63 and Edwards, *Original Sin*, *WJE* 3.
[34] Edwards, *Freedom of the Will*, *WJE* 1.
[35] Marsden, *Jonathan Edwards*, 442, made this comment in relation to Edwards' *Freedom of the Will*.
[36] Brown, *Jonathan Edwards and the Bible*, xv.
[37] Ibid., xvii.
[38] Edwards, "Notes on Scripture," *WJE* 15:423–69.

history so that Moses, entrusted with the law, is likewise entrusted with the history, as "history and law are everywhere so grafted one into another, so mutually inwrought."[39] He argues that it is more reasonable to consider the primeval history in Genesis as Mosaic than not on the grounds that it is attested by the reliable history that follows Gen. 11:26, and referred to as genuine and Mosaic just as Moses is throughout the Old Testament.[40] He catalogs 163 instances, events or themes in the Pentateuch that appear elsewhere in the Old Testament, corroborating their reliability through multiple attestations.[41] He puts forth a further historical argument on the basis of the assertion that "it is certain" that the book of the law that was taken into the Babylonian captivity was the same that came out.[42]

Edwards fervently defended his notions of theological history as he ardently studied the progress of the contemporary Protestant cause of his day, all of this standing in historical continuity with the narrative he constructed concerning biblical, past, and contemporary history as it led to the forthcoming postmillennial triumph of the church.[43] His argument would be unconvincing to anyone who did not assume the authentic spiritual nature of Scripture, but that result coheres with his Calvinistic assumptions about knowledge of God.

While Edwards had as a lifelong project, his development of a grand narrative of history that informed his reading of the Bible and which was a central part of his overall theological hermeneutic, his biblical hermeneutics might also be considered spiritual hermeneutics. For Edwards, spiritual truths came from the believer's perception of Scripture, which is properly spiritual and affective.[44] Right reason did not conflict with revelation, though neither revelation nor the illumination of Scripture could be had without a supernatural light in the first place. Edwards, in fact, held to the tradition that what other religions and deists have that is truth comes from remnants of divine revelation that had been unwittingly absorbed in cultural traditions—that is, the *prisca theologia*.[45] Additionally, the excellencies of the divine were to be found in images and shadows of divine things found in nature as well as Scripture. In his notebook on "Images (or Shadows) of Divine Things," he explains,

> The book of Scripture is the interpreter of the book of nature two ways, viz., by declaring to us those spiritual mysteries that are indeed signified and typified in the constitution of the natural world; and secondly, in actually making application of the signs and types in the book of nature as representations of those spiritual mysteries in many instances.[46]

---

[39] Ibid., 441.
[40] Ibid., 438.
[41] Ibid., 443–53.
[42] Ibid., 457.
[43] Marsden, *Jonathan Edwards*, 481–89.
[44] Brown, *Jonathan Edwards and the Bible*, 76–86.
[45] Holifield, *Theology in America*, 106. Also see, Gerald R. McDermott, *Jonathan Edwards Confronts the Gods: Christian Theology, Enlightenment Religion, and Non-Christian Faiths* (New York: Oxford University Press, 2000).
[46] Edwards, "Images of Divine Things," *WJE* 11:106.

The two books, Scripture and nature, are divine self-communication. Material realities existed at the will of the divine, and so reality is essentially about personal relationships. Passing things are the signs or expressions of divine love. Though Edwards drew from Locke and Newton, he also held that "created reality was not independent of the minds that engage it . . . the universe most essentially consisted of personal relationships. All of creation was a system of powers to communicate."[47]

Edwards held that God especially communicates through types, which are not the product of human imagination but a discovery of God's self-communication. The presence of the Spirit in the exegete could perceive spiritual truths so that there was a harmony between heart and text. To put it in Gadamerian hermeneutical terms, Edwards held to something along the lines of a spiritual "fusion of horizons."[48] The spiritual sense was not limited by the literal, even as the literal held a certain prominence: "The plethora—and indeed, the inexhaustibility—of the Bible's meaning was basic to Edwards' hermeneutics. Without abandoning the foundational role of the literal sense, he showed a tilt toward the spiritual sense. The fecundity of the Bible, its wealth of hidden meaning, overflowed the literal sense."[49] Edwards used typology, in line with Puritan precedent, as a way to avoid fanciful allegories as well as wooden literalism and to honor the spiritual nature of Scripture.[50]

But it was the affections, "the more vigorous and sensible exercises of the inclination and will of the soul," which were Edwards' key to rightly interpreting the Bible, and a key resonance with pentecostal hermeneutics.[51] Edwards is well known for his involvement in the religious awakenings in which he was a key figure. Against the anti-revivalist, conservative Puritan Old Lights, on the one hand, and the more liberal but orderly Anglicans on the other, Edwards and the New Lights sought to be both faithful to the Puritan heritage and fervent in faith so as to eagerly desire awakenings and revivals. Edwards' leadership of the revival in Northampton in 1734–35 and his *Faithful Narrative* of the revival placed him at the forefront of this movement.[52] His subsequent involvement with the awakenings in the early 1740s and his ongoing leadership in the revival movements made him an important advocate of experiential religion. Edwards' work on the proper role of human affections in religion is also telling of his biblical hermeneutics.

Edwards' *Religious Affections*, published in 1746 in the midst of difficult times for him in Northampton, begins, in sermonic fashion, with an exposition of 1 Pet. 1:8, "Whom having not seen, ye love; in whom, though now ye see him not, yet believing, ye rejoice with joy unspeakable, and full of glory" (Authorized Version). Edwards interprets the scriptural text by tending to the spiritual content of the words of the Apostle Peter, taking what later hermeneutic theory would refer to as the text's own literary context at the face value it appeared to have to him, and by swinging the very

---

[47] Marsden, *Jonathan Edwards*, 504.
[48] Hans-Georg Gadamer, *Truth and Method*, 2nd rev. ed., trans. Joel Weinsheimer and Donald G. Marshall (London and New York: Continuum, 2004).
[49] McClymond and McDermott, *Theology of Jonathan Edwards*, 173.
[50] Cherry, "Symbols of Spiritual Truth."
[51] Edwards, *Religious Affections*, WJE 2:96.
[52] Edwards, *The Great Awakening*, WJE 4:96–210.

meaning of the words he is interpreting (i.e., love, joy, and others) as proper Christian affections back onto the text in his hermeneutical method.[53] True religion and true knowledge of Scripture is affected and fervent: "That religion which God requires, and will accept, does not consist in weak, dull and lifeless wouldings, raising us but a little above a state of indifference: God, in his Word, greatly insists upon it, that we be in good earnest, fervent in spirit, and our hearts vigorously engaged in religion," upon which he cites, in full, quotations Rom. 12:11, Deut. 10:12, then 6:4-5, and 30:6 as scriptural demonstration of this truth.[54] The bulk of *Religious Affections* is, first, an exposition of a dozen things that are not but may pretend to be genuine signs of gracious, that is, divinely given, affections, followed by twelve genuine ones. The gracious signs are God-centered and produce good spiritual fruit while the signs that offer no proof focus on appearances.[55] In these, we have the integration of spiritual, biblical, theological, and philosophical hermeneutics in Edwards' signs and false signs, together in a comprehensive paradigm in which his biblical hermeneutics continually funded and was continually funded. For Edwards, those who have the power of godliness are baptized in the Spirit:

> The Spirit of God in those that have sound and solid religion, is a spirit of powerful holy affection; and therefore, God is said to have given them the spirit of power, and of love, and of a sound mind (2 Tim. 1:7). And such, when they received the Spirit of God, in his sanctifying and saving influences, are said to be baptized with the Holy Ghost, and with fire; by reason of the power and fervor of those exercises the Spirit of God excites in their hearts, whereby their hearts, when grace is in exercise, may be said to burn within them; as is said of the disciples.[56]

Edwards, then Pentecostals, both read the scriptural texts which spoke of Spirit baptism and saw their importance. Both made connections between Spirit baptism and the affections, recognizing that a living and affected experiential faith is what is needed to rightly interpret Scripture.

Edwards and pentecostal hermeneutics

In the humble conditions of the revival that took place among the holiness Christians led by William Seymour at Azusa Street (1906–09) in Los Angeles, scriptural passages that spoke of a baptism in the Spirit had been reinterpreted as teaching an empowerment from God that followed God's gracious works of salvation and sanctification.

---

[53] Edwards, *Religious Affections*, WJE 2:93–99.
[54] Ibid., 99.
[55] Edwards, *Religious Affections*, WJE 2:127–461. McClymond and McDermott, *Theology of Jonathan Edwards*, 676, consider *Religious Affections* (1746) as tending toward caution concerning charismatic manifestations as compared to more openness in his earlier *Distinguishing Marks* (1741) with a middle ground between the two found in *Some Thoughts Concerning the Revival* (1743).
[56] Edwards, *Religious Affections*, WJE 2:100.

This hermeneutical and doctrinal move, combined with other social, theological, and practical factors, originated a new movement within Christianity that blossomed into the manifold movements that comprise contemporary Pentecostalism, though modern pentecostal origins also came from beyond Azusa Street.[57] I have contended that this original pentecostal hermeneutic ought to be understood as the original pentecostal paradigm, and as one that has since organically developed into other hermeneutical types: evangelical-pentecostal, contextual-pentecostal, and ecumenical-pentecostal hermeneutics.[58]

As with Edwards, the place of the affections in pentecostal hermeneutics cuts across Enlightenment rationalisms. This can be seen in Land's thesis that orthopathy has been as essential to pentecostal identity as orthodoxy and orthopraxis. Or in James K. A. Smith's claim that, against the "de facto naturalism of market-driven, technological construals of the world . . . pentecostal spirituality fosters a more expansive, affective understanding of what counts as knowledge and a richer understanding of what we know."[59] Or in Wolfgang Vondey's characterization that "the affections inform, shape, and direct the pentecostal worldview as not merely an objective understanding of the world but as active involvement in the world's transformation."[60] Pentecostalism represents a broad tradition of Christianity that has emerged since the turn of the twentieth century. It is difficult to account for the hermeneutical approach of a tradition of roughly a half billion people that has no central structure and allows for a variety of tendencies, even if there are identifiable continuities. This is why Vondey's *Guide for the Perplexed* explains Pentecostalism through a series of contrasts and syntheses: local and global, holistic and extreme, ecumenical and denominational, orthodox and sectarian, socially engaged and triumphalist, egalitarian and institutional, scholarly and anti-intellectual.[61] The variety of pentecostal hermeneutics, moreover, has identifiable resonances with Edwards' hermeneutics.

Among Classical Pentecostals, with roots in the traditional pentecostal denominations coming out of Azusa Street and representing slightly under half of global Pentecostals, I have identified four types. The original classical pentecostal hermeneutic, as aforementioned was a hermeneutic of origination. It moved dialectically between Scripture and experience to construct new doctrines and experiences that came to constitute early Pentecostalism. This openness called for regulation, so an early version of an evangelical-pentecostal hermeneutic did so by arguing for the biblical justification of classical pentecostal doctrines. By the mid-twentieth century, that hermeneutic developed more sophisticated and academic

---

[57] Cecil M. Robeck, Jr., *The Azusa Street Mission and Revival: The Birth of the Global Pentecostal Movement* (Nashville: Nelson, 2006), considers the Revival the "Grand Central Station" of early Pentecostalism. The broader origins are accounted for, among other sources, by Anderson, *An Introduction to Pentecostalism*; Allan Anderson, *To the Ends of the Earth: Pentecostalism and the Transformation of World Christianity* (Oxford: Oxford University Press, 2013); and Walter J. Hollenweger, *Pentecostalism: Origins and Developments Worldwide* (Peabody, MA: Hendrickson, 1997).

[58] Oliverio, *Theological Hermeneutics in the Classical Pentecostal Tradition*.

[59] Smith, *Thinking in Tongues*, 59.

[60] Vondey, *Pentecostalism*, 33.

[61] Ibid.

uses for biblical scholarship and more thoroughgoing methods of integrating interpretations of the intent of biblical authors into doctrinal and systematic theologies in a contemporary evangelical-pentecostal hermeneutic. By the 1990s, a contextual-pentecostal hermeneutic had arisen that emphasized, primarily from a philosophical rather than cultural standpoint, the contextuality of all interpretation, in line with hermeneutic philosophy.[62] The constructive goal of these contextual hermeneutics was to get to the subject matter of the text by legitimizing the contextuality of the interpreter as well as the text, often in line with Gadamer's "fusion of horizons." Picking up on the trickle that remained from the early ecumenical impulses at Azusa Street and other early pentecostal movements, an ecumenical-pentecostal hermeneutic explored pentecostal readings of Scripture alongside those of other Christian traditions in order to broaden, deepen, and mature pentecostal theology.[63] Consonances can be found between Edwards' hermeneutics and each pentecostal hermeneutical type.

The quest for the spiritual sense of Scripture is often found in popular pentecostal hermeneutics as a quest for experience of Jesus and the Spirit through the revelation of the scriptural text and is readily seen in the more original type of pentecostal hermeneutics. An exemplary instance of this can be seen in the founder of the African American Church of God in Christ (COGIC), Charles Harrison Mason (1866–1961). When he visited Azusa Street in early 1907, Masson struggled to accept the new pentecostal doctrine of baptism in the Spirit. Mason wrestled with the spiritual meaning of the Scriptures that were used in the proclamation that this third blessing of the Spirit was available, and that it had *glossolalia* as its "Bible sign." After great endeavor, Mason testified to receiving Spirit baptism after having a deeply affective experience in which his insight resulted in humility before God that brought great joy, so that "from that day until now." He later also testified that "there has been an overflowing joy of the glory of the Lord in my heart."[64] For both Edwards and Mason, biblical interpretation was inextricably linked to the spiritual meaning of the text so that the end sought was a living experience of the spiritual truth that was the result of the gracious work of the Spirit. Such living experience of the text has been paradigmatic for the core of what constitutes "pentecostal" in pentecostal hermeneutics. Lived experiences of the Spirit, moreover, have been essential to the subsequent development of other types of pentecostal hermeneutics. Nevertheless, for reasons developed in *Religious Affections*, Edwards would likely have been a critic of the wider spiritual hermeneutics utilized by early Pentecostals like Mason—for example, the latter's interpretation of unique vegetable roots as spiritual signs from God. But it would also be hard to find deeper testimonies of the living and affected knowledge of Scripture promoted by Edwards

---

[62] Here I refer to the tradition following Gadamer, Ricouer, Westphal, and others as drawn upon by Christian theologians. See the essays in Kenneth J. Archer and L. William Oliverio, Jr., eds., *Constructive Pneumatological Hermeneutics in Pentecostal Christianity* (New York: Palgrave Macmillan, 2016).

[63] Oliverio, *Theological Hermeneutics in the Classical Pentecostal Tradition*, esp. 15–18, 315–18.

[64] Mary Mason, comp., *The History and Life Work of Elder C.H. Mason and His Co-Laborers* (1924; reprint, Memphis, TN: Church of God in Christ, 1987), 27–30 and Ithiel C. Clemmons, *Bishop C.H. Mason and the Roots of the Church of God in Christ* (Bakersfield, CA: Pneuma Life, 1996), 6–23.

than what has been found among early Pentecostals from Seymour and Mason through to the present.[65]

Yet another early founder, Daniel Warren Kerr (1856–1927), who showed more conservative hermeneutical tendencies that helped (re)turn pentecostal hermeneutics toward an evangelical-pentecostal hermeneutical type, is perhaps the Pentecostal whose biblical and spiritual hermeneutics most closely stands in line with those of Edwards. Quietly an influential figure for early Pentecostalism as the primary author of the Assemblies of God's original Statement of Fundamental Truths (1915/16), as well as the founder of several institutions of higher education, Kerr sought the spiritual realities that Scripture revealed for his Bible doctrines while persisting in foregrounding the spiritual realities. That is, for Kerr, the spiritual experiences were primary and the proper ends, while the theology was secondary yet still of importance.

In interpreting the Bible, Kerr did not just want biblical facts, he wanted "facts on fire."[66] While not using the same terms as Edwards' spiritual and speculative theologies, Kerr offered similar categories as he advocated the preeminence of "spontaneous theology" over "systematic theology."[67] It is "spontaneous theology" that should take "first place" as the "Bible is a supernatural revelation from God to men . . . the discourse of God concerning Himself."[68] "Systematic theology" is like the dry, factual structures which, while true, do not contain life. For Kerr, "the secret of 'spontaneous theology' lies in the word of Jesus, 'He that willeth to do His will shall know of the doctrine whether it be of God or whether I speak for myself,' John 7:17."[69] Kerr also drew on images in a manner similar to Edwards' "images" or "shadows," finding the organic nature of "spontaneous theology" to contain spiritual life in images like "fire," "water," and "rain."[70] The quest for a spiritual sense of Scripture, the preeminence of this spiritual knowledge over the systematic or speculative, the development and justification of such as scriptural doctrine, and Kerr's own "modernizing traditionalism" in his theological narrative of history, sound tones quite similar to those of Edwards.[71]

This "modernizing traditionalism" is also another key point of confluence with Edwards and evangelical-pentecostal hermeneutics. McClymond and McDermott consider "hybrid traditionalism," their preferred category for the class of exegetes in which Edwards is properly placed in his approach to the historicity of Scripture, as being defined by holding to traditional views while not merely assuming them but arguing for them.[72] In doing so, Edwards could defend things, like the Mosaic authorship of the Pentateuch, in ways that would strain historical judgments of many believing scholars

---

[65] For instance, McClymond and McDermott, *Theology of Jonathan Edwards*, 172n26, find that "though Edwards might have approved some aspects of the twentieth-century Pentecostal-Charismatic movement, the practice he condemned in *Religious Affections* has a parallel in the contemporary Charismatic notion of the '*rhema* word' or specific text of Scripture that comes vividly to mind—purportedly through the power of the Holy Spirit."

[66] Daniel Warren Kerr, "Facts on Fire," *The Pentecostal Evangel*, April 11, 1925, 5.

[67] See Paul Ramsey, "Editor's Introduction," *WJE* 2:47.

[68] Daniel Warren Kerr, "Spontaneous Theology," *The Weekly Evangel*, April 17, 1915, 3.

[69] Ibid.

[70] Ibid. and Daniel Warren Kerr, *Waters in the Desert* (Springfield, MO: GPH, 1925), 17–20.

[71] Oliverio, *Theological Hermeneutics in the Classical Pentecostal Tradition*, 88–104.

[72] McClymond and McDermott, *Theology of Jonathan Edwards*, 168–72.

today. This "modernizing traditionalism" or "hybrid traditionalism" has also been used in various renditions of "believing criticism" among contemporary evangelical-pentecostal hermeneuts since the development of a more scholarly tradition within Pentecostalism in the mid- to late twentieth century. This development can be seen, for instance, in the way history and biblical interpretation are integrated in the earlier evangelical-pentecostal theologian Myer Pearlman's (1898–1943) works published in the 1930s. Pearlman's oft-used text *Knowing the Doctrines of the Bible* (1937) drew on ancient historical and cultural contexts as they merged with the present so that the text presents a theological, even eschatological, narrative of human history. A more sophisticated use of historical-critical methods, and especially redaction criticism, has since developed in late-twentieth and early-twentieth-century evangelical-pentecostal biblical scholars like Roger Stronstad and Robert Menzies.[73] Edwards and early forms of the evangelical-pentecostal hermeneutic, however, produced readings of history that have often ended in awkward historical judgments, especially regarding their eschatologies. For Edwards, this can be seen not only in his hoped-for Protestant world triumph which came amid his postmillennial schema of history but also among many Pentecostals, often in more cataclysmic readings of history rooted in their forms of premillennialism.[74]

A more fruitful resourcing of Edwards and his legacy for Pentecostals continues to be found in how the substance of Christian theology and the human affections meet, like they did for early hermeneuts like Seymour, Mason, and Kerr. Contemporary pentecostal theologians, including many who can be categorized as doing theology and interpreting the Bible in light of the sense of the utter contextuality of all human understanding, a sense which has become acute in late modernity, have also placed a strong emphasis on the centrality of the affections for pentecostal biblical interpretation. Many of these contextual-pentecostal theologians, like Amos Yong, have understood the affections as not only central to pentecostal theology, but have also emphasized the centrality of love for Christian theology altogether, and for the pentecostal cardinal doctrine of Spirit baptism more particularly. Following Land's lead, Yong and other pentecostal theologians have affirmed that the affections, the "abiding dispositions which dispose the person toward God and the neighbor in ways appropriate to their source and goal in God,"[75] are to be shaped by an orthopathy, that is, right affections, and are to be combined with right practices and right beliefs for fruitful Christian living, theology, and biblical interpretation.[76] Some Pentecostals have turned to an "analogy of love" (*analogia agapē*) not at the exclusion

---

[73] My account of Pearlman's hermeneutics is available in *Theological Hermeneutics in the Classical Pentecostal Tradition*, 121–30. For Stronstad, see *The Charismatic Theology of St. Luke* (Peabody, MA: Hendrickson, 1984); "Pentecostal Experience and Hermeneutics," *Paraclete* 26, no. 1 (1992): 14–30; and Menzies, *Empowered for Witness: The Spirit in Luke-Acts* (Sheffield: Sheffield Academic Press, 1994).

[74] My thanks to Oliver Crisp for pointing to this similarity in history and eschatology during our panel discussion on Edwards and Pentecostalism at the 2016 Annual Meeting of the Society for Pentecostal Studies.

[75] Land, *Pentecostal Spirituality*, 136.

[76] See Amos Yong, *Spirit of Love: A Trinitarian Theology of Grace* (Waco, TX: Baylor University Press, 2012), esp. 75–91.

of the *analogia entis* or the *analogia fidei*, but seeing each as bringing the others to completion in a perichoretical relationship.[77]

The ecumenical-pentecostal impulse in contemporary pentecostal hermeneutics has also, by an almost second nature impulse, turned to the affections in its readings of the Bible. Ecumenical-pentecostal approaches have sought to draw on the historical Christian traditions and contemporary *oikumenē* in order to nurture pentecostal and other churches with rich theology. The overall agenda is exemplified by Simon Chan's call for pentecostal "traditioning."[78] But the Old Testament scholar Lee Roy Martin's post-critical, ecumenically oriented, and nurturing approach to the "hearing" of texts provides a key contemporary exemplar of pentecostal affective hermeneutics that resounds with Edwards' in an approach to Scripture where the affections come to the fore in garnering spiritual fruit from the interpretation of Scripture.

For Martin, "the affective approach calls for the hearer to attend to the affective tones that are present in the text and to allow the affections of the hearer to be shaped by the text."[79] Martin turns to "hearing" over "reading" on account of its more biblical basis, so that the constitution of the text presupposes God's speech and calls for obedience and transformation, while this orality also reflects pentecostal self-understanding.[80] Such an affective hearing can combine with a variety of approaches and take place in different contexts, among diverse traditions. Further, it need not ignore critical scholarship, as Martin advocates a post-critical rather than pre- or a-critical approach. This approach distinguishes itself from other modern ones that tend to focus on the dissection of the structure of a text and other historical-critical issues with little to no attention placed on the emotional dimensions, though such are prominent in texts like the Psalms which Martin focuses on. Rather, a hearing of the text "aims to develop emotional and moral sensitivities" and informs not only belief and action but "the imagination."[81]

Pentecostal hermeneutics that have tended to the affections have understood such as a way of knowing, a positive response in attitude and reception that is compatible with late modern hermeneutics and anthropology, as well as a pentecostal sense of the manifold witness to truth and understanding in order to construct spiritual understanding, discern, and build Christian communities of empowered and loving witness. Edwards' hermeneutics were much more conservative than many late modern, that is, contemporary pentecostal hermeneutics, though the depth of his theological

---

[77] For development of the "analogy of love," see Yong, *Spirit of Love*, esp. 85–91; Frank D. Macchia, *Baptized in the Spirit: A Global Pentecostal Theology* (Grand Rapids, MI: Zondervan, 2006), 257–82; David R. Nichols, "The Search for a Pentecostal Structure in Systematic Theology," *Pneuma: The Journal of the Society for Pentecostal Studies* 6, no. 2 (1984): 57–76; and my "Spirit Baptism in the Late Modern World: A Pentecostal Response to *The Church: Towards a Common Vision*," in Thomas Hughson, ed., *The Holy Spirit and the Church: Ecumenical Reflections with a Pastoral Perspective* (New York: Routledge, 2016), 44–70, esp. 57–60.

[78] Simon Chan, *Pentecostal Theology and the Christian Spiritual Tradition* (Sheffield: Sheffield Academic Press, 2000), esp. 17–39.

[79] Martin, "Longing for God," 55.

[80] Ibid., 55n2; also, Lee Roy Martin, *The Unheard Voice of God: A Pentecostal Hearing of the Book of Judges* (Blandford Forum: Deo, 2008).

[81] Ibid., 59.

vision and the affirmation of the affections, rightly understood, are points where pentecostal hermeneutics might learn from the great American theologian.

Further, Edwards was insufficiently aware of the influence of British-colonial and Puritan cultural norms upon his spiritual and theological interpretations of the Bible. The black pentecostal theologian Estrelda Alexander has noted how, though Edwards preached and sought the salvation of blacks, he theologically interpreted the Bible as implying that the hierarchical social order on earth in fact reflected God's intent, and that even in heaven there would be differing "degrees of glory" for whites and blacks.[82] Contemporary pentecostal hermeneutics would, almost unanimously, be critical of smuggling in these types of cultural assumptions into theological hermeneutics. Nevertheless, popular pentecostal hermeneutics also commonly reflect cultural assumptions quite deeply, loosely interpreting biblical texts in light of contemporary ideas as they take initial spiritual and theological readings of the Bible at face value, oftentimes without suspicion concerning interpretive motives or sufficiently developed theological, biblical, or philosophical resources for discernment.

Dialogue between the dual impulses to relate to culture and affirm the affections can create the desire for an approach, like Martin's, that is unafraid of scholarship and critical readings but is nevertheless productive of sanctified and empowered affections for hearing the biblical text.[83] What Edwards and many Pentecostals have understood is that the affections are a way of knowing. The affections are not reduced to irrational reactions to be overcome by colder and supposedly more rational ways of understanding. The affective is an inevitable aspect of human being-in-the-world. Humans are lovers. Such loves orient us toward the ends that we most greatly desire.[84] They form the agendas of what we read in the Bible, and they open our ears to hear. They tend our intentions to that which we attend.

Conclusion

Edwards' approach to the affections seeks the spiritual sense of Scripture with a discipline that is rigorous and that casts suspicion on mere outward appearances. Pentecostals have tended to openness in interpreting experienced affections as righteous or gracious. The confluence of the attention to the affections here is also met by contrasting theological anthropologies and narratives for the path of salvation and the Christian life. For Pentecostals, Edwards' theology of the affections in *Religious Affections* may be utilized in helpful critique of overly optimistic and accepting readings of the human affections that mistake too wide a variety of feelings for gracious ones, or any spirit for the Spirit. Edwards' Calvinistic approach is untenable

---

[82] Estrelda Y. Alexander, *Black Fire: One Hundred Years of African American Pentecostalism* (Downers Grove: IVP Academic, 2011), 64–65.
[83] See also Chris E. W. Green, *Sanctifying Interpretation: Vocation, Holiness, and Scripture* (Cleveland, TN: CPT, 2015).
[84] James K. A. Smith, *Desiring the Kingdom: Worship, Worldview, and Cultural Formation* (Grand Rapids, MI: Baker Academic, 2009).

for most Pentecostals, yet his theological criteria for identifying affections might lead Pentecostals to develop further theological criteria of their own. Pentecostals do not need to put on the "Saul's Armor" of Edwards' theology for developing a more robust account of the affections, for biblical interpretation or otherwise.[85] Like the best of ecumenical-pentecostal hermeneutics, though, Pentecostals may see an example in the Christian tradition and not merely imitate it but seek to learn from it, to draw salient understanding, and then to reconstruct and integrate a deeper and more theologically sound approach to the affections in tune with pentecostal identity. Martin's work, in particular, exemplifies this as he has integrated such into his scholarly work in interpreting the Old Testament.

---

[85] D. Lyle Dabney, "Saul's Armor: The Problem and Promise of Pentecostal Theology Today," *Pneuma: The Journal of the Society for Pentecostal Studies* 23, no. 1 (2001): 115–46.

2

Speculative Theology and Spiritual Practice: A Reformed, Catholic, and Pentecostal Conversation on an Aspect of Theological Method

Christopher A. Stephenson

Introduction

Jonathan Edwards' treatise on religious affections gives insight into an empirical and inductive theological method for determining whether religious expression is genuine. It also points toward the relationship between religious affections and the method of speculative theology. Pentecostals have historically excelled in the realm of affectivity, while speculative theology is rarely a priority for them even among their academic theologians. My attempt to bring Edwards and Pentecostals into conversation with each other on speculative theology involves an invitation to some of the Catholic sources within the Christian spiritual tradition to join the conversation. I bring Edwards and Pentecostals together through their similarities with this third party with the goal of showing the relationship between speculative theology and spiritual practice informed by the best from Edwards' *Religious Affections*, from select sources within the spiritual tradition's accounts of meditation and affective prayer, and from soaking prayer among Pentecostals.[1]

Jonathan Edwards and *Religious Affections*

My discussion of *Religious Affections* focuses on three of Edwards' signs: the fifth, eleventh, and twelfth. Edwards' fifth sign that affections are truly gracious is that they are accompanied by a reasonable and spiritual conviction of the certainty of divine things. Truly gracious persons have a thorough conviction that particular tenets of the

---

[1] For my attempt to integrate pentecostal theology with meditative and affective prayer in connection with analytic theology, see Christopher A. Stephenson, "Should Pentecostal Theology be Analytic Theology," *Pneuma: The Journal of the Society for Pentecostal Studies* 36, no. 2 (2014): 246–64.

gospel are true, and they no longer consider these truths debatable or simply probable. The certainty with which such truths are held surpasses the mere assent sometimes given to matters of faith that are doubtful speculation, for gracious persons are so firm in their conviction of these truths that they are willing to stake everything on them. Because these truths have such weight, they rule the affections of gracious persons and govern them throughout their lives.[2]

Edwards envisions religious affections as arising from a particular kind of certainty of Christian truth, certainty that is both reasonable and spiritual. By "reasonable," he means conviction founded on good evidence. Persons can have legitimate certainty about genuine truths without sufficient evidence or good reasons. Insufficient reasons for the certainty of a religious belief include being based solely on education or being held because predecessors or neighbors share the belief. While this kind of certainty is not necessarily problematic in and of itself, it should not be taken as an indication that religious affections are truly gracious. Neither does it follow that reasonable certainty is a sign of gracious affections if the certainty is not also spiritual. By "spiritual," Edwards means an illumination of the understanding, because a proper judgment about things requires the correct apprehension of them. Thus, the Holy Spirit gives right apprehension to the mind through a kind of revealing or unveiling. The specific content of this apprehension is "a sense and taste of the divine, supreme and holy excellency of those things" apprehended.[3] Spiritual conviction arises when one rightly understands the beauty and glory of those things understood. This sense, given to believers by the Holy Spirit, is not simply a new principle within their natural senses, such as might be given to an unbeliever. Instead, this spiritual sense is a genuinely new sense beyond any natural capacity believers have on their own.[4]

The sense of glory and beauty convinces the mind of truth both directly and indirectly. It convinces directly because the glory is itself direct and clear; the one who sees this glory knows the truth intuitively. Edwards does not mean that one believes the truth of divine things without argumentation or deduction altogether; rather, one believes "without any long chain of arguments; the argument is but one, and the evidence direct; the mind ascends to the truth of the gospel but by one step, and that is its divine glory."[5] The one who holds a spiritual conviction does so reasonably because the sense of beauty and glory counts as an internal evidence for the truth of the idea believed. Seeing the divine glory of things convinces one of the truth because things pertaining to God have a supreme excellency about them that distinguishes them from things human and mundane, similarly to the way a natural beauty in writing style might distinguish one author from another. It is divine truths that exhibit supreme excellency, and they appear most brightly in the doctrines of the gospel. Edwards maintains that there must be such a direct conviction of the truth of divine things

---

[2] Edwards, *Religious Affections*, WJE 2:291–92.
[3] Ibid., 297.
[4] Ibid., 201–8. Concerning the new spiritual sense and accompanying certainty, see Michael J. McClymond and Gerald R. McDermott, *Theology of Jonathan Edwards* (Oxford: Oxford University Press, 2012), 311–20 and 373–88 and Stephen J. Nichols, *An Absolute Sort of Certainty: The Holy Spirit and the Apologetics of Jonathan Edwards* (Phillipsburg, NJ: P&R, 2003).
[5] Edwards, *Religious Affections*, WJE 2:298–99.

through internal evidence alone; otherwise, the majority of persons would be excluded from knowing divine truth. There must be another way to attain divine truth for the illiterate or uneducated who cannot understand lengthy arguments or who have little or no awareness of external evidences that come through endeavors like historical investigation. According to Edwards, a sense of the glory of divine truth convinces the mind indirectly also. First, it helps remove the prejudices one has against arguments that demonstrate the truth of the gospel due to animosity against the gospel itself. Second, the sense actively assists reason and makes even speculative matters "more lively."[6] It engages the mind's attention and helps the mind see more clearly obtuse ideas and the relations among speculative notions.

Edwards observes that three things are often identified inaccurately as spiritual conviction. First, there is a conviction of truth that arises from more common enlightenings of the Holy Spirit. Some have these general convictions without having a sense of the beauty and excellency of the truths of which they are convinced. Second, there is a conviction of truth that arises from so-called miracles, visions, or other personal revelations. For example, he writes,

> the lying miracles of the Papists . . . beget in the minds of the ignorant deluded people, a strong persuasion of the truth of many things in the New Testament. Thus when the images of Christ, in popish churches, are on some extraordinary occasions, made by priestcraft to appear to the people as if they wept, and shed fresh blood, and move, uttered such and such words. . . . Even the intercourse which Satan has with witches, and their often experiencing his immediate power, has a tendency to convince 'em of the truth of some doctrines of religion.[7]

Third, there is a conviction of truth that arises purely from realizing one's stake in the particular truth. For example, persons believe that heaven exists because they want it for themselves and believe that hell exists and that it is for others rather than themselves.

Edwards' eleventh sign that affections are truly gracious is that they increase one's desire for spiritual things, whereas false affections encourage satisfaction in the affections themselves. Edwards states that the more one loves God with a gracious love, the more she desires to love God and the more troubled she is by her lack of love for God and her lingering love for sin. The more one mourns her sin, the more she desires to mourn her sin and longs to thirst for holiness. No attainment in the present life can completely satisfy such longings, because even the height of perfection within reach here and now is only a foretaste of the glory eventually to be revealed. Gracious affections are like a growing flame; the longer they burn the more fervently they do so. Also, the more one has of holy affections, the greater is her sense of the excellency of divine things.[8]

---

[6] Ibid., 307.
[7] Ibid., 309–10.
[8] Ibid., 376–78.

Edwards' twelfth sign that affections are truly gracious is that they result in Christian practice. He claims that gracious affections result in Christian practice because gracious affections themselves stem from believers' participation in the divine nature by way of Christ and the Holy Spirit dwelling in their hearts in connection with the faculties of our souls. As a lively principle, they bring their nature to bear on the faculties of the soul. Thus, gracious affections have a governing power that shapes human behavior. For Edwards, Christian practice is not simply one indication among others of gracious affections; rather, it is the greatest sign of grace.[9]

Some of the Christian practices that Edwards highlights are expressions of love between persons. For example, in a reference to friendship, he says that a mere profession of love for someone is an inferior evidence of genuine friendship compared to concrete deeds. One should trust gestures like constancy in adversity, readiness for self-sacrifice on behalf of another, and demonstrations of kindness to the detriment of one's own interests far more than "a thousand earnest professions and solemn declarations" or "expressions of friendship in words."[10] Furthermore, Edwards praises the Christian who shows his tenderheartedness toward those undergoing a tragedy by bearing another's burden and using his own resources on behalf of another over the Christian who tells of his love for another while in fact remaining selfish and stingy. It is the former Christian who more reliably manifests a spirit of love.

While advancing his case for the primacy of Christian practice, Edwards distinguishes between two kinds of exercises of grace, namely, immanent acts and acts that are more practical than immanent acts. The first exercise of grace begins and ends within the soul apart from any direct connection to outward actions. For example, says Edwards, one may engage in contemplation without achieving results beyond the thoughts of the mind, although "they may tend to practice (as all exercises of grace do) more remotely."[11] The second exercise of grace concerns things to be done through the actions of the will. For example, according to Edwards, one exercises the grace of charity and gives a cup of cold water to a fellow believer or one exercises the grace of the supreme love of Christ and willfully undergoes persecution in the course of fulfilling her responsibilities. This second exercise of grace produces good works that originate as acts of the will. Edwards states explicitly that Christian practice in this second sense is the chief evidence of sincere religion to those who profess it and that such practices are "much to be preferred to . . . any immanent discoveries or exercises of grace whatsoever, that begin and end in contemplation."[12] Furthermore, Christian practice is the best evidence that one's belief of the truth is of the saving kind of belief. Anticipating the objection that spiritual experience is a better judge of one's standing before God than Christian practice is, Edwards clarifies that the two are closely related. In fact, there is no inconsistency in maintaining that Christian practice is the chief sign of grace and maintaining that spiritual experience is the primary evidence of grace, for Christian practice that is holy is a kind of experience.

---

[9] Ibid., 383, 392–93, and 406.
[10] Ibid., 410.
[11] Ibid., 422–23.
[12] Ibid., 426.

In *Religious Affections*, then, Edwards, first, establishes a close connection between affectivity and the certainty of Christian truth. The certainty surpasses speculation, but Edwards does not disparage speculative theology. On the contrary, the spiritual sense of the glory, excellency, and beauty of divine truth enhances speculative matters and helps the mind see them more clearly. The certainty of Christian truth is related to argumentation and deduction, although based on a special intuition of truth assisted by the Holy Spirit. He also makes suggestive statements about the relationship of this spiritual sense with other spiritual manifestations that might be considered "charismatic," as well as less than favorable comments about one facet of the Catholic tradition. Edwards, second, connects affectivity with an increase rather than a satiation of spiritual longing. Gracious affections prompt us to want more. Edwards, third, makes Christian practice the result of gracious affections, some of the manifestations of which are expressions of love from one person to another. While he gives these kinds of outward acts primacy over immanent acts like contemplation, he does not disparage the latter.

Meditation and affective prayer in the Christian spiritual tradition

Meditation is a discursive form of prayer in which one focuses on some theological or spiritual truth that she wishes to analyze thoroughly, understand better, and reach a firmer conviction about. While greater theological understanding might come from any number of means of academic study, meditation, specifically as a form of prayer, is a process of rousing one's love for God and plotting a course to act on the affection of love roused by the meditation. The goal, then, is not only greater understanding of a theological or spiritual truth but also greater love for that truth along with greater love for God. An occasion of practicing meditation can last as long as one remains in a disposition for devotional reflection and is able to carry it out without distractions interfering. According to Thomas Aquinas, the duration of prayer should match its goal. Thus, prayer should last long enough to raise the fervor of interior desire and end once it cannot be continued without making one weary.[13] However long or short the duration of meditation, the hope is that the affection of love roused by it will endure throughout one's day, resulting in constant prayer. Meditation requires one to turn his attention away from the natural activities of the day in order to focus attention on Christian truth as a means of spiritual growth and sanctification. Jordan Aumann states that those who never focus their attention through meditation may enter states of habitual sin, not because of contempt for the things of God but because they never retreat from daily responsibilities to assess their spiritual condition.[14]

---

[13] Thomas Aquinas, *Summa Theologiae* (New York: Blackfriars/McGraw-Hill, 1964), IIa IIae, q. 83, a. 14.
[14] Jordan Aumann, *Spiritual Theology* (London: Continuum, 2006), 318–27 and 323.

One of the potential results of meditation is affective prayer, a grade of prayer in which love (or some other affection) roused by meditation comes to be predominant over the discursive aspect of meditation. When meditation gives rise to an affection, one ceases discursive prayer in order to yield to the affection until it expires. One can then return to discursive prayer by meditating on another theological or spiritual truth, which might again give rise to an affection. As one yields to the affection, one stops the process of rigorous thinking to allow love (or some other affection) to grow. One may be so overwhelmed by affections that thought is actually hindered or even made impossible as long as the affections endure. Whether one yields to affections by expressing vocal prayer or by becoming silent and contemplating oneself in the presence of God, one is no longer meditating but rather responding to the content of meditation. Aumann states that among the various prescriptions for meditation in the spiritual tradition, three elements predominate: (1) the consideration of a theological or spiritual truth, (2) an application of the truth to one's life, and (3) a commitment to act upon the application somehow.[15]

Teresa of Avila states that grades of prayer such as meditation and affective prayer might be especially suited for those who have actively embraced the life of the intellect.[16] On the one hand, discursive prayer should come quite naturally to them, and on the other, the transition to affective prayer allows them to delight in Christ without pushing the intellect to the point of exhaustion. Offering an example of an object of meditation, she writes,

> Let us begin to think about an episode of the Passion, let's say of when our Lord was bound to the pillar. The intellect goes in search of reasons for better understanding the great sorrows and pain His Majesty suffered in that solitude and many other things that the intellect, if it works hard, can herein deduce. How much more if it is the intellect of a learned man! This is the method of prayer with which all must begin, continue, and finish; and it is a very excellent and safe path until the Lord leads one to other supernatural things.[17]

Her reference here to being led to other supernatural things indicates that meditation and affective prayer are relatively low grades of prayer that should be reasonably accessible to most Christians. That is, they are well within the realm of the ascetical (ways of prayer that are more active than passive and can be practiced without extraordinary divine assistance) rather than the mystical (ways of prayer that are more passive than ascetical ways and are practiced only with extraordinary divine assistance). Surely intellectual capacity and training varies from one person to the next, but meditation and affective prayer can be practiced volitionally, whereas one cannot simply produce by exercise of the will an encounter on the order of, say, Julian of Norwich's revelations

---

[15] William Johnston, *Mystical Theology: The Science of Love* (Maryknoll, NY: Orbis, 1995), 51–52, 66–67, 133–34, and 224–26.
[16] Teresa of Avila, *The Book of Her Life*, chapters 11–22, in *The Collected Works of St. Teresa of Avila*, 3 vols. (Washington, DC: ICS, 1987), 1:128–30.
[17] Ibid., 129.

of divine love or the ecstasy that Teresa herself experienced. This is not necessarily to say that there is a wall between the ascetical and the mystical that only a few are permitted to scale, but rather that meditation and affective prayer are among those grades of prayer that can be practiced with determination, attentiveness, and the basic help of the Holy Spirit and grace.

The spiritual tradition, then, renders a close connection between Christian truth and discursive and affective prayer. These grades of prayer exist within the broader context of ascetical and mystical practices, which the spiritual tradition has not always excelled at integrating with charismatic phenomenon. That is, even when granting the continued legitimacy of *charismata*, it is not always clear how such phenomenon relate to ascetical and mystical practices. There is also a close connection in the spiritual tradition between increasing certainty about and love for theological truths and carrying out concrete actions in response to meditation on theological truths. The former should lead directly to the latter. In light of these grades of prayer, speculative theology can be carried out in the form of prayer.

Soaking prayer in the pentecostal-charismatic tradition

Soaking prayer is not an entirely new phenomenon, but rather an established practice among Pentecostals and Charismatics that has had different names within different pentecostal-charismatic traditions over time. To a certain extent, soaking prayer is what Classical Pentecostals sometimes call "falling under the power," what those in the Latter Rain Movement may call being "slain in the spirit," what members of the Charismatic movement might prefer to call "resting in the Spirit," and what participants in the Toronto Blessing initially called "carpet time." "Soaking" eventually replaced "carpet time" as the name for lying down on the floor voluntarily or involuntarily, alone or with other worshipers, with or without receiving prayer from others, in order to have an encounter with God similar to that usually associated with these other names.[18] When lying down voluntarily, practitioners of soaking prayer may even use pillows and blankets to enhance levels of comfort. Soaking prayer is often accompanied by music, whether live or recorded, that utilizes repetitive phrases to produce a calming effect that is supposed to assist participants in resting or relaxing in God's presence. Sometimes participants actively join the repetition by synchronizing their breathing patterns to the rhythm of the music, which is usually slow. As breathing slows and regulates, participants become more relaxed.[19] Perhaps they will become so relaxed that they fall asleep, which is generally not considered a problem. Sleep may be exactly

---

[18] Margaret M. Poloma, *Main Street Mystics: The Toronto Blessing and Reviving Pentecostalism* (Walnut Creek, CA: AltaMira, 2003), 56n3.

[19] Peter Althouse and Michael Wilkinson, "Musical Bodies in the Charismatic Renewal: The Case of Catch the Fire and Soaking Prayer," in *The Spirit of Praise: Music and Worship in Global Pentecostal-Charismatic Christianity*, ed. Monique M. Ingalls and Amos Yong (University Park, PA: Penn State, 2015), 30, 38, and 40.

what one needs, and God may be simply providing for the needs of those soaking.[20] Michael Wilkinson and Peter Althouse report that no one seemed to be disturbed when someone snored for over an hour during a soaking prayer gathering that they attended in Toronto.

John Arnott, one of the charismatic leaders associated with the origins of soaking prayer, says that soaking in God's presence is resting in God's love rather than "striving" in prayer. When under the influence of the Holy Spirit, one might fall down or lie down on the floor, and God might direct his attention to a portion of Scripture, an internal audible impression, or visual image. One might as easily sit or stand, as long as he can be vulnerable before God. Over time, one is transformed by these periods of soaking. Arnott uses the metaphor of pickling cucumbers to describe the process, writing, "Pickle us, Lord, in the marinade of the Holy Spirit. Soak us in your wonderful presence until we become more like You."[21]

Soaking focuses on the reception of divine love, and while soaking is usually nonverbal, one might also experience a number of charismatic phenomena like glossolalia, laughter, or moaning and groaning while soaking. Yet, the desire is for the benefit of soaking to accrue not only to the one who soaks but also to others. That is, the one who soaks in God's love shares that love with others through altruistic actions. In this respect, the metaphor of "soaking" is pressed to the fullest extent. Just as a sponge that soaks up water can then transfer that water to another location or item when squeezed, the one who soaks in God's love can release divine love to others through forgiveness, compassion, and benevolence. Thus, soaking is not purely reflexive in the sense of "I soaked myself in God's presence and love," but also transitive in the sense of "I soaked someone else in God's love," perhaps through an act of service of which someone was the beneficiary or perhaps through the laying on of hands. Soaking prayer is a response to the Great Commandment to love God and to love neighbor, and some practitioners of soaking prayer refer to it as a baptism into divine love.[22] For example, one woman claims to have received greater compassion for, and in turn ability to forgive, a coworker because she soaked herself in God's love. While not all tension with the coworker dissolved, the woman states that regularly soaking in God's love makes it easier for her to be kind to her supervisor.[23]

Wilkinson and Althouse offer three case studies of the benevolent endeavors of churches that practice soaking prayer. First, River City Church (Jacksonville, FL) began in a neighborhood with low-income housing populated predominantly by African Americans. After relocating, the church remained active in assistance with addiction recovery and providing medical care and training in employment skills. One member of River City Church describes the church's initiatives in a public housing area to give tutoring services, school supplies, and clothing to residents. Another member who

---

[20] Michael Wilkinson and Peter Althouse, *Catch the Fire: Soaking Prayer and Charismatic Renewal* (DeKalb: NIU, 2014), 9 and 88.
[21] John Arnott, "Soaking in His Presence," *Revival Magazine: A Spiritually Alive Perspective on Christian Living*, August 2003, http://revivalmag.com/article/soaking-his-presence (accessed October 3, 2015).
[22] Wilkinson and Althouse, *Catch the Fire*, 4–5, 8, and 110.
[23] Ibid., 85.

devotes her own time to these initiatives is described as doing so "out of an overflow of love."[24] Soaking prayer is practiced by both the church members who participate in acts of benevolence and those whom the members help. Wilkinson and Althouse conclude that soaking prayer is a vital part of the church's outreach to the poor in its area.[25]

Second, Catch the Fire (Montreal) offers an example of racial reconciliation encouraged in part by soaking prayer and a fundamental orientation to sharing divine love. On one occasion, the pastor, Gerry Plunkett, explicitly addressed the racism between black and white Francophone people groups in Montreal, which extend into the church congregation. He apologized to African and Haitian church members for their treatment at the hands of his fellow whites. While some Africans seemed to be uncomfortable with the gesture, many blacks and whites openly wept and embraced each other in love. One black woman expressed to the congregation her love for the white pastor and his apology. The pastor expressed his desire for the black church members to receive the Father's love. Furthermore, Plunkett participated in a conference in Togo, a nation in West Africa, and made a similar apology that was specific to this different context. He discussed the significant number of North American slaves that passed through Togo, the exploitation of resources in Africa by whites, and the imposition of French values on Africans. Again, blacks and whites openly embraced and responded positively to the pastor's message of the Father's love.[26]

Third, Tierra Nueva (Burlington, Washington) exhibits extensive concern for social transformation. The church operates a support center that makes counseling and legal assistance available to its community. The center's staff sometimes arbitrate disputes between tenants and landowners and between employees and employers. The church visits a local county jail, where it proclaims hope and reconciliation for the imprisoned and leads them in practicing soaking prayer. Tierra Nueva also sponsors a seminary that offers rudimentary theological training for persons marginalized within society for various reasons.[27]

Soaking prayer, then, is a form of prayer in the pentecostal-charismatic tradition that is not altogether unlike meditation in the spiritual tradition. It emphasizes the receiving and giving of divine love, both of which may be accompanied by charismatic phenomenon. The sharing of a sense of divine love that one has already received often takes the form of benevolence toward others. As with the spiritual tradition, a form of prayer should lead to concrete actions.

Integrative conclusion

To conclude, I bring together what I consider the best from the three voices above to sketch a possible exercise in speculative theology and spiritual practice. I make no attempt to reconcile points of tension among them. I take for granted that there is

---

[24] Ibid., 143.
[25] Ibid., 140–44.
[26] Ibid., 144–48.
[27] Ibid., 148–50.

enough similarity among them to warrant an attempted integration, especially between Edwards and the spiritual tradition on affections in general and desire for the greatest possible certainty of divine truth, between Pentecostals and the spiritual tradition on quiet, reflective prayer, and between Edwards and Pentecostals on Christian practice in the form of acts of love expressed toward others. My hope also is that using the spiritual tradition as a bridge between Edwards and Pentecostals further develops Edwards' notion that immanent acts like contemplation tend to practice and shows that Pentecostals sometimes follow a form of prayer that is not far from meditation in soaking prayer (even if not usually discursive).

One of Edwards' miscellanies provides a brief speculation that could become the content of meditative prayer directed toward the goal of increasing one's sense of divine love and of sharing it with others. He states that it was both fitting and necessary that the mediator of redemption should be the Son, rather than the Father or the Holy Spirit because the Son mediates both between the Father and fallen humans and between the Father and the Spirit. With respect to the first, it is unfitting for the Father to be the mediator because it is the Father who was offended by human sin and should thus be appeased by a mediator other than himself. It is unfitting for fallen humans to be the mediator since they, as the offending party, need someone to mediate on their behalf. With respect to the second, it is unfitting for the Father to be the mediator because the Son is already mediator between the Father and the Spirit by virtue of mediating between the Father and believers. Believers do all of the holy things that they do only by the Spirit, who is their principle of life and action. Yet, even these saintly things done through them by the Spirit are acceptable to God only through a mediator. Thus, it is fitting and necessary for the Son to be the mediator of redemption.[28]

As one meditates on Edwards' speculative account of the fittingness and necessity for the Son to be the mediator of redemption, her mind might move to another voice earlier in the Christian tradition who also reasoned about the Son as mediator with both similar and different conclusions. For example, Peter Lombard agrees with Edwards that only the Son is called "mediator," whereas Father, Son, and Spirit are rightly called "redeemer." However, he disagrees with Edwards about the Son mediating between the Father and the Spirit. For Peter, since God is one, the Son is not mediator between God and God, only between God and humans. Thus, the Son is mediator according to his human nature only, not with respect to his divine nature.[29] Of course, even the use of a figure like Peter demonstrates a more ecumenical sentiment toward the Catholic tradition than Edwards shows when referring to the "lying miracles of the papists" within a few strokes of his pen's reference to the "intercourse which Satan has with witches."[30]

---

[28] Edwards, "Miscellany 614," *WJE* 18:146–47.
[29] Peter Lombard, *The Sentences*, trans. and intro. W. Becket Soule (Ave Maria, FL: Sapientia, 2016), b3, d19, cc5-7.
[30] Edwards, *Religious Affections*, *WJE* 2:309–10. I do not assume that these isolated statements are representative of Edwards' sentiments toward the Catholic tradition; nonetheless, the statements are relevant given their mention in the context of charismatic phenomenon and my attempt to use Catholic sources as a bridge between Edwards and Pentecostals.

Whether or not she accepts the details from Edwards or Peter, constructs another formulation toward which their suggestions spur her thoughts, or acknowledges that she is not yet ready to reach a conclusion at all, meditation on these ideas has potential to bring to her greater confidence in the appropriateness of the Son's mediation of redemption and greater love for God because of it. As the affection of love increases, she might respond with silence, tears, glossolalia, or some other expression of vocal prayer. Ideally, she will remain awake and focused on meditation and affectivity because she has scheduled prayer for a time that she is well-rested and focused. If she cannot avoid sleep, she should postpone meditation until a time that she can. To paraphrase, Thomas Keating, OCSO in a public lecture on contemplative prayer, if she repeatedly falls asleep while attempting contemplative prayer, she needs to get more sleep at night! This marks a shift away from the pentecostal assumption that sleep should sometimes be a goal of soaking prayer, at least if it is to perform the work similar to discursive meditation.

If she meditates successfully, she may be struck by the beauty and glory of the Son's mediation of redemption to humans. She may also find an increased desire to meditate rather than a sense of complete satisfaction. Her appetite may be whetted rather than her thirst entirely quenched. She may also have an increased desire to progress to other grades of prayer. Perhaps, after soaking in God's love by yielding to affectivity, she might continue to heed the insight of the spiritual tradition and plot a course to act on the affection roused by meditation. She might do so by "soaking" others, that is, by carrying out concrete ways of sharing God's love with others who are not aware of or simply need to be reminded of the Son's mediation on their behalf. Perhaps she might become a minister of reconciliation performing acts of service toward others who feel separated from God or who never imagine themselves as being related to God in any sense. She may have a greater sense of compassion toward everyone she encounters and may attempt to show it by extending additional patience to them when they are irritable or being more sensitive to them when they are hurting. If she does these things, she will also bear witness to a possible point of convergence among three different strands of the Christian tradition—Reformed, Catholic, and Pentecostal—on theological method as it pertains to the relationship between speculative theology and spiritual practice.[31]

---

[31] For my proposal that Pentecostals should employ a variation of *lex orandi, lex credendi* in order to relate spirituality and doctrinal formulation explicitly, see Christopher A. Stephenson, *Types of Pentecostal Theology: Method, System, Spirit* (Oxford: Oxford University Press, 2013), 111–30.

3

Divine Action and Divine Affections: Jonathan Edwards, the Pentecostal and Process Theologian

Joshua D. Reichard

Introduction

This chapter mines the works of Jonathan Edwards and his expositors to explore a theology of divine action in the context of divine affections. The theology of Edwards has deep roots in the affections and religious experience, which makes his theology highly compatible with, if not prototypical of, pentecostal-charismatic theology. But Edwards' theology shares compatibility with process-relational theology. Both traditions may claim him to some degree—and surprisingly, although Edwards is typically aligned with the Calvinists, his view of the God-world relationship is not simplistically monergistic.

Further, this chapter explores Edwards in terms of the free will versus determinism debate with particular emphasis on divine action in creation. Edwards had a peculiar view of *creatio ex nihilo*, a "dispositional ontology," and an equally unusual perspective on the process of "dynamic becoming" versus static being. Edwards will be cast as a process-relational theist in terms of divine action and a pentecostal-charismatic theist in terms of religious affections. Such a reading of Edwards suggests a God that not only acts but also feels; the implications are that human beings, filled with the Spirit, can be both co-creators and co-sufferers with God. Thus, this chapter will propose a pentecostal, process-relational reading of Edwards and a creative synthesis from both vantage points. Edwards' dispositional ontology may thus be read in light of his theology of divine affections; in turn, a pentecostal reading of Edwards supports a process-relational reading.

Setting the stage

Inasmuch as Jonathan Edwards struggled to balance his metaphysical insights and spirituality with his doctrinal confessions, his expositors, especially in contemporary Edwards studies, have attempted to connect dots within his theology. Some have sought to prove that Edwards was someone perhaps he was not and others have sought to prove Edwards was who they want him to be. In this chapter, I propose that it is possible to draw trialogical comparisons between process-relational theology, pentecostal theology, and Edwards' theology without forcing Edwards into any particular theological box.

Sang Hyun Lee's work on Edwards has sparked many passionate theological conversations, including suggestions that Lee's conclusions are influenced by process-relational theology.[1] Lee argues that Edwards emancipated his philosophical theology from the Aristotelian-Thomistic metaphysic (consisting of forms and substances) in favor of a "dispositional ontology," without which "one does not even begin to understand Edwards' world view." In this ontology, Lee contends that Edwards "introduced an essentially new understanding of reality, replacing substance metaphysics with a dynamic and relational conception."[2]

Lee's critics, especially classical theists and Reformed Evangelicals, have endeavored to prove that Edwards was indeed doctrinally, confessionally, and theologically orthodox, at least in the evangelical-Reformed sense. Stephen Holmes, for example, argues that Edwards could not have endorsed the ontology that Lee ascribes to him because of its unorthodox concept of God.[3] Perhaps Lee did not set out to prove anything to the contrary; however, critics fear that he aligns Edwards too closely with what they see as heterodox "process" theologies. The mere association with process-relational theology, although not explicit in Lee's interpretation, has stoked the ire of his critics. Critics of Lee argue that reading a dispositional ontology into Edwards' theology contradicts the traditional Aristotelian-Scholastic (Thomistic) ontology that has dominated Western theology. Such a reading, they argue, elevates relationality above substance. Lee argues that Edwards affirmed a more relational view of reality, and of God; but critics argue that in so doing, Lee aligns Edwards dangerously close to process-relational theology.[4]

Those assumptions have ignited a series of turf-wars, characterized by attempts to defend Edwards' theological purity. However, I will argue that critics of Sang Hyun Lee, for example, have made unfair assumptions about process-relational theology. By clarifying those assumptions, and demonstrating that process-relational theology is not menacing in the ways it is portrayed, Edwards' theology may be clarified and amplified. From this comparison, I will lay the groundwork for comparisons with pentecostal theology. Finally, I will articulate the practical implications for such trialogue.

Oliver Crisp critiques Lee's reading of Edwards thus: "One should not attribute obviously problematic views to a particular thinker unless one has very good reason for thinking that the given thinker actually held such views."[5] I honor Crisp's conviction and

---

[1] Sang Hyun Lee, *The Philosophical Theology of Jonathan Edwards*, expanded ed. (Princeton, NJ: Princeton University Press, 2000).
[2] Ibid., 47.
[3] Stephen R. Holmes, *God of Grace and God of Glory: An Account of The Theology of Jonathan Edwards* (Edinburgh: Bloomsbury/T & T Clark, 2000).
[4] See for example, Oliver D. Crisp, "Jonathan Edwards' Ontology: A Critique of Sang Hyun Lee's Dispositional Account of Edwardsian Metaphysics," *Religious Studies* 46, no. 1 (2010): 1–20.
[5] Oliver D. Crisp, *Jonathan Edwards on God and Creation* (New York: Oxford University Press, 2012), 17.

hope not to make the same mistake in this chapter. For this reason, I will only identify points of contact between Edwards, process-relational theists, and Pentecostals, but will not be so bold as to retrospectively ascribe any such labels to Edwards. I seek only to ask questions, not to impose any such haughty presumptions. Moreover, I do not intend to assail or threaten, in any way, Edwards' historical commitment to theological orthodoxy. My intention is not to present another exposition of Edwards or to try to prove that Edwards was a process-relational theist or a Pentecostal.

Instead, I intend to bring contemporary Edwards studies, especially Lee and his critics, into deeper dialogue with both process-relational and pentecostal theologies. I will focus primarily on the issue of the God-world relation, Edwards' doctrine of creation, and its process-relational and pentecostal counterparts. I will primarily engage Edwards' *Dissertation Concerning the End for Which God Created the World*, but such engagement does not constitute a comprehensive survey of Edwards' work. I assert that a trialogical exploration of the doctrine of creation may lay the groundwork for future theological conversations between Edwards' scholars, process-relational theists, and Pentecostals.

Clarifying criticisms: Whose Edwards, whose process-relational theology?

Critics of Lee's analysis have generally been classical theists attempting to defend Edwards' theology as classical and orthodox. Orthodoxy, in this sense, is typically defined by Reformed and Neo-Calvinist Evangelicals, inasmuch as they claim Edwards as their own. The standard critique leveled against Lee is that he anachronistically misplaces Edwards in a twentieth-century context; Edwards could not have been a process-relational theist because he was an eighteenth-century theologian. While this argument is technically accurate, I believe it is ill conceived.

As John Cobb notes, when investigating historical theology for compatibilities with contemporary theology, we must accept the fact that "history does not work backwards."[6] However, it is not unreasonable to conjecture that Edwards could have been an influence on contemporary process-relational thought (although there is scant evidence of such influence). Of course, any comparison of historical theology to contemporary theology is an anachronistic exercise; but that is not a justifiable reason to reject such comparison. It does not seem unreasonable to suggest that Edwards' theology may have moved in directions that were articulated more thoroughly by later theologians, even if and though their ideas have no genetic and historical connection. Thus, the point of this chapter is not to argue that Edwards was or was not a panentheist or that Edwards was or was not within the bounds of orthodoxy. There is little harm in making critical comparisons of any theologies or philosophies, simply allowing them to enter into dialogue, and identifying similarities and differences.

---

[6] John B. Cobb, "Wesley the Process Theologian," *Religion Online* (2000), http://www.religion-online.org/showarticle.asp?title=1097.

On the contrary, critics of Lee have failed to consider that Edwards and the contemporary process-relational theists could be approximating similar truths. Whether such truth is contemporary or historical is hardly justification for rejecting any comparison at all. Instead, the real issue is perhaps a knee-jerk reaction against the specter of process-relational theology and its perceived threat to orthodoxy. It is obvious that Edwards knew nothing of Alfred North Whitehead, process-relational philosophy, or the twentieth century; but it may be equally true that Edwards and Whitehead both simply approximated similar ideas in their philosophical explorations. It may be that in his theology, Edwards was merely "reaching always for what he could not put into words."[7]

For example, John Bombaro argues that although Edwards tinkered with a dispositional ontology, he did so within the doctrinal bounds of Calvinism.[8] This goes without saying. Bombaro argues that Edwards came to embrace a "theocentric metaphysics of finality—not dispositions."[9] It is a fallacy to assume that just because a competing philosophy is used to describe metaphysical realities, competing doctrinal confessions must necessarily follow (this is, in effect, a "slippery slope" argument). Because competing philosophies are automatically linked with heterodox theologies, they are assumed to be heterodox as well. This is not, and need not be, the case.

I suggest that such criticisms may be overstated and grounded in a misunderstanding of process-relational thought. Critics ground their objections in the assumption that God is "dependent" on creation in process-relational theism. Although this is a common misunderstanding, it is a mischaracterization of some, but not all, trajectories of process-relational theism. By and large, classical theists fail to understand the basic philosophical and theological constructs of process-relational theology and instead focus on narrow strains of the tradition, such as the Hartshornean school. In fact, I question the extent to which such critics have read the seminal works of process-relational theology; if they had, their critiques may be more tempered. There is no prescriptive confessional statement for process-relational theology and to make broad judgments against the whole corpus of the process-relational tradition is an overreach at best and straw man at worst.

Divine action: Edwards in dialogue with process-relational theology

I have sought to bring process-relational theologies into conversation with orthodox and evangelical theologies, moving beyond "open theism" and engaging "process theology proper" more assertively. I have done this largely in the context of dialogue with pentecostal-charismatic theologies, primarily on metaphysical, not doctrinal,

---

[7] Belden C. Lane, *Ravished by Beauty: The Surprising Legacy of Reformed Spirituality* (New York: Oxford University Press, 2011), 178.

[8] John J. Bombaro, *Jonathan Edwards' Vision of Reality: The Relationship of God to the World, Redemption History, and the Reprobate* (Eugene, OR: Wipf & Stock, 2011).

[9] Bombaro, *Vision*, 12.

grounds.[10] I do not self-identify as a "process theologian." My goal is to recognize valuable perspectives, including the relational nature of both God and the created order, that can help not only Pentecostals but also Evangelicals in general and to articulate a more scientifically sensitive and metaphysically coherent vision of the God-world relationship, especially with regard to divine action. I do not embrace process theology wholesale and will not endeavor to impose it on Edwards in this trialogue.

Generally, process-relational theists hold that God is dipolar: God has a primordial pole that is immutable and a temporal pole that is mutable. The temporal pole is intimately related to creation. The primordial pole consists of those aspects of God's nature that do not change and the aspect of God in which pure possibilities, eternal objects (in technical Whiteheadian terms), are constituted. The fact that God's temporal pole is affected by creation does not mean that God has forfeited any eternal attributes. Eternal objects correspond to those divine qualities that Edwards called God's "dormant" attributes,[11] which only find their expression in God's creative activity and subsequent relation to creation. Having the ability to act a certain way is only as valuable as actually acting that way.[12] God's attributes would never have been manifest had God not created the world.

In *The End for Which God Created the World*, Edwards' dispositional ontology can be articulated thus:

1. God is His own End for Which God Created, creatures are not.
2. God created to express His divine attributes.
3. When creatures perceive God's attributes, and grow in union with Him, they receive pleasure and joy.

God rejoices in the joy of the creatures and thus, rejoices in Himself, His own chief end for which He created the world. It is quite clear that Edwards was not willing to concede God's self-sufficiency, which puts Edwards in apparent conflict with process-relational theology. God is God's own chief end for creating the world.[13] While God may be disposed to create, Edwards qualified such disposition by stating that God "goes not out of [Godself] in what [God] seeks."[14]

Edwards maintained that God cannot seek or find pleasure in any creature, but only by virtue of God "making it and admitting it to a participation of [God's] fullness."[15]

---

[10] Joshua Reichard, "Pentecost, Process, and Power," *Process Studies* 39, no. 2 (2012): 382–83; "An 'Improbable Bond of the Spirit': Historical Perspectives on the Christian Life in Pentecostal-Charismatic and Process-Relational Theologies," in *The Holy Spirit and the Christian Life: Historical, Interdisciplinary, and Renewal Perspectives*, ed. Wolfgang Vondey (New York: Palgrave Macmillan, 2014), 179–98; "Relational Empowerment," *Pneuma: The Journal of the Society for Pentecostal Studies* 36, no. 2 (2014): 226–45; and "Of Miracles and Metaphysics: A Pentecostal-Charismatic and Process-Relational Dialogue," *Zygon: Journal of Religion and Science* 48, no. 2 (2013): 274–93.
[11] Edwards, *Dissertation I. Concerning the End for Which God Created the World*, WJE 8:428–30.
[12] Ibid., 433–35.
[13] Ibid., 445–506.
[14] Ibid., 450.
[15] Ibid., 446.

Edwards emphatically insisted that nothing is added to God, God is not a dependent being, and God receives nothing from the creatures. Further, Edwards contended that no argument could be made that God is impoverished and needy because God has an inclination to communicate God's infinite fullness. Put simply: creatures are unable to change God, increase God, or decrease God in any way.[16] As such, Edwards' position is wholly incompatible with Hartshornian process theism.[17]

Oddly enough, panentheism may actually help resolve this conflict. I contend that if all things are in God, then God does not, in fact, "go outside Godself" to seek anything. Creation itself is constituted by, dependent on, and sustained by God. Thus, although creation is not God, God must never go outside of Godself to seek anything, including an increase in God's own glory or pleasure. Since the process of creation is immanent, taking place within the divine being, God is not perfected by something extrinsic to the divine nature; this, I believe, is the greatest oversight of critics of process-relational theism who attempt to assume that God is dependent on something external to Godself.

Although process-relational theology affirms authentic freedom in creatures, God's causal activity, presenting pure possibilities to each actual occasion, constitutes that freedom. Thus, it is possible for process-relational theists and classical theists to equally affirm this position. For process-relational theists, God makes possible creaturely participation with God. God's continuous creative activity is what enables creaturely participation in God and creaturely freedom. Apart from God, there is no freedom and no novelty in the universe.

Edwards noted that if creatures exist as possibilities in the mind of God, in process-relational terms the primordial nature of God, "God may be conceived of as being moved by benevolence to these creatures."[18] Whether Edwards meant that God's other essential attributes, such as holiness, goodness, and so on, compel God toward benevolence or, as process-relational theists maintain, that such essential benevolence is itself a divine attribute, the problem remains the same. Free creatures, whether possible or actual, invite a divine response; this must not be purely monergistic. Otherwise, God is entirely indifferent toward creation and altogether unconcerned about its current state or its final end. For Edwards, God created moral beings to experience the manifestation of God's own perfections, greatness, and excellent attributes, and enjoy what they see. God never lacked in the fullness of divine attributes, but God's desire to overflow this fullness was what moved God to create the world. Godself is the end for which God created, not created beings. God's acting for God's own glory and God's acting for the benefit of the creature are not set in opposition to one another. Although God may receive pleasure in observing pleasure in creatures, that does not mean that God depends on the creatures to be happy.[19]

---

[16] Ibid., 446.
[17] Some critics may evoke Hartshorne at this point, whose doctrine of contributionism, in which he argued that "true religion is contributing value to God which [God] would otherwise lack." Charles Hartshorne, *A Natural Theology for Our Time* (LaSalle, IL: Open Court, 1967), 274.
[18] Edwards, *Dissertation I. Concerning the End for Which God Created the World*, WJE 8:440.
[19] Edwards, *Dissertation I. Concerning the End for Which God Created the World*, WJE 8:436–44.

Reformed theologian Belden C. Lane notes that "panentheist amazement" is close to the heart of Edwards' theology.[20] Because the Reformed tradition elevates God's glory in creation, Lane argues that the Calvinists, the Puritans, and Edwards himself struggled to keep their theology from devolving into pantheism. But it is critical to note that panentheism is not pantheism; God is not creation and creation is not God. Rather, creation is contained in God and in God creation is constituted. This is the simple biblical idea that "in God we live and move and have our being" and that in Christ "all things hold together" (Acts 17:28; Col. 1:17).

Moreover, Lane highlights that Edwards spoke of "God's glory as a refulgence that flows from the divine being into the world and back again to its luminary."[21] This is not dissimilar to Charles Hartshorne's theory of contributionism, whereby the actualization of creation returns to God and enriches God's being; in other words, Hartshorne argued that "true religion is contributing value to God which [God] would otherwise lack."[22] In this model, in process-relational terms, God offers eternal objects from the primordial pole to the created order and as actual entities in the created order concretize, they return to God as new data. The circular flow of data from God to the world to God again is highly compatible with Edwards' notion of divine refulgence. While not a typical conception of *creatio ex nihilo*, I do not believe it is incompatible with orthodox convictions.

But Edwards' emphasis extends beyond mere input-output; Lane notes that implicit in Edwards' theology is an intuitive perception that God is enhanced by God's glory being celebrated in creation. For example, Edwards proclaims that "God stands in no need of creatures, and is not profited by them; neither can his happiness be said to be added to by the creature. But yet God has . . . a real delight in his own loveliness, and he also has a real delight in the shining forth or glorifying of it."[23] Lane notes of Edwards' theology: "In creating the world and sharing the divine glory with it, God's happiness is 'enlarged,' God's pleasure made richer."[24] There is inherent joy in such kenotic activity; God gives of Godself and seeks to increase the joy of creatures by calling them to self-give as well.[25]

Classical theists that argue for a God who is entirely immutable and unmoved by creation assume that such attributes are divine perfections. But process-relational theists argue to the contrary: on what philosophical basis should it be assumed that immutability is a great-making property? In fact, process-relational theists argue, and Lee concurs, that such assumptions are based purely on Aristotelian, Augustinian, and Thomistic philosophy where categories of divine perfections elevate invincibility and invulnerability.

---

[20] Lane, *Ravished*, 25. Lane may be an ally in the Edwards-panentheistic dialogue, though not necessarily an ally to process-relational theism per se.
[21] Ibid., 25.
[22] Hartshorne, *A Natural Theology for Our Time*, 274.
[23] Edwards, "Miscellany 679," *WJE* 18:237–38.
[24] Lane, *Ravished*, 176.
[25] Edwards, *Dissertation I. Concerning the End for Which God Created the World*, *WJE* 8:443.

But should Christian theologians affirm invincibility and invulnerability as divine perfections? Why not affirm perfect vulnerability? Critics of Lee assert that Edwards merely used analogical method to suggest that God essentially self-communicates to creation. But by analogy, what parents are not perfectly vulnerable to their children's needs, feeling their children's suffering and rejoicing in their children's joys (Mt. 7:9)? What parent is not enhanced by their children's existence and would otherwise be impoverished? The argument that God is invincible and invulnerable does not adequately match experience; and, it is no less anthropocentric to affirm that God is like Hercules or Superman.

The analogical method extends further to the classical attribute of divine self-sufficiency. If God is unmoved, unaffected, and entirely self-sufficient, what imperative do human beings have to do otherwise? Put crassly, should not human beings model the divine attributes and simply work on behalf of their own self-glorification, and seek to be entirely self-sufficient without need for or regard for others? In fact, according to this line of reasoning, the human expression of altruism should not be for the ultimate benefit of others, but solely for the benefit of the self. When taken to its theological extreme, the classical pentecostal position more strongly supports a Darwinian worldview than a Creator-centered worldview. Edwards acknowledged that "if the world had not been created, [some divine] attributes never would have had any exercise."[26] In this regard, it seems that classical theists need to do more hermeneutical acrobatics than Lee to justify their interpretation of Edwards' doctrine of creation. Edwards himself addresses these concerns in the objection of "selfishness" and, according to his own formulation, the good of the creature is one end God has in mind in the final end of God's own glory.[27] Such a reality compels moral agents to have the same goal: doing good to their fellow moral agents.[28]

Lee asserts that Edwards' dispositional ontology suggests that God is predisposed to create and relate: to create something other than Godself and to relate to something other than Godself. This is the point at which classical theists bristle because they affirm that God must be self-sufficient. However, it is arguable that any of God's essential or dispositional properties require external relations. For example, is it reasonable to speak of God's justice in purely intra-trinitarian terms? Without a creation, there would be no need for God to exercise judgment at all and therefore, God is not just without something to judge. Edwards supposes, nevertheless, that it was not merely God's love of justice and hatred of injustice that originally motivated God to create; instead, Edwards points back to a "more original" motivation for God's creation: the self-expression of divine attributes for God's own glory.[29]

---

[26] Ibid., 429.
[27] Ibid., 445–50.
[28] Ibid., 442.
[29] Ibid., 413.

As Lee argues, Edwards intuited that God must have some essential properties of self-expression.[30] In this regard, Tom Oord's theory of essential kenosis is exceptionally helpful.[31] Oord, like Edwards, argues that creativity is an essential property of God's nature, in fact, not only the physical creative act but also the ongoing self-emptying and divine vulnerability implicit in God's relationship with the creation. This expression of divine suffering is most vivid in the cross of Christ, "in that act of yielding himself up to these sufferings," but continues in God's suffering relationship with the suffering of creation.[32]

Contrary to the assumption that necessary creation constitutes a creation-dependent God, Oord notes that "the world depends utterly on God's noncoercive, enabling, kenotic love."[33] Critics of Lee assert that Edwards seemed to affirm a dispositional ontology only for purposes of God's self-glorification. But Tom Oord affirms a similar ontology not because God must necessarily self-glorify, but because God must necessarily love. Creation is an essential product of God's dispositional self-emptying love, not God's dispositional self-glorification. While God may be able to self-glorify within the Trinity, the extent to which God can self-empty within the Trinity is questionable. This, it seems, is a critical difference between Edwards and process-relational theology.

It is accurate to assume that if God is predisposed to create, and creativity is essential to God's nature, that God must always be necessarily related to some creation other than God. Process-relational theists do not disagree with this assertion. For example, Oord rejects the idea that God is voluntarily self-limited. If God's kenotic activity is self-imposed, then "nothing about God's eternal nature provides grounds to trust that God loves creation."[34] If God is not ontologically disposed to create, then nothing in God's own nature compels God to sustain or love creation. In fact, without such disposition, it is difficult to imagine why God created in the first place.

Because God is predisposed to create, "the gift of Godself to creation is essential to what it means to be God."[35] God gives of Godself in the act of creation; that act does not make God dependent on creation. Instead, God's self-giving makes creation fully dependent on the gift of God's dispositional creative activity. Quite simply, "God's essential relation to creation need not mean God ontologically depends on the world."[36] Oord clearly affirms an orthodox position in this case and that position, I argue, is fully compatible with Edwards.

---

[30] As Oliver Crisp and others argue, the self-communicative aspect of the divine nature finds eternal and full expression in the procession of the Son and the Holy Spirit. Oliver D. Crisp, "Jonathan Edwards' God: The Trinity, Individuation and Divine Simplicity," in *Engaging the Doctrine of God: Contemporary Protestant Perspectives*, ed. Bruce L. McCormack (Grand Rapids, MI: Baker Academic, 2008), 83–103. Tension exists in Edwards' thought on this issue. See Steven M. Studebaker and Robert W. Caldwell III, *The Trinitarian Theology of Jonathan Edwards: Text, Context, and Application* (Burlington, VT: Ashgate, 2012), 191–211.

[31] Thomas J. Oord, *The Nature of Love: A Theology* (St. Louis, MO: Chalice, 2010), 154.

[32] Edwards, *The Excellency of Christ*, WJE 19:576 and Edwards, *Images of Divine Things*, WJE 11:52.

[33] Oord, *Nature*, 129.

[34] Ibid., 110.

[35] Ibid., 125.

[36] Ibid., 107.

Critics of Lee also contend that because God suffers and is expanded by God's relationship with creation, God must be dependent on creation. This is not only the process-relational theological position. On the contrary, in panentheism, all things are in God and owe their existence, sustenance, and freedom to God. Without God's eternal pole, there are no eternal objects, thus, no pure possibilities. Without pure possibilities, there is no free actualization of actual entities, without which mechanistic naturalism must ultimately prevail, even if all such causes are merely efficient causes precipitated by God's primary causation. What classical theists may not understand is that process-relational theists are their allies in affirming the utter dependence of creation on God. Quite simply, without God, there is no creation and certainly no creaturely freedom.

Edwards intuited a dispositional ontology because of its logical coherence. Although Edwards affirmed an otherwise classically determinist position, he also predated Wesley's theology of prevenient grace.[37] Prevenient grace allows for God as the first causal and enabling agent, but preserves creaturely freedom. Prevenient grace proceeds from God's eternal nature, meaning that "God lovingly acts first in each moment to provide agency, freedom, values, and relationship."[38]

Lee's critics also argue that Edwards was an occasionalist: all efficient causes are merely illusions that arise out of God's initial cause, thus, rendering all causes God's causes. While Edwards sought to balance his own philosophical insights with the confessional constraints of his own tradition, it may well be process-relational theology that allows Edwards' insights to move past occasionalism into deeper philosophical sophistication.[39] Process-relational theology does not affirm linear causation in the traditional sense; instead, it embraces a multiplicity of causes that converge in a complex nexus of influence in the concrescence of each actual occasion. God, being one of these many causes, always has (even persuasively powerful) influence but never has coercive determinative control.

Although Edwards may have held to an occasionalist theory of causation, a process-relational perspective may be complementary, rather than contradictory to Edwards' insights. While in occasionalism, all efficient causes are merely by-products of God's primary cause, process-relational theists assert that God makes efficient causes possible, but not deterministically: God never coerces, either by primary or efficient causation, to determine the sufficient cause. In process-relational theology, "to coerce is to act as a sufficient cause. If God were to coerce a creature, God would deny that creature freedom and/or agency."[40]

Classical theists who are critical of Lee's analysis of Edwards are perhaps so preoccupied with defending orthodoxy, they fail to see that neither Edwards nor contemporary process-relational theists overtly attack orthodoxy per se; instead,

---

[37] Since Wesley regularly argued that his doctrine of prevenient grace was "but a hair's breadth away from Calvinism," it may be possible that Edwards was grasping toward a similar truth. However, Wesley's "Calvinism" may not be Edwards' Calvinism—and neither may be Calvin's Calvinism.

[38] Oord, *Nature*, 129.

[39] Stephen Daniel, "Edwards' Occasionalism," in *Jonathan Edwards as Contemporary: Essays in Honor of Sang Hyun Lee*, ed. Don Schweitzer (New York: Peter Lang, 2010), 1–14.

[40] Oord, *Nature*, 127.

they seek to more accurately ascribe God's attributes in rationally and even biblically coherent ways. Instead of maneuvering to make Edwards fit into an orthodoxy understood in certain delimited confessional terms, it may be more prudent to allow Edwards' insights to speak for themselves and make comparisons with contemporary theological constructs on that basis. It is possible to say that Edwards shared insights with process-relational theology without saying that Edwards was a process-relational theist. Anachronism is not a viable argument against Lee's insights.

Part of the argument surrounding Lee's treatment of Edwards concerns the extent to which Edwards affirmed a substance metaphysic.[41] It is not surprising that Edwards used both substance-materialist terminology and idealist terminology; the great illusion of reality is that of enduring substances over time. Crisp proposes a more theo-centric reading of Edwards, arguing that Edwards was an essentialist and did not reject a substance metaphysic. Crisp calls for an "amending" of recent Edwardsean scholarship that relies on Lee's interpretations. I affirm Crisp's motive and approach to Lee's work.

Edwards defines substances as "something that really and properly subsists by itself and supports all properties." Edwards implies here, as Bombaro and others have concurred, the only "real" substance for Edwards is Godself. God alone meets the definition of "substance" according to Edwards' own criteria. This is Crisp's central criticism of Lee: at least one substance does exist for Edwards and that substance is God. But from a panentheistic perspective, this seems to be splitting hairs. The dispositions of creation exist in and are held together by Godself, in whom the creation participates moment by moment.

Lee's account renders Edwards wholly compatible with neither a process-relational nor a pentecostal vision of reality. However, the notion of dispositions being "made actual" would ring familiar to process-relational theists: actual occasions concretize moment by moment in a complex nexus of relations, including the past, God, measure of self-determination, no matter how insignificant.[42] Crisp notes that Lee's reading presumes that substances do not have "habits and laws" but are ontologically "habits and laws." Process-relational theists would tend to agree metaphysically: even God obeys the same metaphysical laws as all other entities. God is not the exemption to all metaphysical principles (i.e., "habits and laws"), but their chief exemplification.[43] From a panentheist perspective, all things are in God and Crisp's notion of "at least one (immaterial substance), namely, God" is not entirely inconsistent.

From either the perspective of the natural sciences (contemporary physics) or from the perspective of process philosophy, it is not difficult to quickly reject a substance metaphysic in favor of an idealist or minimally, immaterialist perspective. Must Edwards be constrained to a substance metaphysic in order to be defended as

---

[41] Bombaro, *Vision*, 13.
[42] In the process metaphysic, all "actual occasions" have contributed to each moment of processive "becoming" by "prehending" the immediate past and God's persuasive influence of possibilities for the future. See John B. Cobb, Jr., *The Process Perspective: Frequently Asked Questions about Process Theology* (St. Louis, MO: Chalice, 2003), 34.
[43] Alfred North Whitehead, *Process and Reality*, 2nd ed. (New York: Free Press, 1979), 343.

orthodox? It does not seem to be a battle worth the fight. Crisp notes, however, that one could still be an idealist and affirm immaterial substances. In the end, Crisp argues that "none of the evidence Lee musters in favor of this dispositional account requires a dispositional ontology in order to make sense" and on that point, Crisp is entirely correct.

Another point of contention with Lee's thesis concerns the extent to which Edwards affirmed a doctrine of continuous creation. Edwards' theory of continuous creation is strongly linked to his theory of divine refulgence and theological occasionalism: as God's glory returns to Godself, God recreates the world anew in each moment. The same Being who is the first cause of all things is also their final end.[44] Lee argues that for Edwards' occasionalism, God does not simply create the universe anew moment by moment; instead, the material world consists of enduring and continuous dispositional states.[45] Paul Helm and Oliver Crisp argue that a continuous creation does not adequately deal with a doctrine of original sin.[46]

But Edwards himself struggled in this regard and toyed with "exceptions" to ontologically grounded fallenness. While creatures are naturally capable of knowing and loving their creator, they are not morally capable.[47] Again, however, the point hardly seems to be whether or not Edwards' thought was entirely consistent with doctrinal orthodoxy. Is it unreasonable to accept that Edwards may have made contradictory or inconsistent conjectures? Edwards may have been attempting to uphold his commitment to determinism while affirming God's essential relation to the creation. Whether God operates according to Edwards' model or the process-relational model, the fact remains that God is deeply involved in ongoing creative activity with the creation. Therefore, it is not unreasonable to conclude that "God everlastingly creates, because God is essentially the Creator."[48]

Divine affections: A process-relational interpretation of Edwards in dialogue with Pentecostalism

If Edwards cannot be uncritically compared to contemporary process-relational theology, then what justifies a comparison with contemporary Evangelicalism or Pentecostalism? Evangelicals, especially in the Reformed tradition, handily claim Edwards as their own, but there is little more justification for any twentieth-century movement to stake its claim than for process-relational theism. Edwards was simply a forerunner to many traditions, including, perhaps, process-relational theology in his metaphysics, Pentecostalism in his religious affections, and Evangelicalism in his emphasis on conversion. But no single emphasis qualifies or disqualifies

---

[44] Edwards, *Dissertation I. Concerning the End for Which God Created the World*, WJE 8:421.
[45] Lee, *Philosophical Theology*, 63.
[46] Paul Helm and Oliver D. Crisp, *Jonathan Edwards: Philosophical Theologian* (Burlington, VT: Ashgate, 2003), 58.
[47] Edwards, *Freedom of the Will*, WJE 1:156–62.
[48] Oord, *Nature*, 80.

any tradition from making comparisons with Edwards' theology. He is, after all, "America's theologian."[49]

I contend that a pentecostal reading of Edwards supports a process-relational reading of Edwards and thereby underscores Lee's reading. While this may not satisfy Lee's Reformed-evangelical critics, reading Edwards' ontology in light of his emphasis on "divine affections" not only supports pentecostal convictions, but builds a natural bridge between process-relational and pentecostal thought. As unlikely as it may seem, Edwards' theology affirms the simple notion that God's love predisposes God's actions—and thereby invites creaturely responses. Dispositional ontology is undergirded by divine affections.

Simon Chan notes that pentecostal spirituality "is not just a twentieth-century reality that has to be reckoned with because it has become so widespread" but "encapsulates an essential component of the Christian tradition."[50] This is certainly the case for dialogue between Pentecostals and Jonathan Edwards. I will argue that the revivalism purported by Jonathan Edwards has compatibility with both process-relational theology and pentecostal spirituality, especially with regard to divine affections. These notions converge in an aesthetic of divine love that characterizes both Edwards and the pentecostal tradition. While differences certainly exist, I contend that the trialogue between Edwards, process-relational theology, and pentecostal theology may find practical expression in religious experience. In Edwards' dispositional ontology, the constitution of the human person in relation to God, his theological-philosophical anthropology, is essential to understanding the reorientation of affections.

Michael Welker contrasts the "modern consciousness of the distance of God" with the "vivid, almost childlike enthusiasm of God's presence here and now" of Pentecostals and Charismatics.[51] Welker notes a "disconnect" between modern human experience and the biblical testimonies wherein the "action of God's Spirit" is described in terms of the "Spirit entering into diverse realities of human life."[52] Pentecostal adherents have been broadly successful in communicating and replicating direct experience of the Spirit in a global context. In fact, process-relational theists such as Bruce Epperly and John Cobb have noted that the process-relational tradition lacks the spiritual enthusiasm and profound experientialism of the pentecostal tradition. Pentecostals have "appreciated Edwards' notion that the Holy Spirit may be not only a conserver of tradition, but an innovator of the status quo."[53] It may be that in the same manner Edwards and Whitehead approximated metaphysical truths, Edwards and Pentecostals approximated similar spiritual experiences.

---

[49] Robert Jenson, *America's Theologian: A Recommendation of Jonathan Edwards* (New York: Oxford University Press, 1992).
[50] Simon Chan, *Spiritual Theology: A Systematic Study of the Christian Life* (Downers Grove, IL: IVP, 1998), 39.
[51] Michael Welker, *God the Spirit*, trans. John F. Hoffmeyer (Minneapolis, MN: Augsburg Fortress, 2004), 1.
[52] Ibid., 6.
[53] Michael J. McClymond and Gerald R. McDermott, *Theology of Jonathan Edwards* (New York: Oxford University Press, 2012), 724.

While process-relational theists value rational metaphysics, Pentecostals affirm the authoritativeness of mystical experiences. However, these polarities are not mutually exclusive and in fact, Edwards embraced both as well.[54] Process-relational theists "locate reality, and therefore also value, in experience."[55] As a forerunner to Pentecostalism, John Wesley's mature conception of the Christian life was thoroughly experiential, what he affectionately called "heart religion." Wesley himself moved from a purely rationalistic interpretation of love, as was fashionable in Enlightenment-era Oxford, to a focus on the affections, experience, and the heart. Wesley related experientialism to a "spiritual sense" through which human beings directly and personally experience God's love.[56] This emphasis on experience is characteristic of both pentecostal and process-relational theists and fits Edwards' emphasis of dynamic becoming.

Process-relational theology also affirms radical empiricism, the experiencing of more than sense data, to validate rationalistic claims and constructs. Although empiricism was the order of the day during the Enlightenment, Edwards and Wesley both sought deeper empirical validation of God's loving presence in direct experience.[57] Moreover, Edwards "endeavored to identify what constitutes true and authentic spirituality."[58] Edwards sought to "show what are the true, certain, and distinguishing evidences of a work of the Spirit of God."[59] Edwards judged revivals empirically, by the fruits they produced.[60] In like manner, Pentecostals have embraced the verificational approach to revivalism proposed by Jonathan Edwards, and will likely continue to inform pentecostal spirituality.[61]

Sam Storms notes that "one of the more distinguishing features of the awakening was the acceleration or intensification of God's activity."[62] This distinction is important in light of Edwards' doctrine of continuous creation: it may be that God does not decide to act during revivals (as opposed to not acting during other times), but that God's activity is more keenly felt and perceived by human beings. Edwards notes of this revival, "God has also seemed to have gone out of his usual way, in the quickness of his work, and the swift progress his Spirit has made in his operations on the hearts of many. It is wonderful that persons should be so suddenly and yet so greatly changed."[63]

---

[54] Jonathan Edwards, "Essay on the Trinity," in *Treatise on Grace and Other Posthumously Published Writings*, ed. Paul Helm (Cambridge: James Clarke, 1971), 118; see also Helen Petter Westra, "Jonathan Edwards and 'What Reason Teaches,'" *Journal of Evangelical Theology* 34, no. 4 (1991): 495–503.
[55] John B. Cobb, "Process Theology," http://www.religion-online.org/showarticle.asp?title=1489 (accessed March 5, 2013).
[56] John Wesley, "Great Privilege," §I.6-10; Sermon 45, "The New Birth," §II.4, http://www.umcmission.org/Find-Resources/John-Wesley-Sermons/Sermon-45-The-New-Birth (accessed March 6, 2013).
[57] Randy L. Maddox, "Seeking a Response-able God: The Wesleyan Tradition and Process Theology," in *Thy Nature and Thy Name is Love: Process and Wesleyan Theologies in Dialogue*, ed. Bryan Stone and Thomas J. Oord (Nashville, TN: Kingswood, 2001), 12.
[58] Sam Storms, *Signs of the Spirit: An Interpretation of Jonathan Edwards' "Religious Affections"* (Wheaton, IL: Crossway, 2007), 21.
[59] Wilson E. Kimnach, "General Introduction to the Sermons," *WJE* 10:164.
[60] McClymond and McDermott, *Theology of Jonathan Edwards*, 725.
[61] Amos Yong, *Spirit-Word-Community: Theological Hermeneutics in Trinitarian Perspective* (Burlington, VT: Ashgate, 2002), 203–07.
[62] Storms, *Signs*, 25.
[63] Ibid., 25.

Edwards concluded, "I am bold to assert that there never was any considerable change wrought in the mind or conversation of any person that had not his affections moved."[64]

Out of these experiences, Lane argues that Edwards urged people to follow an "ordered pattern of affection by putting God first in their lives."[65] Storms documents a pattern of such altered affections, which include a "deep and penetrating conviction of sin" and a "degree of fear," followed by a "sense of God's love, mercy, and saving grace in Christ."[66] Edwards believed this was God's own affection: "We may suppose that a disposition in God, as an original property of his nature, to an emanation of his own infinite fullness was what excited him to create the world."[67] In other words, God's affection excites creative divine activity. God's creative activity thereby excites the affections of human beings in the process of becoming.

Amos Yong points to the work of Donald Gelpi, who examined the conversion of affections in terms of pentecostal initiation: "A dispositional reorientation toward being assimilated into the mind of Christ."[68] Edwards' own religious experience was, according to Lane, "very down to earth, embracing the religious affections of delight and joy, reverberating with the sensuous world around him."[69] Edwards' philosophical theology, namely, his dispositional ontology and perhaps his doctrine of continuous creation, nurtured his own religious affections: it may be that Edwards' understanding of the God-world creation was at the root of his religious experience.

As in Joseph Bracken's brand of process-relational metaphysics, however, God and the world are interactive subjects, not a pantheistic amalgam.[70] This intersubjectivity permits the reorientation of affections because God and human beings are ongoing activities rather than mere entities.[71] Whitehead's metaphysic was largely aesthetic: there is no end-state, only ongoing process. For Whitehead, the emergence of complexity has less to do with competing ends and more to do with a striving for increased feeling and qualitative perception. Edwards said: "In the more ordinary influences of the Spirit of God on the hearts of sinners, he only assists natural principles to do the same work to a greater degree, which they do of themselves by nature."[72] This, I believe, is a metaphysical interpretation not unlike Whitehead's description of aesthetic satisfaction. While Randy Maddox argues that changes in affections cannot be reduced to "rational control" or "philosophical" schemes of moral psychology,[73]

---

[64] Edwards, *Religious Affections*, WJE 2:102.
[65] Lane, *Ravished*, 108.
[66] Storms, *Signs*, 25.
[67] Edwards, *Dissertation I. Concerning the End for Which God Created the World*, WJE 8:435.
[68] Amos Yong, "In Search of Foundations: The Oeuvre of Donald L. Gelpi, SJ, and Its Significance for Pentecostal Theology and Philosophy," *Journal of Pentecostal Theology* 11, no. 1 (2002): 3–26.
[69] Lane, *Ravished*, 202.
[70] Joseph A. Bracken, *The One in the Many: A Contemporary Reconstruction of the God-World Relationship* (Grand Rapids, MI: Eerdmans, 2001).
[71] Joseph Bracken, *The Divine Matrix: Creativity as Link between East and West* (Maryknoll, NY: Orbis, 1995), 93–111.
[72] Edwards, *The Religious Affections*, WJE 2:207.
[73] Randy L. Maddox, "Heart Religion," in *The Methodist Tradition and Related Movements*, ed. Richard Steele (Metuchen, NJ: Scarecrow, 2001), 3–31.

I believe that metaphysical or ontological starting points do not necessarily exclude spirituality; on the contrary, in Edwards' case they are complementary. Rooted in philosophical constructs, Edwards was stricken by a sense of worship that reoriented his own affections in the direction of God's own: the internal disposition of God that causes God to delight in God's own glory also causes God to delight in the exhibitions, expressions, and communication of God's glory.[74] This, I believe, is an essential tridirectional connection between Edwards, process-relational theology, and Pentecostalism. Mature Christians would, as Lane notes of Edwards, "express the beauty of proportioned affections in their relationships with others."[75] This is precisely where Edwards' theology of religious affections converges with the process-relational and pentecostal traditions. Pentecostal scholars, such as Yong, are reformulating the work of the Spirit not as much in terms of bizarre manifestations, but in terms of divine love.[76] Moreover, Frank Macchia notes that "love is the greatest miracle that all extraordinary signs of the Spirit serve."[77]

Edwards observed that at the Northampton revival, worship services were "greatly enlivened" and people exhibited an "unusual elevation of heart and voice."[78] Edwards argued: "Now if such things are enthusiasm, and the fruits of a distempered mind, let my brain be evermore possessed of that happy distemper! If this be distraction, I pray God that the world of mankind may be all seized with this benign, meek, beneficent, beatifical, glorious distraction!"[79] Edwards' own style of revival preaching was uncoercive and non-manipulative.[80] From a pentecostal perspective, Yong argues that Bracken's metaphysic can be cast pneumatologically: "The Spirit makes God present and active, not substantively, but relationally." As such, "the Spirit is the 'between' which enables creaturely relationality and human interrelationality."[81] In like manner, Lee argues that Edwards' dispositional ontology affirms that the actual existence of all of creation is a result of the "continuing and immediate exercise of God's own power."[82]

---

[74] Edwards, *Dissertation I. Concerning the End for Which God Created the World*, WJE 8:436.
[75] Lane, *Ravished*, 193.
[76] In terms of contemporary pentecostal scholars, Amos Yong leads this discussion. I would argue that a handful of others, including Frank D. Macchia, for example, have also been working in this direction. See Amos Yong, *Spirit of Love: A Trinitarian Theology of Grace* (Waco, TX: Baylor University Press, 2012).
[77] Frank D. Macchia, *Baptized in the Spirit: A Global Pentecostal Theology* (Grand Rapids, MI: Zondervan, 2006), 149.
[78] Storms, *Signs*, 12–14.
[79] Edwards, *Some Thoughts Concerning the Revival*, WJE 4:341.
[80] Without going into detail, Edwards' emphasis on non-coercion is highly compatible with process-relational values: Persuasion over coercion is an important distinction for both God's power and the preferred modes of power exercised by human beings. This stands in contrast, to some degree, with the typical preaching modes of Pentecostals, which can be bombastic and coercive. See also Reichard, "Relational Empowerment."
[81] Amos Yong, *The Cosmic Breath: Spirit and Nature in the Christianity-Buddhism-Science Trialogue*, Philosophical Studies in Science & Religion 4 (Leiden: Brill, 2012), 191.
[82] Lee, *Philosophical Theology*, 49.

Although Edwards' revivals and religious experiences were prototypical of pentecostal worship, Edwards scholars such as McClymond and McDermott argue that Edwards was in fact a cessationist.[83] Edwards himself noted:

> Therefore I don't expect a restoration of these miraculous gifts in the approaching glorious times of the church, nor do I desire it. . . . I had rather enjoy the sweet influences of the Spirit, shewing Christ's spiritual divine beauty, and infinite grace, and dying love, drawing forth the holy exercises of faith, and divine love, sweet complacence, and humble joy in God, one quarter of an hour, than to have prophetical visions and revelations for a whole year.[84]

However, McClymond and McDermott also note that Edwards may have "taken a different stance on contemporary charismatic gifts had he witnessed at firsthand the growth, impact, and dynamism of the twentieth-century pentecostal-charismatic movement. He would likely have found much to affirm, as well as much to criticize."[85] This may well be the case. But pentecostal scholars can learn much from Edwards as well—and perhaps affirm divine affections as the greatest miracle and manifestation of the Spirit, specifically a disposition toward creative love.[86]

Conclusion and implications

I contend that a reexamination of Edwards from a process-relational perspective may aid the quest for a pentecostal interpretation of Edwards. A reorientation of religious affections may be grounded in a sound metaphysic, in particular, a metaphysic of the God-world relationship. But I stand firm with Crisp in my belief that a creative reading of Edwards, from both process-relational and pentecostal perspectives, can (and should) stay within the bounds of broad Christian orthodoxy. If indeed as Lee contends, Edwards supported a dispositional ontology and a doctrine of continuous creation, such notions find compatibility with the Whitheadean process metaphysic. As such, they may provide sufficient ground for interpreting Edwards pneumatologically. Pentecostals and Charismatics may read Edwards anew, but not just for his emphasis on revivalism; instead, Edwards may serve to inform a more philosophically grounded perspective. God's creative activity and relationship to the world are essential starting points for formulating a critical theology of God's activity in revivals: past, present, and future.

---

[83] McClymond and McDermott, *Theology of Jonathan Edwards*, 725; Guy Chevreau, *Catch the Fire: The Toronto Blessing: An Experience of Renewal and Revival* (London: Marshall Pickering, 1994), 79, 112.
[84] Edwards, *The Distinguishing Marks*, WJE 4:281.
[85] McClymond and McDermott, *Theology of Jonathan Edwards*, 725.
[86] Reichard, "Relational Empowerment" and Reichard, "Toward A Pentecostal Theology of Concursus," *Journal of Pentecostal Theology* 22, no. 1 (2013): 95–114.

4

Discerning the Signs of the Spirit: Pentecostal Experience Engages Edwardsean Religious Affections

David J. Courey

Introduction

In 1994, I became pastor of a pentecostal church in the heartland of the Toronto Blessing.[1] I attended the historic meetings with John Wimber, and then over the next two years returned several times to experience and witness what was taking place. Pentecostal officialdom had little to say about the Airport phenomenon[2] until something similar and yet quite different took place in Pensacola, Florida, at Brownsville Assembly of God.[3] For sedate pentecostal churches these related occurrences posed a quandary. Denominationally they saw themselves as the most recent heirs of the revivalist impulse, and while some regarded the Toronto events in continuity with that impulse, others were skeptical, or jealous, and still others uncertain how to evaluate the matter.

Then in 1995, Guy Chevreau's book *Catch the Fire* both chronicled the Toronto Blessing and offered an apologetic for it. Chevreau, a Wycliffe College ThD, found support in the work of Jonathan Edwards.[4] He saw in the Great Awakening a parallel with the Toronto renewal, pitting Edwards' revivalist defense against Charles Chauncy's Old Light attacks on the one hand and James Davenport's wildfire excesses on the other

---

[1] For a brief survey, Margaret Poloma, "Toronto Blessing," in *New International Dictionary of Pentecostal and Charismatic Movements*, ed. Stanley M. Burgess and Eduard M. van der Maas (Grand Rapids, MI: Zondervan, 2002), 1149–52, hereafter *NIDPCM*.

[2] The revival began in January 1994 at the Toronto Airport Vineyard, which, after dissociating with the Vineyard, became known as the Toronto Airport Christian Fellowship, and since 2010 has been called "Catch the Fire Toronto."

[3] Margaret M. Poloma and John C. Green offer perspectives on the Brownsville revival within a larger consideration of Assemblies of God spirituality in *The Assemblies of God: Godly Love and the Revitalization of American Pentecostalism* (New York: New York University Press, 2010).

[4] Guy Chevreau, *Catch the Fire: The Toronto Blessing: An Experience of Renewal and Revival* (Toronto: HarperCollins, 1995), chapter 4, "A Well-Travelled Path: Jonathan Edwards and the Experiences of the Great Awakening."

hand. Reaction from the Reformed wing was swift and generally negative.[5] Michael A. G. Haykin and Gary W. McHale wrote to show clear distinctions between the two that made it obvious (to them) that Edwards, a cessationist, could not be a supporter of charismatic renewal.[6] John MacArthur reflected on the Toronto Blessing in his plea for biblical discernment, *Reckless Faith*.[7] While predating Chevreau, he took William DeArteaga to task for his similar use of Edwards. Nick Needham took a comparable tone in his essay, "Was Jonathan Edwards the Founding Father of the Toronto Blessing?"[8]

Without re-traveling the same contentious ground, this chapter seeks a deeper rapprochement between Jonathan Edwards' notion of holy and gracious affections as the distinguishing mark of genuine spiritual experience and contemporary pentecostal paradigms of affective spirituality. Pentecostalism turns affections that arise from encounters with God to pragmatic, ethical ends while Edwards, far from disparaging the ethical dimension, sees the affections and their concomitant moral responses as aspects of a larger aesthetic dynamic that underlies his theology. Edwards and Pentecostals offer divergent yet complementary perspectives on affections. Considering each as unique, for the moment, I wish to explore the differences between Edwardsean and pentecostal reflections on "religious affections."

Edwardsean affections

"True religion," Edwards tells us in an oft-quoted epithet, "in great part, consists in holy affections."[9] This is the burden of his masterwork concerning experiential Christianity, *A Treatise Concerning Religious Affections*, published in 1746 amid controversy over the issue of revival. In 1742, Charles Chauncy, pastor of Boston's First Church of Christ and champion of Old Light orthodoxy, had proposed a calm, rational response, if somewhat polemical, to the "many Irregularities and Disorders" that "the late religious Stir has been attended with."[10] Chauncy's *Seasonable Thoughts* were a response to Edwards' *Some Thoughts Concerning the Present Revival*, released the previous year. Promoting "the Stir," and whipping it into frenzy, were the radical New Lights, such as James Davenport, a particular object of Chauncy's spleen. Davenport had modeled his ministry after the redoubtable George Whitefield whose New England campaign, begun in the fall of 1740, had spread revival across Connecticut and Massachusetts, igniting the Great Awakening. Davenport, however, pursued a more aggressive

---

[5] A remarkably generous review came from Iain H. Murray, who, while demurring from the emphasis on "physical phenomenon," finds much good in Chevreau's grasp of Edwards: "Review of Guy Chevreau, *Catch the Fire*," *Banner of Truth* 378 (March 1995): 28–29.

[6] Michael A. G. Haykin and Gary W. McHale, *The Toronto Blessing: A Renewal from God?* (Richmond Hill, ON: Canadian Christian, 1995).

[7] John F. MacArthur, *Reckless Faith: When the Church Loses Its Will to Discern* (Wheaton, IL: Crossway, 1994).

[8] Nick Needham, "Was Jonathan Edwards the Founding Father of the Toronto Blessing?" http://www.banner.org.uk/tb/edwards.html (accessed March 13, 2017).

[9] Edwards, *Religious Affections*, WJE 2:95.

[10] Charles Chauncy, *Seasonable Thoughts on the State of Religion in New-England: A Treatise in Five Parts* (Boston: Rogers and Fowle, 1743), 35.

antiestablishment tone, calling out ministers he considered unconverted by name. The pitched emotionalism of his meetings, though, drew the most attention. Large crowds would break into spontaneous hysterics: "Some singing, some screaming, some crying, some laughing and some scolding, made the most amazing Confusion."[11]

Sounds like the Toronto Blessing—and where do we find Edwards? Firmly in the middle. Clearly there were physical manifestations, even among moderates.[12] But both opponents and supporters of affective revival call on Jonathan Edwards as the authoritative voice that settles the matter. How is this so? Within the Edwards corpus, there exists a "revival canon" written between 1737 and 1746.[13] These works fit on a scale from the earlier works, which take a more affirmative tone to physical manifestations, to the later writings that express a more measured and guarded approach. Secondly, Edwards' "open but cautious" attitude, displayed throughout the "revival canon," results in passages, which, taken out of context, reflect opposite emphases.[14]

Thus Edwards could encourage receptivity to the Spirit's work, as he does in *Distinguishing Marks* (1741): "'Tis no sign that a work is not a work of the Spirit of God, that it is carried on in such a way as the same Spirit of God heretofore has not been wont to carry o his work."[15] Edwards appears prepared to accept the premise that authentic encounters with God may be occasioned through experiences not explicitly foreseen in Scripture—a highly charismatic assumption. Chevreau cites the same passage in defense of the Toronto Airport revival: "What the *church* has been used to, is not a rule . . . because there may be new and extraordinary works of God."[16] Yet, Edwards also expresses extreme suspicion regarding the revelatory power of visions and prophecies. The powerful interactions claimed in the revival may be genuine, but may be improperly interpreted. Some, inspired by the Spirit to an "extraordinary frame of mind," and experiencing "a strong and lively sense of divine things," may, through the purely human excitation of the imagination, wrongly interpret such experiences as though they were "prophetical visions . . . [or] divine revelations."[17] Phillip A. Craig, writing from the cessationist point of view, appeals to this same passage as Chevreau.[18]

---

[11] *Boston Weekly Post-Boy*, September 28, 1741, cited in Harry S. Stout and Peter Onuf, "James Davenport and the Great Awakening in New London," *Journal of American History* 71, no. 3 (1983): 570.

[12] For examples Edwards' testimony to all manner of physical, emotional, and religious phenomena attending the revival including "outcries, faintings, convulsions, and such like, but with distress, and also with joy," see Edwards, "To the Rev Thomas Prince of Boston," *WJE* 4:546–47, 550.

[13] These include "A Faithful Narrative of a Surprising Work of God" (1737); "The Distinguishing Marks of a Work of the Spirit of God" (1741); "Some Thoughts Concerning the Revival" (1743); *Religious Affections* (1746); and a "preface" along with some letters, all found in Edwards, *The Great Awakening*, *WJE* 4 and *Religious Affections*, *WJE* 2.

[14] Michael J. McClymond and Gerald R. McDermott, *Theology of Jonathan Edwards* (New York: Oxford University Press, 2011), 424, 693–94.

[15] Edwards, "Distinguishing Marks," *WJE* 4:228.

[16] Ibid., 228, cited in Chevreau, *Catch the Fire*, 100 (emphasis original).

[17] Ibid., 237–38.

[18] Philip A. Craig, "'And Prophecy Shall Cease': Jonathan Edwards on the Cessation of the Gift of Prophecy," *Westminster Theological Journal* 64, no. 1 (2002): 177.

Religious affections and holy affections

Resolving the apparent ambiguity takes us to the heart of the matter for Edwards. Affections, he claims, "are no other, than the more vigorous and sensible exercises of the inclination and will of the soul."[19] Affections are the excitement of those dimensions of our being that incite us to action. Religious affections mark a range of human responses that may be of two kinds, (1) natural or supernatural and (2) merely religious, or holy and gracious. As he has already told us, "true religion . . . consists in holy affections"—but how do such affections arise, and how do they differ from other religious affections? "Affections that are truly spiritual and gracious, do arise from those influences and operations on the heart, which are *spiritual, supernatural*, and *divine*."[20] Holy affections come "from the Spirit of God"; and "as the mind continues in its holy frame, and retains a divine sense of the excellency of spiritual things, even in its rapture," one might properly expect that these religious affections not only will elevate the spirit but may, for some, excite physical reactions as well. At their most intense, as affections may be during revival, the human mind, "under a true sense of the glorious and wonderful greatness and excellency of divine things, and soul-ravishing views of the beauty and love of Christ" might become overwrought, the body overwhelmed, and the imagination overcharged. The experience may be forceful, the Spirit may be active, but these natural human responses "are but accidental."[21] They are not ultimately transformational.

Edwards makes an essential distinction between "religious affections" and "holy" or "gracious affections," the latter a subset of the former.[22] He is capable of speaking of religious affections as both positive and negative, but holy affections appear to be those religious affections which are transformational.

> [For] persons to despise and cry down all religious affections, is the way to shut all religion out of their own hearts. . . . There are false affections, and there are true. A man's having much affection, don't prove that he has any true religion: but if he has no affections, it proves that he has no true religion. The right way, is not to reject all affections, nor to approve all; but to distinguish between affections, approving some, and rejecting others.[23]

The key question in revival is distinguishing between "natural" and "spiritual" religious affections. The natural affections may or may not be aroused by the work of the Holy Spirit; the supernatural affections, on the other hand, have no other source. No manner of outward religious language, expression, or feeling is proof of the Spirit's presence "as a principle of new nature, or as a divine supernatural spring of life and action"—what Edwards often calls "the sense of the heart." The presence of physical manifestations,

---

[19] Edwards, *Religious Affections*, WJE 2:96.
[20] Ibid., 197, emphasis original.
[21] Edwards, "Distinguishing Marks," WJE 4:237-38.
[22] "'Tis no sign one way or the other [that affections are gracious], that religious affections are very great, or raised very high;" Edwards, *Religious Affections*, WJE 2:127.
[23] Ibid., 121.

or prophetic speech, even if they are Spirit-inspired, is no sure indication that God has produced holy affections. "Not all those persons who are subject to any kind of influence of the Spirit of God, are ordinarily called spiritual in the New Testament."[24] Even Balaam may prophesy.

Affections and the beatific vision

Correlating "religious affections" with the encounter with the beauty of the trinitarian God is one of the leitmotifs of Edwards' "revival canon." As Gerald McDermott has said, for Edwards, "all thinking about the affections must start with the inner-trinitarian life of God."[25] Sang Hyun Lee has developed the notion of "dispositional ontology" for describing God's trinitarian relations *ad intra* and *ad extra*.[26] While I do not wish to enter the considerable debate Lee's philosophical interpretation has occasioned, his account speaks to Edwards' views about religious affections.[27]

This dispositional approach is of necessity relational. If, as Edwards claims, God is the "foundation and fountain" of all beauty and being,[28] there must be a beholder of this beauty, so that there may be, in the philosophical terms of Edwards' day, *proportionality* and *consent* to that beauty. The perfect beholder of this beauty must itself be perfectly beautiful: this is the matter of *proportion*. God has an eternally actual and perfect idea of his excellency and that idea is the repetition of himself, the Son. The Son's joyful reflection of the Father's beauty and the Father's delight in that beauty are *consent*, and in true Augustinian form, this eternal bond is the Holy Spirit.[29] The immediate *ad extra* experience of this *ad intra* beauty for the glorified saint is called the beatific vision.

It is the Father's dispositional essence to express his beauty that begets the Son, and the Father and Son's dispositional essence to share joy and love from which the Holy Spirit proceeds. Thus, the perfection of the Trinity repeats the excellencies of divine

---

[24] Ibid., 199–201.
[25] Gerald R. McDermott, "Jonathan Edwards on the Affections and the Spirit," in *The Spirit, the Affections, and the Christian Tradition*, ed. Dale M. Coulter and Amos Yong (Notre Dame, IN: University of Notre Dame Press, 2016), 279.
[26] Much of what follows on dispositions is informed by Sang Hyun Lee, "God's Relation to the World," in *The Princeton Companion to Jonathan Edwards*, ed. Sang Hyun Lee (Princeton, NJ: Princeton University Press, 2005), 59–71.
[27] Sang Hyun Lee, *The Philosophical Theology of Jonathan Edwards*, expanded ed. (Princeton, NJ: Princeton University Press, 2000). Extensive discussion is found in the following: Kin Yip Louie, *The Beauty of the Triune God: The Theological Aesthetics of Jonathan Edwards* (Eugene, OR: Pickwick, 2013); John J. Bombaro, *Jonathan Edwards' Vision of Reality: The Relationship of God to the World, Redemption History, and the Reprobate* (Eugene: Wipf & Stock, 2011); and Kyle C. Strobel, *Jonathan Edwards' Theology: A Reinterpretation* (London: Bloomsbury T&T Clark, 2014).
[28] Edwards, *Dissertation II. The Nature of True Virtue*, WJE 8:551.
[29] Louis J. Mitchell, "The Theological Aesthetics of Jonathan Edwards," *Theology Today* 64, no. 1 (2007): 38–40. Steven M. Studebaker carefully summarizes Herbert Richardson's 1962 Harvard dissertation, which marked the beginning of contemporary assessments of Edwards' Trinitarianism: *Jonathan Edwards' Social Augustinian Trinitarianism in Historical and Contemporary Perspectives* (Piscataway, NJ: Gorgias, 2008), 44–54. Studebaker's critiques of Richardson do not mitigate his contribution here.

glory, and the knowledge and love of this beauty has gone on and will go on *ad intra* for eternity. But the divine disposition to communicate this beauty means that it must also be repeated *ad extra*, resulting in the act of creation in space and time. God's communication of his beauty in creation is the eternal project of the self-enlarging God extending his actuality *ad extra*, as the creation asymptotically[30] achieves its repetition of the divine glory as it is taken up in the beatific vision. It is here that dispositional ontology touches on the question of religious affections.

God is pursuing the repetition of his internal beauty in the external world. A secondary beauty is revealed through all creation, but the proportion and consent of intelligent, sensible, spiritual beings is much more profound. Since this takes place in a limited, fallen world, it results in an eternal process of redemptive growth tending to but never actually attaining the glory of the divinity. This asymptotic repetition climaxes the drama of redemption, and is the ultimate goal of history. God brings about seasons of intense religious affection, so that humanity may experience a more penetrating encounter with the beauty of God revealed in Christ. This is the proper work of the Holy Spirit whose purpose is to seek the repetition of the *ad intra* glory *ad extra* in the elect. One might call this the incipient beatific vision, the foretaste of the fullness of eternity.

As individuals find themselves in a climate of religious intensity, it is to be expected that their emotions will be stirred, possibly their bodies will be overwhelmed, and their imaginations overwrought. Edwards' psychology of religious experience anticipates that the body and soul are related at the point of affections:

> Such seems to be our nature, and such the laws of the union of soul and body, that there never is any case whatsoever, any lively and vigorous exercise of the will or inclination of the soul, without some effect upon the body, in some alteration of the motion of its fluids, and especially of the animal spirits.[31]

Thus experiences, physical, emotional, or religious, are neither positive nor negative indicators of a truly spiritual work, but merely religious affections that may (or may not) also include holy, gracious affections that bring about a repetition, a transformational encounter with the beauty of God.

The result, Edwards calls a "new sense of the heart," and it represents the ever-increasing proportion and consent of the regenerate soul. It is ultimately a gift from God. Unregenerate individuals may have real experiences of the Spirit producing all manner of religious affections, but a true encounter with the primary beauty of God depends on gracious affections that can only "arise from special and peculiar influences of the Spirit, working that sensible effect or sensation in the souls of the saints."[32] Whatever the other accompaniments of religious affections, true holy and gracious affections create "the sense of the heart of the supreme beauty and sweetness

---

[30] The word, in this context, is Strobel's: *Jonathan Edwards' Theology*, 144.
[31] Edwards, *Religious Affections*, WJE 2:98.
[32] Ibid., 210.

of the holiness or moral perfection of divine things."[33] The sense of the heart combines affective delight (the mind and heart, that is, *consent*) with dispositional action (the inclination and the will, or *proportion*).[34] While the Spirit may influence others from without, through natural means, and the kind of experiences and knowledge that may be naturally apprehended, holy affections arise from the work of the Spirit within. The Spirit himself becomes "so united to the faculties of the soul, that he becomes there a principle or spring of a new nature and life." Thus, the Spirit is the means by whom we participate "of God's spiritual beauty and happiness, according to the measure and capacity of a creature."[35] This is nothing less than the implantation of a new nature, rather than improvements on the old. Nor is it "a new faculty of will, but a foundation laid in the nature of the soul, for a new kind of exercises of the same faculty of will."[36]

Revival then is a powerful mediator of holy affections, the evidence of which is a profound engagement with the moral excellencies of the Godhead. Such a vision has definite ethical implications in the increasing (and through eternity, asymptotic) repetition in the believer that results from the incipient beatific vision. This conformity to the divine image in the moral habitus of professing believers is "the sign of signs," persuading both believers and others.[37]

> Seeing holiness is the main thing that excites, draws, and governs all gracious affections, no wonder that all such affections tend to holiness. That which men love, they desire to have and to be united to, and possessed of. That beauty which men delight in, they desire to be adorned with. Those acts which men delight in, they necessarily incline to do.[38]

So, the greatest measure of true revival is not to be found in phenomena, but in holiness.

This vision is also the driver of sacrificial ministry. While not a theme in *Religious Affections*, this is a recurring motif in the *Life of David Brainerd*, his son-in-law-to-be, whose early death prompted Edwards to craft of his journals a tale of spiritual passion amid emotional and physical adversity. Brainerd's spiritual sustenance was "the affecting considerations and lively ideas of God's infinite glory, his unchangeable blessedness, his sovereignty and universal dominion . . . and the pleasing prospects or hopes he had of a future advancement of the kingdom of Christ, etc."[39] Truly religious affections do not end in the meeting house, but have remarkably practical results in terms of mission.

---

[33] Ibid., 272.
[34] John E. Smith, "Religious Affections and the 'Sense of the Heart,'" in *The Princeton Companion to Jonathan Edwards*, ed. Sang Hyun Lee (Princeton, NJ: Princeton University Press, 2005), 105.
[35] Edwards, *Religious Affections*, WJE 2:203.
[36] Ibid., 206.
[37] Ibid., 443.
[38] Ibid., 394.
[39] Edwards, *The Life of David Brainerd*, WJE 7:506.

Pentecostal affections

To what of the above could a pentecostal possibly quibble? Or add? At its most basic, Edwards provides a theological basis for something Pentecostals have said all along: "I don't care how high you jump, if you walk straight when you hit the ground." But, a closer look suggests meaningful differences between Edwardsean and pentecostal approaches to religious affections.

The seminal treatment of affections in pentecostal theology is Steven Land's *Pentecostal Spirituality*. Land agrees with Edwards that Christian spirituality is largely a matter of divinely inspired affections, and these offer a particularly applicable model for thinking about Pentecostalism. Land argues that "the righteousness, holiness, and power of God are correlated with distinctive apocalyptic affections which are the integrating core of Pentecostal spirituality."[40] He proposes a model of orthodoxy and orthopraxy growing out of an eschatologically oriented orthopathy. At the outset, Land frames the problem as a tension between the language of holiness and the language of power. He sees this as a rapprochement between its Wesleyan past and its pentecostal present.[41]

Land credits Edwards and Wesley with contributing to "a deep stream of evangelical thought" that still awaits a fuller development. The primary vector of Edwards' affections is Godward, creating passionate affections of love for Christ, and a response of holiness. On the other hand, "power" terminology is ubiquitous in pentecostal vocabulary.[42] It also signifies an intense affective experience, often attended with phenomena, and is emotionally, if not always physically, overwhelming. Power encounters are motivational, persuasive, and vindicating. While they may result in a sense of awe, they are most often outwardly directed. The holiness-power dialectic parallels three areas of ambiguity, first between objectivity and subjectivity touching on the postmodern context of Pentecostalism; second between transcendent and immanent reflecting on embodied spirituality, and finally between telic and apocalyptic eschatologies, underscoring the missional dynamic of Pentecostalism.

Objectivity and subjectivity

Holiness and power as affective encounters present a challenge in sorting out their objective and subjective dimensions. While contemporary Pentecostals may appreciate the depth of Edwards' analysis of spiritual experience, they may find it too precise in describing an ultimately incommunicable encounter. Edwards does a commendable job of expressing the affective raptures of the beauty of holiness within an Enlightenment engagement with Locke and Berkeley, but he comes short of an existential account of the ineffability of spiritual experience. Ron Kydd captures an

---

[40] Steven Jack Land, *Pentecostal Spirituality: A Passion for the Kingdom* (Cleveland, TN: CPT, 2010), 23, 184.
[41] Ibid., 10–11.
[42] Peter Althouse, "The Ideology of Power in Early American Pentecostalism," *Journal of Pentecostal Theology* 13, no. 1 (2004): 97–115.

essential pentecostal perspective: power encounters evade full rational disclosure; they are, as the old preacher said, "better felt than telt."[43] Peter Neumann sets this in tension with Douglas Jacobsen's countervailing observation. Not unlike Edwards, even early Pentecostals endeavored to make rational distinctions. "Not just any experience" could be considered valid. Pneumatic experiences must be qualified through a biblical/theological framework. Thus, both the ineffability of affections and their rational evaluation were necessary concomitants of early pentecostal reflection.[44]

Somehow in the context of late modernity, the first generation managed to balance objectivity and subjectivity. This ambiguity is reflected in the distinctly postmodern matrix of contemporary Pentecostalism. The effort to bring closure to pentecostal self-definition has been fraught with difficulties, yet, for the most part, Pentecostals and Charismatics generally seem to tell one another apart from those who "don't belong." The ambiguity also parallels Edwards' openness to experiences not explicitly biblical, and his effort to qualify truly religious affections. In this regard, Pentecostals seem still to have problems locating themselves between charismatic openness and pentecostal discernment. The challenges of the Toronto Blessing continue, only the cast has changed. Definitions and boundaries, though, seem to be among the casualties of the postmodern mood, an observation that couches the pentecostal situation in a very different intellectual world than Edwards', which sought for increasingly fine distinctions. The possibility of any genuine objectivity slips into the subjective morass.

This is the quandary of pentecostal theology, though it is neither a pentecostal nor a postmodern *novum*. It is the perennial journey of the theologian—*fides quaerens intellectum*—yet with a distinctly pentecostal tone. As Clark Pinnock movingly wrote in *Flame of Love*,

> Theology must always be more than rational. . . . For we are speaking of a reality that is active in our lives and that cannot be captured altogether in cognitive ways. There are depths of the mystery that cannot be accessed by reason alone. As well as studying the Scriptures on the Spirit, we must be prayerful and open, longing to fall in love with the One who frees and surprises, delights and searches, energizes and purifies us. We have to be sensitive to things that are only spiritually discerned (1 Cor. 2:14). Let us learn to operate on two levels simultaneously. Even as we are thinking, deep within we can be at prayer and be receptive to the divine breath.[45]

In the accompanying footnote, Pinnock references both the Toronto Blessing and the *apophatic* tradition in orthodox theology as sources in his personal pilgrimage.[46] He reflects an attitude we saw in Edwards. "In terms of theological method, this means

---

[43] Ronald A. N. Kydd, "Better Felt than Telt," *Eastern Journal of Practical Theology* 4 (1990): 30–34, cited in Peter D. Neumann, *Pentecostal Experience: An Ecumenical Encounter* (Eugene: Pickwick, 2012), 101–2.

[44] Neumann, *Pentecostal Experience*, 101–04. See Douglas G. Jacobsen, *Thinking in the Spirit: Theologies of the Early Pentecostal Movement* (Bloomington, IN: Indiana University Press, 2003), 3–7.

[45] Clark H. Pinnock, *Flame of Love: A Theology of the Holy Spirit* (Downers Grove: IVP, 1996), 13–14.

[46] Ibid.

that a theologian is not limited to biblical data alone but also reflects on the experiences generated by it."[47] Here, again we find the value of subjectivity and objectivity illuminating one another.

Edwards, working from a distinctively Enlightenment objectivity, claims to be able to separate truly holy affections from the merely religious by the depth of one's engagement with Christ. Something both he and Chauncy fail to notice is how affections themselves, or their lack, may shape spiritual perception. Contemporary pentecostal reflection, on the other hand, not only values, but trades significantly on the "situatedness" of the "participant/observer." Pentecostalism has become the spirituality of subjectivity.

This is illustrated by a fascinating series of articles by Randall Holm, Matthew Wolf, and James K. A. Smith exploring frontiers in tongues research.[48] Smith notes that both Holm and Wolf seem concerned that construing tongues as merely human, learned language somehow denies its miraculous dimension. Smith proposes tongues as both human and divine. The model of tongues he offers is incarnational—human-divine. Such a paradigm uncovers the power of tongues as subversive language, as kenotic language on the margins. Conversely, Smith suggests the inchoate content of such language is purely human.[49] The extreme subjectivity of glossolalic experience, then, is precisely what the speech-act signifies, but it is no longer, in any objective sense, communication with God. In Pinnock's terms, Smith implies that the only meaning in tongues is in the theological reflection the experience engenders, yet conversely, its objective scriptural significance as meaningful communication is lost. The way forward, Pinnock recommended, is a synthesis of both objective and subjective dimensions.

Transcendence and immanence

Both Pentecostals and Edwards navigate questions of transcendence and immanence, yet resolve ambiguities differently. Pentecostals translate their encounter with the transcendent into immanent expressions of worship, holiness, and service. Power encounters arouse religious affections that lead to embodied expressions of spirituality. Edwards' "new sense of the heart," however, causes believers to experience immanent encounters of creational beauty (nature, the arts and sciences, etc.) in transcendent ways.[50] Michael McClymond and McDermott capture this well: "Believers are able to perceive a holy beauty in God that is invisible to nonbelievers, and in this sense believers and nonbelievers live in two different universes. Subsequent to regeneration, the believer comes to appreciate even the beauties of the natural world in new ways."[51] The secondary beauty of creation leads the worshiper to the *ad*

---

[47] Ibid.
[48] Randall Holm, Matthew Wolf, and James K. A. Smith, "New Frontiers in Tongues Research: A Symposium," *Journal of Pentecostal Theology* 20, no. 1 (2011): 122–54.
[49] Ibid., 152–54.
[50] Strobel, *Jonathan Edwards' Theology*, 12n27.
[51] McClymond and McDermott, *Theology of Jonathan Edwards*, 317–18.

intra beauty of the Trinity.[52] Certainly Pentecostals could appreciate meditation on the beauty of Christ, but even then, their orientation follows the old holiness chorus, "Let the beauty of Jesus be seen in me."

Pentecostal worship connects religious affections to physical expressions. For Edwards, affections are notably not reducible to mere emotion, and may, in fact, call one to act against feeling. On the other hand, emotion, if not a sine qua non, is at least a significant component of pentecostal affection. Personal experience of the Spirit as the central dimension of true spirituality accents the emotive component of religious affection.[53] Daniel Albrecht indicates the delicate balance involved. "In the affectively charged dimension that Pentecostals call worship, human sensations and emotions are encouraged and believed to help in the communicative process with the divine. The need to rightly discern an authentic 'move' of the Spirit is opposed to self-deceiving impulses."[54] The salient point for Pentecostals is that such transcendent encounters translate into embodied practices.

In Edwards' notion of religious affections, the outward phenomena associated with revival are the overflow of human "motion of the fluids" and in his mature reflection, are at best incidental and no indication of spiritual reality. For Pentecostals, embodied manifestations such as the raising of hands; anointing with oil, or laying on of hands; spontaneous praise; glossolalia or prophecy; and in some circles, dancing, are all viewed as biblical means of worship.[55] The human-divine interface between Spirit and spirit is not always clear for Pentecostals. The spectrum of human cooperation with divine impetus runs from purely human, as in hand-raising, to what some consider to be significantly divine, such as "falling under the power," with many experiences falling in between, such as singing in tongues or dancing in the Spirit.

The physicality of pentecostal spirituality reveals a consecration of materiality, or embodiment unknown in Neoplatonic thought or Gnosticism, and to some extent shunned in modernist, rationalist Evangelicalism. As James K. A. Smith notes, "There is a sacramentality of pentecostal worship that sees the material as a good and necessary mediator of the Spirit's work and presence."[56] This extends from embodied worship practices to practical holiness and mission. Pentecostalism is an embodied theology—a theology that has not reached its goal until it has received physical manifestation involving the human body. Rather than seeing physical manifestation as incidental, or possibly superfluous, Pentecostalism, in its essence, is a form of Christian spirituality that deliberately connects profound spiritual encounter with concrete bodily expression.

For Pentecostals, transcendent encounters have directly immanent consequences. All aspects of pentecostal spirituality have affective roots seeking effective embodiment.

---

[52] Louie, *The Beauty of the Triune God*, 59–60.
[53] Russell Spittler, "Spirituality, Pentecostal and Charismatic," in *NIDPCM*, 1097.
[54] Daniel E. Albrecht, *Rites in the Spirit: A Ritual Approach to Pentecostal/Charismatic Spirituality* (Sheffield: Sheffield Academic Press, 1999), 228n19.
[55] "Many of the eccentricities of Pentecostalism . . . can be understood as contemporized forms of biblical precedents," in Spittler, "Spirituality," in *NIDPCM*, 1098.
[56] James K. A. Smith, *Thinking in Tongues: Pentecostal Contributions to Christian Philosophy* (Grand Rapids, MI: Eerdmans, 2010), 81–82.

Pentecostal affections result in a more immediate response, while for Edwards, the affections lead to a more extended contemplation of the divine. Edwardsean theology sees ethical expression as the result of the incipient beatific vision believers experience in this life. Embodiment is ancillary. As Sang Hyun Lee points out, "Beauty . . . is a dynamic, active reality that has practical, ethical, and political consequences."[57] For Edwards, secondary creational beauty invites the believer to participate in the primary divine beauty, and, by a more profound consideration, to ethical acts, which repeat that beauty in creation. Thus Edwards, by indirect means, also proposes a consecration of materiality. Transcendence for Edwards arises from Spirit-inspired experience of the immanent, while for Pentecostals immanent expressions of spirituality are rooted in transcendent encounters with the divine.

Telic and apocalyptic eschatologies

Edwards and Pentecostals share an intense interest in eschatology, shaping their notions of the affections. The ambiguity here is between the eschaton as the *goal* of all things and the *end* of all things. Does it draw us to fulfillment in Christ, or drive us to fulfill the mission of Christ? The apocalyptic urgency of Pentecostalism results in its missional dynamic, while the Edwardsean telic draw of the Spirit into the beatific vision produces inner longings for the divine. This ambiguity is reflected in pentecostal and Edwardsean affections.

Land understands pentecostal affections sequentially. A God-directed gratitude for justification leads to an others-directed love proceeding from holiness, and together these create the need for power that stimulates a self-directed courage for witness. Mobilizing, focusing, and providing urgency to these affections is the apocalyptic orientation of pentecostal spirituality.[58] Edwards also shared a surprisingly vivid eschatology.[59] Like Pentecostals, he is capable of reading the signs of the times, but rather than fueling end-time urgency, Edwards' postmillennialism contributes to the teleological goals of the beatific vision. He places his account of affections and revival within the drama of history from creation to redemption and consummation.

Pentecostalism's controlling metaphor was the Latter Rain motif, which provided its eschatological hermeneutic.[60] The latter-day outpouring of the Spirit signaled the end times, empowering believers to complete the Great Commission before the rapture of the church. Eschatological immediacy became a profound driver of missional zeal.[61]

---

[57] Sang Hyun Lee, "Edwards and Beauty," in *Understanding Jonathan Edwards: An Introduction to America's Theologian*, ed. Gerald R. McDermott (New York: Oxford University Press, 2009), 123–24.
[58] Land, *Pentecostal Spirituality*, 133–59.
[59] McClymond and McDermott, *Theology of Jonathan Edwards*, 566–79.
[60] The classic treatment of pentecostal eschatology is D. William Faupel, *The Everlasting Gospel: The Significance of Eschatology in the Development of Pentecostal Thought* (Sheffield: Sheffield Academic Press, 1996).
[61] The pentecostal hermeneutic of immediacy and its attenuation are discussed in chapter 2 of David J. Courey, *What Has Wittenberg to Do with Azusa? Luther's Theology of the Cross and Pentecostal Triumphalism* (New York: Bloomsbury, 2015).

By 1908, only two years into the Azusa revival, early Pentecostals had sent missionaries from various centers of fervor to at least twenty-five nations.[62] By the 1930s, though, in the face of another delayed *parousia*, Pentecostals, reflecting on their eschatology, adopted a revised dispensationalism. Expectant Pentecostals studied dispensational charts, watching world events for end-time events. This attenuated immediacy reduced the heat of apocalyptic fervor but extended its effects over a longer period.

Edwards, too, connected current events to biblical prophecy, but through a historicist lens. Wars and rumors of wars in America and Europe caught his attention. British conflict with Catholic nations was interpreted in terms of the battle between truth and error.[63] Revelation is the only book on which he wrote an entire commentary. Still, the millennium would not come for another 250 years, awaiting the full 6,000-year cycle of the present age.[64] Edwards' unfolding eschatological vision fit with the larger project of his *A History of the Work of Redemption*, and its telic, rather than apocalyptic objectives. Revival and its affections play an indispensable role here: "It is not unlikely that this work of God's Spirit, so extraordinary and wonderful, is the dawning, or, at least, a prelude of that glorious work of God, so often foretold in Scripture, which in the progress and issue of it, shall renew the world of mankind."[65] The *end* of all things, that is, the terminus of space-time history (*eschaton*), as well as the *goal* and purpose of creation (*telos*), only find resolution in the repetition of the beatific vision, resulting in the greater glory of God. The fulfillment of the church's mission fits within this framework, as a function of its reflection of the dispositional urge to communicate the grace and glory of God and so to bring all things *ad extra* into alignment with the *ad intra* beauty of divinity. Even Hell serves this purpose by exhibiting the full beauty of divine justice. The telic nature of Edwards' eschatology provides a God-directed impetus to Christian ethics and mission.

Apocalyptic speculation over end-time events did not waste eschatological immediacy—it also led to a pragmatic immediacy. Pentecostals were known for their entrepreneurial, can-do attitude. Early leaders were often savvy business people who, impelled by a sense of prophetic urgency and empowered by the Spirit, were willing to go anywhere, and do anything, often with unquenchable pentecostal optimism. Winnipeg realtor A. H. Argue was a tireless itinerant; editor, pastor of a major church; and a founder of the Pentecostal Assemblies of Canada.[66] Amy Semple McPherson became the first to win a large non-pentecostal following through the nascent medium of radio.[67] As television emerged, so did pioneers like Rex Humbard and Oral Roberts, whose weekly series neatly plied the spontaneity of a healing crusade with

---

[62] Allan Anderson, *Spreading Fires: The Missionary Nature of Early Pentecostalism* (Maryknoll, NY: Orbis, 2007), 64.
[63] Christopher B. Holdsworth, "The Eschatology of Jonathan Edwards," *Reformation and Revival* 5, no. 3 (1996): 123–24.
[64] McClymond and McDermott, *Theology of Jonathan Edwards*, 572–73.
[65] Edwards, *Some Thoughts Concerning the Revival*, WJE 4:353.
[66] Courey, *What Has Wittenberg*, 126.
[67] Grant Wacker, *Heaven Below: Early Pentecostals and American Culture* (Cambridge, MA: Harvard University Press, 2001).

the production needs of television.[68] This kind of creative entrepreneurial engagement was a direct consequence of pentecostal affections articulated through eschatological immediacy.

Conclusion

The boundaries of pentecostal experience continue to be contested territory, theologically and pastorally. As Chevreau discovered, Edwards provides means of assessing religious affections that resonate with hard-won pentecostal wisdom. Religious affections come in two varieties: those that produce manifestations only and those gracious and holy affections that perform a transformative work. These lead the regenerate to such a contemplation of God's internal beauty that they seek its repetition in the external world through holy life and mission. Conversely, pentecostal thought offers a revised notion of affections, which rather than pointing inward aims outward in an embodied spirituality expressing itself in worship, holiness, and ministry. For Edwards, affections are primarily meaningful if they are inwardly reflective, while for Pentecostals, they find principal significance in being outwardly effective.

Edwards' analysis provides ways of refining a pentecostal understanding of religious experience by calling postmoderns to balance subjective situatedness with objective revelation. Meanwhile, Edwards' aesthetic theology contributes to a pentecostal instinct about the basis of worship. A consideration of Edwardsean affections has implications for both arts and sciences, and adds to a fuller and more nuanced sense of pentecostal embodiment. His notion of reflection deepens pentecostal ethical imperative with a transcendence beyond the merely experiential and pragmatic. Finally, Edwards' Godward teleology offers a corrective to on over-immediate eschatology, balancing apocalyptic *end* and telic *goal*.

But Pentecostalism also enlightens the Edwards paradigm. It reasserts the subjectivity of experience, sometimes neglected in Edwards' scholarship. It also reinterprets the affections in the light of more strictly biblical categories. While Edwards was concerned with offering an apologetic for the revival and its phenomena, and Chevreau and others have similarly applied his model to charting the borderlands of charismatic experience, Pentecostals also wish to apply his observations to the normal and possibly normative dimensions of biblical pneumatic spirituality. They may find Edwards instructive, and inspiring, but not sufficiently useful without modification to the contemporary situation. What is the relation between religious affections, holy affections, and the phenomenal manifestations of spiritual experience outside the context of revival? Edwards' cessationism and the propriety of Congregational worship did not foresee such questions. Finally, the intensely missional character of pentecostal affections provides a useful adjunct to its secondary place in Edwards' paradigm. The telic orientation of Edwardsean affections offers a corrective to Pentecostalism, but the

---

[68] David Edwin Harrell, Jr., *Oral Roberts: An American Life* (Bloomington, IN: Indiana University Press, 1985), 126–31.

corollary is that the activist dimension of Pentecostalism becomes essential before the overwhelming needs of the world for the embodied gospel of Jesus Christ.

Edwards and Pentecostals form two sides of one coin, each enhancing the other. The source of pentecostal affections is power encounter, while Edwards is mostly concerned with an aesthetic encounter. Power is coercive, whereas beauty is attractive. Power is pragmatic and active, while beauty is idyllic and passive. Beauty calls us to the Mount of Transfiguration; it is transcendently transformative, an experience of contemplation, adoration. Power calls us to the valley below; it is immanently transformative, an encounter equipping for witness, mission. Both Pentecostals and Edwards are occupied with divine encounter, both are engaged in a kind of supernatural exchange with God, and both are concerned that transformed lives should be the result of that engagement. The differences are more matters of accentuation, the one, not being completely devoid of the other's emphases.

Part Two

God and Salvation

5

The Holy Spirit and the Trinity: A Pentecostal Improvement on Edwards

Steven M. Studebaker

Introduction

Edwards' pneumatology was progressive. It developed within the Reformed Puritan tradition, but that tradition could not contain it. His progressive pneumatology motivated developments in the immanent and the economic Trinity. Although reflecting traditional Augustinian trinitarian tendencies, his pneumatology inspired him to push beyond the emphases of that tradition. Edwards developed social images that supported a relational vision of the triune God. Community, the personal sharing of love, defines the trinitarian God. This relational nature of God finds eternal expression in the community of the Father, the Son, and the Holy Spirit. Edwards' relational vision of God and the Spirit's identity in the immanent Trinity informed a relational understanding of the economic Trinity as well. In the economy, the fecundity and harmony of creation manifests God's communicative and relational nature. Grace is primarily the communication of the Holy Spirit that not only transforms individual human beings but also draws them into fellowship with the trinitarian God and the community of the church. Grace and redemption are relational because they are fundamentally communion with persons, both divine and human.

Edwards' progressive pneumatology has important connections with pentecostal theology—indeed, the pneumatological instincts and directions of this theology qualify him as a proto-pentecostal. In important respects, Edwards' pneumatology is more fundamental and richer than traditional pentecostal pneumatology, which locates the Spirit's primary work in the subsidiary doctrine of Spirit baptism. Edwards' pneumatology contributes to contemporary pentecostal theologians working to achieve a more *pneumatological* and thus a more *pentecostal* theology of the Holy Spirit. Thus, the conversation is not unilateral. The global pentecostal movements suggest that the Holy Spirit is central to Christian experience. The Spirit should be a theological afterthought in neither the economic nor the immanent Trinity. Pentecostal theological instincts can complete Edwards' progressive pneumatology and proto-pentecostal instincts with a more robust understanding of the Spirit's identity in the triune God (immanent Trinity) and role in the work of redemption (economic Trinity).

This chapter has three sections. The first section brings the traditional and progressive elements of Edwards' pneumatology related to the immanent Trinity into conversation with pentecostal trinitarian theology. The second section turns to the economic Trinity and characterizes Edwards' pneumatology as progressive and proto-Pentecostal. The third section shows the synergy between Edwards' proto-pentecostal pneumatology and the constructive pneumatologies of pentecostal theologians Frank D. Macchia and Amos Yong.

Augustinian and more

Edwards' trinitarian theology carries on the major characteristics of the Augustinian trinitarian tradition—the psychological analogy and the mutual love model. But it was more than that as well. Edwards was a creative theologian. He thought from and within the Puritan tradition, but also beyond it. Like other areas of his theology (e.g., promoter of Awakenings), Edwards' trinitarian theology was progressive. It extended elements of trinitarian theology that, although not ignored, were not areas of focus for most of the preceding tradition of Western trinitarian theology.[1] Edwards developed a relational and social vision of the triune God. That he did so on the basis of pneumatology makes his theology of particular interest to pentecostal theology. Setting Edwards' trinitarian theology in relief with the Augustinian tradition helps showcase its progressive elements. To do so involves addressing four areas of Edwards' trinitarian theology. The first is the foundational and relational theological ontology that is the basis for not only Edwards' vision of the Trinity but also other areas of his theology, such as creation, grace, ecclesiology, and eschatology. The second describes the Augustinian elements of his trinitarian theology—for example, the Holy Spirit as the mutual love of the Father and the Son. The third highlights the innovative or progressive features of his social vision of the Trinity. This section concludes with a pentecostal solution to the problem of the Spirit's personal identity, which Edwards identified but never resolved.

Relational ontology

Although reflecting traditional Augustinian trinitarian tendencies, Edwards' pneumatology inspired him to push beyond the emphases of that tradition. He developed social images that supported a relational vision of the triune God. Relations and reciprocal communication of love define the trinitarian God. This communicative nature of God finds eternal expression in the community of the Father, the Son, and the Holy Spirit.[2] Foundational for Edwards' trinitarian theology are two principles:

---

[1] In an important sense, however, Edwards built on the work of some of his Puritan predecessors, who had turned not only to the social nature of the Trinity but also to its implications for a relational soteriology, for example, Kelly M. Kapic and Justin Taylor's edition of John Owen's *Communion with the Triune God* (Wheaton, IL: Crossway, 2007).

[2] See Edwards, *Dissertation I. Concerning the End for Which God Created the World*, WJE 8:432–35 and 526–36, for his definitive statements on the nature of God's communicative being.

the dynamism of the divine disposition for self-communication and divine goodness. Edwards believed that the divine being is relational and the Trinity is the structure of that relational ontology. The Trinity is the eternal product of the divine being's intrinsic dynamism for self-communication. God's being is never static. It is eternally active in sharing being that takes place in the subsistence of the divine persons. The communication of goodness begins with the sharing of being that creates the other and the opportunity for reciprocal relations.

For Edwards, the divine nature's disposition for self-communication and divine goodness are nearly interchangeable ideas. Divine goodness resides in the self-communicative nature and activity of the divine being. Goodness is sharing happiness with other persons; it is to "delight in communicating happiness."[3] True happiness is not self-enclosed and selfish, but oriented to another. Goodness is inherently interpersonal and consists in the desire and act of sharing happiness or love with another person.[4] Edwards closely aligned goodness with the concepts of joy, happiness, and most significantly love. Love constitutes goodness; it is the act whereby one person shares his or her joy with another. Love, moreover, is social in nature because the beloved desires to return love to the lover, which makes their love mutual. The sharing of love between two persons consummates goodness. Since God is the highest order of being, God must manifest the interpersonal sharing of goodness. This principle, argues Edwards, makes the diversity of persons in the Godhead necessary: "God must have a perfect exercise of his goodness, and therefore must have the fellowship of a person equal with himself."[5]

A plurality of divine persons are necessary because God's disposition to communicate goodness must have an infinite exercise. If it did not, it would not actualize the fullness of goodness, which would leave God an imperfect being. Created persons, whether angelic or human, are worthy objects of love. But because they are finite communications of beings, they are neither infinite communications of goodness nor suitable partners for the infinite sharing of interpersonal love. The only object that meets the criterion of an infinite communication of happiness is the divine being itself.[6] Therefore, plurality in the Godhead is necessary because the communication of being and of the infinite happiness of God—divine love—can only become manifest in the eternal personal diversification of the divine persons.

The link between the interpersonal nature of divine goodness and the disposition of the divine nature for self-communication is a centerpiece of Edwards' Trinitarianism. Edwards believed that the divine disposition to communicate goodness can find realization only in a community of three divine persons.[7] Integrating divine goodness and self-communication with the Trinity places Edwards within the tradition of

---

[3] Edwards, "Miscellany 96," *WJE* 13:263.
[4] Edwards, "Miscellany 87," *WJE* 13:251–52, "Miscellany 97," *WJE* 13:264, and "Miscellany 104," *WJE* 13:272.
[5] Edwards, "Miscellany 96," *WJE* 13:264.
[6] Edwards, "Miscellany 117," *WJE* 13:283–84.
[7] Edwards, "Miscellany 96," *WJE* 13:262–63.

Richard of St. Victor (d. 1173) and Bonaventure (1221–74).[8] Edwards' trinitarian theology also bears the familiar analogies and images of Western trinitarian theology. It does however also contain emphases that are less common and these elements are not peripheral but central to his theology of the trinitarian God. But first I turn to the more familiar elements of his trinitarian theology.

Augustinian elements

Edwards uses a version of the psychological analogy. The psychological analogy assumes that a rational being or mind has a twofold structure—the capacities for thought and will. A rational being, therefore, has two powers of operation, the understanding and the will. When the understanding and the will operate, they subsist in a particular way. The understanding terminates or subsists in an idea or logos. The will subsists as the desire (or love) for whatever is held by the understanding.

This structure of a rational being or mind becomes the basis for Edwards' articulation of the divine processions in terms of the Augustinian mutual love model. God the Father correlates with the mind. As the mind generates thought (understanding) and desire (will), so the Father is God "absolutely considered" and the unbegotten font who generates the processions of the Son and the Spirit.[9] The Son proceeds by way of the divine understanding and the Holy Spirit by the divine will. Accordingly, the Father begets the Son as the perfect idea or Word of the divine essence through the eternal act of the divine understanding. As a perfect idea, the procession of the Son "repeats" or yields a subsistence of the divine nature that possesses the fullness of the divine nature. The Son, like the Father, possesses the ability to know and to love and to communicate being, which enables the Son, along with the Father, to co-spirate (i.e., *filioque*) the Holy Spirit.[10] The Son, however, shares these capacities with the Father in a derivative way. The Father retains the exclusive character of unbegottenness, whereas the Son's principal identity is begotten Son of the Father. The Holy Spirit subsists as the mutual love of the Father and of the Son. The subsistence of the Holy Spirit as mutual love fulfills the disposition of the divine nature to communicate goodness. The Holy Spirit is the eternal fellowship of love shared between the Father and the Son. The Spirit

---

[8] Richard of St. Victor, *On the Trinity*, trans. and intro. Christopher P. Evans, in *Trinity and Creation: A Selection of Works of Hugh, Richard, and Adam of St Victor*, ed. Boyd Taylor Coolman and Dale M. Coulter (Turnhout: Brepols, 2010), 3.1 (p. 247), *Prologue* (p. 211), and 1.1 (p. 213); *The Works of Bonaventure*, trans. José Vinck, vol. 2, *The Breviloquium* (Paterson, NJ: St. Anthony Guild, 1963), 36; and *The Works of St. Bonaventure*, ed. George Marcil, vol. 3, *Disputed Questions on the Mystery of the Trinity*, trans. Zachery Hayes (1979; reprint, St. Bonaventure, NY: The Franciscan Institute St. Bonaventure University, 2000), 254–57.

[9] Edwards, *Discourse on the Trinity*, WJE 21:130–31 and *The Threefold Work of the Holy Ghost*, WJE 14:379.

[10] Edwards, *Discourse on the Trinity*, WJE 21:131; "Miscellany 363," WJE 13:435 and "Miscellany 370," WJE 13:442; and *Notes on Scripture*, WJE 15:335, 319–20. Edwards' theory of the Son as an ideal repetition of the divine nature has led critics from Horace Bushnell and Benjamin Warfield to contemporary Oliver D. Crisp to charge his theology with implying modalism, tritheism, or infinite multiplication of divine persons. For details, see Steven M. Studebaker and Robert W. Caldwell III, *The Trinitarian Theology of Jonathan Edwards: Text, Context, and Application* (Burlington, VT: Ashgate, 2011).

completes the communication of divine goodness.[11] Edwards uses the processes of the psychological analogy to articulate the subsistence and personal relations to the divine persons.[12]

Progressive elements

Central to Edwards' trinitarian theology are social and relational language and emphases. Amy Plantinga Pauw initiated the contemporary revival in Edwards' trinitarian theology. The nineteenth century saw intermittent interest in Edwards' trinitarian theology, but after a hiatus of nearly a century, Plantinga Pauw's *"The Supreme Harmony of All"* was the first book dedicated to Edwards' trinitarian theology.[13] A solid starting point for research on Edwards and the Trinity, her key contribution is that Edwards drew on social and psychological models of the Trinity. The psychological (western/Augustinian) model takes the oneness of God as foundational in reflection on the Trinity, and the social (Eastern/Cappadocian) model takes the plurality of the divine persons as the central category of trinitarian theology. Edwards alternated between these two models to articulate the immanent and economic Trinity and doctrines related to creation and redemption. His eclectic and "multilingual" use of the distinct social and psychological models provides an inclusive model for contemporary trinitarian theology. He serves as a historical source to transcend the impasse that characterizes contemporary debates between proponents of these differing models of the Trinity.[14]

Plantinga Pauw and I share the conviction that Edwards is a valuable resource for contemporary theology both in respect to the creative style of his theology and the content of his trinitarian theology. Edwards developed the social and relational nature of God in an uncommon way in the Western tradition of trinitarian theology. Regrettably Edwards gained notoriety for being a regressive Calvinist Puritan through the widespread dissemination of the hell fire and brimstone sermon, "Sinners in the Hands of an Angry God." The popular image is unfortunate. Edwards was a Calvinist and perhaps at times austere. But the heart of his theology was a God of abundant and overflowing love and joy. This God of love and happiness, moreover, shared that social

---

[11] Edwards, *Discourse on the Trinity*, WJE 21:113, 116–17, and 121–22; "Miscellany 94," WJE 13:260–61; and *Charity and Its Fruits*, WJE 8:373.

[12] For people unfamiliar with the traditions of trinitarian theology, Edwards' use of the internal operations of a mind to portray the divine persons sounds far-fetched. When I teach this part of Edwards' theology or introduce this material in teaching the wider traditions of trinitarian theology, the eyes of students invariably and almost instantly glaze over. Despite the opacity of the psychological analogy, Edwards' trinitarian theology was the source of some of his most creative theology.

[13] Amy Plantinga Pauw, *"The Supreme Harmony of All": The Trinitarian Theology of Jonathan Edwards* (Grand Rapids, MI: Eerdmans, 2002). For the history of scholarship on Edwards and the Trinity and the key issues under discussion, see Studebaker and Caldwell, *The Trinitarian Theology of Jonathan Edwards*, 6–18 and Michael J. McClymond and Gerald R. McDermott, *Theology of Jonathan Edwards* (New York: Oxford University Press, 2012), 193–206.

[14] Plantinga Pauw, *"Supreme Harmony of All,"* 11–15, 30–35, and 183–92.

goodness by creating a world with human beings that can participate in and manifest that social goodness with the world, each other, and their God.

Pentecostal improvement

Although adeptly using the mutual love model and the psychological analogy to develop a social vision of God, Edwards also recognizes their shortcomings. A person has an "understanding" and a "will."[15] But the psychological analogy makes the Son and the Holy Spirit relative operations of the mind of the Father. The problem is the same for the mutual love model because it relies on the structure of the psychological analogy for articulating the identities of the divine persons—for example, the Son proceeds and subsists as the Word of the divine understanding and the Holy Spirit as the love of the volitional capacity of the divine mind. As Edwards points out, "This [psychological analogy and mutual love model] makes the understanding one distinct person, and love another."[16] In an effort to resolve the conundrum, Edwards suggests that the understanding and the will share a "wonderful union between them that they are after an ineffable and inconceivable manner one in another."[17]

This approach also portrays the personal identity of the Son primarily and the Spirit entirely in passive terms.[18] The Father begets the Son. The Son's primary identity is derivative; he is the one begotten by the Father. Secondarily, the Son's identity includes agency as he participates in the procession of the Holy Spirit (i.e., *filioque*). But the Father retains the principal role in the Spirit's procession, thus underlining the Son's derivative and primarily passive identity in the immanent Trinity. Where the Father and the Son play, more and less, active roles in the Trinity, the Spirit, as their mutual love, does not. The Spirit is not an agent at all. The Spirit is the Father and the Son's mutual act of love. The Spirit is the product of their personal agency. The mutual love model is a relational model of the Trinity. The Father and the Son exist in an eternal fellowship of love. That fellowship, however, is binitarian. The Father and the Son love each other, but the Spirit is neither a lover nor a beloved.

But even dropping the structure of the psychological analogy and just retaining the notion of mutual love, Edwards' goal is forestalled. Edwards maintained that love, the excellency of the divine nature, requires giving and receiving goodness and happiness. The exchange of goodness comes to most sublime expression in the mutual love of the Father and the Son.[19] Edwards' relational principle of love, however, does not apply to the Holy Spirit. The Spirit neither receives nor gives love. The Spirit is love; the Spirit is

---

[15] Edwards, *Discourse on the Trinity*, WJE 21:132-33.
[16] Ibid., 133.
[17] Ibid. Edwards was not the first theologian to recognize this problem; indeed, even Augustine, widely attributed with popularizing the psychological analogy, identified this problem. See *The Works of Saint Augustine: A Translation for the 21st Century*, ed. John E. Rotelle, vol. 5, *The Trinity*, ed. Edmund Hill (Brooklyn, NY: New City, 1991), 9.2-8 (pp. 271-75).
[18] Wolfgang Vondey also makes the same point about the passivity of the Spirit in traditional trinitarian theology in "The Holy Spirit and the Physical Universe: The Impact of Scientific Paradigm Shifts in Contemporary Pneumatology," *Theological Studies* 70, no. 1 (2009): 32-33.
[19] Edwards, "The Mind," WJE 6:336-38 and 362-65 and "Beauty of the World," WJE 6:305.

the mutual love that binds the Father and the Son in eternal fellowship. The society of Edwards' Trinity is, therefore, two divine persons united in loving communion by the third person that is identical with their mutual love. If receiving and giving love is the essence of personhood, then the Spirit does not attain it.

The solution to this theological problem is twofold. First, theology should jettison the psychological analogy. It works neither as an analogy of the Trinity (since it reduces the Son and the Spirit to relative operations of the Father's mind) nor as an ontology for human persons. Theological minds from Augustine and Aquinas to Edwards, Barth, and Rahner have come up short trying to resolve the problems created by the psychological analogy in Western trinitarian theology.[20] Perhaps it is time to recognize that they are insurmountable. The problem here, however, is not with the Trinity, but the way the psychological analogy problematizes it.

Second, making a pentecostal contribution to Edwards' trinitarian theology means turning to the narrative of the Spirit of Pentecost. The story of the Spirit begins with the Spirit stirring over the primal elements and catalyzing creation (Gen. 1). The promise of the Spirit in the Hebrew prophets renews the land and restores the life of the cities (Ezek. 37:1-14). The investiture of the Spirit on Mary brings about the Incarnation of the Son of God in Jesus Christ. By the same Spirit, Jesus Christ carried out his messianic ministry (Lk. 4:14-19 and Mt. 12:1-28). The Spirit redeems Jesus from his god-forsakenness and brings the resurrected Christ from the tomb (Rom. 1:4 and 8:11). The risen Christ sends the Spirit of Pentecost to all people so that all people can participate in the grace realized in the life of Jesus Christ (Acts 2:17). In the eschaton, the Spirit renews creation (Rom. 8). Biblical pneumatology, therefore, portrays the Spirit as a personal agent in the history of creation and redemption.

The economic activities of the divine persons reveal their immanent personal identities. If this principle is invalid, then the very notion of the Christian theology revelation becomes unhinged. Why? Because theology could posit no intrinsic connection between what God does and is. But assuming the validity of the principle, the consequence for pneumatology is that since the Spirit is a personal agent in the economic Trinity, then so also in the immanent Trinity.

But what does this activity of the Spirit in the economy of redemption mean for the immanent Trinity? It has pneumatological and trinitarian implications. From the perspective of pneumatology, the narrative of the Spirit reveals that the Spirit is an active agent. The Spirit moreover plays a central, not a derivative, role relative to Christ and the Father. The Spirit is the personal agent that creates and unites the humanity of Jesus with the Son of God. The Holy Spirit in other words is the principal personal agent that constitutes Jesus the Christ. As the Spirit anointed Christ, Jesus lives in loving fellowship with the Father throughout his incarnate life. The pneumatological implication for the immanent Trinity is that the Spirit plays an active role in the Trinity. As the Spirit's activity in the economic Trinity contributed to shaping the identity of

---

[20] These very problems with the analogy led Augustine to turn to the analogy of co-operational subsistence of memory, understanding, and will. They operate and subsist simultaneously and inseparably, even though remaining relative operations of one mind. See Augustine, *The Trinity* 14:15 and 14:21–25 (5:383 and 386–91).

Jesus Christ as the Incarnate Son of God—from Incarnation, to life and ministry, and resurrection, so the Spirit contributes to the formation of the Father's and the Son's eternal identities in the immanent Trinity. The Spirit's activity in relation to the Father and the Son, drawing them into their relationship and constituting the eternal fellowship of the trinitarian God, also contributes to the Spirit's identity. The Spirit is not the mutual act of love between the Father and the Son, but the divine person who facilitates their relationship through relationship with them. Being and activity are indivisible in the Trinity. The Spirit's personal agency as the one who constitutes the triune fellowship of God indicates the Spirit's personal identity. The formation of the personal identities of the Father, the Son, and the Holy Spirit is complete only when the Spirit achieves the fullness of the eternal fellowship of the trinitarian God. The Spirit's identity does not derive from being the mutual act of love, but from the Spirit's activity of bringing to completion the communion of the trinitarian God.[21]

The eschatological place of the Spirit of Pentecost in the history of redemption also has implications for trinitarian theology. The outpouring of the Spirit of Pentecost is not only an eschatological moment in the history of redemption but also a revelation of the Spirit's immanent identity. The economic work of the triune God culminates in the outpouring of the Holy Spirit because the Spirit completes the triune fellowship of God. Trinitarian theology maintains the reciprocity between the immanent and economic Trinity. The divine persons transcend their work and revelation in the economic Trinity, but never in a way that introduces disjunction between their economic work and immanent identities. The outpouring of the Spirit of Pentecost was and remains an eschatological event in the history of redemption. Given the symmetry between the economic and the immanent Trinity, the Spirit's eschatological role in the economic Trinity points to the Spirit's role in the fellowship of the trinitarian God.[22] The implication for the immanent Trinity is that the Holy Spirit constitutes the fullness or fulfills the fellowship of the trinitarian God. Just as the outpouring of the Holy Spirit on the Day of Pentecost is a threshold and eschatological moment in the economy of redemption, so also the coming forth of the Spirit in the immanent Trinity is a liminal procession that consummates the triune God. Without the Spirit, the trinitarian fellowship is incomplete. In the person of the Spirit, the divine life crosses the threshold to full trinitarian love. Not by simply adding a third to a fellowship otherwise had between the Father and the Son. In the person of the Holy Spirit, the personal fellowship of the Godhead transcends a binary relational dynamic and achieves a trinitarian one.

---

[21] For a full development of this argument, see Steven M. Studebaker, *From Pentecost to the Triune God: A Pentecostal Trinitarian Theology* (Grand Rapids, MI: Eerdmans, 2012), 53–100.

[22] Wolfhart Pannenberg also speaks of the Spirit playing a consummative role in the economy of redemption. He suggests that the Spirit "completes the revelation of the Father by the Son." His point, however, is quite different than mine. The work of the Spirit is entirely oriented to the revelation of the Father. The Spirit and the Son for that matter are subordinate to the Father. The Spirit's economic subordination to the Father occurs through the Spirit's obeisance to the Son as the vice-regent of the Father's kingdom. The Holy Spirit completes the revelation *of the Father* by the Son and does so by glorifying the Son. Pneumatology is ultimately subordinate to Patrology via its penultimate subordination to Christology. See Wolfhart Pannenberg, *Systematic Theology*, vol. 1, trans. Geoffrey W. Bromiley (Grand Rapids, MI: Eerdmans, 1991), 315, 321–25.

The trinitarian implication is that the Trinity is a *trinitarian* fellowship of the Father, the Son, and the Holy Spirit. In the mutual love model, the Spirit is instrumental. The Spirit is the bond of love between the Father and the Son, the interpersonal relationship of love between the Father and the Son. The problem, as Edwards identified, is that it does not provide a unique and additional relational dynamic that is proper to the Spirit. The Spirit, however, is constitutional, not instrumental. The Spirit fulfills the fellowship of the trinitarian God by expanding the relational dynamic from mutual fellowship between two to the fellowship of the three divine persons. The Spirit not only fulfills the relationship between the Father and the Son by uniting them in eternal love, but also the fellowship of the *trinitarian* God by adding to that fellowship a trinitarian relational dynamic. Even if retaining the traditional categories of divine processions, only in the subsistence of the Holy Spirit does the Godhead cross the trinitarian threshold and "become" the fellowship of the Father, the Son, and the Holy Spirit. The Holy Spirit, therefore, constitutes the triune fellowship of the trinitarian God. The Spirit is the person who completes the fellowship of not only the Father and the Son but the Trinity as such.

The use of "become" connotes no temporal chronology, but the ontological and relational order of the divine persons. For example, the Father must beget the Son or, alternatively, the Son must be from the Father. The terms "Father" and "Son" otherwise mean nothing. The ontological order intrinsic to the Father-Son relation does not negate the Son's eternal nature. The Son has been from the Father from eternity. In the same way, although the Spirit is third in the ontological order, the Spirit is eternal. Being third in ontological order reflects the Spirit's personal activity and identity in the immanent Trinity. The Spirit's role in facilitating the fellowship of the Father and the Son presupposes their subsistence. Ontological order, moreover, implies no subordination. That the Spirit is third does not mean the Spirit is third in a divine hierarchical power structure. The divine persons are ontologically and functionally equal. Although their relational activities and, thus also, personal identities are unique, they are equal.[23]

Proto-pentecostal pneumatology and theology of grace

Edwards' relationship to traditional Protestant theology is not simple. On the one hand, he embraced a forensic theology of justification that privileges Christological, legal, and penal categories. On the other hand, he affirmed a pneumatological and, indeed, trinitarian theology of grace. The immanent identities of and relations among the divine persons frame their work in the economy of redemption. The duality between the traditional and progressive elements in Edwards has sparked an ongoing debate on the orthodoxy of Edwards' doctrine of justification. The fundamental divide

---

[23] For more on the order and equality of the divine persons, see Studebaker, *From Pentecost to the Triune God*, 95–96.

being scholars who regard Edwards as moving toward a transformative theology of justification and scholars who see him remaining within the Protestant forensic trajectory. In short, did Edwards go Catholic or remain Protestant? The answer depends on the Edwards' texts one reads.[24] This section describes the traditional and progressive elements of Edwards' soteriology, with the latter showcasing the relationship between the immanent and the economic Trinity and his proto-pentecostal pneumatology.

Edwards and traditional Protestant soteriology

When specifically addressing the doctrine of justification, Edwards is traditional. Justification is a legal and penal transaction. Justification takes a judicial relationship between God and human beings as fundamental. The essence of salvation, therefore, is rectifying the judicial scales between God and human beings. God loves human beings, but demands perfect obedience to divine law and punishment or payment for violating that law.[25] Being justified before God requires payment for sins and obedience to the law. Jesus Christ, through his life of perfect obedience to God's law and penal death on the cross, assuages the wrath of God for human sin and fulfills the requirements of divine law. Salvation consists in having faith in the efficacy of Christ's work. Through faith the believer receives the forgiveness of sins and the imputed righteousness of Christ. The legal and forensic doctrine of justification is the essence of salvation in traditional Protestant theology. The righteousness that saves the believer is the imputed righteousness of Christ and not the righteousness of sanctification.

Edwards affirms this traditional Protestant theology of justification. For Edwards, justification derives from the extrinsic righteousness of Christ that through faith God imputes to cover sins. Imputed righteousness, moreover, remains extrinsic. The receiver of Christ's righteousness "is looked upon as destitute of any righteousness in himself, by that expression, 'it is counted' . . . 'for righteousness.'"[26] God regards or counts as righteousness sinful human beings by imputing Christ's righteousness to their accounts. Justification is being "approved of God as free from the guilt of sin, and its deserved punishment, and as having that righteousness belonging to him that entitles to the reward of life."[27] In adopting this traditional Protestant view of justification and sanctification, Edwards embodied a Christocentric tradition of theology that subordinates the Spirit to Christ as well as the transformational and relational to the legal and penal.

---

[24] For scholarship on this debate, see Studebaker and Caldwell, and the recent books by Michael McClenahan, *Jonathan Edwards and Justification by Faith* (Burlington, VT: Ashgate, 2012) and Josh Moody, ed., *Jonathan Edwards and Justification* (Wheaton, IL: Crossway, 2012).
[25] Edwards, *Justification by Faith*, WJE 19:150.
[26] Ibid., 148.
[27] Edwards, *Justification by Faith*, WJE 19:151 and 147–48.

Edwards' progressive and proto-pentecostal pneumatology

Edwards' pneumatology was also progressive. His thinking on the role of the Holy Spirit in the economy of redemption yielded his best constructive theology. Edwards begins with the problem:

> If we suppose no more than used to be supposed about the Holy Ghost, the honor of the Holy Ghost in the work of redemption is not equal in any sense to the Father and the Son's. . . . Merely to apply to us, or immediately to give or hand to us, [the] blessing purchased after it is purchased . . . is but a little thing to the purchaser of it by the paying an infinite price by Christ.[28]

Edwards identifies the pneumatological problem of the traditional Protestant paradigm. For Edwards, the model in which Christ achieves redemption through his life of obedience and death on the cross and the Holy Spirit applies the gifts of redemption subordinates the Spirit to Christ.

Edwards' solution to this problem is that the Spirit is the "great purchase of Christ."[29] The Holy Spirit is the item purchased by Christ on behalf of human debtors. This progressive pneumatology reflects continuity and discontinuity with his tradition. The legal-contractual language and conceptual framework (i.e., the Holy Spirit is purchased by Christ) stand in continuity with the penal-substitutionary and Anselmian traditions of atonement theology. The divergence resides in shifting the nature of redemption from a conferred judicial status to the gift of a divine person. He remarked, "The sum of all that Christ purchased is the Holy Ghost."[30] Grace, therefore, is not essentially pardon from sin, imputed righteousness, sanctification, or any other group of benefits, but a divine person—the Holy Spirit. Edwards affirmed that "grace . . . is no other than the Spirit of God itself dwelling and acting in the heart of a saint."[31] In *Religious Affections*, Edwards argues that "the Son is the purchaser and the price; and the Holy Spirit is the great blessing or inheritance purchased." The Holy Spirit is "grace itself." He then identifies the Holy Spirit as the gift of grace with the Spirit of Pentecost.[32] According to Edwards, making the Spirit the purchase of redemption brings equality to the Spirit relative to Christ. It does so because the gift of salvation—the Spirit—is equal to the value of its cost—the suffering of Christ. In both circumstances, a divine person is the currency of redemption.[33] By casting salvation in terms of the gift of a divine

---

[28] Edwards, *Treatise on Grace*, WJE 21:191.
[29] Edwards, *Charity and Its Fruits*, WJE 8:353 and "Miscellany 706," WJE 18:326.
[30] Edwards, "Miscellany 402," WJE 13:466 and "Miscellany 706," WJE 18:326.
[31] Edwards, *Treatise on Grace*, WJE 21:192.
[32] Edwards, *Religious Affections*, WJE 2:236. He also identifies the communication of the Holy Spirit as the grace of Christ with the Spirit of Pentecost in *An Humble Attempt*, WJE 5:341 and *God Glorified in Man's Dependence*, WJE 17:209.
[33] Edwards, *Charity and Its Fruits*, WJE 8:353–54; *Discourse on the Trinity*, WJE 21:130–31, 135–37, 142, and 144; *God Glorified in Man's Dependence*, WJE 17:202, and 207–08; "Miscellany 364," WJE 13:436 and "Miscellany 402," WJE 13:466–67; "Miscellany 706," WJE 18:326 and 328–29, "Miscellany 755," WJE 18:403–4, and "Miscellany 772," WJE 18:419–20; "Miscellany 1062," WJE 20:43–40; and *Treatise on Grace*, WJE 21:188–91.

person, Edwards at once overcomes the subordination of the Spirit in his tradition and radically alters the nature of redemption. At the same, Edwards did retain the forensic doctrine of justification. Whether or not he saw the tension between his traditional forensic and Christocentric and progressive transformational and pneumatological ways of framing grace is not evident in his writings.

How does Edwards' theology of grace relate to his trinitarian theology? Edwards' theology of the immanent Trinity shapes the trinitarian structure of the economy of redemption. His trinitarian theology not only led him to critique traditional Christocentric soteriology but also to develop a pneumatological concept of grace and a trinitarian vision of redemption. The trinitarian nature of Edwards' theology of grace can be summarized in the following. The Holy Spirit unites the Son of God to the humanity of Jesus Christ so that the risen Christ can share the Spirit with all people (for Edwards, the elect) and thereby provide the way for their union with the Son of God and fellowship with the Father. Thus, grace is pneumatological because the Holy Spirit is the personal point of contact. But the Spirit of grace also unites believers with each other, the Son, and the Father, thus establishing and extending the triune fellowship of God with creation. Based on the progressive nature of his pneumatology, I have called Edwards' a proto-Pentecostal. Edwards was not a Pentecostal. But his pneumatology gives the Spirit a central role in the work of redemption, from Incarnation to grace, ecclesiology, and eschatology in a way that complements recent developments in pentecostal theology.

Edwards, pentecostal theology, and the Holy Spirit

Edwards' pneumatology was proto-Pentecostal and progressive. His account of the Spirit's role in the economy of redemption provides a resource that can contribute to the efforts among pentecostal theologians, such as Frank Macchia and Amos Yong, to fortify the *pentecostal* nature of pentecostal theology.[34] This final section highlights the way that traditional pentecostal pneumatology subordinates the Spirit and that Edwards, Macchia, and Yong can resolve it.

The classical pentecostal doctrine of Spirit baptism

The traditional pentecostal doctrine of Spirit baptism putatively showcases the Holy Spirit. Spirit baptism is a second of work grace after conversion that imparts empowerment for mission and manifesting spiritual gifts. Classical Pentecostals

---

[34] See Frank D. Macchia, *Justified in the Spirit: Creation, Redemption, and the Triune God* (Grand Rapids, MI: Eerdmans, 2010); *Baptized in the Spirit: A Global Pentecostal Theology* (Grand Rapids, MI: Zondervan, 2006); and Amos Yong, *Spirit of Love: A Trinitarian Theology of Grace* (Waco: Baylor University Press, 2012).

affirm also that the initial physical evidence of Spirit baptism is speaking in tongues (*glossolalia*), although insistence on tongues is increasingly less common. This theology of Spirit baptism has served as the distinctive doctrine for many Pentecostals, which is ironic because it subordinates the Spirit even more so than the wider tradition of Protestant soteriology.[35] Spirit baptism, understood as a second work of grace, renders the Holy Spirit an add-on to the redemption otherwise provided by Christ. I am speaking specifically about pentecostal pneumatology and not pentecostal experience and practice. My focus is the theological implication of the pentecostal theological way of expressing its experience of the Spirit. The classical pentecostal doctrine of Spirit baptism subordinates the Spirit to Christ and, in respect to salvation as such, makes the Spirit almost irrelevant. Spirit baptism is distinct from and subsequent to salvation. Salvation happens at the cross. Baptism in the Spirit happens at Pentecost. Traditional pentecostal theology has an accentuated experience of the Spirit, but an impoverished theology of the Spirit.

A case in point is Robert P. Menzies' argument that Spirit baptism is a *donum superadditum* to the salvation provided by Christ.[36] His purpose is to safeguard the integrity of Luke-Acts' pneumatology vis-à-vis Pauline pneumatology. In other words, he rejects the subordination of Luke-Acts to Paul. In that respect, he is on the mark. The problem, however, is that Menzies reads Luke-Acts and Paul through a Protestant paradigm of justification and sanctification. Paul is about justification. Luke-Acts is about sanctification. Specifically, Luke-Acts focuses on the experience of Spirit baptism and charismatic empowerment, which fall under the broader category of sanctification in the Protestant order of redemption (*ordo salutis*). Since the Spirit's work relates to sanctification, it has little to do with the substance of salvation. The irony here is that although maintaining the independent and unique theological voice of Luke-Acts relative to Paul, this pentecostal pneumatology remains subordinated to a deeper Protestant Christocentrism. Menzies is correct that Luke-Acts adds something important to New Testament pneumatology and should not be read through a Pauline paradigm. But neither Luke-Acts nor Paul, for that matter, should be read through a Protestant paradigm that privileges Christological to pneumatological and legal to transformational categories.

The doctrinal distinctive of Classical Pentecostalism is Spirit baptism, understood as an experience of the Spirit subsequent to conversion-salvation and evidenced by speaking in tongues. Although providing a clear confessional identity, this doctrinal definition has unfortunate consequences. First, it is elitist. It recognizes as authentic "Pentecostal" only experiences of the Spirit that fit the classical pentecostal paradigm

---

[35] See my "Pentecostal Soteriology and Pneumatology," *Journal of Pentecostal Theology* 11, no. 2 (2003): 248–70 and "Beyond Tongues: A Pentecostal Theology of Grace," in *Defining Issues in Pentecostalism: Classical and Emergent*, ed. Steven M. Studebaker (Eugene: Pickwick, 2008), 46–68.

[36] Robert P. Menzies, *The Development of Early Christian Pneumatology, with Special Reference to Luke-Acts*, Journal for the Study of the New Testament Supplement Series 54 (Sheffield: Sheffield Academic Press, 1991), 48.

of Spirit baptism. Second, and consequently, it cannot accommodate the variety of charismatic experiences within the wider pentecostal movements.[37] For these reasons and others, pentecostal scholars in the 1990s and first decade of the twenty-first century shifted from this doctrine to charismatic experience as the essence of Pentecostalism.[38] Walter J. Hollenweger's work on global Pentecostalism that demonstrated the variety of pentecostal theology, practices, and historical trajectories was a key factor in the search for a more ecumenical and inclusive understanding of pentecostal identity.[39] Shifting the essence of Pentecostalism to charismatic experience does not deny the importance of pentecostal theology. But it does mean that, given the diversity of pentecostal theologies, reaching a doctrinal definition of Pentecostalism (such as the classical pentecostal one) is beyond reach.[40]

These two approaches—classical pentecostal and charismatic experience—to defining Pentecostalism present pentecostal theology with a twofold problem. On the one hand, the downside of the move to the phenomenological definition of Pentecostalism—charismatic experience—rather than theology renders theology an epiphenomenon to Pentecostalism.[41]

On the other hand, the classical pentecostal doctrine of Spirit baptism makes the Spirit subsidiary to redemption. It subordinates the Spirit to Christ and, in respect to salvation as such, makes the Spirit almost irrelevant. This doctrine leaves Pentecostals with an accentuated experience of the Spirit, but an underdeveloped theology of the Spirit. For these reasons and others, pentecostal theologians, such as Frank Macchia and Amos Yong, have begun to argue that the pentecostal experience of the Spirit

---

[37] See my discussion of the implications of the diverse experiences of the Spirit in global Pentecostalism for the traditional classical pentecostal doctrine of Spirit baptism in "Globalization and Spirit Baptism," in *Pentecostalism and Globalization: The Impact of Globalization on Pentecostal Theology and Ministry*, ed. Steven M. Studebaker (Eugene, OR: Pickwick, 2010), 87–108.

[38] Allan Anderson, *Pentecostalism: An Introduction* (2004; reprint, New York: Cambridge University Press, 2006), 13–14, and 187–88; Mark J. Cartledge, *Encountering the Spirit: The Charismatic Tradition* (Maryknoll: Orbis, 2007), 19–32; Steven Jack Land, *Pentecostal Spirituality: A Passion for the Kingdom* (Sheffield: Sheffield Academic Press, 1993), 23–32; and Keith Warrington, *Pentecostal Theology: A Theology of Encounter* (New York: T&T Clark, 2008), 18–27.

[39] Walter J. Hollenweger, *The Pentecostals* (London: SCM, 1972) and *Pentecostalism: Origins and Developments Worldwide* (Peabody, MA: Hendrickson, 1997). Harvey Cox's interpretation of Pentecostalism as a manifestation of primal religion was also an early contribution to this trend—*Fire from Heaven: The Rise of Pentecostal Spirituality and the Reshaping of Religion in the Twenty-First Century* (Reading, MA: Addison-Wesley, 1995), 81–83.

[40] For example, see Douglas G. Jacobsen's argument that doctrinal diversity in early Pentecostalism precludes reaching a doctrinal definition of Pentecostalism in *Thinking in the Spirit: Theologies of the Early Pentecostal Movement* (Bloomington, IN: Indiana University Press, 2003), 10–12; cf. Veli-Matti Kärkkäinen's statement that "the best thing to do is to acknowledge and live with the lack of consensus. Diversity is the hallmark of this Spirit movement;" Kärkkäinen, "Pneumatologies in Systematic Theology," in *Studying Global Pentecostalism: Theories and Methods*, ed. Allan Anderson, Michael Begrunder, André Droogers, and Cornelius van der Laan (Berkeley, CA: University of California Press, 2010), 232.

[41] Simon Chan, "Whither Pentecostalism," in *Asian and Pentecostal: The Charismatic Face of Christianity in Asia*, ed. Allan Anderson and Edmond Tang (Oxford: Regnum, 2005), 579 and Macchia, *Baptized in the Spirit*, 55.

bears theological implications.[42] Theology and experience cannot be separated. Spirit baptism, so central to pentecostal experience, has implications for pentecostal pneumatology as well as a contribution to make to the wider traditions of Christian theology.

Edwards and progressive pentecostal pneumatology

But what does Edwards have to do with this intramural discussion among pentecostal scholars? Edwards made the Holy Spirit the essence of grace and the centerpiece of the work of Christ and redemption. In pneumatological terms, Edwards' theology was more *pentecostal* than traditional pentecostal theology. Edwards, therefore, provides a historical resource that can contribute to and deepen these efforts among contemporary pentecostal theologians to articulate a pneumatology that captures the theological significance of the pentecostal experience of the Holy Spirit. Highlighting Edwards' connection with contemporary constructive efforts in pentecostal theology is the task of the remaining section of this chapter.

Edwards made the Spirit the primary end of the work of redemption. Christ's work culminates, not on the cross or even resurrection, but in the gift of the Holy Spirit. The Spirit does not administer the gifts of grace, but is the gift of grace. Where traditional pentecostal theology, however unintentionally, relegates the primary work of the Spirit—Spirit baptism—to a secondary experience that is not only distinct from but also unnecessary to salvation, Edwards makes receiving the Spirit the fundamental experience of grace. Doing so was the result of Edwards' trinitarian theology of grace. Although he retained traditional legal and penal themes, he achieved a trinitarian vision of redemption, ecclesiology, and eschatology. Edwards' theology of grace was pneumatological because his larger vision was trinitarian. Inspired by the Spirit's identity and role as the mutual love that unites the Father and the Son, Edwards argued that the Spirit united the humanity of Jesus with the Son of God (thus advancing a Spirit Christology) and unites all believers to Christ, thereby enabling them to participate in the fellowship of the Father and the Son both now in the community of the church and later in the everlasting kingdom.

Pentecostal theologians Frank Macchia and Amos Yong come to similar conclusions with Edwards. Although representing different traditions of Christian theology, they fundamentally deal with the same twofold problem—Protestant soteriology's Christocentrism and subordination of the Holy Spirit. As outlined above, Edwards begins with the Protestant tradition of soteriology and its subordination of the Spirit to Christology. Macchia's starting point is the effect this broader tradition of soteriology

---

[42] Macchia, *Justified in the Spirit* and Yong, *Spirit of Love* and *Spirit-Word-Community: Theological Hermeneutics in Trinitarian Perspective* (Eugene, OR: Wipf & Stock, 2002). I also make the argument that the pentecostal experience of the Spirit has theological implications for pentecostal trinitarian theology and political theology. See Studebaker, *From Pentecost to the Triune God*, 11–52 and *A Pentecostal Theology for American Renewal: Spirit of the Kingdoms, Citizens of the Cities* (New York: Palgrave Macmillan, 2016).

has on the pentecostal doctrine of the Spirit baptism as well as the tendency to favor charismatic experience over Spirit baptism as the essence of pentecostal theology. Macchia's solution is to articulate the doctrine of Spirit baptism from the perspective of the Trinity. In doing so he releases it from its confinement in a narrowly defined second experience of grace and speaking in tongues.[43] He draws on Athanasian and Augustinian theology. Macchia turns to the Athanasian notion of the "mutual dependence" of the divine persons.[44] Mutual dependence means that the Father is Father only in relation to the Son and the Son in relation to the Father. Applied to the Spirit's work in justification, Macchia argues that the Spirit opens up to the world the love enjoyed and shared between the Father and the Son. He also adopts Augustine's view of the Spirit as the mutual love of the Father and the Son with an important qualification. He recognizes that portraying the Spirit as a "bond" of love runs the risk of depersonalizing the Spirit. His solution to overcome the tendency to depersonalize the Spirit in the mutual love tradition is to assign the Spirit an active role in the economy of grace. The Spirit justifies people through Spirit baptism and includes them in the *koinonia* of God.[45] The result is a pentecostal theology of justification that moves beyond the traditional Catholic view of moral transformation and Protestant emphasis on a forensic declaration of righteousness. Justification consists in Spirit baptism that brings a renewal of life and inclusion into the divine *koinonia*.

Yong begins with the pentecostal tendency to associate the Holy Spirit with spiritual gifts and empowerment for ministry. For Yong, the experience of the Holy Spirit as divine love is at the root of pentecostal experience and ministry. What Pentecostals often identify as empowerment are the "performative explications of encounters with divine love."[46] Pentecostal experiences, such as Spirit baptism, arise from the presence of God in the Holy Spirit. Spirit baptism is the nurturing and tangible presence of God, a presence that God makes evident in signs and gifts of the Spirit. Pentecostal worship and prayer is the relational and reciprocal expression of gratitude for God's loving presence. The Spirit of Pentecost, therefore, is fundamentally the presence of God's love. But that love is active. It gives and renews life. It is not without empowerment, but the enabling of the Spirit arises from the embrace of the Spirit as God's love. A loving presence that heals, cares, and leads Pentecostals into a renewed life of God's Spirit. Being baptized by the Spirit of Pentecost is the gift of gifts.

Edwards, Macchia, and Yong affirm that the Spirit is central, and not an adjunct, to Christian salvation. They do not displace Christology, but make the Spirit an equal partner in the work of redemption. The Holy Spirit contributes to the substance of salvation. For Edwards, the essence of saving grace is the communication of the Holy Spirit as the mutual love of the Father and the Son. For Macchia and Yong, the gift of the Spirit establishes the trinitarian community of divine presence and love. Together, Edwards, Macchia, and Yong advance a theology of the Holy Spirit on trinitarian

---

[43] Macchia, *Baptized in the Spirit*.
[44] Ibid., 303.
[45] Macchia, *Justified in the Spirit*, 302.
[46] Yong, *Spirit of Love*, 51; see especially the chapters in Part two for Yong's development of a pentecostal and pneumatological theology of divine love.

foundations. The result, therefore, is a contribution not only to pneumatology but also to trinitarian theology. Pentecostal pneumatology should continue in the direction advocated by Edwards, Macchia, and Yong. Why? Because it better captures the place of the Spirit in the biblical narrative of redemption and in pentecostal experience.

Conclusion

Edwards' pneumatology and trinitarian theology is progressive and proto-Pentecostal. The Trinity was not just a mysterious doctrine of Christian confession for Edwards. His vision of the Father, the Son, and the Holy Spirit as an eternal community of love provided the foundation for his soteriology, ecclesiology, and eschatology. Edwards' trinitarian theology and pneumatology is progressive because he developed the theological substance of his received tradition with respect to the immanent and economic Trinity. But Edwards' reliance on the Augustinian mutual love prevented the full development of his trinitarian theology. A contribution from pentecostal theology, however, can help resolve them. He also transcended the forensic and legal soteriology of traditional Protestant theology (though he also retained certain of its elements) and achieved a relational and pneumatological and thus also a trinitarian theology of grace. In that respect, he was a proto-Pentecostal. The progressive and proto-pentecostal character of his theology connects with developments in contemporary pentecostal theology, especially the work of Frank D. Macchia and Amos Yong.

6

Divine and Human Excellencies: Jonathan Edwards and the Challenge of Spirit Christology

Gerald R. McDermott

Introduction

I am glad to have been invited to write on this subject for two reasons. First, for seven years I lived in charismatic Christian communes where the Holy Spirit was given the kind of prominence that is unusual outside of pentecostal and charismatic circles. It is refreshing to do analysis here that might be a tiny bit of help for a movement that helped me grow in faith, and that is having an enormous impact on the universal Church. Second, it is good to remind scholars of the unusually significant place for the Holy Spirit in the work of a theologian readers of this book might not know well. Ross Hastings, Robert Caldwell, and Michael McClymond have pointed some of this out, but knowledge of this is still not what it should be.[1]

The Holy Spirit is integral to Jonathan Edwards' Christology. According to America's theologian, Christ's beauty is from the Spirit, the love of the messiah *is* the Spirit, and the Incarnation was (and is) made possible by the Spirit.[2] This same Spirit created, as it were, the hypostatic union.[3] The Holy Spirit is an equal partner in the ongoing history of the work of redemption, which for Edwards is the secret to all of history, both sacred and secular. Christ grows through history as he builds his church, and the Holy Spirit is not only the energy that drives the growth but the glue that holds the building together. While Steven Studebaker is right to charge that Edwards' pneumatology is

---

[1] Hastings' and Caldwell's works are cited below. McClymond's work on Edwards and the Spirit can be found in *Theology of Jonathan Edwards*, which is also cited below.
[2] Robert W. Jenson gave Edwards this designation in *America's Theologian: A Recommendation of Jonathan Edwards* (New York: Oxford University Press, 1988).
[3] "If [Christ's] human understanding and will was directed and moved by the Holy Ghost, and yet it might be said to be done as of his own wisdom and will, the Holy Ghost must in this act as a means of conveyance of the understanding and will of the divine Logos, to the understanding and will of the human nature, or of the unions of these understandings and wills." Edwards, "Miscellany 766," *WJE* 18:412. Unless otherwise noted, there will be one footnote per paragraph, to provide locations for all the quotations in that paragraph.

not as full-bodied (and perhaps not as implicitly biblical) as those of recent pentecostal theologians such as himself, I think its connection to Christology has things to offer pentecostal theologians.

In this chapter I will first try to show the deep connections to the Spirit in Edwards' Christology—in aesthetics, Incarnation, and atonement. Then I will argue that the joint work of Christ and the Spirit is central to his philosophy of history, which is the work of redemption. In that connection I will discuss how the Spirit contributes to what I call ontic enlargement. Third, I will discuss the ways that Edwards tried to correct the West's undervaluation of the Spirit and his work, and consider whether he was successful. Finally, I will suggest four ways that Edwards' pneumatological Christology might be useful to pentecostal theology: its theology of revival, discernment, missions, and aesthetics.

Christology, aesthetics, and the Spirit

Edwards taught that the greatest event in all the history of redemption was Christ's satisfaction of divine justice by his perfect life of obedience to God's law and his propitiatory suffering and death. This was the primary focus of his Christology. Edwards wrote of satisfaction in terms that Anselm had made famous (violating the honor of a lord), in mercantile terms (incurring a debt), and in terms of moral government (upholding respect for law), the last of which eventually became the dominant model for the atonement in the hands of his theological disciples.[4]

While none of these models was unprecedented, Edwards' linking them to beauty was. The atonement was not limited to the passion, but began with the "humiliation" of an obscure birth and continued through thirty years of poverty and reproach. All of Christ's life of humble and self-denying obedience was beautiful, but the last hours of his passion were the most meritorious and beautiful. These provided the "principal" part of the propitiation. This "last act of obedience" was "that by which principally he merited heaven." It was then, in the suffering that was more than in all the rest of his life, that the saints see the "brightest effulgence" of Christ's "beauty and amiable excellency." They realize that "Jesus Christ is infinitely the most beautiful and glorious object in the world," and it is more pleasant to see him than "to look on the sun in his meridian glory." They now have the pleasure "of considering that this lovely virtue is imputed to them. 'Tis the lovely robe, and robe of love, with which they are covered. Christ gives it to them, and puts it upon them, and by the beauty of this robe recommends 'em to the favor and delight of God the Father, as well as of all heaven besides." His beauty covers our "deformity," and it is only because of his beauty that we are "accepted and loved."[5]

This return to Christ's beauty is one of several ways that Edwards' theology of the atonement differed from that of his predecessors. Stephen Holmes has noted that while

---

[4] For a fuller discussion of these, see Michael McClymond and Gerald McDermott, *Theology of Jonathan Edwards* (New York: Oxford University Press, 2013), 249–51.
[5] Edwards, "Miscellany 791," *WJE* 18:488; *Christ, the Light of the World, WJE* 10:539; "Miscellany 791," *WJE* 18:495; and "Miscellany 385," *WJE* 13:454.

the Western theological tradition had stressed the atonement as a legal transaction, and post-Reformation Protestants had emphasized the juridical and declarative dimensions, Edwards highlighted the aesthetic, rational, and personal aspects of the passion. Edwards' mercantile metaphor (Christ "purchasing" heaven and the Holy Spirit for the elect) "is no more than an insistence that atonement is personal."[6]

The significance of this is twofold. First, Patrick Sherry and others have argued that Edwards did more to relate God and beauty than anyone else in the history of Christian thought. Augustine and Balthasar have also been noted for their theological aesthetics, but according to Sherry beauty was more central to Edwards' vision of God than for either of those great Catholic divines. As Edwards himself put it, "God is distinguished from all other beings and exalted above 'em, chiefly by his divine beauty."[7]

Second, according to Edwards the Spirit is the source of all true beauty. His work is to "beautify all things." He did so at the creation, bringing the waters and chaos "out of its confusion, into harmony and beauty." The Spirit is fitted to *give* beauty because he *is* beauty: "Whose office can it be so properly to give all things their sweetness and beauty, as he who is himself the beauty and joy of the Creator?"[8] Edwards wrote that the Spirit is also the source of all true love. This is because, once again, the Spirit *is* love: "The divine nature subsists in love . . . this love is the Spirit. . . . God's love, or his lovingkindness, is the same with the Holy Ghost." Edwards insisted that divine love is not simply an attribute of God but a "distinct divine person." So the love of the Son and the love of the Father are simply the subsistence of the Spirit *in* the other two persons: "The Father loves because the Holy Ghost is in him. So the Son loves because the Holy Spirit is in him and proceeds from him." Similarly, the Holy Spirit *understands* "because the Son, the divine *idea*, is in him."[9]

Incarnation and atonement

Edwards placed enormous emphasis on the Incarnation and atonement as expressions of love—and therefore the Spirit—in his Christology. For example, in his early notebooks he wrote that Christ's hanging on the cross "was the most wonderful act of love that ever was." In it Christ showed his infinite love for the Father. "There he made an offer of his love to the world." Far from being an abstract declaration of peace, Christ taking on suffering flesh was a passionate and touching act of love—comparable to our love for the "other sex," the union of a husband and a wife, and the affections of a friend or a brother. But even more, this was a love of heart-wrenching sacrifice. Christ lost on the cross infinitely more than the damned lose, since "his blessedness in the love and

---

[6] Stephen R. Holmes, *God of Grace and God of Glory: An Account of the Theology of Jonathan Edwards* (Grand Rapids, MI: Eerdmans, 2000), 143 and 148–47. Holmes is not discounting the penal and transactional atonement in Edwards, but asserting that Edwards emphasized the aesthetic and personal dimensions.

[7] Patrick Sherry, *Spirit and Beauty: An Introduction to Theological Aesthetics* (Birmingham: SCM, 2002) and Edwards, *Religious Affections*, WJE 2:298.

[8] Edwards, *Discourse on the Trinity*, WJE 21:123.

[9] Ibid., 122, 128, and 132–33 (emphases added).

communion with God was infinitely greater." When his passion was approaching and he could foresee the horrendous suffering he was to endure, and then when he actually felt the torments and cruelties and insults, "his love did not fail." He still yielded himself to the infinite pain. "He waded through the sea of blood and wrath." Edwards asked, "Where is there anything that can parallel this love?"[10]

If the Spirit constituted the love and beauty of Christ, he was also the creator of the hypostatic union. Edwards explained the inner workings of this hypostatic union (from the Greek *hupostasis*, translated as "reality" or "person") by saying that the Logos speaks and acts by using the human nature of Christ, both body and soul, as an "organ." The Holy Spirit is the "means of conveyance" of the Logos' will and understanding to Christ's human will and understanding. Another way Edwards put it was to say that the Holy Spirit conveyed the Son's power and knowledge and will and acts to the faculties of Christ's human soul. Because Christ's human consciousness received the consciousness of the Logos, there was between them what "we call identity of consciousness." Because of this identity there are not two wills or persons but one. So when "the divine person" laid down his life, "there was the act of Christ as God in it as well as man."[11]

Steven Studebaker and others have observed that this way of thinking about the hypostatic union parallels and perhaps follows Edwards' way of seeing Christ's union with his church and the inner-trinitarian union—subjects on which Edwards wrote far more.[12] For Edwards the Spirit is the bond of union as the love between the Father and the Son, and the "internal, spiritual harmony between Christ and the soul" is a union held in place by the Holy Spirit. Indeed, for Edwards, it is not the nature of Christ but this *spiritual* harmony between Christ and his church that is "the nature and genius of Christianity." The purpose of all doctrines, even the doctrine of the hypostatic union, is "to bring about this sweet harmony between the soul and Jesus Christ"—a harmony created and sustained by the Holy Spirit.[13]

The Spirit was also important—but perhaps not important enough—to Edwards' version of another aspect of the hypostatic union, its "communication of attributes." This follows from the standard conception that in one divine person are two natures, gloriously luminous and majestic, but distinct. The human nature—not the divine—suffered and died. Yet while distinct, the two natures shared with one another. This is the *communicatio idiomatum* that, as Robert Jenson has remarked, has been acknowledged by the theological tradition but held at arm's length. The West (including most of the Reformed tradition) has generally restricted its meaning to the notion that attributes

---

[10] Edwards, "Miscellany 304," *WJE* 13:390; "Miscellany 189," *WJE* 13:332; *The Excellency of Christ*, *WJE* 19:585, 588–89; "Miscellany 265," *WJE* 13:371; "Miscellany 762," *WJE* 18:408; and *The Free and Voluntary Suffering and Death of Christ*, *WJE* 19:511.

[11] Edwards, "Miscellany 738," *WJE* 18:364; "Miscellany 766," *WJE* 18:412; "Miscellany 738," *WJE* 18:364; and *The Free and Voluntary Suffering and Death of Christ*, *WJE* 19:497.

[12] Steven M. Studebaker and Robert W. Caldwell III, *The Trinitarian Theology of Jonathan Edwards: Text, Context, and Application* (Burlington, VT: Ashgate, 2012) and Steven M. Studebaker, *From Pentecost to the Triune God: A Pentecostal Trinitarian Theology* (Grand Rapids, MI: Eerdmans, 2012).

[13] Edwards, "Miscellany 817," *WJE* 18:528; "Miscellany 766," *WJE* 18:412; "Miscellany 738," *WJE* 18:364; and *The Sweet Harmony of Christ*, *WJE* 19:447.

from both natures can be ascribed to the person of Christ, while Lutherans have said Christ's human nature takes on the predicates of the divine nature. Edwards stepped boldly where angels feared to tread, sounding like a Lutheran when he proclaimed that the same person who made the world and fills heaven and earth is "a child in bodily clothes . . . sucking the breasts of a woman," both "a worm of the dust and . . . the King of Glory." There are many intimations in his sermons and notebooks that the humanity of this King was the same as ours. He is able to pity us because he has experienced the same "difficulties" he dwelt in a frail body like us and took upon himself "its weak, broken state." He was subject to hunger, thirst, weariness, pain, and death as other human beings are. Just as believers increase in holiness, Christ increased in the holiness of his nature. His sufferings "purged him from imputed guilt," and he was "made perfect by sufferings." When the thoughts of the Logos were communicated to his human soul *by the Holy Spirit*, the man Christ Jesus could grasp those thoughts only in finite ideas; he was conscious of them only "after the manner of a creature," so that he could not remember all the details of his pre-incarnate conversations with the Father "[precisely] as they were in the infinite mind."[14]

But there are other suggestions in the Edwardsean corpus that the divine nature so nearly overwhelmed the human nature that Christ's humanity was distant from ours. Edwards told his parishioners that Moses' burning bush was never consumed as a demonstration that Christ's human nature could never perish because of the divinity in it. He preached that Christ never had to deny lust or practice mortification because he had no sin. Today's readers might wonder why Christ's sinlessness, which of course Edwards assumed, would require that he never have lustful temptations. Would he not have denied lustful desires? If not, he might not have inherited a morally fallen human nature, as Calvin, Owen, and Barth assumed he did. Calvin believed the sinful nature was cleansed by the Holy Spirit either before or during conception, while Owen and Barth argued that the Spirit over time gradually purified Christ's fallen human nature. Edwards seems to have accepted only what W. Ross Hastings calls a "metaphysically" fallen nature, not a morally fallen nature. That is, Christ inherited a human nature that was subject to physical decay but was "morally impeccable." For he wrote that at birth the Holy Spirit protected the Christ child from his mother's "pollution," that because of his divine nature Christ "was not liable to fall and commit sin," and "the human soul of Jesus Christ [was] *necessarily* holy."[15] Did Christ, then, suffer the same temptations as we, if he did not struggle with a morally fallen nature?

---

[14] Edwards, *Sermons Series II*, WJE 54:499; "Miscellany 1219," WJE 23:153; Robert Jenson, "Christology," in *The Princeton Companion to Jonathan Edwards*, ed. Sang Hyun Lee (Princeton, NJ: Princeton University Press, 2005), 78; Edwards, *Christ's Sacrifice*, WJE 10:599; *The Sweet Harmony of Christ*, WJE 19:443; and "Miscellany 1005," WJE 20:333.

[15] Edwards, *The Free and Voluntary Suffering and Death of Christ*, WJE 19:500; *A History of the Work of Redemption*, WJE 9:320; W. Ross Hastings, "'Honouring the Spirit': Analysis and Evaluation of Jonathan Edwards' Pneumatological Doctrine of the Incarnation," *International Journal of Systematic Theology* 7, no. 3 (2005): 297; Edwards, "Miscellany 767," WJE 18:414; *Religious Affections*, WJE 2:949; and *Freedom of the Will*, WJE 1:281 (emphasis added). For more from Hastings on Edwards and the Spirit, see chapter 3 in his *Jonathan Edwards and the Life of God: Toward an Evangelical Theology of Participation* (Minneapolis, MN: Fortress, 2015).

Edwards would have rejected the strong kenotic theology of the nineteenth and twentieth centuries, in which Christ was said to have relinquished most or all divine prerogatives. Edwards believed that Christ retained his divine knowledge and omnipotence but chose not to exercise them. "When the Apostle says, Christ emptied himself, as Phil. 2:7, he means he *appeared* in the world without his former glory and joy." At the cross Christ did not have the "full enjoyment of his Father," for "God hid his face and withdrew the comfortable and joyful tokens of his presence, which made him cry out, 'My God, [My God, Why hast thou forsaken me?']" But throughout that unspeakable ordeal Christ kept his divine happiness nonetheless.[16]

There are several dangers to this approach. Hastings warns that it runs the risk of blurring the persons of the Spirit and the Son, disconnecting the God-man from fallen humanity and making Jesus Christ appear distant and not fully human.[17] The incarnate Son could seem to be more like God acting *on* a man than *as* a man. There is also the possible impact on soteriology. For, as Gregory Nazianzus famously declared, what is not assumed is not redeemed. If Christ did not assume our morally fallen nature, then it is not redeemed. If Edwards had used at this point a stronger Spirit Christology, something like what Calvin, Owen, and Barth used, this potential break in the redemptive chain could have been filled.

Yet Edwards' privileging of the divine nature must be seen in the light of his apologetic battles against Arians and Unitarians who denied Christ's deity. And his conviction that the man Christ Jesus needed his divine nature to be holy was a call to Arminians, convinced of the self-determining power of their wills, to realize they would fall without union with deity. Edwards' Christology was similar to that of John of Damascus, who described *perichoresis* as Christ's divine nature penetrating his human nature but not conversely. Both the Damascene and Edwards realized that "universal truth is constituted and found precisely as some particular"—not the union of the Son of God with some abstract human "nature," but with the unique humanity created for the one person Jesus Christ. If there are still problems with Edwards' answer to the question of how two natures could be united in one person, it is well to consider that "a fully satisfactory answer has never been given."[18]

The Spirit in the history of Christ's redemption

Edwards' treatment of the Spirit's role in Christ's work of redemption was less problematic. Here the dynamic efficiency of the Spirit was crucial to his philosophy of history and the purpose of creation. God created, he argued, in order to glorify himself by communicating the inner-trinitarian knowledge, joy, and love among the divine persons to his human creatures. By seeing the beauty of God, understanding his

---

[16] Edwards, "Miscellany 513," *WJE* 18:57; *Notes on Scripture, WJE* 15:186; *Sermons, Series II, WJE* 51: no. 412; and *The Free and Voluntary Suffering and Death of Christ, WJE* 19:500 (emphasis added).
[17] Hastings, "Honouring the Spirit," 293, 295, 297.
[18] John of Damascus, *On the Orthodox Faith*, book III, chapters 4 and 7, in http://www.orthodox.net/fathers/exactidx.html and Jenson, *America's Theologian*, 83, 73.

ways, and delighting in his love, those creatures were to be made anew through union with Christ and his Father by the Spirit. The primary way that people would see this beauty and be caught up into the trinitarian reality would be by hearing and receiving the gospel. For this purpose, God appointed gospel ministers as successors to the apostles—to preach, teach, and baptize all nations. When the church called and sent preachers of the gospel to new places and peoples, it was doing the work of missions. For Edwards, therefore, missions were the engine that drove history toward the ends for which God created the world.

And if missions drive history, even secular history, the Holy Spirit drives missions. The history of missions is dynamized by periodic revivals powered by the Holy Spirit, who first inspires men and women to pray for them. The revivals usually come after times of irreligion and moral laxity, are directed by a prophet or some other "eminent" person, and proceed principally through preaching. In ancient Israel they were first seen under Joshua when the Jews first came into Canaan. Another revival preceded "the second settlement of [God's] church in the same land in the time of Ezra." Revivals typically inspired renewals of the covenant: "We find that such solemn renovations of the covenant commonly accompanied any remarkable pouring out of the Spirit, causing a general reformation."[19]

The Spirit inspires and animates at every point along the way, and by so doing drives the course of history because revivals change the world. Revivals in ancient Israel's history changed world history because Israel was at the intersection of the world's three most important continents: Africa, Asia, and Europe. Even Israel's apostasies were influential: her exile to Babylon, caused by her failure to keep covenant, spread her influence to Babylon and Persia as residents of those lands came into contact with the Jewish exiles.[20] The rise of Christianity in its first three centuries was one long revival, which changed the world order when it absorbed the Roman Empire in the fourth century. The Reformation was a revival that formed modern Europe.[21] Edwards kept insisting that all of this history, and hence all the history of the world, is Christological because it is Christ's work of redemption and also pneumatological, for "the Work of Redemption in its effect has mainly been carried on by remarkable pourings out of the Spirit of God."[22]

Enlargement in Christ by the Spirit

Although Edwards did not say explicitly that the Spirit determined Christology, his theology suggests this, for, in one of his most provocative loci, Edwards argued that Christ *increased his being* as the Spirit directed the growth of the church through

---

[19] Edwards, *A History of the Work of Redemption*, WJE 9:266, 192.
[20] Ibid., 266, 192.
[21] Ibid.
[22] Ibid., 143.

this history of redemption. This is what could be called ontic enlargement.[23] Or as Michael Bush has put it, "Whatever begins in Christ, and whatever is true of Christ, soon *grows*."[24] This is true of his own manhood during the Incarnation, the progressive union of the saints with the Trinity, and his own mystical body. In his treatise on the end of creation, Edwards wrote that Christ is completed and enlarged by the gradual growth of the church.

> God looks on the communication of himself, and the emanation of the infinite glory and good that are in himself to belong to the fullness and completeness of himself, as though he were not in his most complete and glorious state without it. Thus the church of Christ (toward whom and in whom are the emanations of his glory and communications of his fullness) is called the fullness of Christ: as though he were not in his complete state without her; as Adam was in a defective state without Eve.[25]

Edwards explained that the trinitarian God is, in one sense, eternally complete and perfect, fully actual and self-sufficient. Yet, at the same time, God *ad extra* (God's action by the Son *and* the *Spirit* in creation and history) is the external *repetition* of his own being, and therefore a kind of ontic self-enlargement, just as the beams of light from the sun are an "increase, repetition, or multiplication" of its glory: God, "from his goodness, as it were *enlarges himself* in a more excellent and divine manner ... by flowing forth, and expressing himself in [his creatures], and making them to partake of him, and rejoicing in himself expressed in them, and communicated to them."[26]

This means that Christ's work by the Spirit in redemption is the temporal extension of God's actuality, repeating in time God's internal actuality without improving it. The external exercise of God's internal disposition through the Son and Spirit is the temporal repetition of the divine fullness. What happens in the history of redemption does not add to God's being *ad intra* but constitutes the external extension of God's internal fullness.[27] God is not timeless self-identity, as in some Platonic versions of the Christian deity, but the infinite sum and comprehension of all being and beauty for whom the Incarnation was something new. God's glory is enlarged through the Incarnation, and Christ is enlarged by the growth of the church through time. This is why, Edwards proposed, the church is said by Scripture to be the completeness of Christ (Eph. 1:23), "as if Christ were not complete without the Church." The church is the fullness of Christ, and therefore adds to the completeness of Christ as the further increase of that completeness.

---

[23] I use this word rather than "ontological" to denote expansion in God's relations to other beings rather than change in God's essence, which could be suggested by "ontological."
[24] Michael D. Bush, "Jonathan Edwards' Christology," 197 (unpublished manuscript).
[25] Edwards, *Dissertation I. Concerning the End for Which God Created the World*, WJE 8:439.
[26] Ibid., 433, 461–62 (emphasis added).
[27] Sang Hyun Lee, *The Philosophical Theology of Jonathan Edwards* (Princeton, NJ: Princeton University Press, 1988), 170–242.

Correcting the undervaluation of the Spirit

Pentecostals will be interested to know that Edwards believed that the Western Christological tradition, especially in its Reformed branches, had undervalued the Holy Spirit and did what he could to bring correction. He thought his Puritan predecessors had diminished the Holy Spirit's role in redemption by restricting it to the application of the work of the Father and the Son. In his essay "On the Equality of the Persons of the Trinity," Edwards dramatically asserted that the Holy Spirit has "superiority" among the Three, as the "principle that as it were reigns over the Godhead and governs his heart, and wholly influences both the Father and the Son in all they do." As Sang Lee has noted, this is a Spirit who is not just a bond of love but an active agent—a full-fledged Person who reigns and governs and influences. While the Father and the Son have superiority in their own roles, Edwards said "the Holy Ghost, that is, divine love, has the superiority" because he "reigns over the Godhead and governs his heart, and wholly influences both the Father and the Son in all they do." In this respect, the Spirit is "highest . . . though he be last, as he is the messenger sent by the other two." And because the Spirit is not only the "internal spring" and "moving cause" of the covenant of redemption but also "the great good covenanted for," his honor is all the greater.[28]

In his *Treatise on Grace*, Edwards wrote that the Spirit is "the fullness of God . . . the sum of all good . . . the fullness of Christ . . . the good purchased [by Christ] . . . the comprehension of all good things." Edwards observed that the tradition's reduction of the Spirit's role to "merely . . . apply to us" the work of Christ was to make the Spirit "subordinate to the other two Persons." But in his proposal, he thought, "there is an equality." For he had proposed that the Spirit is the love of God, and "to *be* the wonderful love of God, is as much as for the Father and Son to *exercise* wonderful love; and to be the thing purchased, is as much as to be the price [Christ's blood] that purchases it."[29]

Edwards also did his part to reduce the sting of the *filioque* clause in the Creed, thereby enhancing to some degree the role of the Spirit. The controversy began when the Western church added *filioque* (and from the Son) to the Nicene Creed (in 589 and then again in 1017), asserting that the Spirit proceeds not only from the Father but also from the Son. The Eastern church protested not only that this was a politically imperialistic act (since the West acted unilaterally, ignoring protests from the East) but also that it subordinated the Spirit to the Son and detracted from the harmony of the Trinity.

Edwards no doubt recognized that there are biblical grounds for *filioque*. It was Christ who poured out the Spirit upon the church (Acts 2:33), and Christ said in Jn 15:26 that he would send the Spirit. But the same verse says that while Jesus would send (*pempsō*) the Spirit from the Father, the Spirit of truth proceeds (*ekporeuetai*)

---

[28] Amy Plantinga Pauw, *"The Supreme Harmony of All": The Trinitarian Theology of Jonathan Edwards* (Grand Rapids, MI: Eerdmans, 2002), 121; Edwards, *On the Equality of the Persons of the Trinity*, WJE 21:147; Sang Hyun Lee, "Editor's Introduction," WJE 21:19; and Edwards, *On the Equality of the Persons of the Trinity*, WJE 21:147.

[29] Edwards, *Treatise on Grace*, WJE 21:188, 189, 190, 191 (emphases added).

from the Father. Edwards tried to do justice to both statements by saying that while the Spirit "proceeds both from the Father and the Son," that procession is "from the Father originally and primarily, and from the Son as it were secondarily." Hence the Eastern Fathers' basic instinct was right. Yet the Spirit proceeds from the Father "mediately by the Son" but from the Son "immediately." So "the Son hath this honor that the Father hath not: that that Spirit is from the Son immediately by himself." By contrast, the Father sends the Spirit only "by his beholding himself in the Son," thus the necessity for the Western *filioque*.[30] Edwards' refusal to dismiss *filioque* will not please some Pentecostals, but his interpretation of it might cheer others.

Did Edwards go far enough?

Steven Studebaker is a leading pentecostal theologian and expert on Edwards' Trinitarianism. Studebaker recognizes Edwards' contributions to trinitarian thought and the value of his corrections to his previous tradition. He says that Edwards' greatest contribution was to see the Spirit as the "great purchase of Christ" so that redemption was not just a juridical judgment but the gift of a divine person. Grace was not simply pardon but a person. Furthermore, says Studebaker, Edwards lifted the role of the Spirit to become the goal of the work of both the Father and the Son.[31]

At the same time, however, Studebaker believes that Edwards' use of idealism to depict the Son and the Spirit as the Father's understanding and will reduces these two Persons to functions of the Father. In addition, Edwards' use of the mutual love model (the Spirit as the mutual love between the Father and the Son) in which the Spirit neither gives nor receives love, diminishes the full personhood of the Spirit. Finally, Edwards' depiction of the history of the work of redemption renders the Spirit's role to be merely "instrumental," to facilitate the work of Christ. Hence Christ's giving of the Spirit at Pentecost and the ongoing distribution of the Gift through church history constitute the return of Christ's love to the Father. All in all, then, Edwards' pneumatology is "constrained" by the mutual love model so that there is an "implicit subordination of the Spirit to Christ."[32]

I think Studebaker's criticisms are legitimate. If I were to defend Edwards, I might suggest that Edwards is more attentive to the explicit biblical narrative on the relative roles of Christ and the Spirit and less attentive to the implications that Studebaker and others have recently found for the work of the Spirit in Christ's conception, temptations, baptism, and ministry. In other words, if Edwards had paid more attention to these biblical markers, he might have conceived of what Studebaker has called the Spirit's "constitutional role in Christology."[33]

---

[30] Edwards, *Discourse on the Trinity*, WJE 21:143. See also Edwards, *Justification by Faith Alone*, WJE 19:150.
[31] Studebaker, *From Pentecost to the Triune God*, 159.
[32] Ibid., 152–54, 157, 160.
[33] Ibid., 80.

Contributions of Edwards' Christology to pentecostal theology and churches

Nevertheless, I think there are several significant contributions that Edwards' use of the Spirit in his Christology can make to pentecostal theology in the twenty-first century. First, Edwards provides what might be the most robust theology of revival on offer in the history of Christian thought. When European churches are dying, and ways are being sought to reach Muslims and other hard-to-reach people groups, Edwards' theology of revival could be particularly useful. For Edwards revival is Christological and not only pneumatological because it is the principal method God uses by his Spirit to bring knowledge of the Christ to human beings. And the history of revival is what drives the history of *Christ's* work of redemption. Pentecostals already speak of the Spirit's work in revival to bring knowledge of Jesus to a wider world. But with the use of Edwards' theology of revival, they might more easily connect the dots in Scripture and theology between the works of the second and third persons of the Trinity. Edwards might help them do this more theocentrically than nineteenth-century Arminians did in Charles Finney–inspired revivals. Edwards highlighted the surprising work of God in revival, while Finney stressed "the right exercise of the powers of nature."[34]

Edwards' theology of revival can be found chiefly in *Faithful Narrative of a Surprising Work of God* (1737), *The Distinguishing Marks of a Work of the Spirit of God* (1741), *Some Thoughts Concerning the Present Revival* (1743), *Religious Affections* (1746), and *Humble Attempt to Promote Explicit Agreement and Visible Union of God's People in Extraordinary Prayer* (1747), which were all writings devoted primarily to experiences, ideas, and debates arising out of the 1730s–40s revivals. More than three centuries after his birth, Edwards has continued to be cited as an authority on revival, and might be regarded as the most influential author of all time on the topic. Furthermore, these writings are not exclusively pastoral in character but touch on a wide spectrum of theological issues and debates. These include the nature of conversion, the respective roles of mind, affections, and imagination in spiritual experience, visions and other extraordinary experiences, bodily manifestations, the proper interpretation of Scripture, the nature of religious practice, the laity's relation to the clergy, the pattern and progress of redemptive history, eschatological expectations connected with revivals, the importance of unity in the church, and the role of prayer in spiritual awakening. The 1730s–40s revivals not only offered a pastoral challenge but a provocation to theological reflection. Since we have many of the same issues today, these reflections can still profit.

Second, with revival comes spiritual warfare and confusion. Here too Edwards' employment of the Spirit in his Christology can be of use at the point where it offers spiritual discernment. In other words, how can Christ as Word enable his church to test the spirits? Because knowledge of truth is the principal role of the Word as second person of the Trinity, discernment is inherently Christological. Edwards taught discernment by reflecting on his experience from the revivals of the Great Awakening

---

[34] Charles G. Finney, *Lectures on Revivals of Religion*, ed. William G. McLoughlin (Cambridge: Belknap Press of Harvard University, 1960), x–xi, 13.

in his *Religious Affections* (1746), where he outlined twelve "negative signs" (unreliable signs) of the work of the Spirit and twelve "positive" or reliable signs. This has come to be recognized as one of the greatest of the church's manuals of spiritual discernment. Pentecostal churches in Asia and Latin America that have experienced revival and confusion have discovered this treatise to be particularly useful.[35]

Third, Edwards' reflection on the work of redemption by Christ and the Spirit has been, and can continue to be, a great stimulus to Christian missions. Perhaps Edwards' most productive stimulus was his extraordinary historical optimism and fervent expectation of imminent revival. Beginning in the late 1730s and continuing through the Great Awakening and much beyond, Edwards prophesied that the world was on the verge of massive religious revival. The era was like that of the first century, he wrote: there had just been a quantum leap in learning, and it was a dark time again for religion. There was nothing in the biblical prophecies that had to be fulfilled before this great outpouring of the Spirit, only prayer and preaching. The revival would bring the "church's prosperity" and at the same time violent opposition because the "great revival" will "mightily rouse the old serpent." The long-term result would be awakening in every nation—among Jews, Muslims, and heathen, and throughout Africa, Asia, and Australia. Repeatedly he projected the conversion of American Indians, as well as the inhabitants of Africa and South Asia: "Many of the Negroes and Indians will be divines, and . . . excellent books will be published in Africa, in Ethiopia, in Turkey."[36] Missions are Christological because it is the work whereby God brings knowledge of his Christ to those who have not heard. Because it is driven by revival, its story is the story of *Christ's* work of redemption.

Here we come full circle to the explosion of Christianity in the Global South today. It is intriguing to see that the revival of missions in the two centuries after Edwards led at least indirectly to revival in Africa and Asia, so that African and Asian divines (typically, Anglican archbishops) are now giving religious direction to American Christians and their churches. Edwards' predictions were not too far off the mark. However, it is not his uncanny prophecies that have excited interest in his missiology among many today, but his bold historical optimism and his challenge to all the church to catch the vision of mission. Pentecostals have done magnificent work in missions; perhaps they can do even more with help from Edwards.

Fourth, Edwards' Christological and pneumatological emphasis on beauty can be helpful in apologetics and evangelism. I find that of the three Platonic transcendentals—truth, goodness, and beauty—the last is the most compelling to millennials. This seems to be true not only for non-Christians but also for believers in the church. I would suggest that this Edwardsean aesthetic can shed new light in a number of ways. First, for example, it means that *conversion* is not simply doing our duty of submitting to the Creator but seeing, by the Spirit, the beauty of his infinite love in Jesus Christ.

It also means that *grace* is not just supernatural help to do the right thing but having the Spirit, who shows us the beauty of Jesus Christ. And it is not a one-time seeing,

---

[35] I have used the *Affections* when leading retreats for pastors and church workers in Singapore, Brazil, and Cuba. Many have been Pentecostals, and all have found Edwards' insights to be illuminating.
[36] Edwards, *A History of the Work of Redemption*, WJE 9:480.

but a growing vision of the beauty of the depths of God—like going deeper and deeper into a cell with an increasingly powerful microscope, seeing more and more of its astoundingly ordered complexities.

The Spirit's revelation of God's beauty in Christ means that *community* takes on new shape. If the source of all beauty is the Trinity, then God's beauty is relationship. In fact, God *is* relationship. To experience God is to participate in the inner life of the Trinity. And if God displays His beauty most vividly in His own community of Persons, then we can experience and display God's beauty only in the community of the church, which itself is participation in the trinitarian community because it is the body of Christ.

The Spirit's opening to Christological beauty gives special meaning to *the arts*. All cultural gifts—music and literature and drama and the fine arts—can be seen as reflections of the beams of the divine beauty. So, for example, we can say that despite his moral failures and theological myopia, Mozart gave us something of a taste of the music of heaven. Beautiful music conveys something of God's beauty, even if the composers do not know the full beauty of the triune God.

This changes the way we think of *justice*. We can think of it as not simply fidelity to a set of abstract principles, but as Christ's Spirit imparting a vision of the beauty of the divine trinitarian community. In a community reflecting the divine community, each person gives herself wholly for the good of the others, and therefore reflects, knowingly or unknowingly, the purposes of Being-in-general. So the pursuit of justice in our fallen and broken world is, among other things, allowing the beams of the beautiful divine light to be displayed in human communities. As we seek justice for others and our own communities, we open space for reflections of the trinitarian beauty to be seen and enjoyed.

Conclusion

In sum, Edwards' Christology was integrally connected to his pneumatology. According to Edwards, the Spirit is the beauty of God, who is "distinguished from all other beings, and exalted above [th]em, *chiefly* by his divine beauty."[37] Hence the Spirit constitutes God's most distinguishing characteristic, and that characteristic is most vividly seen in "the excellency of Christ."[38] Not only is the Spirit central to Edwards' theological aesthetics and therefore his Christology, but the Spirit is also the love that drives and constitutes the Incarnation and atonement. Furthermore, the Spirit is the soul of revival, which is the engine of missions, Edwards' secret key to human history. The American theologian's attempts to correct the Western tradition's undervaluation of the Spirit enjoyed mixed success. Nevertheless, his work in theology of revival, spiritual discernment, missions, and aesthetics can be of help to pentecostal theology and its churches.

---

[37] Edwards, *Religious Affections*, WJE 2:298.
[38] Edwards, *The Excellency of Christ*, WJE 19:560–95.

7

The Spirit of Power and Love: Edwards and Pentecostals on Constructive Pneumatology

Andrew K. Gabriel

Introduction

When discussing pneumatology Pentecostals have historically emphasized an empowering of the Holy Spirit that comes through Spirit baptism subsequent to conversion. As a result, Pentecostals have often emphasized dramatic encounters of the Spirit and have at times spoken of the Spirit only as a *power* that fills Christians. Despite all of their talk about the Spirit, however, traditional pentecostal theology has suffered for a lack of pneumatology. Historically, Pentecostals have focused on Spirit baptism, speaking in tongues, and spiritual gifts. That is, their focus has been on interpreting certain *experiences* of the Spirit. As a result of these historic emphases, pentecostal theology has done well in promoting the connection of the Spirit and power, but, until more recently, they have been weak in developing an understanding of the divine person of the Holy Spirit. Combining the strengths of both pentecostal pneumatology and the pneumatology of Jonathan Edwards can lead to a more robust doctrine of the Holy Spirit.

Pentecostals share a common concern with Edwards with respect to pneumatology. Like contemporary Pentecostals, who have been at the forefront in developing pneumatological theology in contemporary theology, Edwards attempts to address what he perceived to be a lack of pneumatological reflection in Christian theology of the eighteenth century. Michael McClymond and Gerald McDermott observe, "Many of Edwards' contemporaries affirmed the deity and personality of the Spirit but had little more to say."[1] By contrast, the Holy Spirit played a central role in Edwards' theology, even though sometimes in hidden and implicit ways.[2] With respect to the person of the Spirit, in particular, Edwards emphasizes that the Spirit is the love of God that bonds

---

[1] Michael J. McClymond and Gerald R. McDermott, *Theology of Jonathan Edwards* (Oxford: Oxford University Press, 2012), 263 (cf. 200). Similarly, Amy Plantinga Pauw, *"The Supreme Harmony of All": The Trinitarian Theology of Jonathan Edwards* (Grand Rapids, MI: Eerdmans, 2002), 121.
[2] Robert W. Caldwell III, *Communion in the Spirit: The Holy Spirit as the Bond of Union in the Theology of Jonathan Edwards* (Milton Keynes: Paternoster, 2006), 9.

the Father and the Son as well as God and creatures. Although some Pentecostals might be concerned that viewing the Spirit as the bond of love (in an Augustinian manner) could lead to a subordination of pneumatology to Christology or to a depersonalized portrayal of the Spirit, Edwards' emphasis complements a recurring theme that is emerging among Pentecostals (especially Amos Yong and Frank Macchia) of relating the Spirit to the love of God. The pneumatologies of Pentecostals and Edwards, then, can support one another to present the Holy Spirit as the Spirit of love and power. This resulting pneumatology can contribute to a concept of Spirit-empowered holiness and supports an integration of pneumatology into the doctrine of the divine attributes.

Edwards on the Spirit

Mind analogy

Edwards explicates his understanding of the person of the Spirit primarily within the context of his doctrine of the Trinity. Edwards largely follows the typical Augustinian approach to the Trinity, which views the Spirit as the love that unites the Father and the Son. Edwards is so much a product of the Western trinitarian tradition that Patricia Wilson-Kastner remarks that "when one quotes from Edwards on the Trinity, one 'could be quoting Augustine, Calvin, or any one of his sixteenth or seventieth century Puritan ancestors.'"[3] Nevertheless, even though Edwards largely follows the Augustinian model of the Trinity, Amy Plantinga Pauw submits that "the role of the *Holy Spirit* is in many respects the most original and the most problematic aspect of Edwards' trinitarianism."[4] This is because Edwards identifies the Spirit as the personal love of God, a conclusion that most of his contemporaries would not have been comfortable with.[5]

Even though Edwards draws on the Augustinian tradition, Edwards engages modern philosophy to illustrate and defend the doctrine of the Trinity. Many modern philosophers had come to conclude that the doctrine of the Trinity was of little use to Christianity, and, therefore, some had abandoned this doctrine in favor of deism.

---

[3] Patricia Wilson-Kastner, *Coherence in a Fragmented World: Jonathan Edwards' Theology of the Holy Spirit* (Washington, DC: University Press of America, 1978), 29.
[4] Pauw, *The Supreme Harmony of All*, 14 (emphasis added). I speak of Edwards "largely" following Augustine because although Edwards clearly follows Augustine, numerous Edwardsean scholars have suggested that Edwards supplements the mutual love model of the Trinity with a social model of the Trinity. This includes Pauw, *The Supreme Harmony of All*, 12–15; Sang Hyun Lee, "Editor's Introduction," *WJE* 21:11, 19–20; Robert Jenson, *America's Theologian: A Recommendation of Jonathan Edwards* (New York: Oxford University Press, 1988), 91–98; William J. Danaher, Jr., *The Trinitarian Ethics of Jonathan Edwards* (Louisville, KY: Westminster John Knox, 2004), 67–116; and McClymond and McDermott, *Theology of Jonathan Edwards*, 198–99. Those who conclude that Edwards does not engage a social doctrine of the Trinity include Caldwell, *Communion in the Spirit*, 37, 39; Steven M. Studebaker and Robert W. Caldwell III, *The Trinitarian Theology of Jonathan Edwards: Text, Context, and Application* (Burlington, VT: Ashgate, 2012), 63, 81–82, 119; and Steven M. Studebaker, *Jonathan Edwards' Social Augustinian Trinitarianism in Historical and Contemporary Perspectives*, Gorgias Studies in Philosophy and Theology 2 (Piscataway, NJ: Gorgias, 2008), 255.
[5] Pauw, *The Supreme Harmony of All*, 48.

To counter this, Edwards engaged idealism in order to present an *a priori* argument for the doctrine of the Trinity. Steven Studebaker and Robert Caldwell explain, Edwards "attempts to derive the eternal generation of God the Son from his idealism by drawing out the ontological implications associated with God's self-reflection."[6] With this *a priori* argument Edwards stands apart from the majority of the Reformed tradition who thought that God's triunity could not be discerned from reason alone, but only through divine revelation.[7]

Edwards begins his *a priori* defense and explication of the doctrine of the Trinity with the claim that "it must be supposed that God perpetually and eternally has a most perfect idea of himself."[8] Since this idea, or image, that God has of Godself is perfect, Edwards reasons, this image much be exactly like God in every way. This image of God that comes forth in God the Father's understanding is the second person of the Trinity—God the Son.

Edwards continues his rational defense of the doctrine of the Trinity by describing the Spirit as the eternal delight that God has in beholding the image or perfect idea of Godself. Edwards' analogy for the Trinity is that God is a mind with two modes of activity: God's intellect (God's understanding and perfect idea of Godself) and God's will (God's love of and delight in the perfect idea of Godself). More importantly, for the purpose of this chapter, for Edwards the Spirit is "an infinitely holy and sacred energy [that] arises between the Father and Son . . . in mutually loving and delighting in each other."[9] Or, to use more traditional language, the Spirit is the mutual love of the Father and the Son.

Spirit and love in Scriptures

While Edwards aspires to explain the doctrine of the Trinity using reason alone, he finds his conclusion that the Spirit is the love of God confirmed in Scripture. The first Johannine letter provides the biblical texts that Edwards appeals to most consistently: 1 Jn 4:8 states that "God is love," which implies, for Edwards, that "the divine nature and essence does subsist in love." The letter continues, "If we love one another, God lives in us" (v. 12) and clarifies that the way God lives in us is that God "has given us of his Spirit" (v. 13) for God "abides in us, by the Spirit that he has given us" (1 Jn 3:24). And again, "God is love, and those who abide in love abide in God, and God abides in them" (1 Jn 4:16). In light of how this biblical letter describes both love dwelling in believers and the Spirit dwelling in believers, Edwards concludes that these passages of Scripture confirm "not only that the divine nature subsists in love, but also that this love is the Spirit, for it is the Spirit of God by which God dwells in his saints."[10]

---

[6] Studebaker and Caldwell, *The Trinitarian Theology of Jonathan Edwards*, 68. Cf. McClymond and McDermott, *Theology of Jonathan Edwards*, 193 and Oliver D. Crisp, *Jonathan Edwards on God and Creation* (Oxford: Oxford University Press, 2012), 118–27.
[7] Studebaker and Caldwell, *The Trinitarian Theology of Jonathan Edwards*, 137.
[8] Edwards, *Discourse on the Trinity*, WJE 21:113.
[9] Ibid., 121. Cf. Edwards, "Miscellany 94," WJE 13:260.
[10] Edwards, *Discourse on the Trinity*, WJE 21:122. On 1 John see also Edwards, *Treatise on Grace*, WJE 21:181–83.

Edwards contests that the name "Holy Spirit" also confirms that the Spirit is the love of God. First, Edwards considers the term "Spirit." He observes that when we speak of an individual's "spirit," we are generally referring to the "disposition, inclination or temper" of that person's mind. Likewise, when the Scripture refers to the "Spirit" of God, Edwards supposes, it refers to the "disposition or temper or affection of the divine mind," which is love. Second, Edwards considers the term "holy." He suggests that holiness is found in the "disposition of a mind" and that it is "in God's infinite *love to himself* that his holiness consists."[11] Hence, the terms "holy" and "Spirit" allude to the Spirit's personal identity as love. Edwards continues to demonstrate the nature of the Spirit as love by describing the Spirit in quickening and sanctifying creatures and by exploring various biblical symbols of the Spirit (dove, oil, a river of water, communion).[12] Aside from these implicit references to the Spirit, Edwards observes that "Scripture seems in many places to speak of love in Christians as if it were the same with the Spirit of God in them."[13] For example, Rom. 5:5 reads, "God's love has been poured into our hearts through the Holy Spirit that has been given to us" (cf. Col. 1:8, 2 Cor. 6:6, Phil. 2:1).

Love that creates unions

According to Edwards, within the immanent Trinity the Spirit is the bond of love that unites the Father and the Son. Edwards presents the Spirit playing the same role of creating various unions within the divine life *ad extra*. He maintains, the Spirit "that proceeds from the Father and the Son is the bond of this union, as it is of all holy union between the Father and the Son, and between God and the creature, and between the creatures among themselves."[14] In other words,

> In the theology of Jonathan Edwards, the Holy Spirit's activity as the bond of the trinitarian union between the Father and the Son is paradigmatic for all other holy unions in his theology. In the personal union of Christ's two natures, the mystical union believers have with Christ, and the union of fellowship that believers have with each other, the Holy Spirit works *ad extra* in a manner that is patterned after his inner-trinitarian work.[15]

To summarize, for Edwards, the Spirit is the love of God that unites the Father and the Son within the divine life *ad intra* and the love of God that creates holy unions in the divine life *ad extra*.

---

[11] Ibid., 123 (emphasis added).
[12] Ibid., 123–30 and, *Treatise on Grace*, WJE 21:183–88.
[13] Edwards, *Treatise on Grace*, WJE 21:185.
[14] Ibid., 186.
[15] Caldwell, *Communion in the Spirit*, 8; cf. Pauw, *The Supreme Harmony of All*, 146.

Pentecostals on the Spirit

Unlike Edwards who emphasizes that the Spirit is the love of God, Pentecostals have traditionally tended to associate the Spirit with power.[16] Consider, for example, the very title of Robert and William Menzies book *Spirit and Power*, with the subtitle *Foundations of Pentecostal Experience*. In addition, I can attest to this in my own formative pentecostal experience. Growing up, next to Jn 3:16 the verse that was most prominent in pentecostal preaching was Acts 1:8: "You will receive power when the Holy Spirit has come upon you." Aside from various biblical narratives that relate the Spirit to power coming upon people, such as Samson (Judg. 14:6, 19; 15:14) or Jesus (Lk. 4:14, Acts 10:38), Scripture speaks explicitly of the "power of the Spirit" (Lk. 4:14; Rom. 15:13, 19; 1 Cor. 2:4).[17] There is, then, significant biblical precedent for pentecostal theology to associate the Spirit with power.

One can find, nevertheless, some association of the Spirit and love within pentecostal theology. Historically, some early North American Pentecostals described the baptism of the Holy Spirit not only as experiences of glory and power, but also as a reception of divine love.[18] For example, one anonymous testimony in *The Apostolic Faith* paper (published by William J. Seymour, leader of the Azusa Street Revival) recounts an experience of baptism in the Holy Spirit saying, "Jesus and I are united. He baptized me with love."[19] Another person describes their experience of being baptized in the Holy Spirit using similar language: "It was a baptism of love. Such abounding love! Such compassion seemed to almost kill me with its sweetness! . . . This baptism fills us with divine love."[20]

Although this association between Spirit baptism and the love of God was not maintained in much of pentecostal theology (especially among the Finished Work Pentecostals who followed William Durham[21]), the association is finding renewed emphasis in contemporary pentecostal theology. For example, Amos Yong in *The Spirit Poured Out on All Flesh* (2005) did not explicitly define Spirit baptism in terms of the love of God. By contrast, more recently as Yong developed his pneumatological theology of love in his *Spirit of Love: A Trinitarian Theology of Grace* (2012), he proposes "the Day of Pentecost outpouring is God's excessive and universal gift of love to the world,

---

[16] As observed by Frank D. Macchia, *Baptized in the Spirit: A Global Pentecostal Theology* (Grand Rapids, MI: Zondervan, 2006), 82 and Amos Yong, *Spirit of Love: A Trinitarian Theology of Grace* (Waco, TX: Baylor University Press, 2012), 39, 42, 76.

[17] I explore the relationship of the Holy Spirit to divine power in Andrew K. Gabriel, *The Lord Is the Spirit: The Holy Spirit and the Divine Attributes* (Eugene, OR: Pickwick, 2011), chapter 7, with pages 183–86 focusing on "The 'Spirit' and 'Power' in Theology and Scripture."

[18] Kimberly Ervin Alexander, "Boundless Love Divine: A Re-evaluation of Early Understandings of the Experiences of Spirit Baptism," in *Passover, Pentecost, and Parousia: Studies in Celebration of the Life and Ministry of R. Hollis Gause*, ed. Steven Jack Land, Rickie D. Moore, and John Christopher Thomas, Journal of Pentecostal Theology Supplement Series 35 (Blandford Forum: Deo, 2010), 152, 158–161.

[19] *The Apostolic Faith* 1.2, October 1906, 3.

[20] *The Apostolic Faith* 1.1, September 1906, 1.

[21] Yong, *Spirit of Love*, 67.

in and through the gift of the Spirit of God."[22] In part, Yong is here following the work of Frank Macchia who (2006) contends that "Spirit baptism is a baptism into the love of God that sanctifies, renews, and empowers until Spirit baptism turns all of creation into the final dwelling place of God."[23]

Pentecostal concerns

Concern 1: Filioque

Clearly, there are some parallels between Edwards' pneumatology and contemporary pentecostal pneumatology when Pentecostals associate the baptism of the Holy Spirit with the love of God. Nevertheless, there are a few points in Edwards' pneumatology that might hinder Pentecostals from following Edwards wholeheartedly.

To begin, since Edwards follows the Western Augustinian trinitarian tradition, Edwards accepts the *filioque*—an expansion to the idea that the Holy Spirit "proceeds from the Father" (as originally stated in the Nicene-Constantinopolitan Creed) to state that the Holy Spirit proceeds from both "the Father *and the Son*" (*filioque*). For Edwards, the Holy Spirit is "that personal energy, the divine love and delight, [that] eternally and continually proceeds from both" the Father and the Son.[24]

For many Pentecostals, the *filioque* has not been a key theological issue for reflection, but rather a sign of dead creedal orthodoxy.[25] Veli-Matti Kärkkäinen observes that some pentecostal denominations do include the *filioque* within their statements of faith and many pentecostal manuals on systematic theology accept it as well, though generally without much theological reflection.[26] Nevertheless, when Pentecostals have taken more time to contemplate the *filioque*, in contrast to Edwards, they have often resisted the *filioque*. On the one hand, Yong writes that he has "come to see the value of the *Filioque*" and that he is "very sympathetic to the substance of Aquinas' handling of the *filioque*."[27] On the other hand, Frank Macchia concludes that "the *filioque* from [sic] Pentecostal perspective is inadequate to describe the coming forth of the Son

---

[22] Ibid., 98; cf. 89.
[23] Macchia, *Baptized in the Spirit*, 60, cf. 17. For Yong's reflections on Macchia's *Baptized in the Spirit*, see Yong, *Spirit of Love*, 85–90.
[24] Edwards, "Miscellany 143," *WJE* 13:298–99. Cf. Edwards, *Treatise on Grace*, *WJE* 21:185–86 and *Discourse on the Trinity*, *WJE* 21:135, 143. On Edwards' acceptance of the *filioque*, see Lee, "Editor's Introduction," *WJE* 21:17; Caldwell, *Communion in the Spirit*, 46–47; and Studebaker and Caldwell, *The Trinitarian Theology of Jonathan Edwards*, 72.
[25] Jeffrey Goss, "A Pilgrimage in the Spirit: Pentecostal Testimony in the Faith and Order Movement," *Pneuma: The Journal of the Society for Pentecostal Studies* 25, no. 1 (2003): 36–37 and Veli-Matti Kärkkäinen, "Trinity as Communion in the Spirit: Koinonia, Trinity, and Filioque in Roman Catholic-Pentecostal Dialogue," *Pneuma: The Journal of the Society for Pentecostal Studies* 22, no. 2 (2000): 210–12.
[26] Kärkkäinen, "Trinity as Communion in the Spirit," 223, 229.
[27] Amos Yong, *The Spirit Poured Out on All Flesh: World Pentecostalism and the Possibility of Global Theology* (Grand Rapids, MI: Baker Academic, 2005), 226; Yong, *Spirit of Love*, 169n20; and Amos Yong, *Spirit-Word-Community: Theological Hermeneutics in Trinitarian Perspective* (Burlington, VT: Ashgate, 2002), 72.

and the Spirit from the Father."[28] Macchia reaches this conclusion because he believes "the *filioque* privileges the Son in a way that does not match the mutual dependence between the Son and the Spirit in the Scriptural narrative of Spirit baptism and its effects in creation." [29]

Articulating a solution to the *filioque* debate or attempting to discern the most appropriate pentecostal response to the *filioque* is beyond the scope of this chapter. What is pertinent to this chapter, however, are the reasons that Pentecostals have sometimes hesitated to affirm the *filioque*, particularly as they relate to the person of the Spirit. Even though these reasons may not be unique to Pentecostals, they do indicate how Pentecostals might receive Edwards' pneumatology.

First, Yong expresses the concern that the *filioque* might hinder a quest for a pneumatological theology (Yong offers Karl Barth, who defended the *filioque*, as an example).[30] Second, and more pertinent to this chapter, Macchia acknowledges that his concern is not so much the *filioque* itself, but rather the need to affirm the interdependence of the persons of the Trinity.[31] That is, in the economy of salvation, the Son not only gives the Spirit to believers as believers are baptized in the love of God, but the Son is also baptized in the Spirit when he is anointed and empowered for his ministry as the Christ. I will return to this point below as I engage the question of the personal nature of the Spirit in Edwards' pneumatology. Third, consistent with Orthodox concerns regarding the *filioque*, Howard Ervin and Yong note that they wish to avoid subordinating the Holy Spirit to the Son.[32]

While Pentecostals might be concerned that Edwards' position regarding the *filioque* could indicate a subordination of the Spirit in Edwards' theology, this is not the case. Rather, as noted above, Edwards shares pentecostal concerns regarding subordinating the person and work of the Spirit in both theology and life and he seeks to overcome a possible subordination of the Spirit, which he identifies among his Reformed contemporaries. First, Edwards contends that the "the Holy Ghost is equal" to the Father and the Son, for, as the love of God, the Spirit "is that divine excellency and beauty itself."[33] Second, with respect to the Spirit's work in salvation, in contrast to

---

[28] Frank D. Macchia, "Baptized in the Spirit: A Pentecostal Reflection on the *Filioque*," in *Ecumenical Perspectives on the* Filioque *for the Twenty-First Century*, ed. Myk Habets (London: Bloomsbury, 2014), 155.

[29] Macchia, "Baptized in the Spirit," 155. Given that Macchia accepts the idea of "the Spirit as proceeding from the Father *through* the Son" (Macchia, *Justified in the Spirit*, 305 [emphasis original]), and that Edwards similarly believes that the Spirit proceeds "from the Father originally and primarily, and from the Son as it were secondarily" (Edwards, *Discourse on the Trinity*, WJE 21:143), I am unconvinced that Macchia's conclusions require him to reject the *filioque*. Similarly, Yong, *Spirit of Love*, 192n35, believes that Macchia was defending a variant of the *filioque* in *Baptized in the Spirit*. While coming to a conclusion regarding the *filioque* is beyond the scope of this chapter, my own inclination is to agree with Yves Congar (*I Believe in the Holy Spirit*, 3 vols., trans. David Smith [New York: Seabury, 1983], 3:87 and 131) who claims that the Eastern and Western churches have historically expressed the same faith but through two different dogmatic structures.

[30] Yong, *The Spirit Poured Out*, 225–26.

[31] Macchia, *Justified in the Spirit*, 305.

[32] Yong, *The Spirit Poured Out*, 226. On Howard Ervin's position, see Kärkkäinen, "Trinity as Communion in the Spirit," 225.

[33] Edwards, *Discourse on the Trinity*, WJE 21:135.

other Reformed theologians in his day, Edwards argued that the Spirit does not give us the blessing that Christ purchased, but rather that the Spirit is the thing purchased. The Spirit is not, therefore, subordinate to the Son, for "to be the thing purchased, is as much as to be the price that purchases it."[34] Caldwell explains, "Far from being the agent who merely applies the work of Christ to the elect," for Edwards, "the Spirit *is* the sum of all the good that believers commune in, all the grace that believers benefit from, and all the love that they enjoy in God."[35] To summarize, Edwards overcomes a possible subordination of the Spirit by emphasizing the identity of the Spirit as the divine excellency or love of God and as the purchase of salvation.

Concern 2: The Spirit as love

Another point in Edwards' pneumatology that might hinder Pentecostals from following him wholeheartedly is that Edwards not only associates the Spirit and love but also concludes that the Spirit is the mutual love of the Father and the Son. Aside from their conclusions that being baptized in the Spirit is an experience of being baptized into the love of God, both Yong and Macchia also, like Edwards, describe the Spirit as the mutual love of or bond of love between the Father and the Son and between God and creation. Macchia, for example, speaks explicitly of "the Spirit as the bond of love between the Father and the Son as well as between God and the world (Rom. 5:5)."[36] Here is another parallel between Edwards' pneumatology and some contemporary pentecostal pneumatology. Nevertheless, it is one thing to associate the Spirit with love, but it is quite another to say that the Spirit is the love of God, as Edwards does. So, for example, Yong is more apt to speak of the Spirit as "the Gift of Love to the world"[37] or of the "Spirit *of love*."[38] He does, however, also state more strongly "of the gift of the Holy Spirit, *who is love*."[39]

Macchia cautions that when speaking of the Spirit as the mutual love of the Father and the Son one must be careful to "not de-personalize the Spirit by eliminating the Spirit's participation as person in the *koinonia* of Father and Son, relating to them in ways appropriate to the Spirit"[40] thereby portraying the Spirit as an impersonal force. Some Edwardsean scholars also note that Edwards might depersonalize the Spirit in the way that he refers to the Spirit as mutual love of the Father and the Son.[41]

Caldwell makes a noteworthy observation regarding this concern. Edwards "never thought that to speak of the Holy Spirit as divine love threatened the personhood of

---

[34] Edwards, *Treatise on Grace*, WJE 21:191. Likewise, Edwards, *Discourse on the Trinity*, WJE 21:136–38.
[35] Caldwell, *Communion in the Spirit*, 35. Cf. Studebaker and Caldwell, *The Trinitarian Theology of Jonathan Edwards*, 80 (emphasis original).
[36] Macchia, *Baptized in the Spirit*, 124. Cf. 135, 159, 265. Also, Macchia, *Justified in the Spirit*, 132, 142, 203, 234, and 300. Yong develops this most fully in chapter 2 of *Spirit-Word-Community*, though it is also present in his *Spirit of Love* (e.g., 159).
[37] Yong, *Spirit of Love*, 19, 129.
[38] Ibid., 19, 98, 162.
[39] Ibid., 98 (emphasis added).
[40] Macchia, *Justified in the Spirit*, 302.
[41] McClymond and McDermott, *Theology of Jonathan Edwards*, 198 and Pauw, *The Supreme Harmony of All*, 43.

the Spirit."[42] Edwards explicitly affirms that "we ought to look upon him [the Spirit] as a distinct personal agent. He is often spoken of as a person, revealed under personal characters and in personal acts, and it speaks of his being acted on as a person, and the Scripture plainly ascribes every thing to him that properly denotes a distinct person."[43]

At the same time, Edwards was aware that viewing the Spirit as love does not "seem well to consist with [the notion] that a person is that which hath understanding and will."[44] In making this admission, Edwards moves from his usual ontological way of describing each divine person as a subsistence of the divine nature to a modern understanding of person as a conscious center of thinking.[45] Edwards responds to this modern way of thinking about personhood by contending that the three divine persons do not have three distinct understandings, but that they all share the same understanding by virtue of sharing the same divine essence and by virtue of the perichoresis of the divine persons.[46] To support his conclusion, Edwards observes,

> We often read in scripture of the Father loving the Son, and the Son loving the Father, yet we never once read either of the Father or the Son loving the Holy Spirit, and the Spirit loving either of them. It is because the Holy Spirit is the divine love itself, the love of the Father and the Son. Hence also it is to be accounted for, that we very often read of the love both of the Father and the Son to men, and particularly their love to the saints; but we never read of the Holy Ghost loving them, for the Holy Ghost is that love of God and Christ that is breathed forth primarily towards each other, and flows out secondarily towards the creature.[47]

Likewise, Edwards continues, we read of "the saints having fellowship and communion with the Father and with the Son; but never of their having fellowship with the Holy Ghost, because the Holy Ghost is that common good or fullness which they partake of, in which their fellowship consists."[48] Hence, for Edwards, it seems the Spirit is not a third center of divine consciousness, although the Spirit is a person in the sense that the Spirit does share the understanding of the divine life.[49] Edwards has, thereby, addressed the concerns of Pentecostals that viewing the Spirit as the mutual love of the Father and the Son (with its corollary of the *filioque*) might depersonalize the Spirit.

---

[42] Caldwell, *Communion in the Spirit*, 198.
[43] Edwards, *Treatise on Grace*, WJE 21:181.
[44] Edwards, *Discourse on the Trinity*, WJE 21:133.
[45] Studebaker and Caldwell, *The Trinitarian Theology of Jonathan Edwards*, 77, 142. Studebaker and Caldwell observe that "the definition more fundamental to his theology is the scholastic, ontological definition. . . . He does not completely affirm a 'modern' understanding of person" (78).
[46] Edwards, *Discourse on the Trinity*, WJE 21:133-34. Regarding the divine essence, see Edwards, "Miscellany 308," WJE 13:392.
[47] Edwards, *Treatise on Grace*, WJE 21:186.
[48] Ibid., 188.
[49] I say "it seems" because, as noted in a footnote above, some Edwardsean scholars have suggested that Edwards supplements the mutual love model of the Trinity with a social model of the Trinity.

Constructive conclusions and proposals

Spirit of love and power

Edwards' pneumatology responds well to some concerns that Pentecostals might raise when encountering his emphasis on the Spirit as love. Pentecostals would do well, then, to draw on Edwards by further integrating the idea of the Spirit as love within their pneumatology while recognizing that speaking of the Spirit as the love of God is a limited, but helpful addition to pneumatology. The Spirit is, then, the one who empowers the church in its witness and the one who, as the love of God, binds the church into union with God and one another. One should not view these two perspectives of the Spirit as power and love as antithetical, for one can view these works of the Spirit as synergistic—the Spirit empowers the love of believers leading them to witness effectively in works of love.[50] Pentecostal and Edwardsean pneumatologies support one another. The Spirit is not only the love of God who creates love, as Edwards emphasizes, but the Spirit is also, as Pentecostals' tend to emphasize, the power of God who empowers others to draw all people into an encounter with divine love.

Spirit of love and holiness

One advantage that Pentecostals would gain by speaking more regularly of the Spirit as love is that it could contribute to a renewed emphasis on holiness in the pentecostal tradition. This is a needed correction in many parts of the pentecostal-charismatic movement. As Larry Hart observes, "If the charismatic movement had taught the power of the Spirit for holy living with the same diligence with which it taught the power of the Spirit for signs and wonders, it probably would not find itself on some of the shoals in which it is presently floundering."[51]

Emphasizing the Spirit as the love of God should lead not only to a renewed emphasis on holiness, but also to a revised view of what constitutes holiness. Yong notes that in early North American Pentecostalism, when Pentecostals spoke of baptism in the Spirit, "twin themes of power and purity" marginalized the theme of love.[52] Edwards gives caution to any Pentecostals who might view holiness simply as purity or fleeing from "worldliness." For Edwards, the Holy Spirit does not shape believers' character as some sort of *external* influence. Rather, as the embodiment of divine love, the Spirit becomes the "vital principle" dwelling *within* believers and believers participate in the nature of the Spirit, which is love.[53] This union between the Spirit of love and humanity leads believers to affections and actions of love. The result, Edwards writes, is that "all creature holiness consists essentially and summarily

---

[50] Likewise, Yong, *Spirit of Love*, 89–90.
[51] Larry D. Hart, *Truth Aflame: Theology for the Church in Renewal*, rev. ed. (Grand Rapids, MI: Zondervan, 2005), 396.
[52] Yong, *Spirit of Love*, 42.
[53] Edwards, *Discourse on the Trinity*, WJE 21:124 and *Treatise on Grace*, WJE 21:194–96. Cf. Bruce M. Stephens, *The Holy Spirit in American Protestant Thought, 1750–1850*, Studies in American Religion 59 (Lewiston, ME: Edwin Mellen, 1992), 8.

in love to God and love to other creatures."⁵⁴ Another chapter in this volume expands on Edwards' theology of sanctification in more detail, but here is it important to note that Edwards' pneumatology provides the foundation for viewing holiness as a work of love and resulting in love.⁵⁵

Spirit of love and the divine attributes

Following his emphasis that the Spirit is the love of God, Edwards identifies the attributes of God's love specifically with the person of the Holy Spirit. Edwards observes, "We find no other attributes of which it is said that they are God in Scripture or that God is they, but *logos* and *agape*."⁵⁶ There are, then, for Edwards, only two "real attributes of God": understanding (or *logos*) and love (*agape*).⁵⁷ Edwards identifies "the sum of God's understanding," including God's wisdom and omniscience, with the divine person of the Son. Similarly, Edwards identifies God's will, which is love, with the Spirit. Hence, Edwards identifies God's holiness and justice and the divine attributes of goodness, mercy, and grace all as coming forth from "the overflowings of God's infinite love," who is the Spirit.⁵⁸ Edwardsean scholars observe that Edwards here departs from the scholastic and Reformed traditions of attributing the divine attributes to the divine essence rather than to the divine persons.⁵⁹

The primary difficulty with Edwards' proposal is that one cannot distinguish between the divine persons based on the divine persons having different attributes. Oliver Crisp is, then, rightly concerned that Edwards' theology of the "real attributes" of God "threatens to divide the works of God between the persons of the divine Trinity."⁶⁰ There is, however, a theological intuition in Edwards' theology that can be maintained and serve well for a pentecostal and pneumatological approach to the doctrine of the divine attributes. Namely, as Stephen Holmes observes, Edwards seeks to "subsume the doctrine of the divine perfections under the doctrine of Trinity" rather than under a doctrine of the divine essence.⁶¹ This implies that when someone seeks to expound an understanding of the divine attributes one must consider the divine persons who are the very subsistence of the divine essence.

If it is acceptable to appropriate certain divine works (like creation) or attributes (like omnipotence) to "God the Father Almighty" (as in the Nicene Creed), then it should be acceptable to, in some sense, appropriate the attribute of divine love with the person of the Holy Spirit. It appears this might be what Edwards is doing

---

[54] Edwards, *Treatise on Grace*, WJE 21:186.
[55] Yong provides pentecostal reflections on the Spirit of love leading to holiness as works of love in *Spirit of Love*, 59–74.
[56] Edwards, *Discourse on the Trinity*, WJE 21:132.
[57] Ibid. In contrast to these two "real distinctions," Edwards writes, "[God's] attributes of infinity, eternity and immortality ... are mere modes of existence" (ibid., 131).
[58] Ibid., 131.
[59] Crisp, *Jonathan Edwards on God and Creation*, 127–35; Studebaker and Caldwell, *The Trinitarian Theology of Jonathan Edwards*, 76, 81; and Pauw, *The Supreme Harmony of All*, 72.
[60] Crisp, *Jonathan Edwards on God and Creation*, 135.
[61] Stephen R. Holmes, *God of Grace and God of Glory: An Account of the Theology of Jonathan Edwards* (Edinburgh: T & T Clark, 2000), 70.

when he claims, "Though all the divine perfections are to be attributed to each person of the Trinity, yet the Holy Ghost is in a peculiar manner called by the name of love."[62]

While Edwards might be incorrect to suppose that the attributes of divine love may be attributed to the Spirit (if he means the Spirit *alone*) as a means of recognizing the Spirit as a divine person distinct from the Father and the Son, the life of the Spirit should contribute to our understanding of the attributes God.[63] For example, if one thinks about the attributes of divine love, one finds that it is through the Spirit that God's *grace*—love as unconditioned and unhindered—takes sinners and gives them freedom (2 Cor. 3:17). Also, God's love is *holy* as God creates and seeks fellowship with humanity by overcoming their resistance to God's will as the Spirit convicts of righteousness, judgment, and sin (Jn 16:8). As an expression of God's *merciful compassion*, like a mother giving birth to her child, the Spirit of God groans that there might be new birth (Rom. 8:22-26).[64] There is much to be gained by further following Edwards' intuition of associating the Spirit with the divine attribute of love and the attributes of God more generally. Likewise, one might follow the pentecostal intuition of associating the Spirit and power by considering how pneumatology can inform the doctrine of divine omnipotence.[65]

Conclusion

In conclusion, those engaging pneumatology would do well to integrate both a pentecostal emphasis on the Spirit and power and Edwards' view of the Spirit as the love of God while continuing to maintain the equality and interdependence of the divine persons within both the economic and the immanent Trinity. The Spirit of power (the historic pentecostal emphasis) is also (as Edwards emphasizes) the bond of love that unites humanity with God and one another. This pneumatology can contribute to a renewed understanding of Spirit-empowered holiness as including love for God and others and supports the development of a pneumatological approach to the doctrine of the divine attributes.

---

[62] Edwards, *Treatise on Grace*, WJE 21:181. Similarly, he writes, "The Father loves because the Holy Ghost is in him. So the Son loves because the Holy Spirit is in him and proceeds from him" (Edwards, *Discourse on the Trinity*, WJE 21:133). Holmes, *God of Grace*, 71, believes Edwards' doctrine of the "real attributes" may express instances of appropriation.

[63] Gabriel, *The Lord Is the Spirit*, 89-122.

[64] Andrew K. Gabriel, "Pneumatological Insights for the Attributes of the Divine Love," in *Third Article Theology: A Pneumatological Dogmatics*, ed. Myk Habets (Minneapolis, MN: Fortress Academic, 2016), 39-54.

[65] See, for example, Gabriel, *The Lord Is the Spirit*, 186-201.

8

Transformation by the Spirit in Justification and Sanctification

James M. Henderson

Introduction

Robert Jenson has stated that American Revivalism has been explicitly "Arminian" in the sense of being "dedicated to salvation by the cheapest sort of works," in contrast to the thought of Jonathan Edwards.[1] Is this true of American Pentecostals, or is there common ground between some American Pentecostal thinkers and Jonathan Edwards in terms of their theology of justification and sanctification? In this chapter, I explore the thought of Jonathan Edwards on the topics of justification and sanctification, and compare or contrast Edwards' ideas with those of twentieth- and twenty-first-century Pentecostal thinkers. At the end of this analysis, I will show significant agreement between Edwards and Pentecostals of both the Holiness and Finished Work schools. I will show that, while Edwards maintains the language of a forensic declaration, meaning that the Christian's salvation coming from the Father's declaration of "not guilty" based solely on the imputation of Christ's merits to the saint, Edwards grounds justification primarily in the idea that the work and presence of the person of the Holy Spirit unites the soul with Christ. This presence and work of the Spirit unites the human soul to Christ and transforms the soul in regeneration (without forming a *habitus* in the Thomistic sense), and so the presence and work of the Holy Spirit is what constitutes both justification and initial sanctification in the person and life of each Christian.[2]

Justification

This section compares and contrasts the thought of Jonathan Edwards on justification with that of Pentecostal authors. To begin with, both Edwards and Pentecostals assume

---

[1] Robert W. Jenson, "Mr. Edwards' Affections," *Dialogue* 24, no. 3 (1985): 169.
[2] I use the term "initial" sanctification to contrast the transformation that I believe Edwards understands is the result of justification with "sanctification" as it is normally used in Holiness thought, as acts of love and a godly lifestyle.

that an unconverted person cannot achieve true holiness or obedience. This makes justification necessary. Whether or not justification is a legal imputation of Christ's righteousness that does not also transform the soul in some sense (only and wholly "forensic") or is a transformative event is a contested issue.[3] Whether the work of the Holy Spirit in justification is sufficient to free the converted Christian from bondage to sin or to empower the saint to live in obedience is a point at which Edwards agrees with some Pentecostals and disagrees with others. As I show, however, all the parties in this debate would agree that transformation in some sense comes before (or is logically simultaneous with) justification.

Jonathan Edwards on justification

The thought of Jonathan Edwards has been the subject of study for the last two centuries, and opinions vary widely. For some, like Jenson, Edwards was and is the only significant evangelical American theologian. Perhaps this is because Jenson sees Edwards as part of the theological school of John Calvin.[4] Others portray Edwards as more of a mystic,[5] or perhaps as a metaphysical idealist,[6] and not someone who is at home with Reformed theology. My purpose in this section is not to examine the entire corpus of Edwards' work, but to attempt to see how one can understand Edwards' view of justification and sanctification, especially in the context of the work and presence of the Holy Spirit.

Justification comes by a deeper sense than rational knowledge. Those who read Edwards from a Reformed position tend to emphasize the idea that justification comes because the Holy Spirit communicates to the mind a kind of knowledge.[7] In this, Reformed thinkers appear to be saying that saving knowledge is primarily rational knowledge. However, Edwards appeals to something deeper than the rational.[8] Salvation comes as the mind, perhaps a metonymy for the whole person in Edwards, experiences a sense that it cannot define rationally such as the taste of sweetness, a sense of delight in or desire for the beauty of God.[9] If this is knowledge, then it is knowledge of a new and

---

[3] I am aware of the debate between Edwards' scholars over this very point. As I state here, I believe that Edwards advocates a "forensic" justification that is not, in the end, a legal fiction. For a survey of the issues and debate on Edwards' views on this question, see Steven M. Studebaker and Robert W. Caldwell III, *The Trinitarian Theology of Jonathan Edwards: Text, Context, and Application* (Burlington, VT: Ashgate, 2012).

[4] Jenson, "Edwards' Affections," 169.

[5] James R. McNerney, "The Mystical Journey of Jonathan Edwards," *Studia Mystica* 1, no. 3 (1985): 27.

[6] Richard A. S. Hall, "Edwards as Mystic," in *The Contribution of Jonathan Edwards to American Culture and Society: Essays on America's Spiritual Founding Father*, ed. Richard A. S. Hall (Lampeter: Edwin Mellen, 2008).

[7] For example, Josh Moody says, "For first, there must be an idea of Jesus Christ in the mind." God gives this knowledge before conversion, and Moody argues that this makes Edwards a Calvinist. Josh Moody, "Edwards and Justification Today," in *Jonathan Edwards and Justification*, ed. Josh Moody (Wheaton, IL: Crossway, 2012), 27.

[8] James Hoopes, "Jonathan Edwards' Religious Psychology," *The Journal of American History* 69, no. 4 (1983): 856.

[9] M. Darrol Bryant, "The Mind of Jonathan Edwards: Beyond America," in *The Contribution of Jonathan Edwards to American Culture and Society: Essays on America's Spiritual Founding Father*, ed. Richard A. S. Hall (Lampeter: Edwin Mellen, 2008), 78.

different kind that goes beyond speculative understanding or rational opinion to the experience, or apprehension of, the loveliness of God that is pleasant to the soul.[10]

This sense goes under or around the rational and does not consist in propositions.[11] While this sense is not "mystical" in that it denies the rational or requires the abnegation of self, it is "spiritual" because it involves an apprehension of the divine glory, which "consists in a *sense* and *taste*" of the divine excellency and beauty, a "*sense of the heart* wherein the mind not only speculates and beholds but *relishes* and *feels*,"[12] in a way different than understanding with the reason as taste is different from one's other faculties.[13] This sense is not a new faculty of understanding, but "a new principle or a new foundation laid in the nature of the soul."[14] This sense of the heart is something implanted in the believer by regeneration, and brings to the believer God's beauty. The believer becomes beautified, and so able to apprehend, appreciate, and desire God in a way that we could not before regeneration.[15] Edwards speaks of this regeneration as having the old nature mortified and a new nature infused.

Edwards wishes to merge the common Puritan concept that salvation comes by knowledge of the gospel/God with the idea that it is an existential, experiential knowledge of God/Christ that justifies, a knowledge of personal relationship such as is the basis of the Pentecostal idea of personal salvation (justification).[16] Because this experience is one of the Holy Spirit entering, restoring, and reordering the soul in its affections, this experience should be considered not only existential but also eschatological, the experience of and participation in a teleological perception of the happiness and glory of God and the fullness of the Christian's final salvation.[17] The regenerated Christian is, then, so thoroughly rebuilt that "he has become quite another man that he was before."[18] All of this means that justification is more than forensic in Edwards' thought.

---

[10] Hoopes, "Edwards' Religious Psychology," 858–59 and Herbert Richardson, "Why Is Jonathan Edwards America's Spiritual Founding Father?" in *The Contribution of Jonathan Edwards to American Culture and Society: Essays on America's Spiritual Founding Father*, ed. Richard A. S. Hall (Lampeter: Edwin Mellen, 2008), 67.

[11] Bryant, "The Mind of Jonathan Edwards," 78; William Breitenbach, "Piety and Moralism: Edwards and the New Divinity," in *Jonathan Edwards and the American Experience*, ed. Nathan O. Hatch and Harry S. Stout (New York: Oxford University Press, 1988), 182.

[12] John Piper, "Jonathan Edwards on the Problem of Faith and History," *Scottish Journal of Theology* 31, no. 3 (1978): 223 (emphasis original).

[13] Edwards, *Religious Affections*, WJE 2:206.

[14] Ibid., 206.

[15] Ibid., 203.

[16] Ibid., 395, 396. Note that Edwards' language of "infusion" is not the same as an infused "habitus" in the soul, but the restoring and reordering presence of the Holy Spirit himself. Note the context of both a "change" in one's nature and "infusion" in Edwards, *Religious Affections*, WJE 2:394, 396. See also Studebaker and Caldwell, *Trinitarian Theology of Jonathan Edwards*, 178. R. Michael Allen notes "justification cannot be premised upon the very participation that it makes not only possible but also actual in Christ Jesus" (citing Rom. 5:1-2). R. Michael Allen, *Justification and the Gospel: Understanding the Contexts and Controversies* (Grand Rapids, MI: Baker Academic, 2013), 61.

[17] J. Lyle Story, "Pauline Thoughts about the Holy Spirit and Sanctification: Provision, Process, and Consummation," *Journal of Pentecostal Theology* 18, no. 1 (2009): 69 and Dane C. Ortlund, *Edwards on the Christian Life: Alive to the Beauty of God* (Wheaton, IL: Crossway, 2019), 43.

[18] Edwards, *A Spiritual Understanding of Divine Things Denied to the Unregenerate*, WJE 14:81. See also Edwards, *Religious Affections*, WJE 2:395, on a change in nature.

Justification is more than a forensic declaration. Edwards appears to have inherited a number of theological assumptions from New England Puritanism.[19] These included an affirmation of an absolute exercise of divine sovereignty and a concomitant belief that salvation depends upon God's grace alone for its cause.[20] Not even faith can be considered a cause of one's salvation.[21] Rather than the sinner seeking God for salvation and attempting to obey the moral commandments, God's act of regeneration is what inaugurates holiness and obedience in the one justified (the saint).[22] In this, Edwards affirms the "legal and transactional" understanding of justification in the Reformed tradition. The Father imputes Christ's righteousness to the Christian and accepts the Christian as though he or she had performed righteously.[23] This makes justification "forensic," a legal declaration rather than an ontological reality. Even faith is a gift to the Christian from God, rather than any sort of righteous work, or godly obedience.[24] The Holy Spirit communicates grace and the character of Christ to the Christian. However, this grace is not something the Holy Spirit mediates or implants in the Christian. This grace, which is the new principle in the heart, is the Spirit, himself, who "communicates himself in his own proper nature."[25] This self-giving of the Spirit becomes a new disposition—a new tendency, inclination, or mode of operation—which becomes a new "foundation" for everything the Christian loves or does.[26] Yet, since the Holy Spirit neither becomes a new "faculty" within the soul nor is the Christian "Godded with God," or made a partaker of the essence of God, these remain alien to the Christian's nature.[27] To illustrate, we might say that the Holy Spirit "re-wires" the soul so that the soul operates differently, but all of the "wiring" is actually the Holy Spirit himself. If we remove the Spirit, we remove the disposition.

Since, in the Reformed view, justification ("salvation" in American revivalist terms) is wholly by grace and not based on any merit or infusion of righteousness in the one justified, all talk of transformation is excluded from the ideation of justification in order to avoid any hint that justification is based on a meritorious work, or even a meritorious being in the sense of ontological good in the Christian or the Christian's nature. Justification is the product of a kind of (intellectual) knowledge or apprehension of God.[28] Reformed theologians strongly assert that the "declaration of justification

---

[19] Norman Fiering, "The Rationalist Foundations of Jonathan Edwards' Metaphysics," in *Jonathan Edwards and the American Experience*, ed. Nathan O. Hatch and Harry S. Stout (New York: Oxford University Press, 1988), 78.
[20] Ibid., 79.
[21] Samuel T. Logan, Jr., "The Doctrine of Justification in the Theology of Jonathan Edwards," *Wesleyan Theological Journal* 46, no. 1 (1984): 41.
[22] Breitenbach, "Piety and Moralism," 179.
[23] Edwards, *Justification by Faith Alone*, WJE 19:174.
[24] Kyle Strobel, "By Word and Spirit: Jonathan Edwards on Redemption, Justification, and Regeneration," in *Jonathan Edwards and Justification*, ed. Josh Moody (Wheaton, IL: Crossway, 2012), 51.
[25] Edwards, *Religious Affections*, WJE 2:201.
[26] Ibid., 200, 206.
[27] Ibid., 206, 203. See Allen, *Justification and the Gospel*, 46, 47, 52.
[28] See, for example, Eberhard Jüngel, *Justification: The Heart of the Christian Faith: A Theological Study with an Ecumenical Purpose*, trans. Jeffrey F. Cayzer (Edinburgh: T&T Clark, 2001), 17–18, 227–29.

itself does not have a transformative power."[29] Because of this, at least one Pentecostal theologian has charged that the Reformed view of forensic justification is "empty" and meaningless.[30]

However, we misunderstand Edwards if we focus on the forensic declaration of justification as "empty" because it does not make a substantial change in the believer.[31] We must remember that, for Edwards and the Reformed tradition, the declaration of justification is one event in a series of saving acts of God, a series that begins with a gift of grace that regenerates the soul, and culminates in the declaration of justification.[32] Forensic justification describes how we are declared righteous without works, but does not express the whole of the transaction between God and human persons. No Reformed view actually leaves out some kind of transformation that is linked to justification. For the Reformed, salvation begins with God's calling and effectual grace, often seen as essentially the same thing. This gift of an irresistible and efficacious grace is not forensic, but is transformative. While this is not considered under the rubric of "justification" by Reformed thinkers, justification is always paired with regeneration, which *is* transformative. Calvin states that repentance "requires transformation . . . in the soul itself," which "comes to pass when the Spirit of God . . . imbues our souls."[33] This imbuement crucifies the old man and restores the soul in regeneration.[34] Both Calvin and Edwards put regeneration before justification in their *ordo salutis*.[35]

By means of this gift of grace, those elected to become Christians are changed. This grace reorders their affections and awakens their consciences. Thus, I point out that justification is never *merely* forensic. Most Reformed writers will not make the link between regeneration with justification explicit, and Edwards himself did not attempt to

---

The stress on reason or knowledge comes from an emphasis on the role of the Word, which engages the rational faculties, including the conscience, in justification (Jüngel, *Justification*, 198–204).

[29] Strobel, "By Word and Spirit," 58.

[30] Frank D. Macchia makes this charge in two recent works, *Baptized in the Spirit: A Global Pentecostal Theology* (Grand Rapids, MI: Zondervan, 2006), 137 and *Justified in the Spirit: Creation, Redemption, and the Triune God* (Grand Rapids, MI: Eerdmans, 2010), 59–60, 72. For a critique and answer to Macchia's position, see Jeffrey Anderson, "Justification as the Speech of the Spirit" (PhD diss., Regent University, 2015).

[31] R. Michael Allen deals with objections to forensic justification as "empty" in *Justification and the Gospel*, 128–37. However, the force of his argument (and that of Eberhard Jüngel whom he cites) is lessened because he seems to understand justification as derived from the knowledge of the good versus a regeneration of the heart, as well as the fact that neither he nor Jüngel explain how a "spontaneous gratitude" (Jüngel, *Justification*, 259, cited in Allen, *Justification and the Gospel*, 129) should arise in the soul.

[32] Josh Moody reminds us that the idea of a supernatural event of a new creation in regeneration is "what rescues justification from the dusty tomes of the law court exegesis to a living entity." See Josh Moody, "Introduction," in *Jonathan Edwards and Justification*, ed. Josh Moody (Wheaton, IL: Crossway, 2012), 13.

[33] John Calvin, *Institutes of the Christian Religion*, ed. John T. McNeil, trans. Ford Lewis Battles, The Library of Christian Classics 20 (Philadelphia, PA: The Westminster Press, 1960), 3.3.6 (pp. 598–99) and 3.3.8 (p. 600).

[34] Ibid., 3.3.9 (pp. 600–2).

[35] Ibid., 3.3.1 (pp. 592–93). Also see Anri Morimoto, *Jonathan Edwards and the Catholic Vision of Salvation* (University Park, PA: The Pennsylvania State University Press, 1995), 110 (cf. 7, 39) and Sang Hyun Lee, "Editor's Introduction," *WJE* 21:40.

relate his thoughts on conversion to the doctrine of justification.[36] However, according to Morimoto, Edwards saw all such terms as calling, regeneration, conversion, and sanctification "all mean one of the same grace infused by the instantaneous work of God."[37] This close association of terms is familiar to Pentecostal thinkers, who generally relate both concepts of conversion and justification to the larger theme, or event, of "salvation." For Pentecostals the distinction between these concepts is negligible. Edwards' understanding of grace as the presence and work of the person of the Holy Spirit means that we may view Edwards as grounding justification in a transforming relationship between himself and the Christian, even while Edwards insists that justification is "forensic." In regeneration, the Holy Spirit unites the Christian to Christ and "infuses" the soul with grace, which gives to the Christian a love for God and holiness.[38] For Edwards, regeneration is an instantaneous act and not a process, but the result is an alteration in the saint's nature.[39] Touched by the light of the sun, the saint's nature is changed and becomes a little sun.[40] Because justification is simultaneous with or even comes after regeneration/conversion, rather than being an "empty" declaration, forensic justification is part of a supernatural and transformative event that alters or restores the human soul. As Edwards puts it, "No light of understanding is good, which don't produce holy affection in the heart; no habit or principal in the heart is good, which has no exercise; and no external fruit is good, which don't proceed from such exercises."[41]

It is Edwards' idea of the work of the Holy Spirit as the grace of the Father that elevates and deepens his view of conversion as regeneration that results in justification.[42] Edwards will maintain that the new principle or disposition that makes one holy is the active presence of the Holy Spirit, and not something owned by the human person.[43] In this sense, justification is "forensic," for the holiness that is the basis of the believer's acquittal never belongs to the believer. There is no "grace" mediated to the person by the Holy Spirit (which becomes part of the human person). The grace is the Holy Spirit himself.[44] Even though conversion appears to come before justification, salvation is dependent on the continual work of God through the Holy Spirit, who is the new disposition of the soul. Grace never becomes "encapsulated in a static human quality,"[45]

---

[36] Morimoto, *Edwards and the Catholic Vision*, 72, 73. Breitenbach, "Piety and Moralism," 191.
[37] Ibid., 39.
[38] Strobel, "By Word and Spirit," 58–59.
[39] Edwards, *Religious Affections*, WJE 2:340.
[40] Ibid., 343.
[41] Ibid., 119.
[42] Studebaker and Caldwell, *Trinitarian Theology of Jonathan Edwards*, 179. This is not to say that Reformed writers completely ignore the transformation worked in the believer's life (see Moody, *Edwards and Justification*, 21, for example). However, they do not grant enough force to the personal work of the Spirit in justification/regeneration as transformation.
[43] Sang Hyun Lee, "Grace and Justification by Faith Alone," in *The Princeton Companion to Jonathan Edwards*, ed. Sang Hyun Lee (Princeton, NJ: Princeton University Press, 2005), 135.
[44] Edwards, *Treatise on Grace*, WJE 21:192. See Steven Studebaker's discussion of David Coffey's theology of the Holy Spirit in "Beyond Tongues: A Pentecostal Theology of Grace," in *Defining Issues in Pentecostalism: Classical and Emergent*, ed. Steven M. Studebaker, McMaster Theological Studies (Eugene, OR: Wipf & Stock, 2008), 64.
[45] Morimoto, *Edwards and the Catholic Vision*, 7; see also Lee, "Grace and Justification," 135.

and the holiness that is the ground of the "forensic" declaration is God's holiness rather than any human achievement. Therefore, in this sense, justification is "forensic," but it is never apart from the transformation of conversion. The fact that Edwards does not explain justification as conversion systematically does not alter this conclusion. This work of the Holy Spirit in the soul unites the Christian to the life of Christ. On the one hand, the Spirit gives a gift of faith in the heart of, or makes faith possible for, the Christian. On the other hand, this faith joins the Christian to the trinitarian life of God by the presence and work of the Holy Spirit.[46] This relationship between the believer and Christ is a union, and this union is "the ground of [the Christian's] right to his benefits," for "our being in him is the ground of our being accepted."[47] Accomplished by the Holy Spirit, this union is not metaphorical but a real, dynamic, and experiential joining that causes the Christian to be "in Christ." This union "makes Christ and the believer one in the acceptance of the Supreme Judge," and is the one "qualification" that allows the Father to accept the Christian and grant him an interest in the benefits of the atonement.[48] Although Edwards does use the term "metaphorical," it seems quite clear that he understood this union as an ontological reality. When "faith unites us to Christ [it is not] a dormant principle in the heart, but as being."[49] The idea of a mystical union seems quite Pentecostal.

Justification comes by the transformation of the indwelling Holy Spirit. Since justification cannot be declared of any person, unless and until the new disposition of the presence of the Holy Spirit abides and works in that person, we must acknowledge that justification is accompanied—at the least—by a transformation. While "forensic" in the sense that the holiness upon which the believer's acquittal rests is never a human accomplishment, justification is grounded in the transforming presence of the Holy Spirit as a new disposition in the soul.

Dane C. Ortlund considers this idea of a new spiritual sense to be one of Edwards' chief contributions to theology.[50] However, Edwards' understanding of justification is not a "spiritual sense" awakened in the human person, but is pneumatological and so is focused on the work of the Holy Spirit. By his presence and work in the soul, the Holy Spirit reorders the affections and joins the justified person to the eschatological fullness of God. The Holy Spirit himself enters into and joins with the Christian, and it is the personal work of the Holy Spirit that restructures or restores the human soul, and so enables the saint to love and to consent to the excellency of God.[51]

Justification comes to the believer as part of the "unition" forged by the Holy Spirit between the believer and Christ.[52] This union is a participation in Christ, and this means that the Christian's holiness and righteousness, on which his justification stands, is something that is always "alien" to the Christian in that it resides in God

---

[46] Edwards, *Justification by Faith Alone*, WJE 19:156. I am indebted to Steven M. Studebaker for this reference and for bringing to my attention the idea of "union," or "unition" as Edwards says, and the references to the idea in Edwards' sermon.
[47] Ibid., 157.
[48] Ibid., 159.
[49] Ibid., 208.
[50] Ortlund, *Edwards on the Christian Life*, 42.
[51] Cf. Hoopes, "Edwards' Religious Psychology," 853 and Breitenbach, "Piety and Moralism," 182.
[52] Edwards, *Justification by Faith Alone*, WJE 19:156; see note 42, above.

and is brought to the Christian only by the abiding presence of the Holy Spirit, and so justifying holiness is still something "outside" of the Christian (*extra nos*) and not a *habitus* or something possessed by the Christian.[53] Even though the Holy Spirit works in and through the natural powers of the regenerate person, acts of love are still the Spirit's work.[54] If we possessed righteousness in ourselves, it would no longer be the work of the Spirit in us, and our union with Christ would fail.

The question is how this alien righteousness is communicated to the Christian and to what extent it changes one.[55] What does it mean to be united to Christ, or to have grace infused into one? We can only understand all of this as the gift of the presence of the Holy Spirit. Not a mere enlightened intellect or restored cognitive faculty, the Holy Spirit himself is the "foundation" or "principle" of new life in the saints, the "vital principle in their souls."[56] He is the Lover that draws the saint into the embrace of and participation in the love of the Trinity.[57] As Steven M. Studebaker argues, the idea that grace is the Holy Spirit himself is at the center of Edwards' doctrine of salvation.[58] The Holy Spirit as grace transforms the disposition of the soul, and that transformation (in regeneration) is the essence of redemption.[59] While I believe that we must maintain a forensic sense in justification, the forensic element is never "empty," that is apart from the transformation of the soul.[60]

This goes beyond the idea of the "seal" or "stamp" of the Holy Spirit spoken of in Eph. 1:13. Although such a seal leaves a permanent stamp or mark on the heart of the converted soul, Edwards makes this more comprehensive and compares the work of the Spirit in regeneration to raising the dead or a new creation.[61] Salvation is restorative; "in the new birth we become human again" as God restores the Christian's "true self."[62] Only divine power is able to grant the soul such a change of nature, and this change means that holiness is in the soul as a disposition that enables the saint to will to do good.[63] While there may be some degree of backsliding, the saint is so transformed

---

[53] Jüngel, *Justification*, 192.
[54] Lee, "Grace and Justification," 135.
[55] Strobel, "By Word and Spirit," 58.
[56] Edwards, *Religious Affections*, WJE 2:201, for his full discussion, see 200–7. Breitenbach comes closer to understanding that it is the work of the Holy Spirit himself when he states that the new principle is holiness, which is communicated to the soul when the Holy Spirit dwells within. See Breitenbach, "Piety and Moralism," 182.
[57] Studebaker, "Beyond Tongues," 57, 62 and Allen, *Justification and the Gospel*, 66.
[58] Studebaker and Caldwell, *Trinitarian Theology of Jonathan Edwards*, 171. Studebaker's pneumatology is robustly trinitarian, and he shows that the entire Trinity is involved in justification and transformation.
[59] Ibid., 185.
[60] Allen states that there must be a forensic element in justification in *Justification and the Gospel*, 59. I doubt that he would agree with the second part of my statement.
[61] Edwards, *Religious Affections*, WJE 2:206 and 232.
[62] Ortlund, *Edwards on the Christian Life*, 49. This is Ortlund's language, but note that Ortlund believes that Edwards falls short of this idea, because Edwards does not acknowledge that the unregenerate are also made in God's image. However, Edwards' Augustinian viewpoint does not mean that he sees the unregenerate as lacking the *imago Dei*, but only that the deranged affections of the broken image mean that the unregenerate are evil in their loves and loyalties.
[63] Roger A. Ward, "Experience as Religious Discovery in Edwards and Peirce," in *The Contribution of Jonathan Edwards to American Culture and Society: Essays on America's Spiritual Founding Father [the Northampton Tercentenary Celebration, 1703-2003]* (Lewiston, NY: Edwin Mellen Press, 2008), 211.

by new desires, changing what he or she fundamentally wants, that he or she cannot entirely return to an untransformed existence.[64] In this way, justification "fuels" sanctification, the presence and work of the Holy Spirit changing the architecture of the soul and making sanctification both possible and imperative in the life of the saint.[65] Yet justification is not the same as the lifestyle of obedience that is commonly referred to as "sanctification."

Edwards' ideas about our union with Christ through the work and presence of the person of the Holy Spirit seem quite congruent with the emphasis on the Holy Spirit in Pentecostal thought. I turn to a consideration of Pentecostal ideas of justification. I first contrast two "classical" Pentecostals, one thinker from the "Finished Work" Pentecostal school and one from the Wesleyan-Holiness tradition. I then examine the more recent work of Frank Macchia.

Pentecostals and justification

In discussing the views of Pentecostals, I will first consider two "classical" pentecostal thinkers who each represent one of the two major schools of classical pentecostal thought, the Holiness-Pentecostal and the Finished Work Pentecostal.[66] As Classical Pentecostals, both streams carry a heritage from the Reformation and emphasize justification by faith. A theology of crisis-conversion influences both, and both stress the cross as the starting place for a new beginning.[67] Along with the thought of John Calvin (and John Wesley), the justification of the sinner is generally seen as a work of the Son, and the sanctification of the saint is seen as the work of the Holy Spirit.[68] As Veli-Matti Kärkkäinen notes, "The theological and Spiritual center of Pentecostalism is Christ and Christology. Consequently, it is Christ who stands at the center of the Pentecostal 'Full Gospel.'"[69] It is in holiness and sanctification, rather than in justification, that Pentecostals primarily see the work and ministry of the Holy Spirit.[70] While a high view of the work of Christ is a Pentecostal hallmark, the exclusion of consideration of the work of the Holy Spirit in justification is a weakness in Pentecostal

---

[64] Hoopes, "Edwards' Religious Psychology," 860 and Ortlund, *Edwards on the Christian Life*, 42, 43.
[65] This is Allen's term in *Justification and the Gospel*, 143. Interestingly, Allen ascribes the Christian's new freedom from bondage to sin to a "conscious self-identification with the person of Jesus." Thus, Allen is stressing the Christian's action after justification, rather than the Spirit's work in justification as with Edwards.
[66] For an analysis of the history and beliefs of these two groups of Pentecostals, see Henry I. Lederle, *Treasures Old and New: Interpretations of "Spirit-Baptism" in the Charismatic Renewal Movement* (Peabody, MA: Hendrickson, 1988). Story, "Pauline Thoughts," also discusses the history and beliefs of the two schools from a Finished Work point of view. For an account of the Pentecostal movement from a Holiness perspective, see Vinson Synan, *The Holiness-Pentecostal Movement in the United States* (Grand Rapids, MI: Eerdmans, 1971) and Donald W. Dayton, *Theological Roots of Pentecostalism* (Grand Rapids, MI: Zondervan, 1987).
[67] Jean-Daniel Plüss, "Pentecostal Grace: From A Forensic Notion to A Pneumatological Reality," *Asian Journal of Pentecostal Studies* 15, no. 1 (2012): 75–76.
[68] Plüss, "Pentecostal Grace," 79.
[69] Veli-Matti Kärkkäinen, "A Full Gospel Ecclesiology of *Koinonia*: Pentecostal Contributions to the Doctrine of the Church," in *Renewal History and Theology: Essays in Honor of H. Vinson Synan*, ed. S. David Moore and James M. Henderson (Cleveland, TN: CPT, 2014), 179.
[70] Ibid., 185.

theology and perpetuates a Western tendency to minimize the role and personhood of the Holy Spirit.[71]

Twentieth-century Finished Work theology. Guy P. Duffield is still considered the chief theologian of the International Church of the Foursquare Gospel. As a Finished Work thinker, Duffield shows a clear affinity with the Reformed understanding of justification and positional sanctification.[72] He discusses both justification and sanctification under "the doctrine of salvation."[73] Sanctification is primarily a result of justification and only treated secondarily under the rubric of the work of the Holy Spirit.[74] Duffield makes justification dependent upon and a result of the work of Christ in his death and, especially, his resurrection.[75] He explains justification and sanctification equally as applications of the provision of salvation through the death of Christ.

Duffield expounds justification in primarily forensic terms, and distinguishes it from regeneration. Justification is God's declaration that the one justified is righteous in his eyes. It is a legal term and has to do primarily with being acquitted of guilt and avoiding condemnation. It is a forensic declaration that restores one to God's favor through the imputation of Christ's righteousness.[76] This righteousness does not make the sinner a righteous person, only one who is acquitted.[77]

Duffield treats regeneration alongside justification, but he does not explain the relationship between the two. Regeneration is the same as the new birth, which is not a change of heart in the sense of changing one's loyalty, but a cleansing and a new creation. Regeneration is a resurrection of the believer into a new kind of life that "makes the believer a new creation, and a partaker of the divine nature."[78] While this regeneration does imply some kind of transformation, he does not explicitly explain it as a transformation and does not consider the question of what changes in the essence or structure of the soul when one becomes a new creation. Duffield implies idea of positional sanctification under the rubric of adoption, which follows regeneration in the text. He explains positional sanctification in the subsequent section on sanctification.[79] The saint is considered "sanctified" in the sense that God sees the saint through the lens of Christ, as it were, and so as absolutely holy and free from defect.

Duffield describes sanctification as having a primary and a secondary meaning. The primary meaning is that of "dedication, consecration, or setting apart for some specific

---

[71] Steven M. Studebaker makes this point in "Beyond Tongues," 46–50; see also "Pentecostal Soteriology and Pneumatology," *Journal of Pentecostal Theology* 11, no. 2 (2003): 250.
[72] Guy P. Duffield and Nathaniel M. Van Cleave, *Foundations of Pentecostal Theology* (Los Angeles: L. I. F. E. Bible College of Los Angeles, 1983).
[73] Ibid., 173–260.
[74] Ibid., 236–45, 276–83.
[75] A discussion of the resurrection of Christ and proofs of the resurrection occupy eleven quarto pages, with the ascension and glorification of Christ extending this section by four pages, at the end of the discussion of the basis and provision of salvation—ibid., 193–206.
[76] Ibid., 220–22.
[77] Ibid., 223–27.
[78] Ibid., 234, see pages 228–34.
[79] Ibid., 234–36.

and holy use."[80] This sanctification is "positional," and refers to the imputation of Christ's righteousness to the believer. Duffield calls the secondary act of sanctification, making the Christian obedient to God's will and Christ-like in character, a "process" and "practical" in the sense that it expresses itself in the Christian's lifestyle.[81]

Regarding justification, both Duffield and Edwards speak of the necessity of God's grace and the work of the Holy Spirit in initiating salvation. The primary differences between Edwards' understanding of justification and Duffield's is that, while Duffield concurs that grace is the first element in justification, grace itself does not bring about a transformation. The gift of grace here is "prevenient" grace, rather than the "effectual" grace that regenerates one without any prior consent. Prevenient grace allows a person the choice of believing or not, what I have called a "resting" in grace, a ceasing to resist the Holy Spirit rather than an act of obedience, but this choice goes before any sort of transformation in regeneration, and does not derive from a regeneration already accomplished.[82] This idea that faith precedes regeneration marks Finished Work Pentecostalism as Arminian, although it is not Wesleyan. Regeneration logically follows the (resting) choice of faith and justification. Regeneration then completes and makes permanent the transformation that the Holy Spirit began as a kind of temporary work in the form of prevenient grace.

Twentieth-century Holiness-pentecostal theology. As an example of the Wesleyan-Holiness-pentecostal view, I turn now to R. Hollis Gause, a theologian of the Church of God (Cleveland, Tennessee). In his work *Living in the Spirit: The Way of Salvation*, the primary focus is living according to the Holy Spirit who is present in one's life through the distinct experience of the baptism in the Holy Spirit.[83] Baptism in the Holy Spirit is the "pinnacle of the mountain." Concerning salvation, the experiences of repentance, justification, adoption, and regeneration are "initial" experiences and not the final experience. According to Amos Yong, seeing salvation as a "way" rather than an event, or series of events, helps one to avoid speculative debates or a seemingly arbitrary sequence of disassociated events and grounds salvation in the human response of repentance that is essential to holiness.[84] Gause begins with repentance as the gift of divine grace, which leads to justification, adoption, regeneration, and sanctification. I will discuss these, briefly, in turn.[85]

---

[80] Ibid., 237.
[81] Ibid., 237–39.
[82] See my chapter, "The Holy Spirit in Election: Renewal and Empowerment," in *Renewal History and Theology: Essays in Honor of H. Vinson Synan*, ed. S. David Moore and James M. Henderson (Cleveland, TN: CPT, 2014), 157–74. For a further discussion, see Chapter 3, "Election as Renewal: The Empowerment of the Holy Spirit," in James M. Henderson, "Election as Renewal: The Work of the Holy Spirit in Divine Election" (PhD diss., Regent University, 2012).
[83] R. Hollis Gause, *Living in the Spirit: The Way of Salvation*, rev. and expanded ed. (Cleveland, TN: CPT, 2009). I am aware that Dr. Gause lived well into the twenty-first century, but I take his viewpoint to be one characteristic of Wesleyan thought of the twentieth century.
[84] Amos Yong, *Renewing Christian Theology: Systematics for a Global Community* (Waco, TX: Baylor University Press, 2014), 229.
[85] I believe that Gause intends "salvation" to be thought of as the entire spectrum of the Christian life, from its beginning and on through the Christian's entire life to its completion. Otherwise, I believe that the terms justification and sanctification refer to the same experiences, though not to the same results, as Edwards, above.

Repentance is a renewal of the mind that convicts one of guilt and corruption. It is not an act so much as a penitential way of life, one of continual assessment of one's manner of living.[86] Repentance is not the same as regeneration, but is a work of grace that changes "the entire nature of human personality: mind, emotions, and will."[87] It is prompted by God's holiness, that is, his ethical purity, as demonstrated in the law which condemns sinful humanity and which requires a human response of continual repentance.[88] This grace allows one to live a penitential lifestyle, which is necessary since "repentance is one of the processes of Spiritual living that is perpetuated in the cultivation of holiness and the Holy Spirit filled life."[89]

Justification is a "judicial act" of declarative judgment, declaring (the believer) to be righteous before God. This declaration is rooted in the act of obedience to Christ, which then further transforms the believer, so that one becomes a partaker in the divine nature, but is still primarily a forensic act, which occurs along with the other "initial" acts of salvation.[90] The link between justification and the penitential lifestyle is that justification—God's declaration of not guilty—"is a judgment concerning past sins, and not future sins. Future sins will be forgiven as they are confessed and forsaken," in the penitential lifestyle, rather than in the initial experience of justification.[91] Gause is quite emphatic that the "obedience of faith" (Rom. 1:5) is necessary to salvation, meaning that one will not continue to commit sins.[92] While the atonement, not merely the death but also the obedient life of Christ, makes the believer "in actual fact righteous" (and is not a judicial fiction), justification does not "carry with it a state of righteousness" in the sense of a fixed identity or ontological state.[93] Continuing justification is based on faith, which always carries with it obedience in repentance and confession.[94] Oddly, Gause will say in one section that justification causes a spiritual transformation that is particularly the product of the love of the Holy Spirit poured out in the Christian's heart.[95] In this sense, justification melds into regeneration, but it appears that this regeneration is dependent on a process of justification through continual penitence. In this way, Gause not only avoids an "empty" forensic justification but also appears to say that justification is entirely dependent on a process of experiential sanctification in the lifestyle of the Christian.

Gause explains regeneration under two rubrics: that of the new birth and that of adoption. Regeneration is a creative act that implants the "seed of the life of Christ" and brings about a new creation in Christ.[96] The agents of this new birth are the Word (the Bible) and the Spirit of God. The new birth is a radical change in both origin

---

[86] Gause, *Living in the Spirit*, 2. The initial chapter on "Repentance unto Life" is immediately followed by a chapter on "Living the Penitential Life," making this emphasis clear.
[87] Ibid., 8.
[88] Ibid., 9–17, 22.
[89] Ibid., 27.
[90] Ibid., 3, 46.
[91] Ibid., 49.
[92] Ibid., 49n18, 52n20.
[93] Ibid., 54n24, 56.
[94] Ibid., 58.
[95] Ibid., 66–67, also see pages 62–64.
[96] Ibid., 4.

and nature. In language that seems to echo that of Edwards, this creative act of God produces a "new heart," as a new "seed of life is implanted in the governing disposition of the soul is made holy."[97] However, Gause does not see this as a permanent change or formation in the heart. This renewal is dependent on an ongoing obedience to God, so that one stops sinning. This idea of living life in complete submission to God is carried on in the next chapter about adoption, which focuses on how the believer comes under the government of God, to come into conformity with the nature of the law of God.[98] The twin bases of this new life (of adoption) are, first, the presence of the resurrected Lord Jesus, whose presence requires the crucifixion of the flesh, and, second, the presence of the Holy Spirit, which is the "route to the fulfillment of the law."[99]

Twenty-first-century pentecostal theology. In the twenty-first century, some Pentecostal authors have begun to examine the idea of what justification means as a relationship to the Holy Spirit.[100] Frank D. Macchia's *Justified in the Spirit* is one such examination, which explains a view of justification that centers more on the work of the Holy Spirit than is usual in Western theology.[101] He addresses his work to the wider Christian body and seeks to take a global point of view. Macchia criticizes many Protestant thinkers for limiting the Holy Spirit's work in justification to the function of inspiring faith in the gospel.[102] Macchia notes that Augustine believed that the Spirit was necessary to assist the will in turning to God, but Augustine took a "distinctly anthropological turn in his understanding of justification" in his debate with the Pelagians.[103] This focus on grace as the creation of human capacity intensifies from the time of Augustine through the thirteenth century, and takes the church's attention away from the person and work of the Holy Spirit himself.[104]

Macchia attributes justification to the reality of the indwelling Holy Spirit. Human cooperation is primarily through participation in the Holy Spirit's interior work, as part of being caught up in "one's participation in the triune life."[105] While this may be a form of synergy, it is not an "autonomous self-acting," which makes the claim of righteousness on God.[106] This is because the Spirit is fundamental to human existence, and grace now "constitutes what it means to be human by the Spirit of God."[107] The presence of the Holy Spirit is a new principle of divine life in the one who is justified.[108] The justified person is caught up into the divine embrace and participates in the

---

[97] Ibid., 74, 76.
[98] Ibid., 80–92, especially 83.
[99] Ibid., 86.
[100] A Foursquare scholar who improves on Guy Duffield's work and anticipates Macchia's *Justified in the Spirit* is J. Lyle Story, in his "Pauline Thoughts." Story discusses both justification and sanctification as works of the Holy Spirit.
[101] Macchia, *Justified in the Spirit.*
[102] Ibid., 5.
[103] Ibid., 16. Macchia refers to Augustine's *De perfectione justicia hominis* in *St. Augustine's Anti-Pelagian Works,* trans. Peter Holmes, and Robert Ernest Wallis, Nicene and Post-Nicene Fathers, 1st series, ed. Philip Schaff (reprint; Peabody, MA: Hendrickson, 1994), 5:19 (p. 40).
[104] Macchia, *Justified in the Spirit,* 18, see also 22.
[105] Ibid., 25.
[106] Ibid., 26.
[107] Ibid., 30.
[108] Ibid., 33.

life of the Trinity.¹⁰⁹ Macchia sees such participation in divine life as contrary to a forensic declaration, God declaring the sinner not guilty, as distinct from a properly pneumatological view of justification. Forensic justification and the imputation of Christ's righteousness are "empty" and do not lead one into spiritual renewal.¹¹⁰ Macchia prefers a view more like the idea of *theosis* promoted by Tuomo Mannermaa's analysis of the thought of Martin Luther.¹¹¹

Justification is, then, primarily, participation in Christ through the pneumatological reality of being caught up into the communion of the Trinity through the presence and work of Holy Spirit. This is the Spirit's distinct work as the "go-between God."¹¹² Macchia emphasizes the idea that justification is a transformation by the work and presence of the Holy Spirit. Part of the reason for this is that he wishes to press against the idea of a theology of "justification by faith" that does not include an interior transformation by the Holy Spirit. Such imputation "removes any possibility of justification involving the renewal of the believer."¹¹³ Macchia adduces the works of Luther and Calvin as well as modern thinkers to support his assertion that "the Spirit is at the very substance of justification as a divine act," first in Christ as Son and in Christ as the Spirit baptizer.¹¹⁴ This grounds justification on an "objective Pneumatology" that is Christological and trinitarian.¹¹⁵

This sounds much like the thought of Jonathan Edwards, noted above. Like Edwards, Macchia rejects the idea that one must first receive a created grace or habitus that elevates the soul and facilitates the indwelling of the Spirit. Such an idea reinforces the "creaturification" of the salvation process and removes it further from a process of divinization (*theosis*).¹¹⁶ Macchia draws from modern Roman Catholic writers such as Hans Küng and Henri de Lubac, as well as Eastern Orthodox thinkers such as Vladimir Lossky, when he asserts that justification is a synergy including the work of the Holy Spirit and the (empowered) individual that arises from the hypostatic union or mutual indwelling of Spirit and human.¹¹⁷ Unlike Edwards, Macchia identifies justification with the "Baptism in the Holy Spirit" and the continuing life of sanctification that this baptism empowers.

---

¹⁰⁹ Ibid., 215.
¹¹⁰ Ibid., 45, 46. Steven Studebaker ("Pentecostal Soteriology," 250) agrees with Macchia, and believes that a "redemptive justification" view, as he puts it, is much more in line with the Pentecostal ethos than a Reformed forensic view of justification.
¹¹¹ Macchia, *Justified in the Spirit*, 51, 52. Studebaker states ("Pentecostal Soteriology," 266–67) that "redemptive justification" is much closer to the Roman Catholic model of justification than to the Reformed forensic model.
¹¹² Ibid., 53, quote p. 54.
¹¹³ Ibid., 59–60.
¹¹⁴ In an earlier work, Macchia accepted James D. G. Dunn's conclusion that "Spirit baptism" refers to justification and regeneration as the initiatory acts of God in saving and rectifying the sinner. See Macchia, *Baptized in the Spirit*.
¹¹⁵ Macchia, *Justified in the Spirit*, 131, 133. Amos Yong, another twenty-first-century Pentecostal voice, accepts Macchia's understanding of justification as primarily participation in the work of the Holy Spirit and the Son (as sanctifier, empowerer, healer, and coming king), in "an encounter with the triune God along the way of salvation." See Yong, *Renewing Christian Theology*, 230.
¹¹⁶ Macchia, *Justified in the Spirit*, 22.
¹¹⁷ Macchia, *Justified in the Spirit*, 23–26, 28.

Sanctification

As I turn to the matter of sanctification, the authors I discuss have an understanding of justification that is strongly rooted in their understanding of sanctification. For Edwards, justification and transformation are simply two ways of describing the same salvific event of the Holy Spirit laying hold upon the individual soul, abiding there, and by his presence and power transforming the inner affections or, one might say, the moral architecture of the soul.

Edwards and sanctification

As we have already noted, Edwards considered justification to be a transformative event where the Holy Spirit becomes present and resident in the soul, and by that presence and power restores the soul or rearranges the deranged affections of the soul. This work of the Spirit changes the "disposition" of the soul, the soul's aims, and its moral architecture. This is congruent with the Reformed idea of a "positional sanctification" that is based on the merits of Christ. However, Edwards appears to move beyond the general Reformed idea to understand that the Spirit has already worked a significant "sanctification" in changing the soul's disposition. What remains is for the Christian to actuate this potential in a lifestyle of obedience and Christ-likeness that becomes outwardly visible.

In some sense, justification is conditioned on obedience, since obedience is the necessary outcome of justification.[118] Edwards expects that the new principle of the heart will result in a life of continuing obedience, flowing out of a continuing repentance and faith.[119] However, the relation here is one of obedience proving that one has been (completely) justified, rather than obedience driving a process of justification, and this is brought about as a result of our "unition" with Christ.[120] The desire for God and to obey God in a lifestyle that grows in outward conformity to God's will is the proof of, as well as the product of, justification. Regeneration "inaugurates holiness and obedience in the saint" by bringing a holy temper to the affections of the heart.[121] Edwards argued in his *Religious Affections* that the best evidence of a genuine conversion was the ability to withstand "trials of grace" because of the new sense of the heart.[122] In fact, having a new sense of the heart or a new principle within the heart would be worthless without the external exercise and fruit of a sanctified lifestyle.[123] Regeneration so transforms the human heart/soul that real obedience is possible. Thus, we are sanctified positionally,

---

[118] Logan, "The Doctrine of Justification," 41. Allen (*Justification and the Gospel*, 127–51) makes this same argument under the rubric of "Freedom for Love."
[119] Edwards, *Justification by Faith*, WJE 19:204, 208.
[120] Ibid., 208.
[121] Breitenbach, "Piety and Moralism," 179, 191.
[122] Ava Chamberlain, "Self-Deception as a Theological Problem in Jonathan Edwards's 'Treatise Concerning Religious Affections,'" *Church History*, 63 no. 4 (December 1994): 544.
[123] Edwards, *Religious Affections*, WJE 2:119. Edwards here proposes that it is a changed lifestyle that is the true judge of whether or not the "high affections" of a person who has a revival experience were given by the Holy Spirit.

but also ontologically to the degree that obeying God from the heart is possible (and so demanded).[124] Thus, the new affections that the Holy Spirit gives to the soul are, indeed, "effectual in practice," since one's lifestyle is simply the expression of the disposition of the soul.[125]

This is neither to say that Edwards viewed sanctification in terms of the adherence to church codes nor that he required perfection from the justified, and so sanctified, saint. Edwards did believe that the Holy Spirit thoroughly changed the disposition, the appetites, aims, and desires of the heart in justification, as the Spirit gave himself to the believer, but, as humans, believers are fallen and one's growth or journey to maturity is "wandering and slow."[126] However, obedience from the heart is possible because of the Christian's participation in the Spirit's work and because of the Holy Spirit abiding in the Christian in a transformative relationship.[127] The Holy Spirit communicates to the saint the love of the Father and of the Son, and so the saint returns that love to God.[128] This return is the natural expression of what is already in the heart of the saint. As Ortlund puts it, "Edwards' legacy . . . was that sanctification is inside-out and we lose it if we make it outside-in." The human person cannot see change by using a crowbar to align one's behavior with an external moral code or set of rules. "We obey as we see and taste beauty."[129]

Such obedience from the heart is the essence of sanctification, but even here, the Christian cannot boast in a righteousness that inheres in or is possessed by the human soul. We have no basis for boasting, because, even while obedience should grow throughout the Christian's life, it is participation in the Holy Spirit that drives the process, rather than the process causing a greater sanctification in the heart of the saint. Holiness is properly ascribed to God the Spirit alone, rather than to the Christian in himself.

Pentecostals and sanctification

For Pentecostals, it is also true that one's view of justification determines one's view of sanctification. Between Duffield, Gause, and Macchia, I can find three differing views of sanctification, all of which derive from their views on justification. None of these

---

[124] By ontological, I am not implying any kind of *hesychastic* absorption into the divine nature. Justification is "ontological" first in the sense that the Trinity takes up residence in the soul through the indwelling of the Holy Spirit, and second in the sense that the "architecture" of the soul (its affections or disposition) is changed by the abiding presence and power of the Holy Spirit.

[125] William Breitenbach, "Religious Affections and Religious Affectations: Antinomianism and Hypocrisy in the Writings of Edwards and Franklin," in *Benjamin Franklin, Jonathan Edwards, and the Representation of American Culture*, ed. Barbara B. Oberg and Harry S. Stout (New York: Oxford University Press, 1993), 20, 21.

[126] Amy Plantinga Pauw, "Practical Ecclesiology in John Calvin and Jonathan Edwards," in *John Calvin's American Legacy*, ed. Thomas J. Davis (Oxford: Oxford University Press, 2010), 93; see also 103–4.

[127] Allen, *Justification and the Gospel*, 46.

[128] Steven M. Studebaker, "Edwards' Pneumatological Concept of Grace and Dispositional Soteriology: Resources for an Evangelical Inclusivism," *Pro Ecclesia* 14, no. 3 (2005): 332n36, citing several of Edwards' works, and Studebaker, "Beyond Tongues," 57, 62.

[129] Ortlund, *Edwards on the Christian Life*, 193.

views will be the same as Edwards' view. Duffield emphasizes the declarative aspect of positional sanctification. Gause emphasizes an ongoing sanctification without which one loses one's justification. Macchia emphasizes union with Christ through the Holy Spirit that enables a lifestyle of following the Spirit, resulting in an ever-increasing Christ-likeness in character.

Finished Work theology and sanctification

Duffield describes sanctification as having a primary and a secondary meaning. The primary meaning is that of "dedication, consecration, or setting apart for some specific and holy use."[130] The initial act of sanctification is "positional," and refers to the imputation of Christ's righteousness to the believer.[131] In this way, Duffield maintains a Reformed perspective on justification in contrast to a Wesleyan-Holiness view.

Duffield refers to sanctification in the sense of Christian obedience under the rubric of a "secondary" meaning of sanctification, which is a "process" and "practical" in the sense that it expresses itself in the Christian's lifestyle. Duffield stresses the Christian's identity as one who is adopted by the Father and one to whom Christ's righteousness is imputed. However, a transformation or even cleansing of the soul is not much in view. It is only through identification with Christ that the believer can have victory over sin, for sinless perfection is something that a believer cannot attain in this life.[132] His assumption seems to be that the Holy Spirit enables obedience without transforming the Christian in any ontological sense. Holiness remains a divine attribute rather than one that adheres to the nature of the Christian.

Duffield does ascribe sanctification to the work of the Trinity in a section on "the means of sanctification."[133] The Father reckons the righteousness of Christ to the account of the one who exercises faith. The Son sheds his blood that the believer might be sanctified. The Holy Spirit is the agent of sanctification through his "indwelling power and anointing."[134] However, little is made of this, and we quickly pass on to the human side of sanctification. This human side requires faith, obedience to the word, yielding to the Spirit, and personal commitment.[135] Yet, this last section does not discuss transformation, but is primarily an argument for the security of the believer in salvation, some of the chief signs of which are the desire to obey God's commandments, and the transformation of life and desires.[136]

Duffield takes up the subject of sanctification again in his section on the doctrine of the Holy Spirit. He first discusses how the Holy Spirit worked in the life of Christ to enable his ministry while on earth. He then applies this to the life of the saint, whom the Holy Spirit sanctifies in that he enables the Christian to "mortify the flesh through

---

[130] Duffield and Van Cleave, *Foundations*, 237.
[131] Ibid., 237–39.
[132] Ibid., 239–42.
[133] Ibid., 242–45.
[134] Ibid., 243.
[135] Ibid., 244–45.
[136] Ibid., 248–60, esp. 248–51.

the Holy Spirit."[137] One short section discusses how the believer is transformed into the image of Christ, but this appears to be primarily a matter of focusing on Christ, a cognitive choice more than an inward transformation. The stress of this section is on the Spirit helping one to understand the Scripture, to pray, and also to serve in connection with spiritual gifts, all emphasizing a cognitive work.[138]

Duffield's treatment of justification is surprisingly less pneumatological than that of Edwards, and his thinking about sanctification as obedience is only slightly better. Edwards' understanding of justification and sanctification could serve as a potent resource for Finished Work thought. It is worth noting that two of Duffield's theological heirs modify his approach in defining "salvation" as a healing that brings one to spiritual wholeness and to participation in the fullness of the eschaton.[139] Stewart, however, does not explain wholeness in terms of either justification or sanctification, but treats them essentially the same as in Duffield's work.

Holiness-pentecostal theology and sanctification. For R. Hollis Gause, objective acts of love coming from a transforming soul are what constitute a continuing and growing sanctification in the Christian. A crisis experience of sanctification (subsequent to justification and regeneration), the last of a series of "initial" acts of salvation, makes this possible.[140] In receiving this experience, the graces that regeneration implants into the soul are released to fruitful growth, and the life of the Christian is characterized by freedom from sinning.[141] The atonement provides for sanctification, but the Christian must appropriate or "claim" sanctification and must then live out sanctification in his lifestyle. The "claiming" of sanctification comes when one seeks the crisis experience of sanctification. In this experience, sanctification transforms the Christian's soul by freeing it from the compulsion to sin, allowing the Christian to live free from sinning thereafter by the exercise of the will in choosing to obey God.[142]

In his first chapter regarding sanctification, Gause does not explain this experience of transformation well.[143] One must infer the experience largely from his emphasis on living out a life of consistent obedience. The second chapter on sanctification focuses on the intercession of Christ and his high priestly role rather than on the believer.[144] Thus, the emphasis in Gause's discussion of sanctification is on obedience rather than on transformation, although he appears to assume the idea of transformation in the whole discussion.

---

[137] Ibid., 279.
[138] Studebaker ("Beyond Tongues," 55, also see 63–64) believes that this lack of emphasis on the transforming nature of the believer's relationship with the Holy Spirit also makes the baptism in the Holy Spirit optional, rather than vital and necessary, for the Christian. Even though Finished Work thought sees the baptism in the Holy Spirit primarily in terms of empowerment for service, rather than sanctification, this point deserves careful consideration by Classical Pentecostals.
[139] Dan R. Stewart, "A Primer on Salvation," in *A Reader on Salvation and Evangelism: Jesus, One World—One Savior* (Los Angeles: International Church of the Foursquare Gospel, 1995); 1–26 and Story, "Pauline Thoughts about the Holy Spirit and Sanctification," 67–94.
[140] Gause, *Living in the Spirit*, 94.
[141] Ibid., 4.
[142] Ibid., 95–99.
[143] Ibid., 93–100.
[144] Ibid., 102–10.

Gause emphasizes transformation more under the rubric of the baptism in the Holy Spirit, in a discussion of the moral and spiritual evidences of the baptism with the Spirit.[145] This may be because Gause considers Spirit baptism as the final experience of salvation, one that enables continual obedience even beyond the experience of sanctification. However, even here Gause deals with the products of the transformation of the experience of sanctification (linked to the final salvific experience of the baptism in the Holy Spirit), rather than the work of the Holy Spirit himself.

Twenty-first-century pentecostal theology and sanctification. In the case of Frank D. Macchia, his ideas of sanctification flow also from his concept of justification. Macchia sees the Reformed idea of imputation as something that works against the idea of renewal in the believer as a transformation of one's being as well as one's character.[146] Macchia both cites and criticizes John Calvin's view, arguing that Calvin's discussion of the work of the Holy Spirit in regeneration means that reconciliation and regeneration must be the same thing as union with Christ through the Holy Spirit. He then proceeds to show that a number of Lutheran and Reformed theologians took this pneumatological turn and saw justification as participation in Christ through the Spirit, and so as a transformational and sanctifying event.[147] For these Reformers, "there is no 'imputation' that is not essentially an indwelling. And there is no indwelling that is not essentially a transformative communion of persons."[148] While Macchia wishes to retain a declarative aspect to justification, justification's primary value is in transformation through the indwelling life of the Spirit.[149]

It is union with Christ through the indwelling Holy Spirit as the basis for truth and justice (right-wising), meaning transformation within the believer, which makes the justified life a sanctified life. Although Macchia cites Henri de Lubac rather than Edwards, like Edwards Macchia presses the idea that justification is based on a "new principle" of life in the believer, which is the presence of the indwelling Holy Spirit.[150] For Macchia, a proper view of justification is the idea of *theosis*, a growing participation in God's own goodness, particularly as the Finnish School of Tuomo Mannermaa understands *theosis* and as Veli-Matti Kärkkäinen works out *theosis* for a Pentecostal context.[151] Justification and regeneration overlap in the healing of reconciliation. "Justification as a relational dynamic is thus essentially transformative."[152] Macchia concludes this chapter by suggesting that we should not exclude the idea of human cooperation from justification, since "justification 'by faith' is justification by way of the faithful life that is liberated by participation in Christ's risen life."[153] Sanctification is then bound up with and advanced by justification, which is a "sanative" process

---

[145] Ibid., 123; see also 144–53 and 177–89.
[146] Macchia, *Justified in the Spirit*, 59.
[147] Ibid., 60–67.
[148] Ibid., 67.
[149] Ibid., 69.
[150] Ibid., 33.
[151] Ibid., 50–55 and Veli-Matti Kärkkäinen, *One with God: Salvation as Deification and Justification* (Collegeville, MN: Liturgical, 2004).
[152] Macchia, *Justified in the Spirit*, 70.
[153] Ibid., 72.

that continues throughout one's life.[154] Throughout the rest of the work, Macchia develops the idea of justification/sanctification as participation in Christ through the Pentecostal metaphor of the "Baptism in the Holy Spirit," which Macchia identifies as the work of the Holy Spirit in regeneration.

Conclusion

In conclusion, I have found Edwards' understanding of justification as a living, transformative presence of the Holy Spirit in the believer to be a surprisingly Pentecostal view, which Pentecostal thinking does not always seem to reflect. It is the Holy Spirit as Lover, as both the active agent of the Trinity and the trinitarian presence in himself, who—in joining himself to the believer in an abiding residence—unifies the justified Christian with the Father and the Son in a participation of eschatological fullness.[155]

Neither of the classical pentecostal views give much attention to transformation in justification, ascribing transformation to later crisis encounters with the Holy Spirit. Duffield allows for a positional sanctification in justification, but, although he joins regeneration with justification as one aspect of one's initial "salvation," he says very little about transformation until he gets to the section on the baptism in Holy Spirit. Gause also downplays the idea of transformation in justification. While regeneration seems to work some change, the believer must seek and depend on the crisis experience of sanctification, and then another experience in Spirit baptism, for the ability to live as a justified Christian.

Despite the work of the Holy Spirit in the crisis act of sanctification and the final act of salvation in the baptism of the Holy Spirit, both justification and sanctification are tenuous, in that only the continuing obedience of a penitential lifestyle will sustain them. The saint can have no confidence before God. This loses something I believe to be important. Story points out that both (positional) justification and (experiential) sanctification are necessary, lest the Christian life become a "repeated circular movement that ends in humility and repentance, with minimal expression of positive growth, victory, and empowerment by the Spirit for Christian character and charismatic service in ministry."[156]

Macchia's view is much better, but seems so concerned about an "empty" forensic declaration in justification that he loses sight of any assurance in his consideration of *theosis*. This appears, to me, to move toward that same tenuous position of being more a sinner than a saint in God's reckoning, and away from a key Reformation understanding that we are secure because we already participate in trinitarian life.

---

[154] Eric Swensson makes this link between Macchia's "pneumatic justification" and what Swensson views as a "movement away from a strict forensic justification toward a more sanative understanding" in the Joint Declaration on the Doctrine of Justification (JDDJ) between the Lutheran World Federation and the Roman Catholic Church. See Swensson, "Pneumatic Justification" (paper delivered at Regent University, Virginia Beach, Virginia, October 2003).

[155] Regarding the community as eschatological, rather than just the individual, see Kärkkäinen, "A Full Gospel Ecclesiology," 187.

[156] Story, "Pauline Thoughts about the Holy Spirit and Sanctification," 71.

Edwards' understanding of justification as the work of the Holy Spirit in transforming the soul should be considered by Pentecostal thinkers as a way of staying within a Reformation heritage of emphasizing the work of God in salvation, and of deepening their understanding of how the Holy Spirit works justification in the believer by motivating and empowering one to trust in Christ. Edwards' view of sanctification is also valuable in that it could help Finished Work Pentecostals understand how a life of obedience to God can be lived out by the power of the Holy Spirit, rather than any sort of *habitus* as a kind of moral "gas" for the engine of the soul (which inevitably runs out, if we trust in our own moral strength).

This emphasis on the work of the Holy Spirit preserves both the confidence of one's approval by God, in the sense that one is "positionally" sanctified, and of one's ability to live a holy life as the saint is motivated and empowered to live a life of moral transformation by the work and presence of the Spirit in his or her soul. This is because justification and regeneration are inseparably linked. As Macchia points out, there is no justification that is not made real in the soul through regeneration. The "union" with Christ that is created and sustained by the relational embrace of the Holy Spirit, whose work and presence transforms the Christian, constitutes this regeneration and the sanctification that flows out into the Christian's lifestyle. This power is the very life of God (I would prefer to say the resurrected life of Christ in God) and so expresses itself in the life of the believer as the saint continues to participate in union with Christ. This makes justification transformative and eschatological, and both grounds and shapes the objective and existential sanctification of the Christian.

Part Three

Church and Culture

9

Edwardsean Charismatic Ecclesiology: The Spirit as Gift

Lisa P. Stephenson

Introduction

The task of bringing Jonathan Edwards' ecclesiology and a pentecostal ecclesiology into dialogue can initially appear to be fraught with a number of difficulties. First, there is the issue of the absence of any sole work published by Edwards devoted exclusively to ecclesiology. Then there is the matter of a paucity of pentecostal ecclesiology itself. What does it mean to subscribe to a *pentecostal* doctrine of the church? Furthermore, it would seem that a cessationist like Edwards would have little in common with a group of people characterized by a strong charismatic spirituality and theology. Nevertheless, what emerges once these potential obstacles are overcome is that both Edwards and Pentecostals share a common interest in a pneumatology of love that, though expressed in different ecclesiological ways at times, provides a rich opportunity for dialogue.

In this chapter, I proceed first by examining Edwards' ecclesiology, which is strongly shaped by trinitarian and pneumatological themes. Second, I demonstrate how Edwards' conception of a pneumatology of love resonates with various strands of Pentecostalism, both during its early years and today. Finally, I explore the intersection of a pneumatology of love with pentecostal ecclesiology and note the affinities and disjunctions between Edwards and Pentecostalism.

Jonathan Edwards: An "ordinary" account

Surprisingly, Jonathan Edwards' ecclesiology has received little scholarly attention.[1] Part of the reason for the neglect may be due to the fact that Edwards himself did not

---

[1] The exception is Thomas A. Schafer, "Jonathan Edwards' Conception of the Church," *Church History* 24, no. 1 (1955): 51–66; Douglas A. Sweeney, "The Church," in *The Princeton Companion to Jonathan Edwards*, ed. Sang Hyun Lee (Princeton, NJ: Princeton University Press, 2005), 167–89; Amy Plantinga Pauw, "Jonathan Edwards' Ecclesiology," in *Jonathan Edwards as Contemporary: Essays in Honor of Sang Hyun Lee*, ed. Don Schweitzer (New York: Peter Lang, 2010), 175–86 and

publish a work elaborating fully on this subject. Admittedly, he did publish various pieces related to ecclesial matters, especially as it connected to the Northampton communion controversy, and these are assembled in a large volume in the Yale edition of Edwards' works entitled *Ecclesiastical Writings*.[2] But absent still among his corpus is a detailed work that reflects on the nature of the church at large. In order to gain a broader understanding of Edwards' ecclesiological views, one must search throughout his writings to gather together the dispersed pieces in order to comprehend the picture as a whole. One need only to examine the table of contents of Rhys Bezzant's *Jonathan Edwards and the Church*—the only book to be published on Edwards' ecclesiology to date—in order to appreciate the scope of such a project.

Due to the space limits of this chapter, I do not attempt to present a comprehensive account of Edwards' ecclesiology. Instead, I focus on how Edwards' ecclesiology intersects with a pneumatology of love—especially as this comes to the fore in *Charity and Its Fruits*—and thus examine how Edwards' ecclesiology is fundamentally pneumatological since it is this point that provides a strong connection with pentecostal ecclesiology. I begin by establishing Edwards' pneumatology of love, wherein the Spirit is identified as the mutual love between the Father and the Son and the gift of love to humanity. I then turn to Edwards' ecclesiology and consider how his pneumatology of love informs his doctrine of the church.

A pneumatology of love

In order to understand properly Edwards' pneumatology, one must first gain an understanding of his doctrine of the Trinity. Edwards employs an Augustinian mutual love model for explaining the Godhead and consistently articulates the Trinity in these categories. This model utilizes the ontological structure of the mind as the primary framework for conceptualizing the three persons. Thus, the Father is the *divine mind* who is unbegotten and is the source of the Godhead. The Son is the *divine understanding* who is generated as the product of the Father's self-reflection. The Spirit is the *divine love* who proceeds as the mutual love between the Father and the Son.[3]

However, it is not solely a rationalistic argument that leads Edwards to positing the Spirit as divine love, as he also finds support for this understanding in the scriptures themselves. Edwards looks to 1 John 4 to substantiate his claims. Twice in the chapter God is described as love (vv. 8, 16), and the Spirit is equated with divine love (vv. 12-13).

Plantinga Pauw, "Practical Ecclesiology in John Calvin and Jonathan Edwards," in *John Calvin's American Legacy*, ed. Thomas J. Davis (Oxford: Oxford University Press, 2010), 91–110; and Rhys S. Bezzant, *Jonathan Edwards and the Church* (Oxford: Oxford University Press, 2014).

[2] Edwards, *Ecclesiastical Writings*, WJE 12.

[3] Steven M. Studebaker and Robert W. Caldwell III, *The Trinitarian Theology of Jonathan Edwards: Text, Context, and Application* (Burlington, VT: Ashgate, 2012), 62–65. There is recent debate among Edwards' scholars as to whether or not he employs an additional social model to the psychological model in his doctrine of the Trinity. See Amy Plantinga Pauw, *"The Supreme Harmony of All": The Trinitarian Theology of Jonathan Edwards* (Grand Rapids, MI: Eerdmans, 2002) and Steven M. Studebaker, *Jonathan Edwards' Social Augustinian Trinitarianism in Historical and Contemporary Perspectives* (Piscataway, NJ: Gorgias, 2008).

Edwards also maintains that in Scripture the connection between the Spirit and love is seen in the biblical symbolism of the Spirit in the form of the dove—the dove is seen as the emblem of love or a lover—and olive oil—the olive tree having served as a symbol of love, peace, and friendship. Furthermore, he notes that in Scripture we frequently read of the Father loving the Son and the Son loving the Father, whereas absent is a reference to either of the Father or the Son loving the Holy Spirit or of the Spirit loving either of them. Edwards maintains that this is the case because the Spirit is the divine love itself, the love of the Father and the Son, and so does not need further identification.[4]

As divine love, the Spirit is the principle of union not only in the Godhead between the Father and the Son but also between God and humanity and between one person and another. Edwards says,

> The Spirit that proceeds from the Father and the Son is the bond of this union, as it is of all holy union between the Father and the Son, and between God and the creature, and between the creatures among themselves. . . . Therefore this Spirit of love is the "bond of perfectness" (Col. 3:14) throughout the whole blessed society or family in heaven and earth, consisting of the Father as the head of the family, and the Son, and all his saints that are the disciples, seed and spouse of the Son.[5]

In the economy of redemption, the Spirit is the gift of love itself that Christ purchases and pours out without limits. "The Father appoints and provides the Redeemer, and himself accepts the price and grants the thing purchased; the Son is the Redeemer by offering up himself, and is the price; and the Holy Ghost immediately communicates to us the thing purchased by communicating himself, and he is the thing purchased."[6] Edwards maintains that this understanding of the Trinity preserves the equality of the three persons in respect to their part in the work of redemption and in their part of the glory of this work, for the Spirit *to be the love of God to the world* is equal to the works of the Father and the Son *from love to the world*. The price paid and the thing bought with that price is equal.[7]

An ecclesiology informed by a pneumatology of love

In 1738 Edwards preached a sermon series on 1 Corinthians 13 that consisted of fifteen preachments. This series, *Charity and Its Fruits*, was the second of three series that he preached in the 1730s to remedy what Edwards perceived to be a growing spiritual malaise in his town of Northampton where he pastored.[8] Despite the previous local

---

[4] Edwards, *Discourse on the Trinity*, WJE 21:121–22, 126–27 and Edwards, *Treatise on Grace*, WJE 21:181–82, 186.
[5] Edwards, *Treatise on Grace*, WJE 21:186.
[6] Edwards, *Discourse on the Trinity*, WJE 21:136.
[7] Ibid., 137.
[8] It was published posthumously; see Jonathan Edwards, *Charity and Its Fruits; Or, Christian Love as Manifested in Heart and Life*, ed. Tryon Edwards (New York: Robert Carter & Brothers, 1852).

"awakening" the townspeople experienced (1736–37), there appeared to be a lack of long-term fruit displayed among those affected.⁹ *Charity and Its Fruits* expounded on the virtues and necessity of love within the Christian life and church.

Edwards' vision of the church, especially from a pneumatological perspective, is fundamentally eschatological. The goal is for holy love to be shed abroad in the hearts of all the church, which is perfectly realized in heaven. Heaven is a world of love and a place in which the church is perfected because the Holy Spirit (i.e., divine love) will be given more perfectly and abundantly to the church than is possible on earth. In heaven love is always mutual and returns are always in due proportion. There will be nothing internal or external to block persons' desire and expression of love. This love will be expressed with perfect decency and wisdom. Edwards maintains that in heaven there

> is the Holy Spirit, the Spirit of divine love, in whom the very essence of God, as it were, all flows out or is breathed forth in love, and by whose immediate influence all holy love is shed abroad in the hearts of all the church [cf. Rom. 5:5]. There in heaven this fountain of love, this eternal three in one, is set open without any obstacle to hinder access to it. There this glorious God is manifested and shines forth in full glory, in beams of love; there the fountain overflows in streams and rivers of love and delight, enough for all to drink at, and to swim in, yea, so as to overflow the world as it were with a deluge of love.¹⁰

Therefore, the task for the earthly church is to anticipate the heavenly church by pursuing the outpouring of the Spirit through its most glorious way. That is, for Edwards, that kind of outpouring is found not in the extraordinary gifts of the Spirit, but in the ordinary, saving operations of the Spirit. He says, "This glory is what will make the church more like the church in heaven, where charity or love has a perfect reign, than any measure or degree of the extraordinary gifts of the Spirit could do."¹¹ The task for the church on earth then is to anticipate this eschatological world of love and live a life of love both to God and others. By living this way the church enjoys a foretaste of the heavenly pleasures and delights.¹²

Edwards has much to say concerning why love is the most excellent gift to the church. Taking his cue from 1 Corinthians 13, Edwards notes that Paul establishes this fact in three respects. First, love is the most essential thing and all other gifts are dependent on it (vv. 1-3). Second, love is the fountain from which all good dispositions and behaviors arise and flow from (vv. 4-7). Third, it will continue even after the church is in its most perfect state because it is unfailing and everlasting (vv. 8-12).¹³

Edwards continues by comparing and contrasting what he terms the extraordinary or miraculous gifts of the Spirit (e.g., tongues, prophecy, and working of miracles) with the ordinary (e.g., awakening, convincing, converting, and strengthening the saints).

---

⁹ Bezzant, *Jonathan Edwards and the Church*, 79–80.
¹⁰ Edwards, *Charity and Its Fruits*, WJE 8:368–70, 377–80.
¹¹ Ibid., 170–71.
¹² Ibid., 395–96.
¹³ Ibid., 351.

He grants that during the time in which the Corinthian letter was written the Spirit had been poured out in ordinary influences, as well as in extraordinary ways. During the first age of the church until the death of all the apostles (c. 100 years after Christ's birth) the extraordinary gifts were common among all sorts of people as foretold by the prophet Joel. These extraordinary gifts were called such because they are not given in the ordinary course of God's providence, but only in extraordinary occasions. They were bestowed on the primitive church in order to found and establish the Christian church in the world. However, since the canon of Scripture has been completed and the Christian church fully founded and established, the extraordinary gifts have ceased and there is no reason to expect there to be a need for them to reappear. For Edwards,

> Prophecy and miracles argue the imperfection of the state of the church, rather than the perfection. For they are the means proper and designed by God rather as a stay and support, or as leading strings, if I may so say, to the church in a state of infancy rather than as means adapted to its state in full growth.[14]

Even when the extraordinary gifts were operative, they were not eternal. Those who had them relinquished them when they died, but retained the divine love that was in their heart so that it could be perfected in heaven.[15]

Edwards expands his comparison between the two kinds of gifts further by noting that the extraordinary gifts are not properly inherent to a person, but likens them to garments a person wears or a precious jewel one carries with herself. The nature of the extraordinary gifts stands in contradistinction to the ordinary gifts, namely the true saving grace of God (i.e., divine love), which is a quality inherent in the nature of the one who is the subject of it. Why? Because when the Spirit bestows saving grace, he imparts himself to the soul in his own holy nature and thus becomes an indwelling, vital principle in the soul. The person now partakes of the nature of the Spirit. Edwards says,

> The Spirit of God communicates itself much more in bestowing saving grace than in bestowing those extraordinary gifts. In those extraordinary gifts of the Spirit the Holy Ghost does indeed produce effects in the man, or by the man; but not so as properly to communicate himself in his own proper nature to the man. . . . The Spirit of God may produce effects on many things to which it does not communicate itself.[16]

Additionally, Edwards posits that another reason love is the most excellent gift is because the spiritual image of God consists of grace and holiness (i.e., effects of the ordinary influence of the Spirit) and not in the extraordinary gifts. Looking to make

---

[14] Ibid., 149–51, 153, 171–72, 362. For a detailed view of Edwards' cessationism, see Philip A. Craig, "'And Prophecy Shall Cease': Jonathan Edwards on the Cessation of the Gift of Prophecy," *Westminster Theological Journal* 63, no. 1 (2002): 163–84.
[15] Edwards, *Charity and Its Fruits*, WJE 8:355, 358.
[16] Ibid., 157–58.

a Christological connection, Edwards posits that while one does image Christ in the utilization of supernatural gifts, being in the image and likeness of Christ consists more in "having the same spirit which he was of, in being meek and lowly of heart, of a spirit of Christian love, and walking as Christ walked. This makes a man more like Christ than if he could work ever so many miracles."[17]

Edwards concludes that love

> is the most excellent fruit of the Spirit, without which the best extraordinary and miraculous gifts are nothing. This is the end of which they are the means, and which is more excellent than the means. Let us therefore earnestly seek this blessed fruit of the Spirit; and let us seek that it may abound in our hearts, that the love of God may more and more be shed abroad in our hearts, and that we may love the Lord Jesus Christ in sincerity, and love one another as Christ hath loved us. Hereby we shall possess that which never fails. We shall have that within us which will be of an immortal nature, and which will be a sure evidence of our own blessed immortality, and the beginning of eternal life in our souls.[18]

To summarize Edwards' ecclesiology, the church is a pneumatological community and, as such, is therefore a loving community. Although the church does not embody this identity perfectly, it participates in the eschatological reality as much as is feasible this side of heaven. It is through the ordinary gifts, rather than extraordinary, that the church has been given the primary and optimal means of being gifted with love in the person of the Spirit. This gifting enables persons to be transformed into the image of Christ and the church to be conformed into the body of Christ.

Pentecostalism: An "extraordinary" response

As noted in the Introduction, at first glance Edwards and Pentecostals may appear to have very little in common. However, both sides share a mutual interest in a pneumatology of love. Above I have examined the ways in which this pneumatology has taken shape in Edwards' theology, and I now turn to Pentecostals' understanding between the relationship of the Spirit and love. It is true that Pentecostals generally have tethered their pneumatology to a Luke-Acts presentation, which has been understood primarily through the lens of Spirit baptism and its associated theme of power. But has an emphasis on a pneumatology of power among Pentecostals been exclusive to a pneumatology of love? The answer is "no." While historically love may not be as prominent a theme as power, it is there especially in the early years and among various scholars today.

There are numerous allusions in early pentecostal literature to Spirit baptism as a baptism in the love of God. Within the pages of *The Apostolic Faith*—the paper that was

---

[17] Ibid., 159.
[18] Ibid., 365.

used to proclaim the events of the first two years of the Azusa Street Revival—there are several references. In the very first edition a Nazarene brother who had received Spirit baptism in his own home during family worship time described it as follows:

> It was a baptism of love. Such abounding love! Such compassion seemed to almost kill me with its sweetness! People do not know what they are doing when they stand out against it. The devil never gave me a swet [sic] thing, he was always trying to get me to censuring [sic] people. This baptism fills us with divine love.[19]

In the following edition another similar association was made:

> Jesus says, "Take my yoke upon you and learn of me." The Lord showed me that this yoke was the covenant of the new testament in his blood, and we put this yoke on when we are baptized with the Holy Ghost. This covenant is a marriage covenant. We are married, not for one day or year or life, but eternally married. When I got married to my wife it was settled for this life. So when I got married to Jesus Christ, it was settled forever. Hallelujah! Jesus and I are united. He baptized me with love.[20]

In one of the last editions of the paper a question was asked as to what the real evidence is that a person has received the Holy Spirit. The following answer was given:

> Divine love, which is charity. Charity is the Spirit of Jesus. They will have the fruits of the Spirit. Gal. 5:22. "The Fruit of the Spirit is love, joy, peace, longsuffering, gentleness, goodness, meekness, faith, temperance; against such there is no law. And they that are Christ's have crucified the flesh with the affections and lusts." This is the real Bible evidence in their daily walk and conversation; and the outward manifestations; speaking in tongues and the signs following: casting out devils, laying hands on the sick and the sick being healed, and the love of God for souls increasing in their hearts.[21]

Other pentecostal literature expressed similar sentiments. In one place readers were instructed that

> the baptism of the Holy Ghost does not consist in simply speaking in tongues. No. It has a much more grand and deeper meaning than that. It fills our souls with the love of God for lost humanity, and makes us much more than willing to leave home, friends, and all to work in his vineyard, even if it be far away.[22]

Elsewhere E. N. Bell connects Spirit baptism to Rom. 5:5 and describes it as a regular outpouring of God's love.[23] William Seymour himself even said, "The baptism in the

---

[19] *Apostolic Faith*, 1:1, 1906, 1.
[20] "United to Jesus," *Apostolic Faith* 1:2, 1906, 3.
[21] "Questions Answered," *Apostolic Faith* 1:11, 1908, 2.
[22] *The Pentecost* 1:1, 1908, 4.
[23] E. N. Bell, "Believers in Sanctification," *Christian Evangel*, September 19, 1914, 3.

Holy Ghost and fire means to be flooded with the love of God and Power for Service, and a love for the truth as it is in God's word. . . . For the Holy Spirit gives us a sound mind, faith, love and power."[24]

This pentecostal identification of a pneumatology of love did not disappear after the first generation and more recently has come to the fore in the work of two prominent pentecostal scholars. Both Amos Yong and Frank Macchia have sought to construct a more explicit connection between pentecostal theology and divine love.[25] Amos Yong proposes a rereading of the pneumatology of Luke-Acts through the lens of divine love. In Luke-Acts the Spirit is poured out first on Jesus (Lk. 3:21-22) and then on all flesh (Acts 2:1-41), both of which can be understood as a baptism of love. Jesus' reception of the Spirit takes the bodily form and presence of a dove and is a manifestation of the love of the Father for the Son. The voice from heaven confirms: "You are my Son, *whom I love*; with you I am well pleased." Jesus' baptism in the Spirit thus becomes paradigmatic of what occurs on the Day of Pentecost. However, at Pentecost the disciples' reception of the Spirit takes the form of tongues of fire and is accompanied by the sound of a mighty wind. This outpouring mediates the loving relationship of the Father and the Son not only between each other but also outward toward all of humanity. Yong says,

> So if the gift of the Spirit involves resting upon and filling the Son, then the gift of the Father through the Son to Israel and the world involves the gracious outpouring of the Spirit so that many hearts can experience the same infilling of liberative love and that the world can become a dwelling place of the Spirit and be fully inundated with the shalomic love of God's peace, justice, and righteousness.[26]

Thus the Spirit of Pentecost is the gift of a loving God to the world. The "baptism" or "infilling" of the Spirit is an inundation of the gift of God's love into persons' lives so that they are no longer full of themselves, but of God (i.e., divine love).[27]

Like Yong, Frank Macchia wants to understand the Day of Pentecost as an outpouring of divine love that has its focus on the church's charismatic empowerment. Macchia says, "The Spirit who mediated the love between the Father and the Son

---

[24] William J. Seymour, *The Doctrines and Disciplines of the Azusa Street Apostolic Faith Mission of Los Angeles, California*, ed. Larry Martin (1915; reprint, Pensacola, FL: Christian Life, 2012), 38–39.

[25] Frank D. Macchia, *Baptized in the Spirit: A Global Pentecostal Theology* (Grand Rapids, MI: Zondervan, 2006) and Amos Yong, *Spirit of Love: A Trinitarian Theology of Grace* (Waco, TX: Baylor University Press, 2012). Ironically, while Yong highlights the pneumatology of a number of historical figures (Augustine, Aquinas, and Tillich) in *Spirit of Love*, he only mentions Edwards in a footnote. Yong defends his omission of Edwards by arguing that he, along with a number of other historical figures, did not make "substantive and extensive connections between love and the Spirit; their pneumatological associations were tangential, made in a more explicitly Trinitarian framework, or ad hoc or nonsystematic in nature" (172n44). However, I do not concur with this assessment. Not only is Edwards' pneumatology of love closely connected to Augustine and constitutes a primary component of his theology, but Edwards' pneumatology of love is also eschatologically oriented, which is an aspect that Yong wants to include in his own articulation but laments its absence in Augustine, Aquinas, and Tillich (*Spirit of Love*, 19).

[26] Yong, *Spirit of Love*, 100–1.

[27] Ibid., 98–99.

is now poured out so as to draw humanity into the *koinonia* of God and to gift and empower the church to participate in the mission of God in the world."[28] Spirit baptism is thus a baptism into divine love, which is the very nature of God. Through Christ as Spirit Baptizer, God imparts God's self. Macchia notes that without this understanding, the "power" that is associated with Spirit baptism amounts to nothing more than an emotional release of unharnessed energy.[29]

A pneumatology of love is thus not antithetical or even foreign to pentecostal theology. On the contrary, this approach resonates soundly with certain voices from the tradition—both past and present—and provides a strong connection with Edwards' theology. Since Edwards and Pentecostals both subscribe to a pneumatology of love, one would also expect there to be certain continuities between their ecclesiologies. To this we will now turn.

An ecclesiology informed by a pneumatology of love

Just as Edwards' ecclesiology was influenced by his pneumatology of love, so too is pentecostal ecclesiology. The way in which this happens resonates with Edwards' theology at points and challenges it at others. When a pneumatology of love serves as a foundation for pentecostal ecclesiology, the understanding of the church as empowered is nuanced.[30] In identifying the church as an empowered community, Pentecostals traditionally understand this descriptor to point to Spirit baptism and its associated theme of power. This should come as no surprise when one of the key texts for Pentecostals makes this connection explicit: "But you will receive *power* when the Holy Spirit has come upon you; and you will be my witnesses in Jerusalem, in all Judea and Samaria, and to the ends of the earth" (Acts 1:8). If the Day of Pentecost is the birth of the church, then one of the gifts given to it by means of the Spirit is that of empowerment: for spiritual gifts, ministry, and evangelism.[31]

It is at this point, however, that the Spirit as gift of love should inform a pneumatology of power. To emphasize a pneumatology of love as the foundation for ecclesiology does not negate the theme of power, but specifies the content of that power: the power to love. More specifically, the church is empowered to love God and one another through the gracious gift of the Holy Spirit. This understanding parallels with Edwards' ecclesiology. If it is the outpouring of love (i.e., the Spirit) that births forth the church, then it will be this same outpouring of love that sustains the church

---

[28] Macchia, *Baptized in the Spirit*, 258.
[29] Ibid., 258–59, 261–62.
[30] One approach to pentecostal ecclesiology has been to utilize the paradigm of the fivefold gospel (i.e., Jesus is savior, sanctifier, Spirit baptizer, healer, and soon coming king) to characterize the doctrine of the church. Through this lens, the church is thus delineated by five marks: It is the redeemed community, holy community, empowered community, healing community, and eschatological community. John Christopher Thomas, ed., *Toward a Pentecostal Ecclesiology: The Church and the Fivefold Gospel* (Cleveland, OH: CPT, 2010).
[31] Yong, *Spirit of Love* and Macchia, *Baptized in the Spirit* (emphasis added).

and perfects it in the eschaton. A pneumatology of love thus characterizes the nature and mission of the church.

Macchia comments on the relationship between power and love in his own work and contends that understanding Spirit baptism as a baptism in love is akin to a prophetic call that draws believers close to [God's] heart in deeper love and empathy in order to help them catch a glimpse of the divine love for the world. It is this love that is at the substance of power for mission. It accounts for the sense of wonder and enthusiasm that Pentecostals feel during moments of renewal in the Spirit.[32]

Macchia suggests that Pentecostals' doctrine of subsequence (i.e., Spirit baptism as a charismatic experience subsequent to regeneration) should be interpreted as an experience of the ecstasy of love. That is, Spirit baptism fills one with the love of God, which in turn empowers one to transcend oneself and give abundantly of oneself to God and others. "God as a self-giving fountain of love poured out abundantly begins to shape us into something similar. Jesus pours out the Spirit so that the Spirit may pour forth in our empowered love for others. We become 'Spirit-baptized personalities.'"[33]

Despite the positive contributions that a pneumatology of love makes to pentecostal ecclesiology, does subscribing to this approach force Pentecostals to abandon the extraordinary gifts of the Spirit as Edwards did and maintain a strict division between love and the extraordinary gifts? Can Pentecostals resolve this tension in their own ecclesiology? Edwards' ecclesiology maintains that the church should pursue the outpouring of the Spirit through the ordinary gift of the Spirit as love, and then pits the ordinary gift of the Spirit against the extraordinary on this basis. From a pentecostal perspective, this is unnecessary and shortsighted. A pentecostal theology would maintain that the extraordinary gifts are not superfluous to an ecclesiology that prioritizes love, but rather sustain it. It is in and through the extraordinary gifts that one experiences the outpouring of God's love in the Spirit and, in turn, is moved to turn outwards and share this love with others.[34]

Yong demonstrates this by looking at the biblical texts themselves. He wants to connect the presentation of the Great Commandment in the Gospel of Luke to the activities of the Spirit baptized believers after the Day of Pentecost in Acts. In Luke, Jesus tells the lawyer that in order to inherit eternal life he must love God and his neighbor, and then narrates the parable of the Good Samaritan (Lk. 10:25-37). This Great Commandment is essentially then lived out in Acts when a result of the outpouring of the Spirit is that a love for God and others is generated. In Acts 2:42-47 one can see the gift of the Spirit creating various other gifts, some in response to God and others in response to the surrounding community. Yong says,

> The love of God ignites love for God, expressed in the prayers and praises of the people directed to God, and generates neighborly love, seen in the generosity and

---

[32] Macchia, *Baptized in the Spirit*, 270–71.
[33] Ibid., 281.
[34] I realize that there are other theological arguments that factor into Edwards' cessationist position, but I want to challenge his central tenet that love is to be associated with the ordinary gifts not the extraordinary ones, resulting in a prioritizing of the former over the latter.

solidarity of the people with each other, as well as with those who were added to the community on a daily basis. . . . Is this not also a manifestation of the love of God, even if not explicitly called such here?[35]

Pentecost's baptism of love was not just a gift from God, but the gift of God himself in the gift of the Spirit. When one experiences the baptism of love—even through means of an extraordinary gift (Acts 2:1-13)—that person is enabled to respond in love to the baptizer (i.e., the lover) and also overflow with compassion toward the love of neighbor (as did the Good Samaritan).[36]

Social scientist Margaret Poloma and her colleagues are finding concrete contemporary examples to corroborate this phenomenon. Poloma has been a part of two research teams that have explored the intersection of fundamental aspects of pentecostal spirituality—including the extraordinary gifts—and benevolent service. Among her findings what has come to the fore is that persons encounter divine love as much as power in their experiences of the extraordinary gifts. This is determined by the amount of benevolent behavior demonstrated (i.e., love for others). In one study Poloma comments, "Those who experience more of the charismatic gifts of the Holy Spirit are more likely to report higher scores for reported empathic feelings and altruistic behavior than are those who do not experience God's presence and power in their lives."[37] And in another study, "Measures of charisma—of experiences of the divine such as prophecy, a sense of the divine presence, and glossolalia—consistently helped explain differences in benevolent behavior."[38] Thus, Poloma's research suggests that during an experience of an extraordinary gift one is caught up in love of God and for God, which in turn leads to love for others that manifest itself in the form of benevolent service.

Thus, pentecostal ecclesiology challenges Edwards' strict division between love and the spiritual gifts; one is not more proper to the nature of the Spirit than the other but, rather, both are interrelated. While Edwards is right that the gifts cease in heaven, on earth they serve as a foretaste of the love that one will experience in heaven. They become a means by which the gift of love is made manifest.

Conclusion

There has been speculation as to whether or not Jonathan Edwards would endorse recent religious revivals, especially as they pertain to the pentecostal/charismatic movement.[39] While it may be unclear if Edwards would approve of Pentecostalism if he

---

[35] Yong, *Spirit of Love*, 97–98.
[36] Ibid., 102–3.
[37] Margaret M. Poloma and Ralph W. Hood, Jr., *Blood and Fire: Godly Love in a Pentecostal Emerging Church* (New York: New York University Press, 2008), 116.
[38] Margaret M. Poloma and John C. Green, *The Assemblies of God: Godly Love and the Revitalization of American Pentecostalism* (New York: New York University Press, 2010), 168.
[39] John D. Hannah, "Jonathan Edwards, the Toronto Blessing, and the Spiritual Gifts: Are the Extraordinary Ones Actually the Ordinary Ones?" *Trinity Journal*, n.s., 17, no. 2 (1996): 167–89.

were alive today, there are certainly more continuities between Edwards' theology and the pentecostal tradition than one might initially expect, and, I imagine, Edwards would find much to affirm.[40] Edwards and Pentecostals posit a pneumatology of love that strongly informs their respective ecclesiologies. Both can affirm that the church, first and foremost, must be characterized by its love for God and one another. Through the gift of the Spirit we experience the love of God shed abroad in our hearts, which turns us outward toward others. However, for Pentecostals, this gift of the Spirit also includes the extraordinary gifts. They are not superfluous to a pneumatological ecclesiology, but form an integral part of one's experience and expression of the Spirit. A pneumatology of love is foundational for being a charismatic church; it is not antithetical. And so the earthly church anticipates the heavenly church by pursuing the outpouring of the Spirit through both the ordinary and extraordinary ways. In the words of Edwards,

> At the end of the world . . . divine love shall not fail, but be brought to its most glorious perfection in every individual member of the whole elect church: when in every heart that love, which was but a spark, shall be blown up to a flame, and every holy soul shall be as it were all a flame of divine love, and shall remain in this glorious perfection throughout all eternity.[41]

---

[40] Michael J. McClymond and Gerald R. McDermott make a similar postulation in "Jonathan Edwards and the Future of Global Christianity," *Theology Today* 69, no. 4 (2013): 482–83.
[41] Edwards, *Charity and Its Fruits*, WJE 8:359.

10

Edwards against Himself? Conflicting Appeals to the Writings of Jonathan Edwards during the 1990s Pentecostal-Charismatic Revivals in Toronto and Pensacola

Michael J. McClymond

Introduction

The Christian revival that began in Canada in January 1994 and soon became known as the "Toronto Blessing"—or to some participants, the "Father's Blessing"—soon became controversial. Within two to three years, a large literature of books, essays, and Internet postings appeared, both attacking and defending the revival.[1] A wide-ranging

---

[1] Selected literature on the Toronto Blessing includes the following: John Arnott, *The Father's Blessing* (Orlando, FL: Creation House, 1995); Steve Beard, *Thunderstruck: John Wesley and the "Toronto Blessing"* (Wilmore, KY: Thunderstruck Communications, 1996); Leigh Belcham, *Toronto—The Baby or the Bathwater? Serious Questions about the "Toronto Blessing"* (Bromley: Day One, 1995); James A. Beverley, *Holy Laughter and the Toronto Blessing: An Investigative Report* (Grand Rapids, MI: Zondervan, 1995) and James A. Beverley, "Toronto's Mixed Blessing," *Christianity Today* 39, September 11, 1995, 22–27; Wesley Campbell, *Welcoming A Visitation of the Holy Spirit* (Orlando, FL: Creation House, 1996); Mark Cartledge, "A Spur to Holistic Discipleship," in *"Toronto" in Perspective: Papers on the New Charismatic Wave of the mid-1990s*, ed. David Hillborn (Carlisle: ACUTE /Paternoster, 2001), 64–74; Guy Chevreau, *Catch the Fire: The Toronto Blessing—An Experience of Renewal and Revival* (Toronto: Harper Collins, 1994) and Guy Chevreau, *Share the Fire: The Toronto Blessing and Grace-Based Evangelism* (Shippensburg, PA: Destiny Image / Revival, 1997); William De Arteaga, *Quenching the Spirit: Discover the Real Spirit Behind the Charismatic Controversy* (Orlando, FL: Creation House, 1996); Patrick Dixon, *Signs of Revival* (Eastbourne: Kingsway, 1994); Richard D. Easton, "Jonathan Edwards on Revival: An Analysis of His Thought as Used by Proponents and Critics of the Toronto Blessing," *Reformation and Revival* 8, no. 2 (1999): 23–40; John D. Hannah, "Jonathan Edwards, the Toronto Blessing, and the Spiritual Gifts: Are the Extraordinary Ones Actually the Ordinary Ones?" *Trinity Journal*, n.s., 17, no. 2 (1996): 167–89; Hank Hanegraaff, *Counterfeit Revival* (Dallas, TX: Word, 1997); Michael A. G. Haykin, *Jonathan Edwards: The Holy Spirit in Revival* (Darlington: Evangelical, 2005) and Haykin, *Jonathan Edwards: The Man, His Experience, and His Theology; Volume 3: The "Toronto Blessing"—A Renewal From God?* (Richmond Hill, ON: Canadian Christian Publications, 1995); David Hillborn, ed., *'Toronto' in Perspective: Papers on the New Charismatic Wave of the Mid-1990s* (Carlisle: ACUTE / Paternoster, 2001); Bruce Hindmarsh, "The 'Toronto Blessing' and the Protestant Evangelical Awakening of the Eighteenth Century Compared," *Crux* (December 1995): 3–13; Stephen Hunt,

(but not exhaustive) survey of published literature during the 1990s shows *eleven authors* who viewed the Toronto movement positively, *seventeen authors* who saw the movement negatively, *seven authors* offering some kind of mixed verdict, and another *eight authors* who remained neutral by refraining from drawing overall positive or negative verdicts.[2] Christian revivals have often been controversial, and so there

---

A History of the Charismatic Movement in Britain and the United States of America, 2 vols. (Lewiston, NY: Edwin Mellen, 2009); Bill Jackson, *The Quest for the Radical Middle: A History of the Vineyard* (Cape Town: Vineyard International, 1999); John Kent, "Have We Been Here Before? A Historian Looks at the Toronto Blessing," in *The Toronto Blessing—Or Is It?* ed. Stanley E. Porter and Philip J. Richter (London: Darton, Longman, and Todd, 1995), 86–103; Robert G. Kuglin, *The Toronto Blessing: What Would the Holy Spirit Say?* (Camp Hill, PA: Horizon, 1996); Ronald A. N. Kydd, "A Retrospectus/Prospectus on Physical Phenomena Centred on the 'Toronto Blessing,'" *Journal of Pentecostal Theology* 6, no. 12 (1998): 73–81; Richard F. Lovelace, *Dynamics of Spiritual Life: An Evangelical Theology of Renewal* (Downers Grove, IL: IVP, 1979) and Lovelace, "The Surprising Works of God," *Christianity Today*, September 11, 1995, 28–32; John F. MacArthur, Jr. *Charismatic Chaos* (Grand Rapids, MI: Zondervan, 1992); MacArthur, *Reckless Faith: When the Church Loses Its Will to Discern* (Wheaton, IL: Crossway, 1994), and MacArthur, *Strange Fire: The Danger of Offending the Holy Spirit With Counterfeit Worship* (Nashville, TN: Nelson, 2013); Ryan J. Martin, "'Violent Motions of Carnal Affections': Jonathan Edwards, John Owen, and Distinguishing the Work of the Spirit from Enthusiasm," *Detroit Baptist Seminary Journal* 15 (2010): 99–116; Frank McClelland and Bert Oatley-Willis, *The 'Toronto Blessing': Christian Faith or Charismatic Feeling?* (Toronto: Wittenburg, 1995); Gerald R. McDermott, *Seeing God: Twelve Reliable Signs of True Spirituality* (Downers Grove: IVP, 1995); Gary McHale and Michael A. G. Haykin, *The Toronto Blessing: A Renewal from God? Volume 1: Historical Perspectives; Jonathan Edwards: The Man, His Experience and His Theology* (Richmond Hill, ON: Canadian Christian, 1995); Nader Mikhaiel, *The Toronto Blessing and Slaying in the Spirit: The Telling Wonder*, 3rd ed. (Earlwood: N. Mikhaiel, 1996); Michael Mitton, *The Heart of Toronto: Exploring the Spirituality of the "Toronto Blessing"* (Cambridge: Grove, 1995); B. J. Oropeza, *A Time to Laugh: The Holy Laughter Phenomenon Examined* (Peabody, MA: Hendrickson, 1995); David Pawson, *Is the Blessing Biblical? Thinking Through the Toronto Phenomenon* (London: Hodder and Stoughton, 1995); Tony Payne, *No Laughing Matter: The Toronto Blessing and Real Christianity* (London: St. Matthias, 1995); Martyn Percy, *The Toronto Blessing; Latimer Studies 53–54* (Oxford: Latimer, 1996); Margaret M. Poloma, "Inspecting the Fruit of the 'Toronto Blessing': A Sociological Perspective," *Pneuma: The Journal of the Society for Pentecostal Studies* 20, no. 1 (1998): 43–70; Poloma, *Main Street Mystics: The Toronto Blessing and Reviving Pentecostalism* (Walnut Creek, CA: Alta Mira, 2003); Stanley E. Porter and Philip J. Richter, eds., *The Toronto Blessing—Or Is It?* (London: Darton, Longman, and Todd, 1995); Stephanus Petrus Pretorius, "The Toronto Blessing: An Expression of Christian Spirituality in the Charismatic Movement?" (D. Theol. thesis, University of South Africa, 2002); Bill Randles, *Weighed and Found Wanting: Putting the Toronto Blessing in Context* (Marion: Bill Randles, 1995); David Roberts, *The Toronto Blessing* (Eastbourne: Kingsway, 1995); Jürgen Römer, *The Toronto Blessing* (Åbo: Åbo Akademis / Åbo Akademi University Press, 2002); Stephen Sizer, "A Sub-Christian Movement," in *'Toronto' in Perspective: Papers on the New Charismatic Wave of the Mid-1990s*, ed. David Hillborn (Carlisle: ACUTE / Paternoster, 2001), 45–63; David Swanson, *Next Stop Toronto: The Toronto Blessing—Is It of God?* (Edinburgh: Rutherford, 1997); Don Williams, *Revival, the Real Thing: A Response to Henk [sic] Hanegraaff's "Counterfeit Revival"... An Attack on the Ministry of Rodney Howard-Browne and the World-Wide Impact of the Toronto Blessing of the Airport Vineyard* (La Jolla, CA: Don Williams, 1995); and Eric E. Wright, *Strange Fire? Assessing the Vineyard Movement and the Toronto Blessing* (Darlington: Evangelical, 1996).

2   The *eleven positive authors* include Arnott, Campbell, Cartledge, Chevreau, Davie, DeArteaga, Dixon, Kendall, Mitton, Poloma, and Williams. The *seventeen negative authors* include Belcham, Hanegraaff, Hannah, Haykin, Kuglin, MacArthur, McHale, Mikhail, Oropeza, Pawson, Payne, Pretorius, Randels, Roberts, Sizer, Swanson, and Wright. There are *seven authors offering a mixed verdict*, that is, evaluating the Toronto Blessing as having sizeable positive as well as negative elements: Beard, Beverley, Easton, Hillborn (edited volume), Kydd, Lovelace, and Pawson. *Eight authors are largely neutral in tone* and refrain from drawing any overall positive or negative verdicts. This last group includes historians (e.g., Hindmarsh and Kent) as well as social-scientific researchers

was nothing unexpected in such conflicting reactions to the Toronto movement.[3] Remarkable, though, was that both sides to the debate sought to resolve disputed issues and to clinch arguments by appealing to an eighteenth-century author—Jonathan Edwards (1703–58).

To a surprising extent, the debate over the Toronto Blessing evolved into a debate over the life, legacy, and theology of Jonathan Edwards. Many of those appealing to Edwards in support or in opposition to the Toronto Blessing were unaware of Edwards' own evolving attitudes on Christian revival, ranging from a more open-ended and accepting standpoint in his earlier work, *Distinguishing Marks of the Work of the Spirit of God* (1741), to more the temperate support of revivals in *Some Thoughts on the Revival* (1742), and the even more cautious approach taken in *Religious Affections* (1746).[4] Complicating the analysis of the Toronto Blessing in the light of Edwards' writings, therefore, is the many-sidedness of Edwards' position on revival, combined with the wide range of issues debated in relation to the 1990s revivals—for example, falling to the ground; bodily effects; laughter, crying, involuntary movements, and inarticulate or "animal sounds;" visionary and other unusual spiritual experiences; the laying on of hands and transferability of spiritual blessings; anti-intellectualism and the role of biblical preaching; supposed predictions of the Toronto Blessing prior to its occurrence; conversions of non-Christians; social impacts (or lack thereof) of the Toronto Blessing; and attitudes in the Toronto Blessing toward the established churches and their practices and worship.

Given the complexity of Edwards' arguments on revival, and the multifarious issues pertaining to the Toronto Blessing, it is not surprising that interpreters differed as to how to apply Edwards' ideas and arguments to the 1990s situation. In reviewing the Toronto Blessing debate, Richard Easton commented that "both sides have distorted and misused Jonathan Edwards in making their respective cases."[5] That judgment seems apt, though one might turn this negative statement into a positive assertion by affirming that both sides to the debate *made legitimate claims* that were solidly based on Edwards' writings and insights. On the other hand, neither side to the debate seems to have attained Edwards' remarkable balance of *openness* toward the new and the unexpected, together with *caution* in testing and evaluating all phenomena supposedly deriving from God.

One of the first published defenses of the Toronto Blessing—Guy Chevreau's *Catch the Fire* (1994)—included seventy-five pages of detailed exegesis and interpretation

---

(e.g., Percy and Römer): Hindmarsh, Hunt, Jackson, Kent, Murphy, Percy, Stanley Porter (edited volume), and Römer. Poloma is unusual in being a social-scientific researcher who is sympathetic toward the Toronto Blessing.

[3] See Keith J. Hardman and Michael J. McClymond, "Anti-Revivalism, History and Arguments of," *Encyclopedia of Religious Revivals in America*, 2 vols., ed. Michael J. McClymond (Westport, CT: Greenwood, 2007), 1:20–25.

[4] Michael J. McClymond and Gerald R. McDermott discuss Edwards' evolving position on revival in "Theology of Revival," in *Theology of Jonathan Edwards* (New York: Oxford University Press, 2012), 424–47. The chapter on "Edwards and the Revival Tradition" (675–94) treats the North American reception of Edwards' revival teaching from the 1740s to the present, with some brief comments on the Toronto Blessing (690–94).

[5] Easton, "Jonathan Edwards on Revival," 23–40, citing 23.

of Edwards' writings, along with commentary and comparisons between the 1730s and 1740s revivals and those of the 1990s. In his chapter, "A Well-Travelled Path," Chevreau argued that Edwards' own experiences of revival and the criteria that Edwards used for discerning and distinguishing good from bad, genuine from spurious, and spiritual from fleshly might have led Edwards generally to approve of the Toronto Blessing.[6] Chevreau's opponents rejected this claim, some of them scorning the notion of Edwards' hypothetical support for the 1990s movement.[7] Few of those supporting or opposing the Toronto Blessing thought that Edwards' position was not important. Almost everyone wanted to lay claim to Edwards' revival legacy, as something too significant to ignore. Already in 1994, Chevreau emerged as the pro-Toronto author whom others most often sought either to oppose or to corroborate, and Chevreau's interlocutors perceived his appeal to Edwards as a key element in his argument.[8]

As noted already, debates over the Toronto Blessing were complex, involved many different issues, and appealed to different portions of the vast corpus of Edwards' writings. It will not be possible here to canvass the discussion in all its intricacies. The present chapter will begin by considering some of Edwards' statements on spiritual discernment in Christian revivals, and then the underlying issues involved in an "Edwardsean" approach to discernment. It should become clear that Edwards avoided simplistic "thumbs up" or "thumbs down" judgments on particular spiritual movements. Our concern here will be as much with the *nature* and/or *process* of discernment as with its *outcome*. Some tentative conclusions will be offered at the end. In the future, the author hopes to pursue this topic in greater depth, and the present chapter is merely a propaedeutic to a full-scale analysis of the Toronto Blessing in light of Edwards' criteria for assessing purported Christian revivals.

Jonathan Edwards' position on revival

Was the Toronto Blessing "from God" or was it not "from God"? Edwards' writings are clearly pertinent to answering this question, since his writings over the span of a decade dealt in depth with the question of how to discern—in biblical and Christian perspective—inward experiences and bodily phenomena that were truly gracious from those that were natural, fleshly, or demonic. Edwards' prefatory remarks in *Religious Affections* (1746) stressed the importance of spiritual discernment:

---

[6] Chevreau, "A Well-Travelled Path: Jonathan Edwards and the Experiences of the Great Awakening," in *Catch the Fire: The Toronto Blessing—An Experience of Renewal and Revival* (Toronto: Harper Collins, 1994), 70–144.

[7] To the hypothetical question of Edwards' response to the Toronto Blessing, John MacArthur (*Reckless Faith*, 163) said that "he would be appalled by the movement" and that "he would almost certainly label it fanaticism." MacArthur continued his critique of charismatic revivalism in *Strange Fire* (2013).

[8] Chevreau's book was cited by Beverly, Campbell, De Arteaga (in bibliography), Hanegraaff, Kuglin, Oropeza, Porter (edited volume), and Wright (on no less than twenty-eight pages).

> There is no question whatsoever, that is of greater importance to mankind . . . than this, what are the distinguishing qualifications of those that are in favor with God. . . . Or, which comes to the same thing . . . wherein do lie the distinguishing notes of that virtue and holiness, that is acceptable in the sight of God.

Among Edwards works related to spiritual discernment were *Faithful Narrative of the Surprising Work of God* (1737), *Charity and Its Fruits* (1738), *Distinguishing Marks of a Work of the Spirit* (1741), *Some Thoughts on the Revival* (1743), and *Religious Affections* (1746).[9]

In the presentation here we will begin with some of Edwards' statements suggesting the need for *openness* to the Holy Spirit's work in revival, and then consider some of his counterbalancing statements on the need for *caution* in accepting phenomena as coming from the Holy Spirit. Generally Edwards presumed that the Holy Spirit worked in different ways at different times, with the consequence that Christian revivals did not conform to any single pattern. In a statement often quoted by defenders of the Toronto Blessing, Edwards noted:

> The Spirit of God is sovereign in his operations; and we know that he uses a great variety; and we can't tell how great a variety he may use, within the compass of the rules he himself has fixed. We ought not to limit God where he has not limited himself. If a work be never so different from the work of God's Spirit that has formerly been, yet if it only agrees in those things that the Word of God has given us as the distinguishing signs of a work of his Spirit, that is sufficient to determine us entirely in its favor.[10]

Edwards' open-enededness and affirmation of the *variety* of revival phenomena during the Great Awakening (1740–41) seems to have been the result of the *variety* of revival phenomena that Edwards witnessed, at close hand, while he was pastor in Northampton, Massachusetts, during the so-called Little Awakening there in 1734–35. In surveying the Northampton Awakening, Edwards commented:

> There is an endless variety in the particular manner and circumstances in which persons are wrought on, and an opportunity of seeing so much of such a work of God will shew that God is further from confining himself to certain steps,

---

[9] Edwards, *Religious Affections*, WJE 2:84. The critical edition of Edwards' works, in *The Works of Jonathan Edwards*, 23rd volume [print edition: abbreviated here as WJE] (New Haven, CT: Yale University Press, 1957–2010) or the online, free electronic versions (at http://edwards.yale.edu) are essential for serious scholarship on Edwards. Nineteenth-century editions of Edwards' works—and the easily obtained online reproductions and cheap reprints of these—contain innumerable unacknowledged alterations in Edwards' original words and so are unreliable for academic study. For the original texts, in chronological order, see: *Faithful Narrative* (WJE 4:130–211), *Charity and Its Fruits* (WJE 8:123–397), *Distinguishing Marks* (WJE 4:215–88), *Some Thoughts Concerning the Revival* (WJE 4:291–530), and *Religious Affections* (WJE 2:84–461). The quotation from *Religious Affections* is from WJE 2:84. For an excellent discussion and reinterpretation of Edwards' approach to spiritual discernment in *Religious Affections*, see McDermott, *Seeing God*.

[10] Edwards, *Faithful Narrative*, WJE 4:229.

and a particular method, in his work on souls, than it may be some do imagine. I believe it has occasioned some good people amongst us, that were before too ready to make their own experiences a rule to others, to be less censorious and more extended in their charity. The work of God has been glorious in its variety, it has the more displayed the manifoldness and unsearchableness of the wisdom of God, and wrought more charity among its people.[11]

During the New England revivals, Edwards noted that the application of scriptural or gospel truth in Christian preaching or in the reading of the Bible sometimes produced effects not only on minds but on bodies too:

Very often, some text of Scripture expressing God's sovereignty, has been set home upon their minds, whereby . . . their bodily strength much spent; and sometimes their lives, to appearance almost gone; and then light has appeared, and a glorious Redeemer, with his wonderful, all-sufficient grace, has been represented to them, often in some sweet invitation of Scripture.[12]

Edwards did not presume that all of bodily effects he witnessed were due to the impact of God's biblical truth on physical bodies. Yet he recognized that this was the case in certain instances.

Edwards insisted that all genuine Christian revivals had to some extent a "mixed" character, with "many difficulties" attending them as well as many benefits and advantages. For this reason, Edwards in *Some Thoughts Concerning the Revival* (1743) chided those—some two to three years after the beginning of the Great Awakening in 1740—who were still waiting to make up their minds about it. Just as there might be a *rash hastiness* in drawing conclusions about a given spiritual movement, so too there might be a *sinful slowness* to acknowledge the presence and work of the Holy Spirit. Edwards wrote:

I would pray those that quiet themselves with that, that they proceed on a principle of prudence, and are waiting to see what the issue of things will be, and what fruits those that are the subjects of this work will bring forth in their lives and conversations, would consider whether this will justify a long refraining from acknowledging Christ when he appears so wonderfully and graciously present in the land. 'Tis probable that many of those that are thus waiting, know not what they are waiting for: if they wait to see a work of God without difficulties and stumbling blocks, that will be like the fool's waiting at the riverside to have the water all run by. A work of God without stumbling blocks is never to be expected: "It must needs be that offenses come" [Mt. 18:7]. There never yet was any great manifestation that God made of himself to the world, without many

---

[11] Ibid., 185.
[12] Ibid., 266.

difficulties attending it. It is with the works of God as 'tis with the Word of God; they are full of those things that seem strange and inconsistent and difficult to the carnal things that seem strange and inconsistent and difficult to the carnal unbelieving hearts of men. Christ and his work always was, and always will be a stone of stumbling, and rock of offense; a gin and a snare to many [Hos. 14:9].[13]

On the other hand, Edwards argued that not all "affections"—what people today would generally term as "emotions"—are genuine signs of the work of the Holy Spirit when they appear within a religious context. He wrote:

There are false affections, and there are true. A man's having much affection, don't prove that he has any true religion: but if he has no affection, it proves that he has no true religion. The right way, is not to reject all affections, nor to approve all; but to distinguish between affections, approving some, and rejecting others; separating between the wheat and the chaff, the gold and the dross, the precious and the vile.[14]

How then does one distinguish "holy affections," due to God's grace and the presence of the Holy Spirit, from those "natural affections" that do not signify the Spirit's work? Edwards offered an elaborate answer to this question in his treatise on *Religious Affections* (1746), and one key element lay in discerning the *source* of one's affections: "Holy affections are not heat without light; but evermore arise from some information of the understanding, some spiritual instruction that the mind receives, some light or actual knowledge. The child of God is graciously affected, because he sees and understands something more of divine things than he did before, more of God or Christ."[15]

While Edwards—as noted—held an open-ended attitude as to how the Holy Spirit might work in any given situation, he was far from celebrating affection for the sake of affection or emotion for the sake of emotion. As Richard Lovelace noted in expounding Edwards, "Movements of revival usually center on recovered biblical truth."[16] Edwards would not have had much sympathy with Christian revivals in which leaders stirred people's emotions without informing their minds of God's truth. Revival at its most genuine, for Edwards, involved "heat with light" or "light with heat," that is, both an *informed mind* and an *affected heart*. Emotional reactions in the midst of a revival that were disconnected from perceptions of divine truth were often transient, according to Edwards, and were more likely to be natural rather than gracious in character.

Genuine, gracious, or Spirit-produced "affections" did not arise through appeals to the human imagination. Edwards' position was nuanced, since he maintained that the

---

[13] Ibid., 273–74.
[14] Edwards, *Religious Affections*, WJE 2:121.
[15] Ibid., 266.
[16] Lovelace, "The Surprising Works of God," 32.

imagination might be involved in gracious experiences, even though the imagination did not play the originating or leading role in such experiences. He commented:

> The affections don't arise from the imagination, nor have any dependence upon it; but on the contrary, the imagination is only the accidental effect, or consequent of the affection, through the infirmity of human nature. But when the latter is the case, as it often is, that the affection arises from imagination, and is built upon it, as its foundation, instead of a spiritual illumination or discovery; then is the affection, however elevated, worthless and vain.[17]

During the New England revivals, Edwards encountered people claiming to have had visions of Christ upon the cross, have heard God speaking to them, or have glimpsed heaven. In all such cases, Edwards refrained from judging these experiences as genuinely gracious or as merely natural, seeking first to engage and interview the person in question and investigate more deeply. Someone might be deeply moved in affection and imagination, he thought, by the story of Christ's life and death—much as a person attending a theatrical performance might be emotionally stirred by events on the stage—without however arriving at any settled conviction regarding the truth of what Christ accomplished by his life or death. In this way, Edwards' approach to visionary experience was both open ended and cautious.

In the midst of a Christian awakening, the first person to be awakened was likely to be the devil—the spiritual adversary—and this meant that Christian believers needed to be continually on the lookout for spiritual counterfeits. Edwards wrote that

> he [i.e., Satan] knew he could best play his game, by sowing tares amongst the wheat, and mingling false affections with the works of God's Spirit: he knew this to be a likely way to delude and eternally ruin many souls, and greatly to wound religion in the saints, and entangle them in a dreadful wilderness, and by and by, to bring all religion into disrepute.[18]

Knowing of Satan's evil intention to be "sowing tares amongst the wheat," Edwards thought it essential for all those involved in a spiritual revival to anticipate in advance the various forms of subtle but effective sabotage that the devil might employ. For this reason, Edwards was critical of those who supposed that they themselves were somehow beyond the reach of Satan's schemes:

> 'Tis a mistake I have observed in some, by which they have been greatly exposed, to their wounding, that they think they are in no danger of going astray, or being misled by the Devil, because they are near to God; and so have no jealous eye upon themselves, and neglect vigilance and circumspection, as needless in their case.

---

[17] Edwards, *Religious Affections*, WJE 2:291.
[18] Ibid., 120.

> They say, they don't think that God will leave them to dishonor him, and wound religion, as long as they keep near to him: and I believe so too, as long as they keep near to God in that respect, that they maintain an universal and diligent watch, and care to do their duty, and avoid sin and snares, with diffidence in themselves and humble dependence and prayerfulness. . . . Tis a grand error for persons to think they are out of danger of the Devil, and a corrupt, deceitful heart, even in their highest flights, and most raised frames of spiritual joy. For persons in such a confidence, to cease to be jealous of themselves, and to neglect watchfulness and care, is a presumption by which I have known many woefully ensnared. However highly we may be favored with divine discoveries and comforts, yet as long as we are in the world, we are in the enemy's country.[19]

The greatest danger in any revival lay in the attitude of spiritual pride, because the spiritually proud person presumes himself to be both invulnerable to temptation and to be superior to other people. To the spiritually proud person, even legitimate and well-founded criticism gets reinterpreted as a sign that the critic is spiritually deficient. Every critic of the revival is thus labeled as spiritually blind, unbelieving, or Pharisaical. Edwards urged his readers to exercise extreme caution in not succumbing to spiritual pride:

> Let none think themselves out of danger of this spiritual pride, even in their best frames. . . . Pride is the worst viper that is in the heart; it is the first sin that ever entered into the universe, and it lies lowest of all in the foundation of the whole building of sin, and is the most secret, deceitful and unsearchable in its ways of working, of any lusts whatsoever: it is ready to mix with everything; and nothing is so hateful to God, and contrary to the spirit of the Gospel, or of so dangerous consequence.[20]

As noted above, Edwards over time became more cautious in his assessment of revivals, and his comments regarding "spiritual pride" underscore one of his key reasons for caution. Often it was those who had had the most dramatic or exotic spiritual experiences during the heat of a new revival who, when the collective fervor died down, later proved to be the most intransigent and self-willed persons in the churches. As a good pastor, Edwards felt that it was his duty to warn his parishioners that they must not cling to their past spiritual experiences—however exalted—as badges of pride, proofs of personal rightness, or signs of spiritual superiority over other people. Edwards' warning concerning "spiritual pride" and his call for a humble acceptance of those with spiritual experiences that differ from one's own are themes that still resonate today.

---

[19] Edwards, *Faithful Narrative*, WJE 4:312–13.
[20] Ibid., 277.

Submerged questions: Charismatic gifts, bodily effects, and inner transformation

As debates over the Toronto Blessing unfolded in the 1990s, it became clear that the overriding question—that is, was the movement "from God"?—was intertwined with other issues, that we might think of as the questions behind the question. One was *the issue of cessationism*, that is, the assertion by some conservative Protestants that miracles and charismatic gifts and manifestations existed during the first century CE but rapidly faded and disappeared during church history.[21] Since the early twentieth century, Protestant cessationists have been at odds with pentecostal-charismatic Christians over the reality and genuineness of charismatic experiences in the modern age. For this reason, they are apt to cast a skeptical eye toward any purported Christian revival occurring in the context of a charismatic church—such as the Toronto Airport Vineyard Church. Cessationist Protestants regard the reported experiences of contemporary charismatic Christians in much the way that Protestants regard Roman Catholic accounts of contemporary Marian apparitions: such a thing—though theoretically possible—seems overwhelmingly improbable. In a series of anti-charismatic books, John F. MacArthur, Jr., is one of the few authors explicitly to link his opposition to recent charismatic revivals to skepticism about charismatic Christianity generally and its claim to modern-day spiritual gifts. On an implicit though not always explicit level, cessationist assumptions underlie many of the anti-Toronto texts that labeled the 1990s revivals as fraudulent, deceptive, fanatical, or diabolical.[22]

Edwards' *Charity and Its Fruits* (1738) shows that he did not anticipate a restoration of the first-century charismatic gifts in his own day.[23] There he noted that "the first age of the church till the death of all the apostles, which was about an hundred years after the birth of Christ, is often, by divines and historians, called the age of miracles."[24] He continued by arguing that "the ordinary influence of God's Spirit, working saving grace in the heart, is a more excellent blessing than any of the extraordinary gifts of the Spirit."[25] For "what greater privileges does God ever bestow on natural men than the gifts of inspiration, prophecy, and working of miracles? The saving grace of God in the heart, working a holy and divine temper of soul in the [gift] of faith and love must doubtless be the greatest blessing that ever men receive in this world."[26] Here Edwards repeats the Apostle Paul's insistence in 1 Corinthians 13 that divine love is a

---

[21] On the cessationist question, see Michael J. McClymond, "Charismatic Gifts: Healing, Tongue-Speaking, Prophecy, and Exorcism," in *Wiley-Blackwell Companion to World Christianity* ed. Lamin Sanneh and Michael J. McClymond (Oxford: Wiley-Blackwell, 2016), 399–418, especially 402–3.
[22] See MacArthur, Jr., *Charismatic Chaos* (1992), *Reckless Faith* (1994), and *Strange Fire* (2013).
[23] Edwards' cessationist arguments are the focus of Philip Craig, "'And the Prophecy Shall Cease': Jonathan Edwards on the Cessation of the Gift of Prophecy," *Westminster Theological Journal* 63, no. 1 (2002): 163–84, and, with explicit reference to the Toronto Blessing, John D. Hannah, "Jonathan Edwards, the Toronto Blessing, and the Spiritual Gifts," 167–89.
[24] Edwards, *Charity and Its Fruits*, WJE 8:149.
[25] Ibid., 152.
[26] Ibid., 167.

"nobler fruit of the Spirit" than any external spiritual manifestations.[27] Furthermore, in this context Edwards accepted the cessationist notion that God-given miracles were a sign of "the infancy of the church," when "it needed miracles and prophecies to establish it." Yet the church "being once established, and the canon of Scripture completed, they [i.e., miracles] ceased.... Why therefore should we expect that they should be restored again when the church is come, as it were, to the stature of a man?"[28] He argued further that "gifts of prophecy and working miracles, and others mentioned by the Apostle... were bestowed on the primitive church in order to the founding and establishing the Christian church in the world."[29]

When Edwards gave the commencement address at Yale College in the midst of the Great Awakening—*Distinguishing Marks* (1741)—his tone in discussing charismatic gifts was softer than it had been in *Charity and Its Fruits* (1738). "Extraordinary gifts" in the modern era were not so much *impossible* as *improbable*. While the church's "glorious times" still lay ahead, according to Edwards in 1741, yet "the glory of the approaching happy state of the church don't at all require these extraordinary gifts."[30] Edwards summarized:

> I don't expect a restoration of these miraculous gifts in the approaching glorious times of the church, nor do I desire it; it appears to me that it would add nothing to the glory of those but rather diminish from it.... It don't appear to me that there is any need of those extraordinary gifts, to introduce this happy state, and set up the kingdom of God through the world.[31]

What ought we to conclude from these arguments? The answer seems to be that Edwards affirmed the operation of miraculous and/or charismatic gifts in the first-century church, yet did not see these gifts as operative in his own day, and did not "expect" or "desire" a further restoration of such gifts prior to Christ's Second Coming. Edwards' wording in 1741—"I don't expect a restoration"—suggests that he might be termed a "soft" rather than a "hard" cessationist. Though not inclined to believe that a restoration of charismatic gifts would ever arrive, Edwards was open to further evidence and argument. The door to an end-times revival of charismatic gifts was not tightly shut, but was cracked open just a little.

Edwards' verdict on modern charismatic gifts applied to those in Edwards' own day whose claims he did not accept (e.g., the Quakers and the French Prophets). If someone has reason to doubt the supernatural character of the phenomena associated with the early Quakers and the French Prophets (both of whom claimed to receive and to promulgate "prophetic" messages), then it is possible to argue that Edwards cessationist outlook was *appropriate for the eighteenth century*, yet not for the twentieth or twenty-first centuries. Since pentecostal-charismatic Christians generally hold that

---

[27] Ibid., 362.
[28] Ibid., 361–62.
[29] Ibid., 153.
[30] Edwards, *Faithful Narrative*, WJE 4:280.
[31] Ibid., 281–82.

the *modern mass revival of charismatic gifts* dated from the beginning of the twentieth century, and not from the eighteenth century, Edwards' "no" to charismatic gifts and the pentecostal "yes" to charismatic gifts might not be in contradiction to one another, since these were *judgments made in two different eras* and *judgments based on differing sets of data*. Thus Edwards' judgment regarding charismatic gifts was not simply a question of "What does the Bible say?" but rather a question of applied biblical interpretation, namely "How does what the Bible say apply to what I am seeing in front of me?"

There is, moreover, another implicit line of argumentation that might be developed from the link that Edwards acknowledged between charismatic gifts and the church's missionary expansion. Edwards' argument that the charismatic gifts were given to found and establish the Christian church might support charismatic restorationism rather than cessationism. For if the operation of charismatic gifts is either useful or necessary for establishing the gospel message within new geographical regions, then this would be a rather clear-cut argument for further manifestations of charismatic gifts as Christian missionaries travel into new regions. Edwards lived and died prior to the birth of the large-scale Protestant missionary expansion after 1800. Yet in light of that later movement, one might have expected Edwards to have reevaluated his position on the miraculous manifestations of the Holy Spirit, as Christianity expanded into new global regions, just as it had in the first century. If charismatic gifts were requisite for the first-century spread of the gospel message into new territories, then why not for the nineteenth- and twentieth-century expansions that were even more geographically and culturally far-flung than those of the first century?

If the *Faithful Narrative* (1737) shows us anything, it is that Edwards' approach to revivals was not only biblical but also observational. Not without reason is the *Faithful Narrative* regarded as the first-ever empirical treatise on the psychology of religion, and the first text in a line of succession that would lead to William James' *The Varieties of Religious Experience*.[32] Distinctive to the *Faithful Narrative* was its wedding of the scriptural principle of "thus it is written" with the empirical principle of "look-and-see." An "Edwardsean" discernment process requires both elements. Hypothetically, if Edwards had been teleported from eighteenth-century New England to late-twentieth-century Orange County, California—to have lunch with Toronto critics John MacArthur and Hank Hanegraaff—then it seems inconceivable that Edwards would have drawn conclusions regarding the Toronto Blessing without ever actually visiting Toronto. An in-depth Bible study with MacArthur and Hanegraaff on First Corinthians would not have been enough. Indeed, one might imagine that Edwards would have not only bought a plane ticket to Toronto, but booked a hotel for several weeks, so that he could conduct the sort of in-depth interviews with the participants at Toronto that he did with his own parishioners prior to writing his *Faithful Narrative*.

An Edwardsean discernment process focuses less on *the shorter-term, inward processes* occurring in the midst of a revival, and more on *the longer-term, moral and*

---

[32] See Wayne Proudfoot, "From Theology to a Science of Religions: Jonathan Edwards and William James on Religious Affections," *Harvard Theological Review* 82, no. 2 (1989): 149–68.

spiritual effects of revival experiences in terms of what Edwards called "holy practice." For just this reason, much patience is needed before one can draw definitive conclusions about a purported movement of the Holy Spirit. A person's change in character becomes known only through the sort of pastoral probing and spiritual interview process that Edwards pursued in writing his *Faithful Narrative*. Moral and spiritual effects must be discerned over a lengthy timeframe. So, to return to our counterfactual speculation, Edwards on concluding his meeting with MacArthur and Hanegraaff, and flying off from Los Angeles to Toronto, would not outwardly observe what was happening at the Toronto Airport Church on one night, draw his conclusions, and then fly back to Los Angeles with his report. Edwards would not have made his judgment based on superficial impressions on arriving in Toronto. He stated that "a work is not to be judged of by any effects on the bodies of men; such as tears, trembling, groans, loud outcries, agonies of body, or the failing of bodily strength. The influence the minds of persons are under is not to be judged of one way or the other, whether it be from the Spirit of God or no, by such effects on the body; and the reason is, because the Scripture nowhere gives us any such rule."[33] This process of discernment was not "outward-to-inward" but "inward-to-outward."

For Edwards, the complexities of someone's soul-state could not be untangled apart from a *first-person narrative* that served as the basis on which to judge. In this sense, Edwards was a true heir of the New England Puritan tradition, where, as early as the 1630s, individuals seeking membership in a local Congregational church were asked first to provide a "relation" (i.e., account of experience) as a basis for evaluation by the pastor and elders. In light of the care and caution that Edwards put into researching and composing his *Faithful Narrative*, and the multiple criteria he set out for spiritual discernment—including the "no signs" that were not indicative one way or another—Edwards would likely have been appalled at those who arrived at snap judgments—whether positive or negative—on purported revivals. Someone who never attended a revival meeting, or who showed up at the meeting, scanned the audience, and then drew a positive or negative judgment from this, would be breaking all the basic rules for "Edwardsean" discernment.

Some authors have either opposed or defended the Toronto Blessing based purely on outward observations. Yet Edwards' way of judging revivals was based on inward experiences and was thus *profoundly moral and spiritual*. Doctrinal correctness, taken in isolation, would not mark a spiritual movement as a significant work of the Holy Spirit. Bodily phenomena likewise did not mark a spiritual movement as the Spirit's work. In Edwards' "inward-to-outward" process, a greater love for Christ and greater holiness in one's way of life would indicate that someone's spiritual experiences were significant as a work of the Holy Spirit. Of course, it was possible in the midst of a given revival that *some people* would undergo Spirit-based and gracious experiences while *other people* would not. Because Edwards thought that all genuine Christian revivals had fleshly elements, this implied that a careful observer would need to differentiate among the particular experiences of the particular people involved. Thus Edwards

---

[33] Edwards, *Faithful Narrative*, WJE 4:230.

was cautious about pointing to large-scale spiritual movements and assessing them in sweeping terms as being "from God" or "not from God." In *Some Thoughts Concerning the Revival* (1743), Edwards determined that the Great Awakening of 1740–41 was genuine and Spirit-based *on the whole*, but not that all aspects of this vast and multifarious movement were to be embraced as spiritually salutary or beneficial.

In Edwards' *Religious Affections* (1746)—his culminating work on spiritual experience—he argued that the "chief sign" of a genuine encounter with the Holy Spirit was what he called "holy practice." This implied that the fervor and excitement of the revival meeting itself was not the suitable venue in which to assess the spiritual genuineness of the experiences occurring there. Edwards' principle of "look-and-see" was thus matched by the correlative principle of "wait-and-see." It simply took time to see if a given person was indeed demonstrating "holy character" in the aftermath of their revival experiences. One of the few researchers of the Toronto Blessing who followed a genuinely "Edwardsean" approach to spiritual discernment was the sociologist Margaret Poloma. Her research sought to identify the emergence "godly love" in the lives of Toronto participants as quantifiable in changed patterns of behavior.[34]

Like Edwards at his parish in Northampton in 1734–35, Poloma in the 1990s did in-depth interviews with Toronto participants, so that her survey data was paired with and interpreted through the lens of each person's spiritual narrative. Poloma's data may be summarized as follows, beginning with the most common to least common outcomes among Toronto participants:

> 91 percent said that they had come to "know the Father's love in a new way."
> 89 percent of TB participant-respondents indicated that they agreed with the statement: "I am more in love with Jesus now than I have ever been in my life."
> 87 percent of those who are married claimed to be "more in love with my spouse than ever before."
> 82 percent agreed with the statement that "talking about Jesus to my family and friends is more important to me now than it has ever been before."
> 70 percent (about) reported that "friends and family have commented on changes that they have observed in me."
> 50 percent (about) came to the TAV "experiencing dryness and great discouragement" and left feeling spiritually refreshed.
> 46 percent said that they were more involved with their churches because of the visit.
> 33 percent say that they become more involved in works of mercy as a result of their visit to TAV.
> 28 percent said that they recommitted themselves to Christ.
> 5 percent reported being healed of a medically diagnosed mental health problem.
> 1 percent (about) of the respondents said that they experienced a first-time Christian conversion at TAV.

---

[34] See Margaret M. Poloma, "Inspecting the Fruit of the 'Toronto Blessing': A Sociological Perspective," *Pneuma: The Journal of the Society for Pentecostal Studies* 20, no. 1 (1998): 43–70 and Poloma, *Main Street Mystics* (2003).

Critics of the Toronto Blessing have pointed to the failure of this movement to engage non-Christians in a significant way, and the survey data from Poloma suggests that the objection has a sound empirical basis. The Toronto Blessing did not bring many non-Christians into a new relationship with Christ and with the Christian church.[35] On the other hand, the same data shows that a very large proportion—91 percent—of the Toronto participants who were interviewed indicated an enhancement of their experience of "the Father's love." With 82 percent indicating a greater desire to share their faith by "talking about Jesus" with others, 46 percent "more involved with their churches," and 33 percent saying that they increased their involvement in "works of mercy," it would seem that Edwards' test of "holy practice" was fulfilled for many of those who were touched by the Toronto Blessing.[36]

Conclusions and conjectures on Edwards and the Toronto Blessing

The focus in this chapter lay on an "Edwardsean" process for evaluating the Toronto Blessing. The process, for Edwards, mattered as much as the verdict. Edwards followed a principle of "inward-to-outward," that is, seeking to discern the inner state of the person who might be undergoing outward bodily effects. Edwards' empirical approach to revivals—his "look-and-see"—implied that revivals could not be judged from a distance or on the basis of second-hand reports. Paired with his "look-and-see" was the "wait-and-see," suggesting that only the discernment of long-term "holy practice" resulting from participation in a revival would show that the movement was genuinely due to the work of the Holy Spirit. Edwards would have had a problem with someone who attended a Toronto Blessing meeting and said—"People are falling to the ground! Alleluia! Isn't it wonderful?"—just as he would with someone else who said—"People are falling to the ground! Appalling! How can this be from God?"

Contemporary people may experience a disjuncture with Edwards' approach to revival, yet simply because most of us today would not want to devote *as much time, energy, and effort* as Edwards did in the discernment process. Edwards' *Faithful Narrative* (1737) shows us that he was profoundly concerned to make a careful and accurate determination of the spiritual state of each person he interviewed. Edwards' pastoral heart beats through every paragraph and page of his revival narrative. He was

---

[35] In response to Steven Studebaker's comment on an earlier draft of this chapter, the Great Awakening of the 1740s affected small-town residents who almost all had at least some connection to their local churches and to the strong Christian culture of early America. Outside of strictly missionary contexts, in which the gospel message has encountered adherents of non-Christian religions, not many Christian "revivals" have resulted in the conversion of large numbers of those with no previous contact with Christianity. In judging whether or not the Toronto Movement counts as a "revival," one ought not to use a standard of measure that would exclude virtually all of the purported "revivals" of the past and present.

[36] Mitton, *The Heart of Toronto* (1995) did not offer the sort of detailed statistical analysis that we find in Poloma's sociological work. Yet his narrative-based defense of the Toronto Blessing was more oriented toward inward experiences than outward phenomena.

the shepherd and they were his flock. The eternal salvation of each soul, he believed, was at stake. He spoke with each of them and sought to make informed judgments regarding the genuineness or spuriousness of their experiences. A first step toward becoming more "Edwardsean" in a twentieth-first-century discernment process would be to observe more closely, to differentiate more accurately, and to analyze more patiently—much more patiently!—before drawing overall judgments about any newly emerging spiritual movement or purported Christian revival. Such a cautious and meticulous approach to a revival would not be a sign of spiritual indifference or undue fastidiousness, but rather—as Edwards example shows—a mark of heightened pastoral concern for each of the persons involved in the revival in question.

Judgments about someone's moral or spiritual character cannot—or ought not—to be hastily made. How does one come to know character? A person's character comes to light within a particular situation. Novelists and other writers of fiction understand this. They thrust their imaginary protagonist into a set of circumstances that displays that person's character in some new way. Henry James wrote that "character in itself is plot" and that "character in any sense that we can get at it is action, and action is plot."[37] In fictional narratives as in real life, the discernment of character occurs as one looks at a person's behavior in changing situations and circumstances. This takes time. This requires patience. In an age like our own, where the average person's attention span lasts as long as it takes to surf from one website to another, our instincts are badly out of alignment with the demanding process of spiritual discernment. Spiritual realities must be spiritually discerned. Changes of heart happen inwardly. Tears, tremblings, fallings, or outcries do not mean that a change of heart *has occurred*. Yet the absence of such outward markers does not mean that a change of heart *has not occurred*.

One final application of Edwards' insights on revival pertains to the giving and receiving of criticism. If we presume that Edwards was correct in surmising that all genuine revivals from the Holy Spirit include fleshly as well as spiritual aspects, then it follows from this that *all revivals deserve criticism*. The question then is how criticism will be offered and how it will be received. Disrespectful vituperation against the participants and proponents of revival, on the one hand, and touchy defensiveness by a revival's defenders, on the other hand, are equally unhelpful. Even worse is a cyclic pattern of criticism and countercriticism. Richard Lovelace, in an insightful chapter on "How Revivals Go Wrong" in his *Dynamics of Spiritual Life* (1979), commented on such negative patterns of criticism and reaction against criticism, and how in many past cases this has caused genuine Christian revivals to diminish and lose their effectiveness.[38]

On both sides of any revival debate, there is need for great patience, deep humility, a refusal to judge hastily, a willingness (among critics) to find something good even if it is unaccustomed, and a readiness (among proponents) to accept that criticism of a revival may be constructive and helpful rather than destructive or malicious. To follow

---

[37] Henry James, as cited in James E. Miller, Jr., ed., *Theory of Fiction: Henry James* (Lincoln, NE: University of Nebraska Press, 1972), 13.
[38] Lovelace, *Dynamics of Spiritual Life*, 239–70.

Edwards' strongest piece of advice, there ought to be recognition by all persons of the toxic character of spiritual pride. John Wesley and Jonathan Edwards did not agree with one another in all aspects of their theologies, yet both these leaders counseled gentleness in correcting those in the midst of revivals who had become extreme in their views or practices, as well as meekness on the part of those receiving criticism.[39] For gentleness, peace, and patience are the "fruit of the Spirit" (Gal. 5:22-23), just as are the more conspicuous manifestations that occur in the midst of a Christian revival.

---

[39] In 1786, Wesley wrote from Chapel-en-le-Ferth of those who had been "awakened, justified, and soon perfected in love" adding that "even while they are full of love, Satan strives to push many of them to extravagance." For "frequently three or four, yes, ten or twelve, pray aloud all together. . . . Some of them, perhaps many, scream all together as loud as they possibly can. . . . Several drop down as dead; and are as stiff as a corpse; but in a while they start up, and cry, 'Glory! glory!' perhaps twenty times together. Just so do the French prophets and very lately the Jumpers in Wales, bringing the real work into contempt. *Yet, whenever we reprove them, it should be in the most mild and gentle manner possible.*" John Wesley, as cited in Mikhaiel, *The Toronto Blessing*, 83 (emphasis added). For Edwards' views on giving and receiving criticism in revivals, see *Faithful Narrative*, WJE 4:14–32, especially 4:24–25.

Edwards and Aesthetics: A Critical and Constructive Pentecostal Appropriation

Edmund J. Rybarczyk

Introduction

Pentecostals are not known for their aesthetic contribution. Though zealously motivated by evangelism and care for the poor, the global pentecostal movement has thus far in history been slow to recognize that artistic creativity itself is an avenue of bearing witness to the beauty of, and life in, Christ. This is a glaring lacuna both because Pentecostals are some of the most creative, industrious, and dynamic Christians on the planet and because Pentecostals seek attuning to, and celebrate the leading of, God's Spirit. Perhaps art and aesthetics have been perceived as too worldly, or perhaps Pentecostals are just too busy to bother with aesthetic reflection and design.[1]

Russ Spittler, a pentecostal scholar of the New Testament, once remarked in personal conversation that Pentecostals, their imaginations enflamed by the Holy Spirit, ought to be the most creative Christians. Globally, Pentecostals undoubtedly have many creative-aesthetic members in their midst, members whose contributions to the community might produce dramatic Kingdom-work impacts, but too regularly these members' aesthetic giftings are ignored or disdained. Equally problematic, Pentecostals have not made aesthetics significant to their Christian mission. Pentecostals' failure to understand that human persons and social groupings are profoundly impacted and shaped by the aesthetic realm means that Pentecostals will constantly be working with—if not outrightly following—the aesthetic cues and leads of others who may not themselves be indwelt by the living Christ. Differently put, rather than being salt and light regarding aesthetics, pentecostal subcultures often are being seasoned by someone else's, or *something* else's, values.

---

[1] See my "Pentecostalism, Human Nature, and Aesthetics: 21st Century Engagement," *Journal of Pentecostal Theology* 21, no. 2 (2012): 240–59, for further assessment. Steven Félix-Jager may represent a new turn for Pentecostals and aesthetics. See his *Pentecostal Aesthetics: Theological Reflections in a Pentecostal Philosophy of Art and Aesthetics* (Boston, MA: Brill, 2015).

How might Pentecostals rectify this oversight and bring their Spiritual life to bear on aesthetics?² A simple remedying step contemplates the insights of other believers. Why start from scratch? For its part the Reformed tradition is renowned for embracing the cultural mandate (Gen. 1:28-30). God, per Abraham Kuyper, even gives common grace to facilitate culture-making and the common good.³ The Reformed tradition recognizes that making culture, or even Christianizing culture (considering the Puritan enterprise), is an important way to be salt and light, and to obey Christ's commandment to make disciples of the nations. Specifically, because he was amazingly attuned to beauty's existence—particularly such that beauty is rooted in the Holy Spirit—Jonathan Edwards may serve as a fitting interlocutor for Pentecostals' aesthetic consideration. This chapter examines Edwards on God as beauty and the Holy Spirit as beauty. Following each of those themes we will suggest an interface with Edwards and pentecostal theology.

Edwards on God as beauty

Even before Jonathan Edwards was born, Puritan spirituality and lifestyle took as its central concerns ethics and behavior. Edwards, as Reformed as he truly was, made a distinctive shift within his own immediate Christian tradition: God was beautiful. Or more narrowly constructed, the first of God's own perfections was beauty. Again, to note how innovative this foundational move was, let us recall that Puritans sought to redeem the time God gave them by living every moment in accord with God's will. They sought "maximum effectiveness" by living godly disciplined lives.⁴ The divine will, as early-eighteenth-century Puritan pastors understood it, mandated not a fastidious legalism but a bringing of "all things in subjection under His feet"⁵ (1 Cor. 15:27). Like a good Puritan divine, Edwards was disciplined even in his youth.⁶ And yet his Puritan fixation—one rooted in commitments to God's sovereignty and holiness concerning

---

2   Aesthetics is that branch of philosophical *reflection* that pertains to beauty, symmetry, balance, art, and taste. Aesthetics involves the *mere* aesthetic—the appearance of an object, subject, or scene. There is often far more at work to be experienced than mere appearance suggests. (It is my conviction that people are shaped by form and design and the oft inchoate values at work in those whether or not they are immediately aware.) But seasoned aesthetes know that mere aesthetic apprehension does not probe deep enough, does not perceive acutely. A form's aesthetic dimension involves its quality, *feel*, character, and pulse. Both aesthetics and aesthetes are informed and shaped by worldviews, religious and/or nonreligious value systems, communities with boundaries, philosophic categories, and far more, all of which produce aesthetic sensibilities. Finally, culture-making, aesthetics, and aesthetic awareness are interrelated and profoundly influence one another.
3   Abraham Kuyper, *The Work of the Holy Spirit*, trans. Henri De Vries (1900; reprint, Grand Rapids, MI: Eerdmans, 1973), 38–39.
4   Leland Ryken, "The Original Puritan Work Ethic," *Christian History* 89, 2006; http://www.christianitytoday.com/ch/2006/issue89/7.32.html?start=1 (accessed November 10, 2013).
5   George Marsden, *Jonathan Edwards: A Life* (New Haven, CT: Yale University Press, 2004), 3–4, 7.
6   Ibid., 53. As a young man this pronounced religious drive saw Edwards fluctuate emotionally. For instance, at nineteen years of age Edwards wrote, "that this being so exceedingly careful, and so particularly anxious, to force myself to think of religion, at all leisure moments, has exceedingly distracted my mind, and made me altogether unfit for that, and everything else" (ibid.).

holy living—makes even more remarkable Edwards' having made beauty central to his own theological framework. "His stress on the primacy of the aesthetic over the moral and legal in our experience of God," wrote Douglas Elwood, "places the old Calvinism on a very different footing."[7]

Even into the twenty-first century what evangelical denomination argues that beauty is central to following Christ? Which pentecostal leader argues that God's beauty is the primary way to frame reality or Christian living? We are two thousand years into Christian history and beauty still barely registers on the Christian, let alone pentecostal, imagination. Edwards' commitment to God's being beautiful, then, is rather novel.[8] Kin Yip Louie writes, "Puritan New England is not known for its cultivation of fine arts."[9] Nevertheless, Gerald McDermott holds that Edwards "related God to beauty more than anyone else in the history of Christian thought."[10]

For Edwards the beauty of God was not merely a focal point for piety and devotion, nor was God's beauty just a theological rubric by which life's beauty could be interpreted, true though those were. God's beauty was "fundamental to his understanding of God, as the first of God's perfections, as key to the doctrine of the Trinity, as a defining aspect of the natural world, as basic to the phenomenon of conversion, as visible in the lives of the saints, and as marking the difference between the regenerate and the unregenerate mind."[11] Beauty moved in and from God and then out into creation itself. Beauty was indeed central to Edwards' theological framework.

God is beautiful. What did that assertion express for Edwards? It meant primarily excellence and holiness, terms synonymous in Edwardsean theology.[12] Excellence did not mean simply worthiness, near perfection, or the aesthetically sublime. Using

---

[7] Douglas J. Elwood, *The Philosophical Theology of Jonathan Edwards* (New York: Columbia University Press, 1960), 3. Kin Yip Louie nevertheless cogently argues that Edwards remained solidly theologically Reformed. Edwards was not so much introducing a new vantage point for Enlightenment philosophy as he was developing further nuance within Reformed theology. See Kin Yip Louie, *The Beauty of the Triune God: The Theological Aesthetics of Jonathan Edwards* (Eugene, OR: Pickwick, 2013), 15, 64–93.

[8] Why he emphasized beauty is less clear. Paul Oskar Kristeller reveals that initial taxonomies about the fine arts began in France in earnest in the mid-eighteenth century; Kristeller, "The Modern System of the Arts," in *Aesthetics*, ed. Susan Feagin and Patrick Maynard (Oxford: Oxford University Press, 1997), 96. William A. Dyrness believes that Edwards was working from his Reformed tradition, and "his views contain a highly original formulation that carries forward the best insights of Calvin and the tradition he represents;" Dyrness, *Reformed Theology and Visual Culture: The Protestant Imagination from Calvin to Edwards* (Cambridge: Cambridge University Press, 2004), 284. Louie clarifies that recent scholars have argued, pro and con, about the influence of Francis Hutcheson (1694–1746) on Edwards. Although Edwards was aware of recent published innovations on aesthetics he was writing about aesthetics before he read others. He was also being novel more than he was relying on other writers. Edwards wanted to relate religious affections to beauty, and vice versa, more than develop a precise aesthetic philosophy (Louie, *The Beauty of the Triune God*, 17–18, 31, 47–62, 187).

[9] Louie, *The Beauty of the Triune God*, 18. Louie also provides an encompassing overview of contemporary Edwardsean bibliography on aesthetics (3–14).

[10] Gerald R. McDermott, *The Great Theologians: A Brief Guide* (Downers Grove, IL: IVP, 2010), 115.

[11] Michael J. McClymond and Gerald R. McDermott, *Theology of Jonathan Edwards* (Oxford: Oxford University Press, 2012), 93.

[12] Louis J. Mitchell, *Jonathan Edwards on the Experience of Beauty*, Studies in Reformed Theology and History 9 (Princeton, NJ: Princeton Theological Seminary, 2003), 1–2.

philosophical categories, Edwards held that excellence involves being. Being, for its part, is clearly greater than nonbeing. Being also incorporates volition. And, volition in turn enables choice and love. True beauty, deepest beauty, manifests in agreement, consent, and love—terms all incorporating mutuality and resulting in *primary beauty*, as Edwards called it. Primary beauty, we may summarize, involves consciousness and choices that stem from the conscious being. By way of contrast, *secondary beauty* involves beauty in the material world.[13] Created nature, the physical realm, manifests myriads of instances of proportion, symmetry, harmony, relations, and equality—aesthetic categories as old as antiquity. However nature cannot express primary beauty because nature is not capable of agreement, consent, or love; material things lack mind and volition.[14] This schema did not cause Edwards to disdain physical beauties (indeed, in musing about causation they can lead us to primary beauty), but he did understand them to be less than spiritual beauties: "The world is the language; spiritual beauty is the meaning."[15]

God, specifically the triune God, is primary beauty's archetype and wellspring because God is not only one. Edwards wrote that one "alone cannot be excellent, inasmuch as, in such case, there can be no consent. Therefore, if God is excellent, there must be a plurality in God; otherwise there can be no consent in him."[16] Because the intelligent and volitional "other" in God is capable of agreeing, consenting to, and loving the "still other" in God, God is *not only love itself*, as commonly understood (1 Jn 4:8, 16), but *beauty itself*. God is both the "foundation and fountain of all beauty."[17] Hence, by the Spirit, the Son consents to and loves the Father, and the Father reciprocates. Louis Mitchell aptly summarized Edwards, "The Trinity is an infinite society of being infinitely consenting to being."[18] The beauty of being is found in agreeing to and making oneself vulnerable to the other; again this is primary beauty. Believers, to become disciples and flourish, must consent to, defer to, and honor both God and one another. It is beautiful to be in consensual relationship.[19] Believers thus

---

[13] Secondary beauty could also appear in society through the categories of architecture, wisdom, structure, and organization (see Mitchell, *Jonathan Edwards on the Experience of Beauty*, 4–5). Within his trinitarian theology Edwards rooted his understanding of the Spirit's divine subsistence in God's eternally existing divine initiative and volition. Thus, there is correlation between God's immanent beauty and the beauty of creation. Or again, there is a Holy Spirit-ual correlation between primary and secondary beauty. This is all very ideal, in a philosophic sense, but it results in an aesthetic and beautiful view of all-reality (God and creation). On Edwards' perspective about the Spirit and God's volition see Steven M. Studebaker, *The Trinitarian Vision of Jonathan Edwards and David Coffey* (Amherst, MA: Cambria, 2011), 62–68.

[14] Among other scholars, McClymond and McDermott, *Theology of Jonathan Edwards*, 94, note Edwards' Platonic indebtedness hereon: The spiritual alone is capable of primary beauty; secondary beauty "mirrors and shadows the beauty of primary beauty;" and beings with mind and volition are superior to non-sentient creation.

[15] Louie, *The Beauty of the Triune God*, 80. This schema in mind, Edwards held that human persons are greater than angels because we can love God with our affections whereas angels only can by nature. Cf. Louie, *The Beauty of the Triune God*, 151.

[16] Edwards, "Editor's Introduction," *WJE* 6:84.

[17] Mitchell, *Jonathan Edwards on the Experience of Beauty*, 105.

[18] Ibid., 13.

[19] Marsden, *Jonathan Edwards*, 3, avers that Edwards nevertheless maintained a traditional aristocratic, hierarchical, perspective on society.

participate in God's beauty when they willingly prefer and serve one another; in this way God's beauty is a beautifying beauty.[20] What God does for God as God—love and serve the other in God—is given to created beings who can reciprocate that service and mutuality to and for one another. God's beauty then is aesthetic: it involves harmony, proximity, proportionality, and relationship—categories that are extended out into creation and humanity. But God's beauty is also virtuous and holy; it involves love, care for the other, righteousness, integrity, charity, and reciprocity.

God's being beautiful was not merely theoretical for Edwards. He experienced this beauty, this divine light, in-church services, and nature. Inside Edwards' Northampton Church in October 1740, George Whitfield preached a sermon and noted that "Mr. Edwards wept during the whole time of the exercise."[21] Edwards is renown even today for charting criteria to measure the wonderful effects of revival, the beauty of God's Spirit at work in Christ's bride. Even though Edwards believed divine beauty far surpassed natural beauty he was profoundly moved by nature's beauty. A teenager, he was already aware of God's presence through nature's beauty. He would walk in the fields contemplating God's sweetness, majesty, and grace.[22] However, Edwards always viewed nature's beauties as less than God's higher and truer beauties. Edwards mused,

> The beauty of trees, plants, and flowers with which God has bespangled the face of the earth, is delightful; the beautiful frame of the body of man, especially in its perfection, is astonishing; the beauty of the moon and stars is wonderful; the beauty of [the] highest heavens is transcendent; the excellency of angels and the saints in light is very glorious: but it is all deformity and darkness in comparison of the brighter glories and beauties of the creator of all, for "behold even to the moon, and it shineth not" (Job 25:5); that is, think of the excellency of God and the moon will not seem to shine to you, God's excellency so much outshines [it].[23]

Edwards appreciated nature's beauty, but always as a projection of a truer reality in another realm, emanating from a still more real beauty: God.[24]

Key for Edwards on God's beauty is that he believed it was something that one could experience; it was not an abstraction for mere speculation. God's beauty truly exists, as an extension of God's saving goodness, and it can be apprehended. Edwards

---

[20] That God's beauty is beautifying mirrors Edwards' view that God's being is loving. Put differently, God is neither statically beautiful nor statically love, but as a communicating being both beautifying and loving. My thanks to Steven Studebaker for pressing the nuance of Edwards' thought hereon.

[21] For quote from "Whitefield's Journal," see Edwin S. Gaustad ed., *A Documentary History of Religion in America: To the Civil War*, vol. 1 (Grand Rapids, MI: Eerdmans, 1982), 196.

[22] Edwards, *Christians a Chosen Generation*, WJE 17:320.

[23] Edwards, *God's Excellencies*, WJE 10:421.

[24] Louie, *Jonathan Edwards on the Experience of Beauty*, 216, summarizes Edwards and locates him historically: "Edwards' aesthetics is an idealistic interpretation of Calvin's dogma of the world as theatre of God's glory."

once clearly delineated his sensibilities about God's divine light. It was a spiritual light that consists in

> a real sense and apprehension of the divine excellency of things revealed in the word of God. A spiritual and saving conviction of the truth and reality of these things, arises from such a sight of their divine excellency and glory; so that this conviction of their truth is an effect and natural consequence of this sight of their divine glory. There is therefore in this spiritual light . . . a real sense of the excellency of God and Jesus Christ, and of the work of redemption, and the ways and works of God revealed in the gospel. . . . He that is spiritually enlightened truly apprehends and sees it, or has a sense of it. He don't merely rationally believe that God is glorious, but he has a sense of the gloriousness of God in his heart.[25]

Reason is indeed important, Edwards argued in the same text. It is reasonable to suppose that a God who exists would want to communicate himself to his creation through grace, knowledge, and wisdom.[26] However, sensory perception and participatory perception trump reason when it comes to the knowledge of beauty.

True to his Puritan moorings, Edwards brought his reflections on God's beauty and light round full circle to a life lived for God,

> This light, and this only, has its fruit in a universal holiness of life. No merely notional or speculative understanding of the doctrines of religion will ever bring to this. But this light, as it reaches the bottom of the heart, and changes the nature, so it will effectually dispose to a universal obedience.[27]

God's beauty and light are variously experienced in the word of God, in one's heart, and in one's reason. By God-given reason and particularly via the Bible,[28] people can know something about God's existence and can understand (Christian) matters of religion.[29] But there is a deeper knowledge, a vivified knowledge—one we today might describe as existential—available concerning God. Pertaining to the senses, Edwards called it a sensible knowledge. It is a transforming knowledge. I think it fair to summarize Edwards hereon and say it is an experiential and visceral kind of knowledge. It is a living knowledge precisely because it is a knowledge vivified in relationship with God.

---

[25] Edwards, "A Divine and Supernatural Light," *WJE* 17:413.
[26] Edwards was confident that human minds can understand God's creation; cf., Louie, *Jonathan Edwards on the Experience of Beauty*, 73–74, 105.
[27] Edwards, "A Divine and Supernatural Light," *WJE* 17:424.
[28] Gerald McDermott notes that while Edwards repeatedly professed allegiance to *sola Scriptura*, he nevertheless operated with a tacit recognition "that the Bible can be read only through and with tradition." Church tradition was more significant than Edwards usually admitted. McDermott, "The Emerging Divide in Evangelical Theology," *Journal of the Evangelical Theological Society* 56, no. 2 (2013): 376.
[29] Edwards often uses the word "religion." Unlike contemporary Evangelicals he does not juxtapose religion against relationship. Rather, religion involves the true practice and lifestyle of faith in Christ.

God as beauty: An interface with pentecostal theology

Beauty and aesthetics are undeniably powerful. Westerners unconsciously and consciously define themselves via multiple aesthetic means: movies, automobiles, clothing brands, jewelry, furniture, music, and even coffee brands. Incontestably, aesthetics and beauty captivate hearts. In Eastern Europe young people are frenetic to sport a T-Shirt emblemizing American pop culture. How we conceptualize aesthetic categories then is of dire importance for fidelity to Christ and his mission. Although Edwards did not write anything about art (he did not even know to do that) or the beauty made by non-Christians,[30] Edwards models that beauty can be envisioned in deeply theological categories. He reminds Pentecostals that beauty is worthwhile because God wants us to see, enjoy, and appreciate it. Positing God as beautiful is sheer genius; besides seizing upon biblical sensibilities, it allows us to touch upon the mystery of God without trespassing into an over-reaching rational rigidity. Like God (Edwards would say, emanating from God), beauty can be known, felt, and discussed all the while those perceptions and articulations never exhaust it. Moreover, it was Edwards' theological genius to link love and holiness in the category of beauty:

beauty = love + holiness
holiness = beauty + love
love = holiness + beauty
beauty + love + holiness = excellency

I suggest that that manner of perceiving God removes coercion from the equation. Beauty invites. Beauty never forces itself upon anyone. It must be recognized, but beauty does not insist upon recognition.[31] While he remains Lord of all, God now invites us to consent to his will, to share his beauty, to live in his holiness. Summarily, God invites us into the fellowship that he enjoys as Father, Son, and Spirit. Salvation, or more carefully a life rooted in God, requires recognition of God's love, being, and grace. Yet, it is a free embrace, a sincere give and take. Edwards positing God as beauty is simply brilliant. I wonder, were Pentecostals to present God as the beautiful one, what might transpire in our evangelical, humanitarian, and missional endeavors?

If we agree that all life's goodness is from the Father (James 1:17), must Pentecostals not agree that beauty is, whether directly or indirectly, also a blessing? Why is there *any* beauty? Why does earthly life transcend mere shades of gray? Poets, painters, and aesthetes across the centuries have all reasoned that there is some great artist roaming the cosmos. No raw accident, life is too marvelously bespeckled with grandeur and too enrapturingly lathered with color. Edwards was right to see that God is the source of this effulgent, if oft finespun, beauty. Pentecostals would do well to seize upon beauty as a substantial component of life. Beauty is God's gift, beauty can transform, beauty

---

[30] Though aesthetic sensibilities pervade his theology Edwards never wrote a treatise devoted singularly to aesthetics.
[31] This line of thought derives from David Bentley Hart, *The Beauty of the Infinite: The Aesthetics of Christian Truth* (Grand Rapids, MI: Eerdmans, 2004).

generates worship: there are manifold reasons to embrace beauty within theological categories. For instance, Edwards neither espoused a material-spiritual split nor a secular-sacred split. Beauty, God's beauty, was actively shining in and through creation. True, not all beauty was equal (why should it be?),[32] but Edwards reminds us that God's creation is good, and is a locus for the beautiful. Too often Pentecostals disdain materiality, especially that fashioned by humankind, as a tempting lure. Edwards reminds us that even the mundane and secular (non-churchly) can be loci for God's inbreaking. Most Pentecostals need both a more piercing and an inclusive aesthetic eye. Edwards opens possibilities thereon.

It is further noteworthy that Edwards did not root beauty merely in the aesthetic realm. Instead, he gave beauty a dynamic quality by linking it to being and relationship. True and beautiful relationship involves deference to the other, free consent, and harmony. Indeed, "how good and how pleasant it is for brothers to dwell in unity!" (Ps. 133:1). Thus, beauty incorporates ethical dimensions that Edwards implied but did not much unpack. Overwhelmingly, contemporary ethical formulation is processed in the categories of power and rights: "Who has and shouldn't have those? who has been excluded from having those? and, how much better the world would be if we took power from *them* and gave it to *them*?"[33] Conversely, at the risk of being charged with syrupy ethereal reflection I wonder what might result were Pentecostals to construe ethics along the lines of beauty, volition, consent, and harmony. What if Edwards was right that the excellency of God is beauty, not merely aesthetic beauty but volitional and existential beauty? What if God "let go," and therefore became victorious—through the Incarnation, the crucifixion, and Pentecost—because sharing and making space for others is the most beautiful way of being? Pentecostals historically are not famed ethicists, yet perhaps beauty and beauty of God's Spirit offer lush fruit waiting to be harvested?

Pentecostals might be happily surprised to find a Reformed theologian esteeming experience. Surely Pentecostals would voice a resounding "amen!" to Edwards' emphasis that we cannot only *know about* God with our reason, but that we can sense, feel, and *know* God in our hearts and souls. Especially now into the postmodern twenty-first century, Pentecostals should not apologize for making experience central in their own theological construction. However, Pentecostals would do well to incorporate, as Edwards did, the creational sphere into their theologizing. God makes his presence known not only in preaching, the spiritual realm, charismatic gifts, or signs and wonders. Furthermore, on this experiential vein, philosopher John Dewey (1859–1952) argued that there is no true aesthetic dynamic without a sense of experiential understanding and participation.[34] Pentecostals, with their intuitive and

---

[32] This point here is fine but substantial: Unlike many Pentecostals, Edwards did not espouse a distinct dualism between material and spiritual or between secular and sacred, but he did differentiate between those pairs in hierarchical fashion. The spiritual is greater than the material. The sacred is greater than the secular.

[33] Yes, let's protect our rights and the prudent exercise of power, but Western society's litigious construction consistently posits those as a zero-sum game. Edwardsean beauty might contrastingly argue, "People, there's enough for everyone."

[34] John Dewey, *Art as Experience* (New York: G. Putnam's Sons, 1934), 13, 16, 35–50.

sometimes even mystical orientations and participatory emphases, hereby have ready-made categories for aesthetic framing.

Edwards on the Holy Spirit and beauty

Harkening to his Reformed tradition Edwards believed that the Spirit was the bond of love between the Father and the Son. By extension of that bonding action the Spirit is he who unites believers to God. Edwards was emphatic that God is a communicating being. Anticipating future pentecostal spiritual and theological constructions Edwards made the then remarkable step of arguing that God's communication is not merely about information but of himself. This communication is one of consent: the Spirit is the consent between the Father and the Son.[35] "The Holy Spirit is the act of God between the Father and the Son infinitely loving and delighting in each other. Sure I am, that if the Father and the Son do infinitely delight in each other, there must be an infinitely pure and perfect act between them, an infinitely sweet energy which we call delight."[36] Those in Christ experience God himself, the Holy Spirit. God does not merely infuse us with grace. God pours his Spirit into believers:

> The Spirit of God is given to the true saints to dwell in them, as his lasting abode; and to influence their hearts, as a principle of new nature, or as a divine supernatural spring of life and action. The Scriptures represent the Holy Spirit, not only as moving, and occasionally influencing the saints, but as dwelling in them . . . he becomes there a principle or spring of new nature and life.[37]

Louis Mitchell interprets Edwards such that "union with Christ admits one into the very society of the Trinity."[38] Again, this is a real and authentic experience of God, and not merely a forensic appropriation of Christ's saving work.

Edwards does not argue that believers experience God's essence; Edwards avoids confusing the creator with the creator, even if he does not clarify the boundaries or mechanisms for this intimate indwelling. Believers receive God himself, the Holy Spirit, as a gift given through Christ's person and work. Saints experience "excellency and joy by a kind of participation of God," and "God puts his own beauty, i.e. his beautiful likeness, upon their souls. . . . The saints are beautiful and blessed by a communication of God's holiness and joy . . . by the gift of the Holy Ghost, or the Spirit of God, and

---

[35] McClymond and McDermott, in *Theology of Jonathan Edwards*, 198, argue that Edwards did not narrowly ground his trinitarian doctrine in the divine essence, following the older pattern of Augustine. Rather, Edwards affirmed a more social model of plurality. The Spirit was the bonding agent in that more social model. For a careful engagement with Edwards' trinitarian theology see Amy Plantinga Pauw, *"The Supreme Harmony of All": The Trinitarian Theology of Jonathan Edwards* (Grand Rapids, MI: Eerdmans, 2002); Studebaker, *The Trinitarian Vision of Jonathan Edwards and David Coffey*; and Steven M. Studebaker and Robert W. Caldwell III, *The Trinitarian Theology of Jonathan Edwards: Text, Context, and Application* (Burlington, VT: Ashgate, 2012).
[36] Edwards, "Miscellany 94," *WJE* 13:260.
[37] Edwards, *Religious Affections*, *WJE* 2:200.
[38] Mitchell, *Jonathan Edwards on the Experience of Beauty*, 40.

his dwelling in them."[39] Christians' hearts and souls experience the indwelling of the beautiful one, God's Holy Spirit.

Edwards' theology on the vivifying effects of God's Spirit is beautiful. Christ didn't only atone for our sins, achieve forgiveness for us, or secure our eternal life, glorious as are those all. Astoundingly, we are given the gift of God's Spirit. Indeed, Edwards averred that saving grace "is no other than the Spirit of God itself dwelling and acting in the heart of a saint."[40] Steven Studebaker notes that for Edwards "the gift of salvation (the Spirit) is equal to the value of its cost (the suffering of Christ). In both circumstances a divine person is the currency of redemption."[41] God's gracious act of salvation is beautiful and his giving of his beautiful Spirit to indwell the believer is beautiful further still.

The Holy Spirit's presence as gift opens believers up to a fuller, richer, more intuitively enhanced way of being Christian. When, within a person, God's Spirit takes up his abode that person's heart is ignited. "The sense of the heart," as Edwards so commonly put it, results from God's indwelling Spirit. Indwelling the believer, the Spirit of God comes and awakens the soul to holy dispositions, holy attitudes, and holy habits. The unregenerate do not enjoy the experience of this holy sensibility. But again, for believers there is a new aesthetic and spiritual sensibility, a new way for the mind to perceive reality. This sensibility is "an active tendency of the entire self that determines the direction of all the functions of the human self," said Sang Lee.[42] Whether twenty-first-century contemporaries would agree with Edwards on these fruits and manifestations of the indwelling Spirit as being so certain (or narrow), Edwards was resolute on the facticity of this theological framing. Perhaps we see him processing that reality when he quoted Job 38:7, "the morning stars sang together, and all the sons of God shouted for joy," or when while observing creation's beauty he journaled, "it was always my manner, at such times, to sing forth my contemplations."[43] Edwards knew that God lived in his heart and changed his experience of life.

Further remarkable, Edwards held that *the Holy Spirit is the very beauty of God*.[44] This may seem outlandish but we recall Edwards' definition of beauty as that which involves consent. Beauty is less an abstraction than it is persons in consensual relationship. The Trinity is a society of being in relation to being. Subsequently in acts of love, God extends that relationship to creation and especially to the saints through the Holy Spirit. Developing this Edwards wrote,

> It was more especially the Holy Spirit's work to bring the world to its beauty and perfection out of the chaos, for the beauty of the world is a communication of

---

[39] Edwards, *God Glorified in Man's Dependence*, WJE 17:208.
[40] Edwards, "Editor's Introduction," WJE 21:46.
[41] Steven M. Studebaker, *From Pentecost to the Triune God: A Pentecostal Trinitarian Theology* (Grand Rapids, MI: Eerdmans, 2012), 159.
[42] Sang Hyun Lee, *The Philosophical Theology of Jonathan Edwards* (Princeton, NJ: Princeton University Press, 1988), 150.
[43] See Marsden, *Jonathan Edwards*, 78.
[44] Again, this is historically novel. Aquinas, who developed "the most sophisticated philosophical aesthetics in the West until the rise of modern aesthetics," posited that the Son is the archetype of beauty (Louie, *The Beauty of the Triune God*, 26). Luther and Calvin had little to say about beauty, per se.

God's beauty. The Holy Spirit is the harmony and excellency and beauty of the Deity; therefore, 'twas his work to communicate beauty and harmony to the world, and so we read that it was he that moved upon the face of the waters.[45]

Edwards believed that this beautiful indwelling elicited within believers a new awareness of God's beauty, Christ's beauty, the beauty of divine things, and the beauty present in nature. In short, the Spirit of God produces *a new and heightened aesthetic sensibility*. This sensory work, to Edwards' understanding, was not a by-product of new life in Christ, it was the first effect in regeneration. It causes believers' hearts to "have a relish of the loveliness and sweetness of the supreme excellency of the Divine nature."[46] In all of this we see that God's beauty beautifies. Or still more precisely, God's Spirit beautifies because he is the beauty of the Godhead. Patrick Sherry summed up Edwards thus: "Edwards derives the Holy Spirit's mission as beautifier from his role within the Trinity... being the harmony and beauty of the Godhead, has the particular function of communicating beauty and harmony in the world."[47]

God, the beautiful being who freely shares being, pours his Spirit into the saints who are then both beautified and more attuned to the beautiful. Saints, with their hearts tuned by God's Spirit, are capable both of seeing more beauty and more of God's beauty at work in life than can the unregenerate. And, those beauties, as they appear in nature, are emanations of God's own glory and beauty. "The word 'emanations' ... clearly means 'communications.'"[48] In his corpus Edwards used emanation(s) 102 times; yet, it is not entirely clear whether Edwards was using that in an established Neoplatonist sense or whether that term is a kind of holdover category that, by the eighteenth century, permeated theological discourse. The parallels with and echoes of Pseudo-Dionysius are nevertheless astounding.[49]

Another way to see the verve of God's Spirit within Edwards' theological framing concerned imagination. It takes some imagination—imagination filtered by a heart lit afire by God's Spirit—to see God within and behind the beauty of creation.[50] As I asserted earlier, aesthetes know that practicing a *mere aesthetic* might be either shortsighted or an expression of apathy. Things are not always as they initially seem. Frequently, art students aver, when we know something about the artist herself the

---

[45] Edwards, "Miscellany 293," *WJE* 13:384.
[46] Edwards, *Treatise on Grace*, *WJE* 21:174.
[47] Patrick Sherry, *Spirit and Beauty: An Introduction to Theological Aesthetics*, 2nd ed. (London: SCM, 2002), 93.
[48] Edwards, "Editor's Introduction," *WJE* 8:96.
[49] For an extensive study of Pseudo-Dionysius' use of beauty, see Brendan Thomas Sammon, *The God Who Is Beauty: Beauty as a Divine Name in Thomas Aquinas and Dionysius the Areopagite* (Eugene, OR: Pickwick, 2013). Perhaps Edwards was something of an "old soul" for Studebaker points out similarities between Edwards and Bonaventure. Cf., Studebaker, *The Trinitarian Vision of Jonathan Edwards and David Coffey*, 40–48 and Studebaker and Caldwell, *The Trinitarian Theology of Edwards*, 121–23.
[50] For a far more extensive engagement with Edwards and a pneumatic imagination, see Amos Yong, *Spirit-Word-Community: Theological Hermeneutics in Trinitarian Perspective* (Eugene, OR: Wipf & Stock, 2002), 203–7. Whereas I briefly suggest epistemic possibilities below, Yong also considers possible philosophic and theological affinities with Edwards.

art itself has a more abiding meaning. Edwards was aware of that same dynamic. The source of prejudice is the assumptions taken for granted. He put it this way:

> Make what they can actually perceive by their senses, or by immediate and outside reflection into their own souls, the standard of possibility or impossibility; so that there must be no body, forsooth, bigger than they can conceive of, or less than they can see with their eyes; nor motion either much swifter or slower than they can imagine.[51]

This willingness to consider that there is possibly more at play than surface level made Edwards committed to a life of honest learning. He knew that age can petrify a person's vantage point. A constant of human nature is that we become committed to our way of being and tenaciously cling to that, something characterized as "the curse of knowledge." Contrastingly, Edwards, his imagination made vivid, wrote, "Resolved, if ever I live to years, that I will be impartial to hear the reasons of all pretended discoveries, and receive them if rational, how long so ever I have been used to another way of thinking."[52] In all of this we can see that there can be epistemological ramifications for new life in the Spirit. God's Spirit not only opens us to beauty's existence in ways we never experienced before, it produces internal sensibilities that can make us open to learning across our lives' duration.

The Holy Spirit and beauty: An interface with pentecostal theology

Because God's Spirit comes to indwell the believer in Edwards' theology Pentecostals thus should view Edwards as a fantastic interlocutor. He surpasses the standard Reformed view that the Spirit's work is centrally to illuminate the biblical text, but he also surpasses standard classical pentecostal formulations of the Spirit's coming for spiritual empowerment or sanctification: Edwards brilliantly argued that God's Spirit variously immerses us into the very life of the Trinity, enflames our aesthetic perception, and enlivens our imaginations to discern and our souls to intuit where God is present or active in life. Again, this aesthetic dimension about Edwards' theology is ripe for pentecostal theologians to celebrate and harvest.

Edwards held that beauty was an emanation from God; such framing is admirable because it both seeks God's honor and it seeks to see all things from, in, and through God. Bluntly, it is solid theology proper. Construing beauty as he did, Edwards elided the secular-sacred split that cleaves the imaginations of too many Pentecostals and Evangelicals. Nevertheless, Pentecostals should counter that emanation is not the

---

[51] Edwards, "Of the Prejudices of Imagination," *WJE* 6:196. For Marsden discussion of this matter, see *Jonathan Edwards*, 80. This also evinces Edwards' Enlightenment commitments to learning truth, in whatever form.
[52] Edwards, *Diary*, *WJE* 16:781.

only way to understand beauty. Edwards, even though he believed the Holy Spirit was beauty itself, could have gone further and processed God's work in and through creational beauty in more resolutely pneumatological rubrics. Emanation is a philosophical category; it is not a bad category, but it is neither immediately biblical nor personal. As a constituent part of their worldview Pentecostals have pneumatology, a theological locus that could yield dynamic understandings of beauty. Emanation is helpful because it accounts for indirect presence or causation, but pneumatology might be employed in still more vivid ways. If God's Spirit is *fons vitae*, everything's life-sustainer, and is he in the Godhead who principally hovers over and in creation, why not potentially view beauty as varied actions, lesser and greater breathings even, of God the Spirit?[53] What if out of rollicking delight and overflowing love God's Spirit enfolds beauty into life, enhances aesthetes' minds and eyes, especially the perceiving eyes of Christian saints, and gives artistic and craftsmanship gifts, in order to share the delight and love—the excellency—of the Trinity? Perhaps beauty is the Holy Spirit's way of saying, "even a sin-infected world cannot limit my playfulness and joy! I'm still here. I care. Behold, I make all things new."[54] With pneumatology Pentecostals have a theological paintbrush, so to speak, that ought be employed to the benefit of their spiritual-theological outlook. A more robust pneumatological understanding of beauty, where the person of the Spirit is at work in and through creation, might also help the church overcome the depersonalizing pneumatological effects of Augustinian trinitarian doctrine. Edwards was a trailblazer for linking beauty to and in God's Spirit, but because Edwards' pneumatology relies on Augustine's mutual love model, a model than can both depersonalize and constrict epistemological understandings of the Spirit, there is room and need both for a more fully orbed pneumatological aesthetic understanding and pneumatological framing of aesthetics.[55]

Pentecostal intellectuals especially will find intriguing Edwards' insistence that life in God's Spirit caused him to remain open to further learning. Particularly, pentecostal and/or renewal institutions of higher education could frame their mission and identity in pneumatological lines following Edwards: God's own *excessus*—the Holy Spirit—makes us aware of the *excessus* (my usage, not Edwards') that is present in life. Being indwelt by God's Spirit should make us want not only to be lifelong learners, but to be ever vigilant to ask, "Are we rightly perceiving?" What if "he will guide you into all the truth" (Jn 16:13) concerns not only Christ or God's revelation, but other epistemological

---

[53] Perhaps a pneumatological panentheism captures this dynamic. This would not be the panentheism of Process theology whereby God is sorting himself out in and through the universe. Nor would it be a panentheism of Mainline Protestant theology, say like Marcus Borg, whereby Spirit sustains life but does not intervene in daily human affairs or history. In *Spirit of Love: A Trinitarian Theology of Grace* (Waco, TX: Baylor University Press, 2012), especially 121–24, Amos Yong develops a pneumatological cosmology that my suggested pneumatological panentheism mirrors.

[54] One thinks not only of the Spirit's work in the chaos-to-creation dynamic, but also in resurrection.

[55] Hence, there is an intellectual dimension—theologizing, thinking, and perceiving—that is itself aesthetic (characterized by beauty, symmetry, balance, and structure), but there is too that intellectual dimension targeted particularly toward aesthetics of/in the Spirit. We need both. For a piercing examination of Edwards' reliance on Augustine's mutual love trinitarian model, see Studebaker, *The Trinitarian Vision of Jonathan Edwards and David Coffey*, 15–17, 39–44, 65–68, 88–92, 142–55.

horizons?[56] Let me suggest a pertinent example. Instead of viewing physicality and materiality—and part and parcel of those, aesthetics—as the domain of sin and the evil one, perhaps Pentecostals could view and respect physicality and materiality (i.e., creation) as something breathed by God's Spirit (cf., Gen. 1:2; Job 32:8; 33:4, 14-15; Ps. 104:29-30; Acts 17:28)?[57] Yes, the cosmos is infected by sin and befouled with the evil one, but it is also the good product of a loving God. The Bible itself is consistently more dynamic in its view of created reality than are we Pentecostals. On a similar theme, and volumes could be unpacked and delineated hereon: Pentecostals live in an open universe on spiritual lines,[58] but they do not always live in epistemologically open ways. Amos Yong suggests a pneumatological imagination: "A pneumatological dimension to knowing without which rationality is itself undermined."[59] Perhaps life in Christ's Spirit is one variously that is ever stretching out, moving into new fields of understanding, and both exploring and artistically shaping the beautiful universe designed by the living God. If indeed the Spirit is he who will "guide you into all truth" (Jn 16:13) we need not be fearful of easily lapsing into deceit or heresy just because we are open to see where God is already at work.

Finally, for all his innovative theologizing on beauty Edwards did not suggest a Christian usage of aesthetics for Christian mission or the Great Commission; revivalism was his missional focus.[60] Maybe as a Puritan he was just too busy intellectualizing to broach a distinctly aesthetic employment. Maybe society was already aesthetically "Christianized," however that was understood in Edwards' day. All that notwithstanding, Pentecostals have a pregnant opportunity to now put aesthetics and beauty to missional use.[61] Increasingly, Westerners now live in a post-Christian era where the aesthetic realm presents new opportunities to engage decreasingly literate, increasingly image-driven, societies. At a missiological level Pentecostals must tap and develop their creative wellsprings. In my experience too

---

[56] Always, however, variously tethered to and filtered by God as Trinity, God as supremely manifest in Jesus Christ, and God's self-revelation in and through the Bible.

[57] Yong does precisely this in his *Spirit-Word-Community*. Yong presses us to consider pneumatology in its own right, and not as something only subservient to Christology, as has historically been configured by theologians. See pages 298–300 for Yong's reflections on a theology of nature.

[58] James K. A. Smith, *Thinking in Tongues: Pentecostal Contributions to Christian Philosophy* (Grand Rapids, MI: Eerdmans, 2010), 33.

[59] Yong, *Spirit-Word-Community*, 22; cf., 133–41, 160–63, 206–8, 212–14. Yong qualifies that a pneumatological imagination is "pneumatic in terms of the experiences of the Spirit and the categories drawn from foundational pneumatology" (*Spirit-Word-Community*, 22). Later Yong clarifies, "Foundational pneumatology can now be simply defined as an abstract account of the ways in which human experiences of self, other, and God are structured, mediated, and ought to be expressed" (*Spirit-Word-Community*, 109). Still more, Yong reasons that his foundational pneumatology corresponds to "metaphysical categories of foundational pneumatology: relationalism, realism, and social dynamism" (*Spirit-Word-Community*, 146). To my point above, Yong's multifaceted delineation evinces a readiness to jettison perspectives that are not true and that do not work. Indeed, the pneumatological imagination as developed by Yong is open to surprise and novelty (*Spirit-Word-Community*, 160).

[60] Cf. Edwards, "Editor's Introduction," *WJE* 4:3–4.

[61] Though he does not touch upon aesthetics proper or missional aesthetics, Yong presses us to think dynamically about a pneumatological-missional engagement with creation. See Amos Yong, *The Missiological Spirit: Christian Mission Theology in the Third Millennium Global Context* (Eugene, OR: Cascade, 2014), 183–87.

much of in-church drama harkens ill-performed *Saturday Night Live* skits: it seeks cultural fittingness or humor, but does so at the cost of both excellence and biblical-theological depth. Similarly, too much in-church aesthetic is designed to create a mood at the expense of pedagogical or disciple-making ends. Pentecostals need to become aesthetes, need to become schooled in both design and theological imagination, so that the triune God's salt, light, and excellency are displayed in fresh and relevant ways. Being a disciple, going to the nations and baptizing them in the triune God's name, involves the whole of society and involves artistic enterprise that transcends individualizing frameworks. Thank you, Jonathan Edwards, for your willingness to learn and explore theo-aesthetic realms.

Part Four

Mission and Witness

12

Jonathan Edwards, Pentecostals, and the Missionary Encounter with Native Americans

Angela Tarango

A tree planted [by a river] is never [dry]: so Christ is never [exhausted].
The soul [of the saint] is joined to Christ and they are made one.
As the water enters into the roots [of the tree], so Christ enters the heart and the soul of a godly man and dwells there.
The Spirit of Christ comes into the very heart of a saint as water to the roots of a tree.[1]

Introduction

The emphasis on natural imagery in Jonathan Edwards' sacrament sermon to the Mahican Indians of Stockbridge often surprises upon first encounter. His language is stripped down to a straightforward message and adopts a storytelling mien—both for pragmatic reasons (he preached through a translator) and in order to appeal to his Native audience.[2] Yet, while the sermon appears straightforward, almost deceptively so, "the doctrine is complex."[3] Compared to the other sermons that he left behind, Edwards tailored his "Indian sermons" to the Native people he was trying to reach. In doing so, as historian Rachel Wheeler notes, "he adapted the lessons of Calvinist doctrine to the circumstances of the Indians. Indeed, to the Stockbridge Indians, Edwards preached a doctrinally consistent Calvinism, but it was a Calvinism transformed by both the style of presentation and by the applications drawn for his Indian congregation."[4]

---

[1] Edwards, *Christ Is to the Heart Like a River to a Tree Planted by It*, WJE 25:603.
[2] Rachel Wheeler, "'Friends to Your Souls': Jonathan Edwards' Indian Pastorate and the Doctrine of Original Sin," *Church History* 72, no. 4 (2003): 751.
[3] Ibid., 753.
[4] Edwards, "Christ Is to the Heart Like a River to a Tree Planted by It," *WJE* 25:752.

Arguably the most influential American Protestant theologian, Jonathan Edwards' life and works have been analyzed by historians in order to understand both the man and his ideas.[5] His years at Stockbridge, which commenced after his dismissal from his parish at Northampton, are often seen as his exile—his time in the wilderness that led to the development of his intellectual treatises and not as a moment of fruitful missionary work. If one counted souls converted, or Indians who chose to live as the English, Edwards was a failure; over time his mission dwindled in numbers. But if you look at the way that Edwards expressed his ideas to the Natives that he preached to, and at the mechanics of his theology, then Edwards' mission to the Stockbridge Indians is a historical moment where one can glimpse an Anglo-American minister's attempt to come to grips with Native culture and how to best fuse it, however perilously, to English (which was rapidly transforming into, "American") Calvinism.[6]

As it matures as a system of faith, Pentecostalism has begun to engage with theologians well outside of its own belief structure, including Edwards. In some ways, the Stockbridge years may be one of the more intriguing comparisons between the two, as both Edwards and Pentecostals carried out missions to Native American peoples. Granted, they took place in vastly different time periods, with enormously different cultural variables and by employing different systems of Christian faith and belief. Yet, considering the two together can help historians understand American Protestantism's historically uneasy relationship with the peculiar manifestations of the Holy Spirit, as well as the evolving role of indigenous Christianity, and thus add a new facet in the history of Christian missions to Native Americans in North America.

Surprisingly, Edwards' and Pentecostals' encounters with Native Americans intersected in three major ways, which this chapter explores. The first is in regards to their view of missionary work; it was necessary for revival, and revival was necessary for evangelization and the spread of the Christian message to the world. Yet the unpredictable nature of the Holy Spirit made this complicated for Edwards. Although in the early years of the eighteenth-century revivals, Edwards accepted the manifestations of the Spirit, he eventually seemed to grow weary of them, thus displaying a complicated and idiosyncratic relationship with the signs and wonders of the era. In the case of Pentecostals, they readily accepted a great variety of the manifestations of the Spirit and made them the central focus of their belief system. Secondly, both Edwards and Pentecostals saw missions as a major force within the history of redemption. The purpose of history in both their minds was redemption and conversion of unbelievers and wayward Christians who had not experienced the indwelling of the Spirit. In the case of early Pentecostals this view was urged on by their belief in the coming

---

[5] Hence the reason Robert Jenson called him *America's Theologian: A Recommendation of Jonathan Edwards* (New York: Oxford University Press, 1988).

[6] In many respects, Edwards' most significant and enduring impact on evangelical missions was literary. His *Life of David Brainerd* (1749) became a widely popular exemplar of evangelical piety, sacrificial and selfless devotion to God, and missionary zeal in the nineteenth century. As Joseph A. Conforti notes, "More editions of and reprints of the *Life of Brainerd* have been issued than of any other Edwardsian work." See Conforti, *Jonathan Edwards, Religious Tradition, and American Culture* (Chapel Hill, NC: The University of North Carolina Press, 1995), 68; for his full analysis of the influence of Edwards' account of Brainerd, see 62–86.

end times but in Edwards' case, he saw himself as acting out a specific role within history as a missionary and pastor. But there is an important caveat here—Edwards followed in the footsteps of what was an already well-established missionary outreach to Natives in New England. His work at Stockbridge was not groundbreaking, and in fact it was other Puritan figures who did a better job of incubating forms of indigenous leadership and Christian affiliation. Finally, both Edwards and Pentecostals had an inherently theologically egalitarian outlook toward salvation, and in both cases, that egalitarian outlook was never fully implemented because of their ethnocentrism. They also tried to interact with Native culture on what they saw as being "its own terms" for both pragmatic and practical purposes, again, with mixed results. Thus, a comparison of Edwards' theology and pentecostal missionary work reveals multiple complex themes that emerge when studying Christian missionary work to Native peoples—that missionary work to Native peoples challenged Edwards' and Pentecostals' notions of mission and the role of the Holy Spirit, style of preaching, and understandings of Native Americans' capacity to become Christians.

Edwards, the Stockbridge Indians, and missions

The Holy Spirit

Edwards understood that revival came to Christians and non-Christians periodically, often through periodic outpourings of the Holy Spirit. In sermon three in *A History of the Work of Redemption* he notes that "when the Spirit of God begins or works on men's hearts, it immediately sets them to calling on (the name of the Lord); as it was with Paul after the Spirit of God had laid hold of him."[7] During these moments of revival, men and women would be prompted to turn their hearts toward God and spread the gospel. Like Pentecostals, Edwards also believed that tremendous revival would herald the coming end times: "So it has been in all remarkable pourings out of the Spirit of God that we have any particular account of in Scripture, and so it is foretold it will be at the great pouring out of the Spirit of God in the latter days."[8] Revivals often took place after a period of unbelief or moral laxity, and Edwards believed that they were to be led by a prophet or some other eminent person.[9]

Edwards believed that revival among Native Americans foreshadowed even greater revival among Christians.[10] As historian Gerald McDermott notes: "This revealing claim indicated that missions to Native Americans were for Edwards simply a chapter in the larger story of the history of revival, which was the main story line in the history of humanity itself, all of which Edwards included in what he called the

---

[7] Edwards, *A History of the Work of Redemption*, WJE 9:142.
[8] Ibid., 142.
[9] Gerald McDermott, "Missions and Native Americans," in *The Princeton Companion to Jonathan Edwards*, ed. Sang Hyun Lee (Princeton, NJ: Princeton University Press, 2005), 259.
[10] Ibid., 258.

history of redemption."¹¹ Edwards understood history as having a particular arc to it, and the purpose of history being redemption, which he lays out in detail:

> It may here be observed that from the fall of man to this day wherein we live the Work of Redemption in its effects has mainly been carried on by remarkable pourings out of the Spirit of God. Though there be a more constant influence of God's Spirit always in some degree attending his ordinances, yet the way in which the greatest things have been done towards carrying on this work always has been by remarkable pourings out of the Spirit at special seasons of mercy, as may fully appear hereafter in our further prosecution of the subject we are upon.¹²

For Edwards, the period he was living in was one of these moments of "outpourings of the Spirit" and those who labored under this belief in God's plan had to seize the moment.

Edwards' relationship with the manifestations of the Holy Spirit eventually became complicated by their unpredictability. Historian Douglas Winiarski asserts that Edward grew weary of emotional outpourings of the Spirit and cautioned his audiences against them. As Winiarski states,

> Dreams, trances, and visions assumed an increasingly sinister cast in Edwards's rapidly evolving revival theology. He had witnessed his parishioners in a "kind of ecstasy" in which they were wrapped up even to heaven, and there saw glorious sights." But visionary enthusiasm, he explained in 1741 to the students at Yale College, was seldom an authentic sign of the work of the Holy Spirit.¹³

Edwards also warned against "exercised bodies and piercing outcries" and "although he had worked aggressively to promote bodily distress in the towns of the upper Connecticut Valley earlier this summer, Edwards reversed his position in the Yale address and stated that he had observed such phenomena at a distance."¹⁴ By 1742, Edwards along with many other ministers in New England attempted to check their spirit-filled congregations. Ministerial associations provided testimonies against the overt displays of emotion and denounced itinerant preaching for creating the chaos.¹⁵ Having helped to set off the revivals, Edwards seemed concerned now that those experiencing the Holy Spirit were getting too caught up in the emotion of it—that they were too tangled up into the ecstasy of revival and had not continued on to live more godly and obedient lives. For Edwards, revival was more than just signs and wonders. Revival should lead to new obedience to the church and life-changing outward manifestations of personal holiness.

---

¹¹ Ibid., 258.
¹² Edwards, *A History of the Work of Redemption*, WJE 9:143.
¹³ Douglas L. Winiarski, *Darkness Falls on the Land of Light: Experiencing Religious Awakenings in Eighteenth-Century New England* (Chapel Hill, NC: The University of North Carolina Press, 2017), 271.
¹⁴ Ibid., 269.
¹⁵ Ibid., 275–76.

Missions

If, according to Edwards, the redemption of mankind is the main goal of history, then "the work of missions, which stimulates revival, is the hidden dynamic driving history and the fruit of missions produces more human happiness then the ablest statecraft."[16] Edwards believed that Native Americans were also fully able to comprehend and accept Christianity.[17] He notes that

> though there has been but a small propagation of the gospel among the heathen in comparison of what were to be wished for, yet there has been something worthy to be taken notice of; something remarkable in the first times of New England, and something remarkable has appeared of late here and in other parts of America among many Indians, of an inclination to be instructed in the Christian religion.[18]

For Edwards, the willingness of some Natives to be instructed in Christianity proved correct his belief that history was leading toward the redemption of humanity. Native Americans were a central part of the arc of history as the necessary redemption of the "heathen other."[19] Edwards, like Pentecostals, believed that the work of the Holy Spirit was imperative to the growth of missions, but unlike Pentecostals, Edwards always remained at core a Calvinist. His Holy Spirit was one that worked deliberately, carefully through history, choosing the saved and the damned, whereas the Holy Spirit of early Pentecostalism was raucous, affecting and unpredictable and came down upon those who sought it.

Missions to Native peoples were established in New England from the colony's outset, so Edwards' work in Stockbridge followed a full century of Puritan evangelization. The history of the study of missions to Native peoples in New England has shifted over the years—historians in the 1970s doubted the veracity of Native Christian belief, but this changed as historians in the 1980s and 1990s moved to stress Native agency in understanding forms of indigenous Christianity.[20] Well before Edwards' time, missions were well established in New England, and historians have argued that New England Native peoples developed a fairly sophisticated understanding of Christianity. Historian David Silverman noted that around 1675–76 on Martha's Vineyard, the "Wampanoags took the lead in their own Christianization, establishing churches and courts in which the traditional elite assumed the new duty of punishing sin and spreading their people's indigenized Christianity."[21] He also noted that the Wampanoag's understanding of Christianity did not mean they had to abandon their old beliefs entirely. "Instead it was a process in which the Indians thought they were digging deeper into ancient

---

[16] McDermott, "Missions and Native Americans," 259.
[17] Ibid., 260–61.
[18] Edwards, *A History of the Work of Redemption*, WJE 9:434.
[19] McDermott, "Missions and Native Americans," 261.
[20] David J. Silverman, "Indians, Missionaries, and the Religious Translation: Creating Wampanoag Christianity in Seventeenth Century Martha's Vineyard," *The William and Mary Quarterly*, Third Series, 62, no. 2 (2005): 144.
[21] Silverman, "Indians, Missionaries, and the Religious Translation," 146.

wellsprings of spiritual power to recover its purest, most potent form and truths that had been with them opaquely along," according to David J. Silverman.[22] Historian Linford Fischer showed in his revealing study of the period leading up to the revivals of the Great Awakening that most Native peoples tended to "affiliate" with Christianity, and that affiliation needed to be understood in indigenous terms.[23] Native Christians did eventually form their own separate churches, some with indigenous preachers after the revivals, and were affected in their own ways by the revivals associated with the Great Awakening period. The fact is that Edwards' work with Native peoples followed long established missionary patterns in New England. His work in Stockbridge was not particularly innovative, and in some ways, was an outlier, given that earlier missionaries had enjoyed better success in encouraging Natives to affiliate with Christianity.[24]

Salvation, pragmatism, and ethnocentrism

As historian Rachel Wheeler attests in her excellent *Church History* article on Edwards and his Stockbridge pastorate, Edwards preached a brand of Calvinism that, while harsh to modern ears, treated all of his parishioners equally in the spiritual realm. Edwards certainly believed that traditional Native beliefs were of the devil, and he warned his Stockbridge parishioners of their collusion with the demonic. "I would have you Indians consider how it was with you. Your whole nation was formerly under the power of that strong man armed, and now you are brought under the gospel. Consider how much has been done [for you]. And yet how is it with many of you still? How the devil keeps you under his power!"[25] While his sermons toward the Natives sound harsh, they are no more so than those he had preached to his fellow Englishmen at Northampton. In fact, as Wheeler attests, he often "stressed that the colonists were inherently no better than the Indians, and that the English would suffer all the more in hell for their neglect of Christian duty; with all their advantages, they should know better."[26] He regularly reminded his Native flock that they were no more cursed than the English—the English had simply just known the gospel for a longer period of time.[27]

Despite his spiritual egalitarianism, Edwards was a man of his time. He never learned to speak the Native languages, instead preferring to preach through an interpreter.[28]

---

[22] Ibid., 146.
[23] Linford D. Fisher, *The Indian Great Awakening: Religion and the Shaping of Native Cultures in Early America* (New York: Oxford University Press, 2003).
[24] Along with Fisher and Silverman's work, for a more in-depth look at New England missions, and Native education, please see: Douglas L. Winiarski, "A Question of Plain Dealing: Josiah Cotton, Native Christians, and the Quest for Security in Eighteenth-Century Plymouth Colony," *The New England Quarterly* 77, no. 3 (2004): 368–413; Edward E. Andrews, *Native Apostles: Black and Indian Missionaries in the British Atlantic World* (Cambridge: Harvard University Press, 2013); and John Demos, *The Heathen School: A Story of Hope and Betrayal in the Age of the Early Republic* (New York: Vintage, 2014).
[25] Edwards, "135. To Sir William Pepperrell," *WJE* 16:678.
[26] Wheeler, "Friends to Your Souls," 746.
[27] Ibid., 747.
[28] Ibid., 749.

He believed that English culture was inherently superior and that the Natives needed to take up their education in English and adopt English ways. He noted that a proper education should include teaching the Natives to sing so to encourage them to "renounce the coarseness, and filth and degradation of savage life, for cleanliness, refinement and good morals."[29] He adopted the point of view of his era that Native culture was inherently inferior and thus "savage." But he also thought Natives were capable of academic work and often advocated for the education of both boys and girls at the mission stating in one letter: "And I cannot but think it might be a pretty easy thing, if proper measures were taken, to teach children to spell well, and girls as well as *boys*. I should think it may be worth the while, on various accounts, to teach them to write, and also to teach them a little of arithmetic."[30] He also thought Native children were able to understand complicated historical concepts: "And I can see no reason, why children can't, or mayn't, be taught something in general of ecclesiastical history."[31] Finally, he also stood up for Native rights and against abuses of the English against the Indians at Stockbridge, a fact to which many of his letters and writings attest.[32] Like so many missionaries, Edwards had complicated views of those he missionized. Native Americans were spiritually equal and temporally unequal, yet always capable of improvement in both realms.

There is a distinctive loveliness in Edwards' Stockbridge sermons to the Indians. They are written in straightforward language and they draw heavily from New Testament texts, with a heavy reliance on the Gospels of Matthew and Luke. The imagery is mainly natural, and he utilized the power of storytelling in his sermons.[33] It seems that Edwards believed that this approach would draw the Stockbridge Indians closer to the gospel, and would be more appealing to them as an audience. While such an approach was pragmatic in terms of his Indian audience, it also signifies how Edwards viewed God. It was his intellectual attempt to engage Native culture on its own terms in a way that he thought would make Christianity more appealing. Even if it seems like a weak attempt it is worth exploring.

In the sermon "God is Infinitely Strong," given in January 1753, Edwards solidified his unique preaching style for the Stockbridge Indians. According to Wilson Kimnach the sermon strikes the listener as more of a personal witness, one that evokes natural phenomena, and with straightforward diction—almost as if you would be explaining theological concepts to a child.[34] In the sermon Edwards emphasizes the omnipotence and omnipresence of God, and relates Him to the natural work.

> Because God made all things, he must see and know all things: all the stars, angels, all mankind; beast, birds, fishes, flies: every part of their bodies, their eyes, their legs, every bone, every vein. [He not only knows the] stars, [but] every tree leaf

---

[29] Edwards, "135. To Sir William Pepperrell," *WJE* 16:411.
[30] Ibid., 411 (emphasis original).
[31] Ibid., 410.
[32] Wheeler, "Friends to Your Souls," 747.
[33] Ibid., 750–51.
[34] Edwards, "Christ Is to the Heart Like a River to a Tree Planted by It," *WJE* 25:641.

[and blade of] grass; [every] drop of water [and mote of] dust: [God] must see 'em all when he made [them]; otherwise [he] could not make 'em. Did he know not what he did?[35]

Edwards goes on to note that God's strength appears "by thunder and lightning, [by] wind, [and by] earthquake. [He] shakes the earth [and] mountains [are] overturned."[36] This God is a mighty and powerful God, one fully engaged in the act of Creation and in the minutia of the natural world. No doubt, Edwards believed that this striking imagery would appeal to the Stockbridge Indians, who understood themselves as part of the natural world in a profound, if not-Christian, manner. In using this language Edwards is tailoring the gospel to them, trying to meet them on their own terms.

Despite the fact that Edwards greatly shifted his preaching style, language, and use of imagery while preaching to the Stockbridge Indians, he never diluted his Calvinist Christian message. In the same sermon, his "application" section spelled out the meaning behind his insistence on an omnipresent, omnipotent creator God. This is not a friendly God; instead Edwards exhorts his Native audience to

> fear him; trust in him; be humble. How miserable they are who have this God to be their enemy. [There is] no getting away from God, no hiding: none can deliver [you from his hands]. . . . He sees all you do, sees in the night, sees your heart, [and] remembers all. Here is encouragement to pray to God. . . . He can save you from the devil: he takes the poor soul out of the mouth of the devil as a strong man comes and takes a lamb out of the mouth of a bear.[37]

Those familiar with "Sinners in the Hands of an Angry God" know this God—yet in his Indian sermons Edwards' God comes across as fearsome, but not quite as vengeful. For Edwards, it was of utmost importance that his Indian flock understood the importance of damnation, but also that God had the ability to offer salvation. Native people could be saved too, but they had to embrace Edwards' Calvinist God, a prospect that no doubt, would have demanded significant social, cultural, and spiritual change among the Indians. In the end, it was chiefly his preaching style that Edwards altered to try to interact with Native culture. Like many other missionaries to Native peoples, ethnocentrism and his inability to accept Native affiliation on their own terms kept him from enjoying widespread success among the Stockbridge Indians.

Pentecostals and missions—a comparison

The Holy Spirit

In North America, many Pentecostals, especially in the early to middle decades of the twentieth century, understood speaking in tongues (glossolalia) to be a sign of baptism

---

[35] Ibid., 644.
[36] Ibid., 645.
[37] Ibid., 645.

in the Holy Spirit. Along with baptism in the Holy Spirit, one could receive the gifts of healing, prophecy, or interpretation of tongues. Many Native American Pentecostals in the early twentieth century described their baptism in the Holy Spirit in emphatic terms like Mohawk Rodger Cree, "He recalled, 'I saw a ball of fire that was lodged in the ceiling—when that ball of fire touched my head, I began to speak in a different language, altogether Supernatural.'"[38] While a powerful experience, this understanding of tongues as evidence can be problematic, as theologian Walter J. Hollenweger points out:

> Many pentecostal churches have a great proportion of members (and sometimes even pastors) who have never spoken in tongues. If a third of all members do not speak in tongues, this leads to enormous pastoral problems. It divides the church into first and second-class Christians.[39]

As the movement expanded across the globe, different groups of Pentecostals came to interpret baptism of the Holy Spirit differently, and as scholar Frank Macchia has noted, "There is no universal agreement among Pentecostals worldwide on such questions."[40] Indeed, there is no set doctrine as Hollenweger states: "Talk of 'the doctrine' of the pentecostal churches is highly problematical. What unites the pentecostal churches is not a doctrine but a religious experience, and this can be interpreted and substantiated in many different ways."[41] Therefore, modern theologians acknowledge that baptism in the Holy Spirit and its relationship to tongues can be understood in multiple different ways, mainly depending on the culture it is taking place within.[42] With this in mind, it is important to note that this chapter will be privileging the North American pentecostal experience, where it is common to understand tongues as evidence.

For Pentecostals, there has always been a strong link between their understanding of Spirit baptism and the impetus for missionary work.[43] Like Edwards, early Pentecostals understood missions as key to their role in history. They believed that they were living in the end times and because of that belief they were pressed to evangelize the world. Missionary historian Gary McGee has noted that early Pentecostals pointed to key Bible verses from the books of Mark, Matthew, and Acts as the inspiration for early

---

[38] Angela Tarango, *Choosing the Jesus Way: American Indian Pentecostals and the Fight for the Indigenous Principle* (Chapel Hill, NC: University of North Carolina Press, 2014), 55.
[39] Walter J. Hollenweger, *Pentecostalism: Origins and Developments Worldwide* (Peabody, MA: Hendrickson, 1997), 227.
[40] Frank D. Macchia, *Baptized in the Spirit: A Global Pentecostal Theology* (Grand Rapids, MI: Zondervan, 2006), 34.
[41] Walter J. Hollenweger, "From Azusa Street to the Toronto Phenomenon," in *Pentecostal Movements as an Ecumenical Challenge*, ed. Jürgen Moltmann and Karl Josef Kuschel, Concilium 3 (London: SCM, 1996), 7.
[42] For an example of this see Macchia, *Baptized in the Spirit*, and also Amos Yong, *The Spirit Poured Out on All Flesh: Pentecostalism and the Possibility of Global Theology* (Grand Rapids, MI: Baker Academic, 2005).
[43] Allan Anderson, *Spreading Fires: The Missionary Nature of Early Pentecostalism* (New York: Orbis, 2007), 65.

missionary work.[44] These verses "show the strong link between their view of baptism of the Holy Spirit as an enduement of power for Christian witness, the expectancy of signs and wonders to follow the proclamation of the gospel to the uninitiated, the imminent premillennial return of Jesus Christ and their own work."[45] Noted pentecostal historian Allan Anderson reinforces this viewpoint in his own work that "just as Spirit baptism is Pentecostalism's central, most distinctive doctrine, so mission is Pentecostalism's central, most important activity."[46] Pentecostalism as a movement cannot be disentangled from its missionary impulse—in fact most historians would argue that especially at the beginning it was an entirely mission-driven movement. The Spirit led the way and believers followed, often compelling them to give up the comforts of home in order to plunge forth into new lands.

Missions

Missions to Native Americans were part of the global missionary work that Pentecostals spearheaded during the early twentieth century. Yet, while as a movement Pentecostalism seemed fresh, new, and exciting, missions to Native Americans got off to a rather quiet and low-key start, especially compared with world missions. A few enterprising souls were called to missionize Native Americans (starting mainly in California and later the desert southwest) in the 1920s, and that number grew steadily in the 1930s and 1940s. They were mostly affiliated with the Assemblies of God (AG), although other pentecostal groups had small missions to Native peoples but the AG's missions grew into the largest and most well documented, so for that reason they will be used as the main example in this chapter.[47]

Missions to Native Americans were undergirded by a particular pentecostal theology of missions that lauded what Pentecostals called "the Pauline example."[48] This meant that in theory, a missionary would try to set up a mission that encouraged local involvement, train native pastors, and eventually turn the mission into a locally run church. In essence, the role of a good missionary was to put themselves out of business. Pre-pentecostal Roland Allen along with early Pentecostals Alice Luce and Henry Ball initially promoted this view with some success, but in fact creating an indigenous mission was easier said than done.[49] While it was good in theory, all of these early prominent missionaries were paternalistic or maternalistic, and racist, not unlike Edwards. Edwards certainly believed in the benevolent and civilizing missionary, and paternalism was the standard for his era. While like Edwards Pentecostals believed that Native peoples of all kinds could experience the Holy Spirit and be saved, and therefore were no more damned than white nonbelievers, in reality many missionaries

---

[44] Gary McGee, *This Gospel Shall Be Preached: A History and Theology of Assemblies of God Foreign Missions to 1959* (Springfield, MO: GPH, 2003), 94.
[45] Ibid.
[46] Anderson, *Spreading Fires*, 65.
[47] See Tarango, *Choosing the Jesus Way*, especially chapter 1.
[48] Pre-pentecostal Roland Allen used the Apostle Paul for his argument for indigenous churches in China, which was also picked up by pentecostal missionaries Alice Luce and later Melvin Hodges. See Roland Allen, *Missionary Methods: St. Paul's or Ours?* (Mansfield Center, CN: Martino, 2001).
[49] McGee, *This Gospel Shall Be Preached*, 97.

were loath to hand over full control of a mission to Native pastors. This led to the development of the indigenous principle in the 1950s by Melvin Hodges. Hodges, a former missionary who had served in Latin America, wanted pentecostal missionaries to embrace what he called the indigenous principle without any taint of colonialism, paternalism, or attempts at Americanization.

The ideas behind the indigenous principle were outlined in a series of lectures given by Hodges in Springfield, Missouri. The series was later published in a book entitled *The Indigenous Church* and later, Hodges followed up with *The Indigenous Church and the Missionary*.[50] The main points that undergirded Hodges were that Native peoples "with the help of the Holy Spirit, were completely capable of running their own churches. It harmed the AG missionary system, if missionaries failed to train the converts to do so."[51] In fact, it was anathema to Pentecostalism for missionaries to not allow indigenous churches. If Pentecostals said that they believed that the Holy Spirit fell equally on all peoples and they actually meant it, then local churches needed to be run by local peoples who had experienced the Holy Spirit. Even if those peoples were not white, Westernized or were recent converts to Christianity. Furthermore, to accept this view, Hodges understood that local Christianity at these missions would absorb certain local flavors or customs and look different from the Christianity that missionaries practiced back home. To him it was important to stress that just because local native Christianity might look different from white American Pentecostalism, it was in no meaningfully way "different" so long as the doctrine and theology behind it were the same.[52]

Hodges' ideas for the AG were touted and influential in world missions, especially to Latin America and Africa, but the same cannot be said among white missionaries to Native Americans. The history of paternalism and Americanization was so strong, along with long held racist notions of Native peoples as "savage" and having been "in darkness," which mirrored language that the AG used in their periodicals, that was not unlike the language that Edwards himself used in his sermons.[53] The fact is that the indigenous principle was never fully implemented by white AG missionaries to Native Americans until Native American Pentecostals forced the issue themselves—and transformed the indigenous principle into a theology that addressed their lives as Native Americans living in a modern world that often ignored or denigrated them. This process, which is outlined in detail in my book *Choosing the Jesus Way: American Indian Pentecostals and the Fight for the Indigenous Principle*, took the better part of the twentieth century and even in the twenty-first, it is not fully realized. The difference here is that Edwards had little success in fully training indigenous missionaries, but other missionaries in early New England did enjoy success, and Native people did assert their own spiritual autonomy.[54] In the twentieth century, American Indian

---

[50] Melvin Hodges, *The Indigenous Church, Including the Indigenous Church and the Missionary* (Springfield, MO: GPH, 2009).
[51] Tarango, *Choosing the Jesus Way*, 39.
[52] Ibid., 38–40.
[53] There is a long history of the use of "savage" in American missionary literature when discussing Native Americans. For a classic work on the term see, Robert J. Berkhofer, *Salvation and the Savage: An Analysis of Protestant Missions and the American Indian Response, 1787–1862* (Louisville, KY: University of Kentucky Press, 1965).
[54] For more on this see Andrews, Fisher, and Silverman.

leaders themselves forced the issue, and built missions that became indigenous all on their own, thus making their example closer to that of later Separate Indian churches from the Great Awakening. Both Pentecostals and Edwards did believe that native people in general were all capable of being saved, and equal with others in the eyes of God, yet their practical, actual missionary approaches were very different.

Salvation, pragmatism, and ethnocentrism

Finally, while Edwards tried to connect to Native culture through his engagement with naturalistic language in his sermons, Pentecostals engaged Native culture in a variety of ways, chiefly in their forms of evangelism. We have numerous examples of white pentecostal missionaries holding outdoor camp meetings that were modeled on traditional Native pow-wows or gatherings, pioneering the evangelism of Native believers at Indian rodeos and cattle roundups. Missionaries also placed emphasis on Native foods and traditional crafts, and encouraged their parishioners to enter contests at local fairs promoting those items in order to find ways to conduct more Native outreach.[55] White Pentecostals, like Edwards, translated their sermons into Native languages, but as Pentecostals are known for extemporaneous preaching, almost no copies of the sermons exist; thus, it is hard to see what linguistic styles were used. Native pentecostal leaders even more fully encouraged and embraced Native culture among their flocks, encouraging the preservation of language, food, and other aspects of their own particular tribal culture that they saw as not oppositional to Christianity and therefore could be retained. For many Native Pentecostals, one did not have to give up their traditions and ties to their tribes in order to become Pentecostal—thus advancing Melvin Hodges' ideal of the indigenous principle.

More recently one pentecostal denomination has embraced contextualization and dialogue with Native traditions. In his book, *Native American Pentecost*, Corky Alexander details how the Church of God (Cleveland) has pioneered a specific kind of Native evangelism. In order to appeal more to Native believers Alexander shows how the Church of God has integrated six specific Native American customs into their evangelism: use of Native language, smudging, drums and rattles, dance, talking circles, and the enemy way ceremony. This makes the Church of God more progressive than the AG, which only allows the use of language, but often preaches against dancing and the use of drums (because in traditional Native belief, drums are thought to have a spirit). Alexander argues that such usages are contextualization and not syncretism, which implicitly implies that integrating these Native customs creates a more indigenous Christianity. Although this is small example, as the Church of God is a smaller institution than the AG, and has a smaller mission to Native peoples, it still shows the inherent flexibility of Pentecostalism and how it has tried to connect with Native culture.[56]

---

[55] See Tarango, *Choosing the Jesus Way*, chapters 2 and 3.
[56] Corky Alexander, *Native American Pentecost: Praxis, Contextualization, Transformation* (Cleveland, TN: Cherohala, 2012), chapters 3 and 4.

Conclusion

Edwards' missions to the Stockbridge Indians and pentecostal missions to Native Americans were separated by two centuries and vastly differing theologies, and yet they exhibit some interesting similarities. Both Edwards and Pentecostals understood the Holy Spirit as the prime mover and inspiration to Christians in their particular historical moments. But while Pentecostals came to understand gifts of the Spirit as proof of Spirit baptism, Edwards moved away from endorsing the manifestations of the Holy Spirit after the start of the revivals of the eighteenth century. Both Edwards and Pentecostals saw missions as essential for revival, and thus the galvanizing force for the history of redemption. Edwards' work followed a century of Puritan mission work, and he was less successful than some of his forebears and contemporaries in fostering an indigenous Christianity. Although both Edwards and Pentecostals understood a theology of salvation that was mostly egalitarian, both were plagued by an undercurrent of paternalism, which was not challenged in Edwards' time and was only squarely faced by Native pentecostal leaders, who forced white Pentecostals to grapple with the implications of a paternalistic and ethnocentric message. Finally, both groups attempted to engage Native culture—Edwards mainly through a particular style of language in his preaching and Pentecostals through their methods of evangelization. Later, Native Pentecostals, again, would take this engagement to a more meaningful place in trying to carve out their own place in pentecostal denominations.

This comparison of a Calvinist theologian in the eighteenth century with a spirit-filled twentieth- and twenty-first-century movement unearths particular quirks and nuances within the study of Christian missions to Native people. Both Edwards and early Pentecostals had particular notions of race and these notions could not be overcome by theologies that were ostensibly egalitarian, despite their best efforts, without directly acknowledging how Christianity racially constructs the "other." Therefore, both Edwards and Pentecostals needed Native push back in order to grow and to move toward realizing their more egalitarian notions of Christianity. Native believers and their red bodies, in their particular times and places, challenged and changed both groups. Edwards' time in Stockbridge and his interactions with the Natives likely (gently) shaped his Calvinism (he died before this could really be realized) just as much as Native Pentecostals not-so-gently pushed white Pentecostals toward realizing a more indigenous Pentecostalism. Therefore, Native encounters with Edwards and Pentecostals show that the most important aspect of the history of Christian missionary work in the United States is not who converted or how many converted, or even what theologies were appealing to Natives. But rather how interaction between Native Americans and Christian missionaries shifted both actors and their theologies, sometimes in ways that were positive as well as negative, and oftentimes resulted in confusing, complicated, and deeply rich encounters that cannot be easily teased apart or even fully understood.

"The Grand Design of God in All Divine Operations": Pentecostal Retrieval of Jonathan Edwards' Distinctive Contribution to the Positive Significance of Non-Christian Religions

Tony Richie

Introduction

Jonathan Edwards' efforts to understand all history from the standpoint of God's universal work of redemption, I suggest, implies refusal to view the world's religions apart from God's particular work of redemption in Jesus Christ.[1] Accordingly, does Edwards grant them, in a carefully qualified sense, a positive place of significance in God's ultimate redemptive plan? Certainly, he understands the religions against the backdrop of the truth of the gospel of Jesus Christ and salvation through him. In setting all God's revelatory and salvific work within the context of divine providence and eternal purpose in Jesus Christ, Edwards staunchly maintained his Calvinist heritage. However, Edwards' theology has implications for contemporary Christian theology of religions including within Pentecostalism with its generally Wesleyan-Arminian heritage.[2] This chapter interacts with specialized Edwards' scholarship, pointedly engages Edwards as a primary source, and suggests implications for Christian theology of religions with emphasis on Pentecostalism—specifically narratival/testimonial methodology, ideological compatibility, shared dynamism, vital pivot of grace, essentiality of opposition, and energetic pneumatology.

---

[1] The main title paraphrases Edwards' letter to college faculty describing "A History of the Work of Redemption;" see *A Jonathan Edwards Reader*, ed. John E. Smith, Harry S. Stout, and Kenneth P. Minkema (New Haven, CT: Yale University Press, 2008), xxvii.
[2] Cf. Mildred Bangs Wynkoop, *Foundations of Wesleyan-Arminian Theology* (Kansas City, MO: Beacon Hill, 1967).

Accessing methodology and ideology

This chapter's primary resource is Edwards' *A History of the Work of Redemption* (AHOR).³ Edwards intended a new theological schema "in the form of a history" showing "how the most remarkable events, in all ages" "recorded in sacred and profane history, were adapted to promote the work of redemption."⁴ In other words, it plumbs the testimony of history regarding redemption. His intention entails some attention to the world's religions.⁵ I approach Edwards' distinctive methodology in terms of my own theological utilization of testimony as a pentecostal model for interreligious dialogue.⁶ To an extent, AHOR is a theological analysis of the testimony of history to redemptive realities.⁷

In spite of Edwards' theological Calvinism, I draw implications for pentecostal theology—which overall tends to be Wesleyan-Arminian with some groups commonly designated "Wesleyan-Pentecostals."⁸ This adaptation is not new. John Wesley appreciatively drew on Edwards theologically and philosophically.⁹ Edwards personified an integration of intellectual sophistication and revivalist passion amenable for the Wesleyan tradition.¹⁰ Pentecostals like Steven Land have followed suit in critically appreciating Edwards' spiritual theology.¹¹ Although Pentecostalism has been more influenced by evangelical Arminianism and Wesley than evangelical Calvinism and Edwards, especially regarding the role of the Holy Spirit in Christian experience, clear echoes of Edwards and Great Awakening revivalism can be heard in the nineteenth-century Holiness movement and its twentieth-century offspring,

---

3   Edwards, *A History of the Work of Redemption*, WJE 9:v–ix, 1–555. When quoting others, I retain their use of Edwards' works. My references utilize the Yale critical edition unless the material is only accessible otherwise.
4   These quotes by the junior Edwards appear in the "Preface" of the old print edition of *The Works of Jonathan Edwards*, vol. 1 (Peabody, MA: Hendrickson, reprinted in 2011), 1:532. Cf. George M. Marsden, *Jonathan Edwards: A Life* (2003; reprint, Yale University Press, 2004), 196–97. Fully outlined with brief notes and observations, the complete work was cut short by Edwards' untimely death.
5   Edwards was "enmeshed in partisan international politics and the violent clashes of nations and religions;" Marsden, *Edwards*, 432.
6   Tony Richie, *Speaking by the Spirit: A Pentecostal Model for Interreligious Dialogue* (Lexington, KY: Emeth, 2010).
7   Harry S. Stout, "Jonathan Edwards' Tri-World Vision," in *The Legacy of Jonathan Edwards: American Religion and the Evangelical Tradition*, ed. D. G. Hart, Sean Michael Lucas, and Stephen J. Nichols (Grand Rapids, MI: Baker Academic, 2003), 27–46, especially 27–30.
8   Kenneth J. Archer, "The Making of an Academic Tradition: The Cleveland School," Presented at the 45th Annual Society for Pentecostal Studies Meeting, San Dimas, CA, Life Pacific College (March 10–12, 2016), on Pentecostalism's Wesleyan-Holiness identity (a.k.a. Wesleyan-Arminian) as exemplified by Pentecostal Theological Seminary, a Church of God (Cleveland, TN), academic institution.
9   Justo L. Gonzalez, *A History of Christian Thought III: From the Protestant Reformation to the Twentieth Century*, rev. ed. (1975; Nashville, TN: Abingdon, 1987), 316–17.
10 William C. Placher, *A History of Christian Theology: An Introduction* (Philadelphia, PA: Westminster, 1983), 260–61 and Roger E. Olson, *The Mosaic of Christian Belief: Twenty Centuries of Unity & Diversity* (Downers Grove, IL: IVP, 2002), 118.
11 Steven Jack Land, *Pentecostal Spirituality: A Passion for the Kingdom* (Cleveland, TN: CPT, 2010), 33–34, 128–30, 183, 221.

Pentecostalism.[12] Thus Oliver Crisp notes with congruity that contemporary Edwards' admirers often include Pentecostals.[13]

Here two observations arise. First, I suggest, Edwards' narratival/testimonial theological approach is conducive for fitting the reality of other religions into the larger story of redemption rather than focusing exclusively on debates about obvious propositional differences. A narrative is by definition a spoken or written account of connected events—an interactive plot that makes the story understandable and meaningful.[14] Narrative is particularly conducive for developing Wesleyan and/or pentecostal theology.[15] Connectivity is a key. Plot has systemic development and synchronization. In short, Christians may view the religions together with redemption in Christ as different parts of the same story. Herein, I do not assume that Edwards would agree with my conclusions; but, I do think my conclusions agree with implicative thrusts of his theological analysis of redemption's chronological and ontological trajectory.

Second, I suggest that Edwards' reliance on the theme of providence's acting in all of history, including religious history, toward the ultimate accomplishment of redemption in Christ[16] is essentially affirmable by both Calvinists and Wesleyan Arminians, including Pentecostals. Of course, these interpret aspects of providence in terms of divine sovereignty and human liberty quite differently. Yet a general sense that God works in all history accomplishing God's ultimate redemptive purpose in Christ is indisputable. For the moment, I set aside conflicts over Calvinism versus Arminianism to get at the heart of Edwards' contribution on the possible positive significance of non-Christian religions. Admittedly, Edwards had firm feelings against what he saw as the inconsistencies of Arminianism.[17] Yet this is no reason to preclude recognition of his perceptive insights regarding the religions' place in God's ultimate plan of redemption in Christ. Edwards' frequent attacks on what he loosely called "Arminianism" were not directed at historical Arminianism but rather at a defective version degenerated into theological freethinking and libertarianism.[18] The Wesleyan-Arminianism popular among Pentecostals would be more congenial with his evangelical commitments.[19]

---

[12] Charles Hambrick-Stowe, "The 'Inward, Sweet Sense of Christ' in Jonathan Edwards," *The Legacy of Jonathan Edwards: American Religion and the Evangelical Tradition*, ed. D. G. Hart, Sean Michael Lucas, and Stephen J. Nichols (Grand Rapids, MI: Baker Academic, 2003), 95.

[13] Oliver D. Crisp, *Jonathan Edwards among the Theologians* (Grand Rapids, MI: Eerdmans, 2015), xiv.

[14] Gerald R. McDermott, *Jonathan Edwards Confronts the Gods: Christian Theology, Enlightenment Religion, and Non-Christian Faiths* (Oxford: Oxford University Press, 2000), 7, describes Edwards' theology as drama and story.

[15] Michael Lodahl, *The Story of God: Wesleyan Theology & Biblical Narrative* (Kansas City, MO: Beacon Hill, 1994).

[16] For Edwards, providence has a machine-like quality comparable to the turning of cogs or wheels, Edwards, *History of the Redemption*, WJE 9:118–19, 525. The Jewish Diaspora, secular events, and wars between nations fit into and further God's purpose to advance toward redemption in Christ, Edwards, *History of the Redemption*, WJE 9:282, 289–91.

[17] Edwards, *History of the Redemption*, WJE 9:431–32 and 539. Edwards, *The Freedom of the Will*, WJE 1:129–439. Edwards contrasts Arminians, Roman Catholics, and Muslims together against Calvinism, Edwards, *The Freedom of the Will*, WJE 1:437.

[18] Crisp, *Jonathan Edwards among the Theologians*, 7, 60, 89–94, 141.

[19] Henry H. Knight, *Anticipating Heaven Below: Optimism of Grace from Wesley to the Pentecostals* (Eugene, OR: Wipf & Stock, 2014).

Surveying contemporary scholarship

Contemporary scholarship indicates the complexity and subtlety of Jonathan Edwards. Edwards is part of a theological tradition stressing the "self-communicating, other-affirming, community-forming love" of God in the act of creating. God's own loving nature and eternal love, as inherent in the Trinity and manifested in Jesus Christ, suggest, according to Edwards, a "disposition to abundant communication."[20] Indeed, Christian eschatology points to ultimate, uninterrupted access to and eternal enjoyment of God's being in boundless love.[21] Further, Edwards affirmed reason's limited value, insisting on special revelation's necessity, while viewing the eschatological culmination of history in pneumatological terms—that is, as carried out by the end-time outpouring of the Spirit.[22] Also, Edwards' pastoral and missiological orientation shows in his affection for and efforts among the Stockbridge "Indians."[23]

A strident critic of the papacy, Edwards' soteriology, accenting dynamic participatory process, Anri Morimoto nevertheless describes as Catholic.[24] Uncompromising in his commitment to Christ and Christian redemption, Edwards, according to Gerald McDermott, set forth a remarkable basis for understanding non-Christian religions. Sean Michael Lucas neatly summarizes salient issues in Morimoto and McDermott.[25] Of note is Morimoto's praise for Edwards' Catholic vision of salvation and McDermott's treatment of Edwards' "(sometimes) charitable dealings with non-Christian religions."[26] Encounter with Deism possibly led the later Edwards to move beyond predecessors regarding the relationship of reason and revelation, knowledge of God by "heathen," and possibility of salvation for those without explicit faith in Christ. Further, Edwards drew on ancient *prisca theologia* tradition and dispositional ontology that likely led him to recognize saintliness among non-Christian humans without confessing faith in Christ. Both Morimoto and McDermott agree that Edwards' "dispositional ontology" "provides potential for a soteriology that affirms salvation for the unevangelized."[27] Additionally, Morimoto argues that Edwards' emphasis on infused grace for human

---

[20] Daniel L. Migliore, *Faith Seeking Understanding: An Introduction to Christian Theology* (1991; reprint, Grand Rapids, MI: Eerdmans, 2004), 101.
[21] Migliore, *Faith Seeking Understanding*, 346–47.
[22] Richard A. Bailey, "Driven by Passion: Jonathan Edwards and the Art of Preaching," in *The Legacy of Jonathan Edwards: American Religion and the Evangelical Tradition*, ed. D. G. Hart, Sean Michael Lucas, and Stephen J. Nichols (Grand Rapids, MI: Baker Academic, 2003), 64–78, especially 65–66, 71.
[23] Stephen J. Nichols, "Last of the Mohican Missionaries: Jonathan Edwards at Stockbridge," in *The Legacy of Jonathan Edwards: American Religion and the Evangelical Tradition*, ed. D. G. Hart, Sean Michael Lucas, and Stephen J. Nichols (Grand Rapids, MI: Baker Academic, 2003), 47–63, especially 54, 57.
[24] Anri Morimoto, *Jonathan Edwards and the Catholic Vision of Salvation* (University Park, PA: Pennsylvania State University Press, 1995).
[25] Sean Michael Lucas, "Jonathan Edwards Between Church and Academy: A Bibliographic Essay," in *The Legacy of Jonathan Edwards: American Religion and the Evangelical Tradition*, ed. D. G. Hart, Sean Michael Lucas, and Stephen J. Nichols (Grand Rapids, MI: Baker Academic, 2003), 228–47, especially 239–40.
[26] Ibid., 236.
[27] Ibid., 239.

transformation offers remarkable opportunity for reconsidering the salvation of those who do not explicitly believe in Jesus Christ.[28]

On the theme of grace Calvinist Gerald Bray thinks Edwards' pre-conversion recognition of God's beauty and goodness may be best explained in terms of natural theology or common grace.[29] To Wesleyans and Pentecostals Edwards' natural or common grace sounds a lot like prevenient grace. As Howard Snyder notes, "Creation is suffused with grace as an unconditional benefit of the atonement," adding that "nowhere is God's grace absent, though people can and do close their hearts to God's grace."[30] Bray freely admits that Jonathan Edwards does not always "square with traditional Reformed theology" and that this "distanced him from strict Calvinism."[31] But it brought him closer to Pentecostals.

McDermott emphasizes Edwards' potential ecumenicity historically while Morimoto emphasizes his ecumenical soteriology.[32] Both Morimoto and McDermott apparently begin with earlier assumptions made by Sang Hyun Lee.[33] Lee argued that Jonathan Edwards radically reconstructed metaphysics from classic categories of form and substance toward reality as dispositional forces and habits.[34] The result is a much more modern and dynamic ontology. Subsequently, it will become clear that ontological and revelatory dynamism is consistent with my interpretation of Edwards' Christian theology of religions.

Contrariwise, Marsden portrays Edwards on the religions in considerably darker hues. Edwards had an intense interest in other religions, gathered all the information he could about them, and made numerous entries on them in his various notebooks. His time in Stockbridge, when he was daily with Indian culture, only increased his interest in the topic. Much of his concern was to answer the deist challenge to the particularity of Christianity. Was there not some truth in all religions drawn from the universal light of nature? For his answer Edwards drew on a tradition of *prisca theologica*, that whatever elements of truth were found in other religions were remnants of earlier revelations to the ancestors of all people, as indicated in Genesis. Although reason could provide some limited knowledge of the truth, true religion could only be based on the revelation that pointed to Christ. Moreover, while other religions, such as those of the ancient Greeks or the Chinese, might produce some relatively good people, true

---

[28] Ibid., 239–40. See Anri Morimoto, "Salvation as Fulfillment of Being: The Soteriology of Jonathan Edwards and Its Implications for Christian Missions," *Princeton Seminary Bulletin*, n.s., 20, no. 1 (1999): 13–23.

[29] Gerald Bray, *God Has Spoken: A History of Christian Theology* (Wheaton, IL: Crossway, 2014), 969–70.

[30] Howard A. Snyder, "Wesleyanism, Wesleyan Theology," in *Global Dictionary of Theology*, ed. William A. Dryness and Veli-Matti Kärkkäinen (Downers Grove, IL: IVP Academic, 2008), 933.

[31] Bray, *Spoken*, 969.

[32] Lucas, "Church/Academy," 239.

[33] Ibid., 240.

[34] Sang Hyun Lee, *The Philosophical Theology of Jonathan Edwards*, 2nd ed. (Princeton, NJ: Princeton University Press, 2000), 3–4, 6–7.

virtue arose only from true religion. Most fundamentally, he viewed other religions, such as Islam, as false and pernicious.[35]

Marsden seems concerned to place Edwards in the environs of early American evangelical Christian particularity versus later tendencies toward pluralist relativism.[36] Edwards certainly stands with evangelical Christianity in contrast with later liberal Christianity—including the latter's affinity for pluralistic ideology with its consequent relativism. Yet obviously Edwards' philosophizing about other religions does not reflect fundamentalist rigidity either.[37] It is best, perhaps, to understand Edwards' apparently oscillating tone as congruous with contextual apologetic concerns.[38]

Identifying guiding ideas

McDermott helpfully identifies ideas guiding Edwards' reflections on the religions.[39] He argues that Jonathan Edwards' theology provides a basis for affirming some sort of revelation in at least some non-Christian religions. Therefore, McDermott proposes a category apart from the traditional general or special classes of revelation that he calls "revealed types."[40] Edwards considered the things in this world to be expressions of divine communication as God's thoughts continuously create: quite literally, creation is the ongoing embodiment of divine ideas. This implies that everything is interrelated. Edwards advocated what has come to be called "panentheism," the view that God inhabits but is distinct from creation. Thus, under God's sovereign direction all of creation and history reflects the mystery of God.[41] Further, McDermott favorably compares Edwards' views on "disinterested benevolence" (loving obedience based on God's beauty and splendor apart from self-interest) with single-minded devotion to virtue found in Confucius and Mencius.[42] Yet Edwards' commitment to Christian evangelism and missions remains consistent.[43]

---

[35] Marsden, *Edwards*, 486. Edwards outlines a process of discernment for identifying the Spirit's true presence, even within Christianity; see Amos Yong, *Discerning the Spirit(s): A Pentecostal-Charismatic Contribution to Christian Theology of Religions*, Journal of Pentecostal Theology Supplement Series 20 (Sheffield: Sheffield Academic Press, 2000), 139.

[36] Marsden, *Edwards*, 8–9.

[37] Gerald R. McDermottt and Harold A. Netland, *A Trinitarian Theology of Religions: An Evangelical Proposal* (New York: Oxford University Press, 2014), 6, 20–21.

[38] On Edwards as apologist, see Michael J. McClymond, *Encounters with God: An Approach to the Theology of Jonathan Edwards* (New York: Oxford University Press, 1998).

[39] Gerald R. McDermott, *Can Evangelicals Learn from World Religions? Jesus, Revelation, and Religious Traditions* (Downers Grove, IL: IVP, 2000). Here McDermott primarily draws from *AHOR* and a few selections from Edwards' "Miscellanies." McDermott's *Confronts the Gods*, however, draws heavily from other sections in Edwards' notes, and is primarily concerned to place Edwards' theology of religions, along with his other work, in the context of Edwards' aggressive response to Enlightenment Deism. Without necessarily disagreeing with this project per se, my sense is that it can skew understanding of Edwards' interest in the place of the religions in God's redemptive purpose as a subject worthy of attention in and of itself, especially as it comes across in his latest work, *AHOR*.

[40] McDermott, *Evangelicals?* 13.

[41] Ibid., 141, 145.

[42] Ibid., 174–77.

[43] Ibid., 215.

McDermott specifically identifies three areas in Edwards' thought: covenants, revelation, and typology. Edwards' emphasis on continuity between the Old Testament "covenant of works" and the New Testament "covenant of grace" connects his emphasis on redemption's consistency through Jesus Christ.[44] Although the world's religions are not in the same category, "Edwards' reflections on the covenants contain some pointers" regarding "the consideration of truth in the religions."[45] Thus providential designs revealing God's truth in partial and incomplete fashion among the religions prepare adherents to receive the full revelation of God in Christ in a manner reminiscent of God's progressive unfolding among Old Testament saints (*praeparatio evangelica*).[46]

Edwards affirmed typology, or "a system of representation by which God points human beings to spiritual realities," observable in history, nature, and non-Christian religions.[47] Sacred salvation history is full of such types (e.g., Gal. 4:21-31; 1 Cor. 9:9-10; 10:6). Nature and history are replete with types such as sowing and reaping or the marriage institution which Scripture reveals to have deeper meanings (e.g., 1 Cor. 15:35-49; Eph. 5:22-33).[48] Types appear even in false religions. For example, the horrific practice of human sacrifice pointed toward the atoning death of Jesus Christ and the idolatrous worship of graven images to the incarnation of God's Son. In a sense, God overruled false religion to communicate divine truths for the ultimate good of all humanity. Edwards does not make false religions true or salvific but he suggests that a vague form of divine revelation reaches into gross religious error in order to accomplish God's eternal redemptive purposes.[49]

Edwards' view of typological revelation is consistent with the Calvinist position that the Creator but not the Redeemer is revealed through nature to non-Christians and that such "natural" revelation alone is insufficient for salvation.[50] However, McDermott argues that Edwards' approach may move beyond traditional "natural" or "general" and "special" theological categories.[51] Yet Edwards' typological revelation is maintained consistently with his balancing of objective and subjective revelation. Not only natural revelation (through nature) but even written revelation (through Scripture) is inadequate apart from the pneumatological revelation (by the Holy Spirit's agency). Only the Holy Spirit can convey "the sense of the heart" that truly constitutes the realities of divine revelation.[52]

McDermott concludes that Edwards' typology can be used to claim that "among the religions are scattered promises of God in Christ and that these promises are revealed types planted there by the triune God."[53] He does not make a clear case that Edwards himself necessarily would have gone quite so far. Nevertheless, McDermott presents a

---

[44] Ibid., 96–102.
[45] Ibid., 102.
[46] Ibid., 102–4.
[47] Ibid., 104.
[48] Ibid., 104–5.
[49] Ibid., 106–8.
[50] Ibid., 50–52.
[51] Ibid., 52–53 and chapter four.
[52] Ibid., 61, 68.
[53] Ibid., 114.

persuasive argument that "revealed types" "are akin to the types that Jonathan Edwards found in many world religions."[54] Accordingly, an authentic implicit connection exists but should not be overstated.

McDermott sums up nicely:

> No one in Colonial America—other than Edwards—reflected persistently and systematically on religious others. Only Edwards developed an elaborate scheme for the role other religions had played in the grand scheme of redemptive history. Others denounced non-Christian religions as various shades of darkness, but Edwards regarded them as actors in the grand historical drama. They were not the main players, to be sure, and not the heroic protagonists, but they were important to the story. Apart from them, the story did not cohere; without their mediation, it did not make sense. In Edwards' history of the world, the non-Christian religions were not merely appendices or afterwords, but integral chapters that answered important questions about God and his revelation to creation. In other words, Edwards may have been the first American intellectual to give non-Christian religions positive significance in a Christian understanding of God and history.[55]

Readers will doubtless notice that the subtitle of this chapter expresses substantive agreement with the thrust of the above. As McDermott has said, "Colonial America's greatest mind, of whom it has often been said that his thinking changed little over the course of his career, seems to have been a work in progress on the question of the world religions."[56] Somehow that seems suitable for one for whom dynamism and development characterize his thought on the religions.[57] As a Pentecostal, I find this approach especially inviting.

Engaging Edwards directly

AHOR tells the story of human history from the perspective that everything is interrelated to God's ultimate redemptive purpose in Jesus Christ.[58] Edwards focuses on redemption not in its narrow or limited sense of the historical Incarnation only but in an enlarged sense encompassing all that contributes to the application and success of the actual purchase of redemption in Christ.[59] Not limited to Christ's

---

[54] Ibid., 113.
[55] McDermott, *Confronts*, 7.
[56] Ibid., 13.
[57] For Edwards—as Augustine, Calvin, and Wesley—Christ's kingdom constantly converts and transforms human culture. See Alister E. McGrath, *Christian Theology: An Introduction*, 4th ed. (Oxford: Blackwell, 2007), 120.
[58] More like McDermott's *Evangelicals* but less like his *Confronts the Gods*, I rely mostly on Edwards' *AHOR*. This allows me to interpret Edwards' on the religions in his fullest and latest expressions without superimposing an outside hermeneutical grid, which can tend to skew perception of the religions rather than in their own right as part of God's providentially directed redemptive purpose.
[59] Edwards, *A History of the Work of Redemption*, WJE 9:118.

specific efficacious mediatorial work, it includes pre- and post-Incarnate activities along with the broader preparatory and applicative work of the Father and the Holy Spirit. Yet "it is all one work" with "one design" across the "various dispensations" "to which all of the offices of Christ directly tend, and in which all the persons of the Trinity conspire."[60] Edwards clearly confesses Jesus Christ as the Son of God and the Savior of the world, and Christianity as "the true religion."[61] Thus, Edwards' theology is Christological at its center and trinitarian in its circumference with ample allowances for distinct redemptive roles by the divine persons without violence to their ontological or missiological unity—similar to developing pentecostal trinitarian theology of religions.[62] Yet this comparison does not imply that Jonathan Edwards is necessarily a direct precedent for existing pentecostal theology of religions. Rather, similarities of the latter with the former suggest compatibilities that may be profitably plumbed.

Several questions arise. What is the role of non-Christian religions in God's redemptive purpose? Are they entirely antagonistic? Are they supportive in any sense? Do they contribute anything positive? And, consequently, two more: how are Christian identity and self-understanding affected, and how then should Christians relate to non-Christian religions and their adherents? Finally, what surfaces via pentecostal engagement? A brief overview prepares for these questions.

Edwards sees history as a glorious and gradual advance of redemption accomplished by God's Word and Spirit.[63] At times the progress of redemption abolishes old aspects of religion and establishes new ones.[64] Edwards employs a "rich skein of images" to connect the events of redemption history: the model of a river and its tributaries, a tree and its branches, the construction of a building, the conduct of war, and "a wheel," or "a machine composed of wheels."[65] These illustrate redemption's ancient beginnings, ongoing and progressive, if gradual, nature, and its cumulative impact and consummative goal.[66] Edwards integrates redemptive continuity and preparatory qualities through teleological advancement and anticipatory development. Yet, the "great effects and glorious success" of the preparatory work of redemption were "only preparatory, by way of anticipation."[67]

Edwards argues that non-Jewish nations and religions have elements of divine institution received by way of Noah—in whom he saw a new grant for all the earth

---

[60] Ibid., 118, 156. The "eternal covenant of redemption . . . between the Father and the Son before the foundation of the world" unfolds in redemption history with eternity and time coming together in the Incarnation (cf. Gal. 4:4). See Ibid., 513, 156.
[61] Ibid., 156, 158.
[62] Cf. Veli-Matti Kärkkäinen, *Trinity and Religious Pluralism: The Doctrine of the Trinity in Christian Theology of Religions* (Burlington, VT: Ashgate, 2004).
[63] Edwards, *A History of the Work of Redemption*, WJE 9:192.
[64] For example, David is a type of Christ abolishing elements of Mosaic liturgy to establish new forms, Edwards, *A History of the Work of Redemption*, WJE 9:220.
[65] William Wainwright, "Jonathan Edwards," The Stanford Encyclopedia of Philosophy (Winter 2016 Edition), ed. Edward N. Zalta; https://plato.stanford.edu/archives/win2016/entries/edwards
[66] Edwards, *A History of the Work of Redemption*, WJE 9:160, 349, 391, and 520 (cf. Ibid., 9:181–84, 285, and 508). Gradual and progressive development of redemption-centered religion occurs as "general grace is growing" until perfected in the eschaton, 99 and 145.
[67] Ibid., 344 (cf. 128).

founded on the covenant of grace with Christ as assurance.[68] On the one hand, God frustrates and confounds any religious design which is contrary to the great work of redemption. On the other, God preserves "the true religion," that is, the religion issuing forth in the person and work of Christ, "when the world in general apostasized to idolatry."[69] There is both continuity and discontinuity, both compatibility and opposition.

Edwards is not shy about confronting false religion or affirming the true. Yet qualified openness appears. After refuting the idolatry of Abraham's own ancestors, including Terah and Nahor, he suddenly imposes clarifying limitations on their corruptions: "We are not to understand that they were *wholly* drawn off to idolatry, to forsake the true God. For God is said to be the God of Nahor," referencing Gen. 31:53.[70] Apparently, "they partook" only "in some measure of the general and almost universal corruption of the times."[71] Solomon, Israel in Egypt, and the family of Jacob are additional examples of those infected in part with religious corruption, particularly idolatry, though "the true Church of God" existed among them.[72] False religion is comparable to an infection which spreads and advances little by little more and more. As Babel/Babylon increasingly becomes an infecting influence for false religion, an enemy of redemption, Melchizedek represents true religion still present in Abraham's days apart from Abrahamic lineage.[73] Furthermore, Edwards distinguishes between God's moral law, which is obligatory on all humanity "of all ages and all nations of the world," and the laws which apply to Jews only.[74] Edwards consistently displays nuance and subtlety rather than "all or nothing" assessments.

Arguably, degrees of revelation and righteousness existed in true religion as well as in corrupt religions.[75] Until the eschaton the good and bad mix even in the Lord's own fields (Mt. 13:24-30).[76] God moved to uphold true religion, and to prevent its eventual extinction, separating it from the world's corrupting influence through

---

[68] Ibid., 137, 152–53.
[69] Ibid., *WJE* 9:156.
[70] Ibid., 9:156 (emphasis original).
[71] Ibid., 156.
[72] Ibid., 156.
[73] Ibid., 179. An oppositional pattern throughout history successively issues forth in destructive judgment and redemptive progress, 352, 444.
[74] Ibid., 309. On Christ's rejection Edwards compares Jews unfavorably with Gentiles (ibid., 9:330–31). Elsewhere he hints at (honest?) struggles of first-century Jews to decide about Jesus outlining Roman persecutions against Christians as satanic (Edwards, *The Unreasonableness of Indetermination in Religion*, *WJE* 19:95 and *A History of the Work of Redemption*, *WJE* 9:388, 393). The pendulum swings back and forth. For Edwards, Jews are under divine judgment for rejecting Christ, 9:381–82, but their amazing preservation throughout history, *both before and after the coming of Christ*, evidences the truth of revealed religion and that "the Jewish nation [is] a standing evidence of the truth of revealed Christianity." See "Miscellaneous Observations on Important Theological Subjects," edited by Edwards' son after his death but included in Jonathan Edwards, *The Works of Jonathan Edwards*, 2 vols. (1834; reprint, Peabody, MA: Hendrickson, 2011), 2:459–51 and 2:493–95 (abbreviated *TWJE*); also, available in Edwards, "History of Redemption Book II," *WJE* 31: n.p.
[75] Israel in Egypt progressively lost true religion by degrees, Edwards, *A History of the Work of Redemption*, *WJE* 9:174.
[76] AHOR reflects postmillennial eschatology (ibid., 350–51, 459, and 493).

calling Abraham and preserving his descendants unto Christ's coming.[77] Since Christ's coming redemption is no longer in a "preparatory state" but a rather in a "finishing state," advancing "by various steps and degrees" to the ultimate establishment of "their proper fulfillment."[78] The "state" of things has changed but the same pattern of dynamic progressive development continues.

Nevertheless, Edwards observed that idolatry's apostasizing influence proved resilient. Results were drastic. About the time God delivered Israel from Egypt, choosing them and forming them into a separate nation, all other nations were "wholly rejected and given over to heathenism."[79] True religion continued for a time among non-Israelites but was short lived. The world's nations continued in idolatry until Christ came. Even so, neither were the Israelites exempt ever afterward from a terribly obstinate propensity to forsake God and plunge into horrid idolatry.[80] Had not God moved mightily to revive true religion by proclamation of the Word and by fresh outpourings of the Holy Spirit it still would not have escaped eventual extinction even in Israel.[81]

Most of Edwards' explicit comments about non-Christian religions target the "Heathen" and Jews but several mention Islam. Occasional remarks group Muslims with Heathen, Jews, Catholics, Arminians, and others, including various Christian schisms, as evidence of natural human blindness regarding God and religion.[82] Edwards aims at vindication of the doctrine of human insufficiency and sinfulness as a result of the ruinous effects of the fall.[83] He groups all under sin. Generally, this work does not indicate a high view of Islam. Specifically, Muslim teachings are immature and misleading—although Edwards admits, with exquisite sarcasm, that some in Christian lands are farther from God than some in Muslim lands.[84]

Much more significantly, Jonathan Edwards groups Muslims together with Jews and Christians as "that part of the world which acknowledges the one only true God."[85] Although Edwards explains Islamic monotheism as a result of Christian influence, it is nevertheless a remarkable admission.[86] He further describes Jews, Christians, and

---

[77] Ibid., 159.
[78] Ibid., 348. Religion is not static but constantly progressing or regressing in development or decline, characterized by dynamism and fluidity.
[79] Ibid., 178. "Heathen" nations and their oracles were animated by satanic energies (ibid., 248 and 394), but signs of divine providence appear among them (ibid., 265 and 267). Edwards vacillates on the value of ancient heathen philosophy (ibid., 9:278, 388 and *Freedom of the Will*, WJE 1:372). The influence of true religion is among the Gentiles (Edwards, *A History of the Work of Redemption*, WJE 9:300–1), but they need evangelization and conversion (ibid., 377).
[80] Those who resolutely refused idolatry were all the more remarkable for being rare: Edwards, *A History of the Work of Redemption*, WJE 9:234 (2 Chron. 11:13, 16).
[81] Ibid., 195, 234–35. Like Pentecostals, a pattern of decline and revival appears built into Edwards' religious understanding with the latter bearing a pneumatological accent.
[82] "Man's Natural Blindness in the Things of Religion," TWJE 2:247–56, especially 249–50. A three-part sermon based on Ps. 94:8-11 preached in February 1740 (see Edwards, "Appendix: Dated Sermons, January 1739–December 1742," WJE 22:540, no. 536.
[83] TWJE 2:253.
[84] Ibid., 249, 250: More of a barb against Christian apostates or profligates than a boon to Muslims.
[85] Edwards, *A History of the Work of Redemption*, WJE 9:399.
[86] If Judaism is Christianity's parent, is Islam a younger sibling? Cf. Tony Bayfield, Alan Race, and Ataullah Siddiqui, eds. *Beyond the Dysfunctional Family: Jews, Christians, and Muslims in Dialogue with Each Other and with Britain* (Seattle: CreateSpace, 2012).

Muslims together as having escaped from "heathenish darkness" and from being "sottish and brutish idolaters."[87] Ought not this explicit assertion that Jewish, Christian, and Muslim monotheists, despite deep differences, nevertheless worship "the one only true God" spark initiative and provide momentum regarding potentialities in shared Abrahamic monotheism? However, a few lines later Edwards describes Islam's rise conversely, along with Roman Catholicism, which he terms "Antichrist," as due to Satan's opposing Christ's kingdom.[88]

Edwards' generous assessment of Jewish, Christian, and Muslim monotheism illustrates his ongoing relevance and significance for contemporary Christian theology of religions. Today leading theologians are wrestling with the knotty question of whether Christians and Muslims share in the worship of the same God.[89] Not surprisingly perhaps, the debate sometimes generates more heat than light.[90] The general human instinct appears inclined toward straightforward "all or nothing" style answers. Yet in this case a circumspect response is probably a more carefully qualified "Yes and No." Here Jonathan Edwards' all-too-rare ability to hold development and tension, even opposition, together, as in his incredible affirmation of Muslims as true monotheists, in the same general category with Jews and Christians, while unflinchingly identifying stark contrasts, may provide an assist.[91] At the least, it enables an expanded approach in which theologians may ask deeply probing questions like, "In what sense may the God of Christians and the God of Muslims be similar or perhaps synonymous?" and "In what sense may the God of Christians and Muslims be dissimilar or perhaps antonymous?" And of course this line of inquiry leads to yet another question: "How does the way Christianity or Islam perceives and processes similarities and divergences between the triune God and Allah impact the manner in which their respective faith communities and individual devotees understand and interact with each other in today's world context?"

To return to Edwards' more directly, a theological chapter comparing Islam with Christianity adds detail and depth.[92] Yet Edwards' discussion is not an unbiased or impartial discussion of Islam's nature. Rather, it is a point-by-point comparison of Christianity and Islam in respect to propagation impact. Not surprisingly,

---

[87] Edwards, *A History of the Work of Redemption*, WJE 9:399.
[88] Ibid., 410, 411.
[89] For example, Miroslav Volf, *Allah: A Christian Response* (New York: HarperOne, 2011).
[90] For instance, in the recent, and very public, controversy that erupted over Larycia Hawkins' statement that Christians and Muslims worship the same God, which began at Wheaton College in Illinois but soon enveloped other evangelical institutions of higher learning across the nation. See Emily McFarlane Miller, "Wheaton Professor Who Left College Over 'same God' Flap: 'I Would Do It Again,'" *Religion News Service*, February 26, 2016; http://www.religionnews.com/2016/02/26/wheaton-professor-who-left-college-over-same-god-flap-i-would-do-it-again-and-again-and-again/
[91] For more on these events and the discussion raised thereby, see Tony Richie, "Do All Abraham's Children Worship Abraham's God? Not a Jewish-Christian-Muslim God," *The Pneuma Review*, April 2, 2016; http://pneumareview.com/do-all-abrahams-children-worship-abrahams-god/
[92] Edwards, "Miscellaneous Observations on Important Theological Subjects," WJE 2:459–510, and 2:253, "Mohometanism Compared with Christianity," ibid., 491–93. Labeling Islam "Mohometanism" in Edwards' day was common practice.

Christianity appears everywhere superior.[93] Edwards opines that Islam's rise made no advance on Christianity, although comparing favorably with heathenism. Islam is a dependent religion, borrowing from others, especially Christianity; accommodating and compliant rather than challenging cultural and religious mores; adapted to the sensual in its disposition; rooted in a barbaric and ignorant time and place; spread by force rather than by knowledge, and lacking in miraculous nature. Oddly enough, Edwards suggests that Islam's acceptance of several basic Christian doctrines is a kind of confirmation of Christian revelation.[94] In all of these means and more Christianity is in Edwards' eyes incomparably superior.

Offering observations, hypotheses, and an application

I add four qualifying observations. First, obviously, Edwards assesses not Islam in and of itself but in comparison to Christianity. Even here he is not evaluating truth claims or spiritual devotion but only respective means and methods of religious propagation. Would an analysis of Islam in its own right yield different impressions? Secondly, whenever Edwards does compare Islam to other religions, namely heathenism, he readily acknowledges advance and improvement. There is no suggestion he considered Islam an improvement over Judaism. Was it an improvement over ancient heathenism (Canaanite, Greco-Roman, or Arabian) only? Again, his comments on Islam evidence Edwards' consistent assumption of a continuum of religious value and/or validity.

Third, some of Edwards' observations appear culturally, and perhaps, racially, biased. Here Edwards is a man of his time.[95] Nevertheless, we must insist on transcending prejudicial tendencies. A more objective frame of mind, intellectual acuity aside, would doubtless be more appreciative of aspects of Islam, of Muslims themselves, and of their distinctive culture. Fourth, some of Edwards' comments about Islam and Muslims perceptively lift up legitimate Christian critiques. Acknowledging and addressing differences among religions informs any honest efforts at authentic dialogue. If some err by ignoring religions' differences and others by ignoring religions' commonalities, better approaches consider both. Finally, Edwards recognized Christian-Muslim interdependencies. Exploring the complexities of reciprocating influences in Christian-Muslim identities could provide some interesting bases for theological conversation and development.

Furthermore, how can Edwards, at times in almost the same breath, describe Islam (and Judaism too) so drastically differently? I offer two hypotheses. First, Edwards tends to attribute almost everything to either God or Satan, apparently depending on his conception of its relation to Christ or Christianity. For example, he attributes the pre-historic migration of native peoples to the Americas to a satanic stratagem

---

[93] Perhaps Edwards' claims are best understood in light of his conception of "true Christians" as God's chosen people, Edwards, *Christians a Chosen Generation*, WJE 17:273–328.
[94] Edwards, WJE 2:492–93.
[95] Edwards envisioned an eschatological advance of "the Negroes and Indians" and "the most barbarous countries," Edwards, *A History of the Work of Redemption*, WJE 9:480.

for avoiding Christianity's success in order to ascribe unto Satan their consequently ignorant worship.[96] Without any disrespect, perhaps today's readers should take such statements with "a grain of salt"—that is, for what they are worth, no more and no less. It would certainly be a mistake to attach a too-heavy weight to their value as theological indicators of divine or diabolical features of the religions.[97]

Second, I suggest insight into these (apparent) contradictions lies in the angle of Edwards' comparisons. When he compares Islam to heathenism/paganism, it comes off much better, a monotheistic religion in the category of Judaism and Christianity. When he compares Islam as Christianity's rival, it comes off much worse, an apostate religion that has distorted and perverted original Christian teaching. Notably, Edwards identifies the two greatest, the most obdurate and unrelenting, historical enemies of "the church of God, its religion and its worship," as heathenism and Roman Catholicism ("popery")—waving away first-century Jewish persecution of Christians as exceptional, and not mentioning Islam at all.[98] However, speculating about eschatology, he suggests heathenism, Catholicism,[99] and Islam will unite in hostility against Christianity, and that Christ's triumph in overthrowing Satan's kingdom will include the fall of the empire of Islam[100] and the restoration of the Jews.[101] Rather than being inconsistent, Edwards sees the religions on a dynamic continuum involving varying degrees of truth and falsehood, light and darkness, and good and evil.[102] Apparently, this continuum can involve the *same* religion in *contrasting* states at *different* times. Thus heathen, Jewish, and Islamic religions sometimes appear in very different perspectives.

Finally, note a pneumatological application from a pentecostal perspective. The Holy Spirit's crucial role for Edwards in vivifying actual participants in the history of redemption, and in reviving the process itself when necessary, is abundantly clear. If Christ is at the center of redemption and the Trinity is at its circumference, then the Holy Spirit fills the space therein (so to speak). Perhaps a great deal of vital dynamism in Edwards' approach to the religions is traceable in large part to the energy of his pneumatological accent. I propose that a legitimate implication for pentecostal theology of religions includes specific pneumatological application. If Christology is

---

[96] Ibid., 434.
[97] A relevant question would be whether this binary instinct in Edwards is inconsistent with his dispositional metaphysics? Does it at least call attention to how Edwards' theological and philosophical (e.g., philosophy of nature) assumptions were not always as coherent as they might have been? Here is one place that some Pentecostals might push back a bit on Edwards.
[98] Edwards, *A History of the Work of Redemption*, WJE 9:445; Providential upholding of the Church throughout its oppositional history is a visible sign of its veracity.
[99] Edwards understands both Catholicism and Islam as apostate forms of Christianity, more culpable than "poor heathens, who never enjoyed the light of the gospel." Muslims, with wicked heathens, Jews, and papists, are "enemies of the church" facing eschatological judgment (ibid., 487, 523).
[100] Ibid., 442-44. Difficult to tell is whether, or to what extent, Edwards distinguishes the *religion* of Islam from its *political* support base. Possibly the political is most in view in predicting the fall of "the *Mahometan* kingdom" and "the Mahometan empire," which support "Mahometanism"? Cf. "Christendom" versus "Christianity" in which the former tends to include more sociopolitical inferences than the latter; for example, Peter Brown, *The Rise of Christendom: Triumph and Diversity, AD 200-1000*, 10th anniv. rev. ed. (Malden, MA: Wiley-Blackwell, 2013).
[101] Edwards, *A History of the Work of Redemption*, WJE 9:469; that is, the Jews' conversion to Christ.
[102] Similar complexities occur in John Wesley on Islam; see Tony Richie, "Mr. Wesley and Mohammed: A Contemporary Inquiry Concerning Islam," *Asbury Theological Journal* 58, no. 2 (2003): 79-99.

the recurring motif and ultimate climax in redemption's narrative plot, and it surely is, then pneumatology is the driving force and life-giving power that moves it along from creation to consummation. Thus, Edwards provides Pentecostals with an admirable example integrating the Christological, trinitarian, and pneumatological in Christian theology of religions.

Identifying pentecostal implications

Edwards' "testimony" of history methodological approach has specific implications for pentecostal theology of religions—and vice versa.[103] Edwards studies often focuses on his keen intellect and strict logic. However, here, while not abandoning rational analysis, he utilizes narrative presentation rather than propositional argumentation to demonstrate God's providential and directorial involvement in the religions. Narratival/orality emphases in early Pentecostalism suggest that pentecostal testimony may serve as an interreligious dialogue model.[104] Edwards utilizes historical testimony as a hermeneutical grid by which to approach the religions. These approaches are complementary and mutually reinforcing. A narratival/testimonial approach could involve rethinking or revisioning methodology as well as theology in terms of the religions' place in Christian understanding of God's redemptive *purpose* and the *process* by which divine sovereignty advances it and implements it.

Removing a potential barrier to authentic pentecostal engagement requires understanding that Edwardsean Calvinism (New School variety) and pentecostal Arminianism (Wesleyan-Arminian variety) are not inevitably at odds in pentecostal appreciation of Edwards' theology of religions. Without wandering too far afield, frankly this argument is probably necessary (for Pentecostals) because of Edwards' vigorous reliance on the ubiquitous activity of divine providence in terms of God's eternal purpose in Jesus Christ as the principle grounding for his distinctive theology of religions. That being said, it is critical for consistent, constructive pentecostal theology to affirm the revelatory and redemptive working of divine providence in all of human history.[105]

Edwards' utilization of a doctrine of natural theology or common grace closely resembling Wesleyan-Arminian-pentecostal theology of prevenient grace undergirds the entire engagement. Wesleyan-pentecostal theology turns on the pivot of grace.[106] Pre-conversion, or prevenient (Latin *praevenire*, that which comes before or anticipates), grace is given to all human beings. Prevenient grace gently, lovingly, and persistently draws all people toward God. To state the obvious, "all" includes adherents of other religions. Prevenient grace signifies that "in Christ by the Holy Spirit God has

---

[103] Cf. Tony Richie, *Toward a Pentecostal Theology of Religions: Encountering Cornelius Today* (Cleveland, TN: CPT, 2013), chapter 4.
[104] Richie, *Speaking*, 135–36.
[105] Tony Richie, "Revelation, Redemption, and World Religions: A Pentecostal Perspective on the Inclusive Embrace of Divine Providence," *Journal of Beliefs and Values* 30, no. 3 (2009): 313–22.
[106] Richie, *Toward*, 41–42.

gone ahead of every person, mitigating the effects of sin to the extent that people can be awakened and respond to God's initiative."[107] Pneumatologically, prevenient grace describes pre-conversion activity of the Holy Spirit firmly rooted Christologically.

Similarly, dynamic energy and openness in Edwards' thought could be quite significant. Again, as in prevenient grace, here the presence of the Holy Spirit comes to the fore. Reliance on foundational but dynamic pneumatology has been a characteristic hallmark of leading pentecostal theologians such as Amos Yong on Christian theology of religions.[108] The instinctive turn to pneumatology is more than a pentecostal penchant for the Spirit. Pentecostals, as Edwards did, realize the necessity of pneumatological dynamism in this area.

It behooves Pentecostals to make explicit ramifications of Edwards' implicit pneumatological dynamism regarding Christian theology of religions. If the Holy Spirit works in the world of religions in dynamic and open—rather than rigid and closed—ways, how should that shape Christian understanding of religious others? How should it shape ecclesial mission in a world of multiple faiths? Most importantly, how should it shape Christian understanding of the person and work of the Holy Spirit and of the triune God? What does the Spirit's dynamic openness among or toward religious others indicate about God's nature and character?

Finally, Edwards clearly identifies diabolical elements in the world's religions. Does not this oppositional element invite pentecostal themes of the demonic or spiritual warfare? Pentecostals have a checkered history here. Yong has ably demonstrated that discerning the presence/absence of the divine/demonic is critical for any perceptive pentecostal theology of religions.[109] Unfortunately, dangerous propensities, sometimes with violent consequences, in pentecostal rhetoric and practice, especially at popular levels, tend toward demonizing religious others.[110]

Perhaps Edwards' admirable ability to incorporate both continuity and discontinuity, both compatibility and opposition, can help Pentecostals attain balance? Perhaps Pentecostals' continuing commitment to a regrettable but real pervasive and subversive influence of the demonic in religions can help rescue from rationalistic denials handicapping real interreligious engagement? Thus God works in the middle of this world's messiness to accomplish whatever must be done for "the saving of many lives" (Gen. 50:20 NIV). For me, that last line sums up much of Christian theology of religions.

---

[107] Snyder, "Wesleyanism," 933.
[108] Tony Richie, "A Distinctive Turn to Pneumatology: Amos Yong's Christian Theology of Religions," in *A Passion for the Spirit: Pneumatology, Pentecostalism, and the Promise of Renewal in the Theology of Amos Yong*, ed. Wolfgang Vondey and Martin W. Mittelstadt, Global Pentecostal and Charismatic Studies Series 14 (Leiden: Brill, 2013), 103–21.
[109] Yong, *Discerning the Spirit(s)*.
[110] Tony Richie, "Demonization, Discernment, and Deliverance in Interreligious Encounter," in *Loosing the Spirits: Interdisciplinary and Interreligio-Cultural Mappings of a Spirit-Filled World*, ed. Veli-Matti Kärkkäinen, Kirsteen Kim, and Amos Yong (New York: Palgrave Macmillan, 2013), 171–84.

Conclusion

In Jonathan Edwards' *A History of the Work of Redemption* historical testimony bears witness to the relation between Christianity and non-Christian religions as dynamic progressive development with an oppositional element. There is a continuum or gradating scale regarding the religions and their adherents. Edwards teaches us today to avoid oversimplifications and stereotypes. To categorically demonize or deify any religion or its devotees is a mistake. Reality is just not that simple. There is affinity *and* antagonism with positives *and* negatives. Even these may move around. But there is constancy. God is sovereign over all. Jonathan Edwards resolved his struggle with the back and forth, give and take of the religions through God's all-encompassing narrative of redemption in Christ. The result is an honest, consistent, dynamic, developmental, and, ultimately, progressive attitude toward non-Christian religions rooted in a thoroughly Christian theology of redemption.

For Christians, the criterial norm or standard for relating to all people is God's ultimate redemptive purpose in Christ. What might that imply for Pentecostals today, theologically and missiologically? In sum, it

- affirms and undergirds traditional commitment to evangelistic witness;
- instructs to identify and cooperate with God's redemptive activities in others;
- embraces God's work in all history accomplishing God's ultimate redemptive purpose in Jesus Christ;
- identifies the gracious role of pneumatology in all redemptive history; and
- encourages reliance on the Holy Spirit in interreligious dialogue/cooperation oriented ministries.

Voices Crying Out in the Wilderness and the Public Square: Redirecting Jonathan Edwards' Teleology of the Political after Pentecost

Amos Yong

Introduction

Although Jonathan Edwards has not been known first and foremost as a civil, social, public, or political theologian, scholarship on these dimensions of his thought has intensified over the last generation.[1] Similarly, it is only very recently that scholarship on Pentecostalism has begun to turn in a political direction, but it is increasingly clear that it would be irresponsible to ignore or neglect thinking about the political implications of pentecostal spirituality. This chapter hopes to forge constructive pathways for both conversations precisely through their cross-fertilization. Its three sections sketch the emerging field of pentecostal studies relative to political theological discourses, review the various arguments lodged so far on Edwards as political theologian, and suggest a pneumatological and eschatological framework for reconsidering both pentecostal theology and Edwardsean thought for political theological purposes. I will argue that pentecostal perspectives can provide the theological (pneumatological) credentials for securing Edwards' stature as a political theologian even as the latter's dynamic millennial ruminations can also expand pentecostal eschatology toward a more potent political theology.

---

[1] For the sake of convenience, in this chapter, *political theology* and its cognates are used generally to include the civil, social, and public dimensions, and I will only resort to the latter three descriptors if I mean each more intentionally in the context of my discussion. I make this choice with full awareness that the secondary literature on Edwards (to which we turn in section two of the chapter) adopts the latter categories and classifications, rather than the notion of *political theology*, but do so since that is the approach deployed in my book *In the Days of Caesar: Pentecostalism and Political Theology* (Grand Rapids, MI: Eerdmans, 2010), which includes also the economic domain of human life (that is not discussed here).

Pentecostalism, the "ends" of the Spirit, and political theology

Not so long ago, the notion of a pentecostal political theology would have been an oxymoron for many reasons, not the least of which is related to the predominance of dispensational eschatology across large swaths of at least the classical pentecostal movement, if not in the first generation then thereafter when institutionalization processes ensued.[2] Such a dispensationalist disposition eschewed political engagement due to the belief that the public sphere would continue to spiral out of control under the influence of Satan and his forces until the *parousia*, shortly before which would be the rapture of the church that would precipitate the so-called great tribulation on earth. In this context, the focused energies of believers were to be directed not to "fixing" the earth's social, political, and economic problems but toward the evangelization of souls to prepare human beings for the world to come. Yet even for classical pentecostal denominations that embraced a dispensationalist eschatology, such generalizations have to be qualified particularly across racial lines since African American pentecostal churches, for instance, were and always have been more attentive to at least the civic, social, and economic if not also political aspects of their lives.[3]

The tide began to turn in earnest, however, when during the last decade of the twentieth century, social scientists began to notice the expansion of pentecostal movements across the majority world and in particular how pentecostal spirituality was enabling transition of these believers from rural to urban environments and facilitating adaptation into the global market economy.[4] Political scientists have thus scrambled to understand Pentecostalism as a public phenomenon, not only in terms of studying pentecostal citizenship beliefs and practices but also researching pentecostal participation in formal local and national political processes.[5] Equally intriguing are pentecostal presence and activity in the economic arena, pressing questions about if and how pentecostal spirituality is correlative with, if not also conducive for, globalization and neoliberal market dynamics.[6] Interestingly, majority

---

[2] For a historical overview of early pentecostal eschatology, Larry R. McQueen, *Toward a Pentecostal Eschatology: Discerning the Way Forward* (Blandford Forum: Deo, 2012), chapters 3–4.

[3] See, for example, David D. Daniels III, "Navigating the Territory: Early Afro-Pentecostalism as a Movement within Black Civil Society," in *Afro-Pentecostalism: Black Pentecostal and Charismatic Christianity in History and Culture*, ed. Estrelda Y. Alexander and Amos Yong (New York: New York University Press, 2011), 43–62.

[4] Leading the way here is David Martin, *Pentecostalism: The World Their Parish* (Malden, MA: Blackwell, 2002).

[5] The literature is by now legion, and I survey some of this material in my "Global Pentecostalisms Navigating the Public Square: Revitalizing Political Theology?" in *The Oxford Handbook of Political Theology*, ed. Shaun Casey and Michael Kessler (Oxford: Oxford University Press, forthcoming).

[6] See Katherine Attanasi and Amos Yong, eds., *Pentecostalism and Prosperity: The Socioeconomics of the Global Charismatic Movement*, Christianities of the World 1 (New York: Palgrave Macmillan, 2012), and the literature references therein; cf. also Christopher Marsh and Artyom Tonoyan, "The Civic, Economic, and Political Consequences of Pentecostalism in Russia and Ukraine," *Society* 46, no. 6 (2009): 510–16; Tomas Sundnes Drønen, "Weber, Prosperity and the Protestant Ethic: Some Reflections on Pentecostalism and Economic Development," *Svensk missionstidskrift* 100, no. 3 (2012): 321–35; and Dena Freeman, ed., *Pentecostalism and Development: Churches, NGOs and Social Change in Africa* (New York: Palgrave Macmillan, 2012).

world Pentecostals are much less beholden to the dispensational eschatology of earlier generations but, more importantly, also have a much more this-worldly soteriology that emphasizes the role of the Holy Spirit to empower human efforts in the present life. The bottom line is that scholars of religion and political economists, among those researching in related disciplines, have begun to pay closer attention not only to the sociopolitical and economic by-products of pentecostal Christianity but also to the ways in which Pentecostals have become more intentional about engaging with these issues.[7]

Not surprisingly, then, pentecostal theologians have also gradually, but no less perceptibly, been moving forward in thinking explicitly about what a pentecostal political theology might look like. The earliest to venture along these trajectories, naturally, were those in dialogue with liberation theological traditions, and these observed how pentecostal spirituality engaged the poor and oppressed on the one hand and were suggestive for pentecostal political theology on the other hand.[8] More recently, the emphasis on liberation has widened so that there are now pentecostal scholars working constructively at the nexus of pentecostal peacemaking and social justice even as others are exploring the contours of a distinctively pentecostal political theology.[9] Others also have been at work on the question about whether pentecostal spirituality engenders its own distinctive set of economic practices such that we might ask if it makes sense to talk about a pentecostal economics, if not at least about a theology of economics based on the pneumatological logic discernible in the Lucan Day of Pentecost narrative.[10] The point is that pentecostal engagement with political theological discourses, broadly defined, appear to be sparking initiatives that show every sign of intensification and none of abatement.

My own efforts in these venues have been to propose what might be called a pluralistic pentecostal political theology attentive not only to the divergent arenas of the public square but also to the various pragmatic strategies of pentecostal engagement in these enterprises and the different theological arguments that support and normatively

---

[7] See Donald E. Miller and Testunao Yamamori, *Global Pentecostalism: The New Face of Christian Social Engagement* (Berkeley: University of California Press, 2007).

[8] For example, Eldin Villafañe, *The Liberating Spirit: Toward an Hispanic American Pentecostal Social Ethic* (Grand Rapids, MI: Eerdmans, 1993); Samuel Solivan, *Spirit, Pathos and Liberation: Toward an Hispanic Pentecostal Theology* (Sheffield: Sheffield Academic Press, 1998); and Robert Beckford, *Dread and Pentecostal: A Political Theology for the Black Church in Britain* (London: Society for Promoting Christian Knowledge, 2000).

[9] See the Pentecostals, Peacemaking, and Social Justice series edited by Paul Alexander at http://wipfandstock.com/catalog/series/view/id/37/; cf. also Joseph Quayesi-Amakye, *Christology and Evil in Ghana: Towards a Pentecostal Public Theology*, Currents of Encounter 49 (Amsterdam: Rodopi, 2013) and Steven M. Studebaker, *A Pentecostal Political Theology for American Renewal: Spirit of the Kingdoms, Citizens of the Cities* (New York: Palgrave Macmillan, 2016).

[10] See Daniela C. Augustine, *Pentecost, Hospitality, and Transfiguration: Toward a Spirit-Inspired Vision of Social Transformation* (Cleveland, TN: CPT, 2012), chapter 3, and most importantly, Nigerian pentecostal social ethicist Nimi Wariboko, especially his *The Charismatic City and the Public Resurgence of Religion: A Pentecostal Social Ethics of Cosmopolitan Urban Life* (New York: Palgrave Macmillan, 2014) and *Economics in Spirit and Truth: A Moral Philosophy of Finance* (New York: Palgrave Macmillan, 2014).

inform such initiatives.[11] Pentecostal pluralism in this case, however, is scripturally and theologically generated on the one hand—from the multiplicity of tongues and languages redeemed by the Spirit on the Day of Pentecost outpouring, hence what I call *many tongues and many political theologies and* practices—and empirically *and* confessionally derived on the other hand: from the multiplicity of sociopolitical environments amid which pentecostal communities, congregations, and churches are to be found around the world *and* as correlated with the diversity of self-understandings opened up through the pentecostal "fivefold" gospel of Jesus as savior, sanctifier, Spirit baptizer, healer, and coming king.[12] More precisely, however, I have come to view the explicitly eschatological trajectory of Jesus the coming king as fundamentally orienting pentecostal if not also Christian reflection on political theology.[13] If that is the case, then any theological endeavor will also be eschatologically funded and constituted, including efforts in political theologies and its concomitant discourses.

Here we come full circle to the eschatological issues that initially inhibited pentecostal engagement with, much less reflection on, public concerns and realities. If the earlier dispensationalist sensibilities were convinced that pentecostal efforts in the public, social, and economic arenas were a waste of time, the many strands across the contemporary global pentecostal landscape do not think with one mind on the issue.[14] To be sure, one would be hard pressed to find pentecostal churches or communities that did not hold forth some futurist aspect in their eschatological understanding. Simultaneously, many, if not most, understand that the church as the people of God has been living in the so-called last days since the Day of Pentecost visitation of the Holy Spirit (see Acts 2:17), and in that sense, all ecclesiology and soteriology is both pneumatological and eschatological simultaneously so that there is at least what New Testament scholars call a *partially realized* facet of the reign of God that is manifest in the present age by the work of the Spirit, if also still to come.[15]

In any case, such a widened eschatological scope has implications for pentecostal public and political theology. If, for instance, the baptism of the Spirit empowers

---

[11] Yong, *In the Days of Caesar*; on pentecostal pragmatism and its political implications, see Tony Richie, "Pragmatism, Power, and Politics: A Pentecostal Conversation with President Obama's Favorite Theologian, Reinhold Niebuhr," *Pneuma: The Journal of the Society for Pentecostal Studies* 32, no. 2 (2010): 241–60.

[12] See also Yong, "Salvation, Society, and the Spirit: Pentecostal Contextualization and Political Theology from Cleveland to Birmingham, from Springfield to Seoul," *Pax Pneuma: The Journal of Pentecostals & Charismatics for Peace & Justice* 5, no. 2 (2009): 22–34 and "What Spirit(s), Which Public(s)? The Pneumatologies of Global Pentecostal-Charismatic Christianity," *International Journal of Public Theology* 7, no. 3 (2013): 241–59.

[13] I make the argument for the priority of eschatology for Christian theology as a whole in Yong, *Renewing Christian Theology: Systematics for a Global Christianity*, images and commentary by Jonathan A. Anderson (Waco, TX: Baylor University Press, 2014), chapter 2 and passim.

[14] A range of views are documented in Peter Althouse and Robby Waddell, eds., *Perspectives in Pentecostal Eschatologies: World Without End* (Eugene, OR: Pickwick, 2010); for more on the eschatological dynamics undergirding the shifting nature of pentecostal attitudes vis-à-vis the political, see Rudolf von Sinner, "Pentecostalism and Citizenship in Brazil: Between Escapism and Dominance," *International Journal of Public Theology* 6, no. 1 (2012): 99–117.

[15] See Frank D. Macchia, *Baptized in the Spirit: A Global Pentecostal Theology* (Grand Rapids, MI: Zondervan, 2006), chapters 3–4; cf. also Matthew Thompson, *Kingdom Come: Revisioning Pentecostal Eschatology* (Blandford Forum: Deo, 2010).

Christian witness regarding the kingdom of God to the "ends of the earth" (Acts 1:8), then such witness includes evangelism classically understood but certainly also goes beyond this to engage with the task of holistic, even transformational, mission in the here and now.[16] This is not to collapse the future horizon into a reductionist historicism; it is to say that eschatological considerations impinge on public and political theological formulations, especially when guided pneumatologically and pentecostally (following the Acts 2 narrative, that is). My point is that the many tongues of the Spirit in the present time open up to many public and political stances, attitudes, and postures, and that these penultimate works of the Spirit also herald the coming, and ultimate, reign of God.

Jonathan Edwards, the "ends" of God, and the political

The relatively recent emergence of Jonathan Edwards as public theologian is due in part to the belated, mid-twentieth century, scholarly reception of his work initiated by American intellectual historians like Perry Miller,[17] and in part to the fact that the nomenclature of public theology and political theology did not attain circulation until the post–civil rights era.[18] Even then, arguments specifically about Edwards' social and public theology have gained currency only slowly,[19] especially since Edwards himself "never gave any extended theoretical attention to social, political, or economic problems."[20] Intriguingly, three major proposals have been formulated

---

[16] I borrow *transformational* from Peter Althouse, *Spirit of the Last Days: Pentecostal Eschatology in Conversation with Jürgen Moltmann*, Journal of Pentecostal Theology Supplement 25 (New York: Bloomsbury Academic, 2003), chapter 3.

[17] Particularly Miller's *Jonathan Edwards* (New York: William Morrow, 1949); Miller, a Harvard University professor, is widely recognized as the dean of American Puritanism and intellectual history.

[18] The modern discussion of political theology was initiated in Germany in the 1920s with the work of political theorist and philosopher Carl Schmitt, but the first books in English did not appear until the 1970s; see my discussion of Schmitt's work and legacy in my *In the Days of Caesar*, §2.3.

[19] As we shall see, Edwards scholars have not written about Edwards as *political theologian*; they have rather engaged him as *theologian of society* (Bryant and Hall) or as *public theologian* (McDermott). There is now also an essay suggestive of Edwards as a theologian of civil society: William J. Danaher, "Jonathan Edwards, Francis Hutcheson, and the Problems and Prospects of Civil Society," in *A World for All? Global Civil Society in Political Theory and Trinitarian Theology*, ed. William F. Storrar, Peter J. Casarella, and Paul Louis Metzger (Grand Rapids, MI: Eerdmans, 2011), 178–96; cf. Ava Chamberlain, "Edwards and Social Issues," in *The Cambridge Companion to Jonathan Edwards*, ed. Stephen J. Stein (Cambridge: Cambridge University Press, 2006), 325–44. In my discussion of Edwards' ideas particularly, I will try to follow the extant scholarly nomenclature, although when I resort to talking more inclusively, rather than technically, about the subject matter of this chapter, I will refer to Edwards as *political theologian* or its cognates.

[20] Paul K. Conkin, *Puritans and Pragmatists: Eight Eminent American Thinkers* (1968; reprint, Waco, TX: Baylor University Press, 2005), 71. Although Conkin is correct that Edwards' attention was focused on other matters, yet this does not mean that his writings were bereft of references to or implications for these topics. A recent anthology captures many of the important segments and sections of the Edwardsean *oeuvre* on these matters: Gerald R. McDermott and Ronald Story, eds., *The Other Jonathan Edwards: Selected Writings on Society, Love, and Justice* (Amherst and Boston: University of Massachusetts Press, 2015).

in this regard, all of which were published in the first half of the final decade of the twentieth century. The following section overviews the arguments proffered by M. Darrol Bryant, Richard A. S. Hall, and Gerald R. McDermott, all written initially as doctoral theses, in order to map Edwards' perceived legacy on these matters. As no consensus exists about how to read Edwards vis-à-vis the public sphere, I will suggest that this inconclusiveness is related at least in part to another aspect of Edwards' thought that is perhaps no less opaque, his eschatology.[21] This submission will prepare the way for the dialogue between pentecostal theology and Edwards in the final section of this chapter.

We begin with M. Darrol Bryant's *Jonathan Edwards' Grammar of Time, Self, and Society: A Critique of the Heimert Thesis*, which, while published last of the three texts we will examine, was submitted for the PhD first in the mid-1970s.[22] As noted in the title, the book is a running engagement with the argument of Alan Heimert, a Harvard University Americanist.[23] The latter's work, developed within the trajectory opened up by the retrieval of Edwards (Heimert was a student of Perry Miller), can be read as representative of the reinsertion of America's eighteenth-century theologian and philosopher back into the mainstreams of the nation's intellectual genealogy. In particular, Heimert insisted that far from being marginal to the American intellectual tradition, the Great Awakening revivals, of which Edwards was the primary guide and apologist, were actually central to the nurturing of the nation's democratic ideals and founding aspirations. If correct, then Edwards the (previously obscure) philosopher and theologian is no less political philosopher and public theologian, or at least the implications of his work should be reconsidered in relationship to these aspects of America's "radical, even democratic, social and political ideology."[24]

While accepting Edwards as integral to American intellectual history, Bryant's counterargument is that the "Heimert thesis," if not qualified, misrepresents Edwards as a political ideologue to those otherwise unfamiliar with his *oeuvre*. Three lines of corrective re-readings are provided toward this end: on Edwards' views on history, human nature, and human society. On the first, if Heimert is correct that Edwards' earlier postmillennial eschatology was part and parcel of a more optimistic view of history prevalent within segments of the American tradition and motivated by a sense

---

[21] Stephen J. Stein, "Eschatology," in *The Princeton Companion to Jonathan Edwards*, ed. Sang Hyun Lee (Princeton, NJ: Princeton University Press, 2005), 226–42, at 226, reminds us that Edwards himself did not use the term "eschatology," but his thought ranged widely over what has come to be included in this notion in the last 200 years; we will also talk about Edwards' eschatology in this chapter, albeit with an awareness of its anachronistic character.

[22] M. Darrol Bryant, *Jonathan Edwards' Grammar of Time, Self, and Society: A Critique of the Heimert Thesis*, Studies in American Religion 60 (Lewiston: Edwin Mellen, 1993), initially presented as "History and Eschatology in Jonathan Edwards: A Critique of the Heimert Thesis" (PhD diss., University of St. Michael's College, 1976).

[23] Alan Heimert, *Religion and the American Mind: From the Great Awakening to the Revolution* (Cambridge: Harvard University Press, 1966). Despite Bryant's efforts, note the persisting impact of Heimert's "thesis" in its reprinting as part of The Jonathan Edwards Classic Studies Series by The Jonathan Edwards Center at Yale University and Wipf & Stock (based in Eugene, Oregon) in 2006.

[24] Ibid., viii.

of the imminence of the coming kingdom of God, Heimert fails to see that the later, post-Awakening, Edwards transitioned gradually, initially to a less New England and American centered and more universal or international horizon for thinking about the kingdom in the more distant future, and then toward a transcendent eschatological vision which main lines provided "the basis for a critique of elements which have subsequently come to be identified as central to American's symbolic nexus."[25] Second, while Edwards' *Life of David Brainerd* (1749) is archetypical for Christian piety and his *The Nature of True Virtue* (written initially in the early 1750s but published posthumously in 1765) provides a foundational philosophical anthropology with implications and applications for social theory and political philosophy, the former does not provide a template for civic and social activism (as Heimert proposes) and should be understood instead alongside the latter as pointing *theologically* to human *being* (not only or merely *doing*) as the proper end (*telos*) of humanity *in God*.[26] Last but not least, Heimert misunderstands especially Edwards' *A History of the Work of Redemption* (drafted in the late 1730s and intended to be revised and expanded later in life, although unaccomplished due to his untimely death) as a vision of the good society; interpreted in the context of Edwards' corpus, especially his later thinking about millennial deferral, our protagonist instead "(1) offers a critique of the quest for power and domination in terms of the doctrine of Divine Sovereignty, (2) breaks with the nation of a Holy Commonwealth, thus, desacralizing politics, and (3) articulates a vision of spiritual community as witness and forerunner of the transcendent Kingdom of God."[27] In general, Bryant concludes, any "failure to differentiate the political order of preservation from the religious order of salvation results in a mistaken transformation of Edwards' theological vision into a sanction for a new quest for Holy Commonwealth"; rather, Edwards assumes, "perhaps ahead of his contemporaries, that society is made up of a variety of communities each having its own proper *telos* and integrating principles."[28]

I am less interested in the degree to which Heimert has been accurately read or correctly rebuffed than in Bryant's urging our focus on the overarching eschatological-teleological framework for appreciating the Edwardsean contribution to contemporary theology. On the one hand, there is a clearing of the brush in admonishing against simplistic notions of Edwards as political theologian since "the notion of divine sovereignty is, in Edwards, the basis for a critique of utopianism in politics because of its insistence that the shape of the future is beyond human control."[29] On the other hand, it may also be appropriate to view Edwards as political theologian, except that

---

[25] Bryant, *Jonathan Edwards' Grammar of Time, Self, and Society*, 32; for further explication of this three-part periodization of Edwards' millennialism, see M. Darrol Bryant, "From Edwards to Hopkins: A Millennialist Critique of Political Culture," in *The Coming Kingdom: Essays in American Millennialism and Eschatology*, ed. M. Darrol Bryant and Donald W. Dayton (Barrytown, NY: New Era, 1983), 45–70, esp. 47–54.
[26] This is the argument in ibid., chapter 3.
[27] Ibid., 170.
[28] Ibid., 181.
[29] Ibid., 223.

his internationalist horizons, clearly articulated in his later work, resist an American-centric nationalism, and his transcendentalist eschatological vision functions as "a principle of transtemporal criticism" of any sociopolitical order.[30]

Richard Hall's 1984 doctoral dissertation, published seven years later,[31] is more narrowly focused on Edwards' later Northampton years of 1743-51, specifically on four texts completed during the last half of this period of his pastorate before moving to Stockbridge. He agrees with Bryant[32] that Edwards ought to be read first and foremost as a theologian rather than a social or political theorist (as might have been implied by historical retrievals of Edwards) but yet argues that there is a social vision at least embedded in the later Edwards, if not also clearly explicit at moments in the writings he analyzes. More valiantly, in a running conversation with Edwards' interpreters, Hall believes his analysis "resolves the scholarly disagreement over Edwards' status as a socio-political thinker; synthesizes the various elements of social-political thought previously unearthed from the four texts into a coherent socio-political theory; and describes Edwards' philosophy of community."[33]

Hall's argument proceeds as follows. First, Edwards' *An Humble Attempt to Promote Explicit Agreement & Visible Union of God's People in Extraordinary Prayer for the Revival of Religion & the Advancement of Christ's Kingdom on Earth* (1747) not only clarifies the Northampton minister's millennial vision, however delayed such was thought to have been at this point of Edwards' life, as well as the means through which such might be anticipated, but also provides a blueprint for the "Christian utopia, his metaphor for which is the Kingdom of God," and in that sense, presents a normative theory of society.[34] Second, the *Life of David Brainerd* (1749) turns from the social to the individual, presenting Brainerd as not only exemplary missionary but ideal member or citizen. Third, *An Humble Inquiry into the Rules of the Word of God, Concerning the Qualifications Requisite to a Complete Standing and Full Communion in the Visible Christian Church* (1749) presents both an argument for how the church

---

[30] M. Darrol Bryant, "America as God's Kingdom," in *Religion and Political Society*, ed. Jürgen Moltmann et al. (New York: Harper & Row, 1974), 49-94, at 81; in this essay, Bryant also argues against the prevailing popular retrievals of Edwards and the Puritan tradition, particularly "the presumptuous belief that the American Republic is the realization of an eschatological hope. [But] Is not this the idolatrous assumption which makes the transcendent the underwriter of the political Republic and, thus, transforms Christianity into a civil religion?" Further, here anticipating the thesis-length argument against Heimert, he contests "that on historical grounds, the assumption that the millennial impulse gains fulfillment in the American Republic is unwarranted, at least in relation to Jonathan Edwards, and we shall argue, on theological grounds, that such an identification involves an idolatrous confusion of the politics of God and the politics of man" (56, 59).

[31] Richard A. S. Hall, "The Idea of Community in the Thought of Jonathan Edwards: The Neglected Texts from Northampton" (PhD diss., University of Toronto, 1984), published as *The Neglected Northampton Texts of Jonathan Edwards: Edwards on Society and Politics*, Studies in American Religion 52 (Lewiston: Edwin Mellen, 1990).

[32] At least with the dissertation form of Bryant's argument, since the book version of the latter actually appeared after Hall's own book, and interestingly, as urged and received by Hall in the book series he edited (Mellen's Studies in American Religion series); see Bryant, *Jonathan Edwards' Grammar of Time, Self, and Society*, 227.

[33] Hall, *The Neglected Northampton Texts*, 68.

[34] Ibid., 62.

might historically embody the eschatological community in anticipation of the coming reign of God (no matter how far off) and, in that sense, suggests an ecclesiological set of guidelines that have implications and applications for social organization. Finally, *A Farewell Sermon Preached at the First Precinct in Northampton, after the People's Public Rejection of Their Minister* (delivered in July 1750 but published in 1751) can be understood in terms of a normative theory of sociality, culled from Edwards' thinking about the final judgment when moral disagreements will be adjudicated and social injustices rectified. Hall thus urges: if Edwards' *The Nature of True Virtue* and other works (such as his 1746 *Religious Affections*, the culmination of his thinking about the revivals) "are concerned with delineating the nature of true piety or virtue, then *Humble Attempt*, the *Life of Brainerd*, and *Humble Inquiry* are concerned respectively with its promulgation, illustration, and social embodiment,"[35] and the *Farewell Sermon* with the theory of justice against which human piety and virtuosity will be judged.

Hall concludes that his efforts "substantiate, amplify, and in places qualify, the revisionist argument [of Heimert et al.], thereby resolving the conflict by establishing once and for all that Edwards' thought indeed has considerable socio-theoretic merit."[36] His achievements are, in my estimation, to have teased out elements of Edwards' thought that are applicable toward a social or public theology, particularly in light of Edwards' eschatological commitments. Insisting from this that Edwards presented himself as a social or public theologian, what Hall (barely) avoids implying, would be saying too much. Yet there is nothing to prevent extension of Edwards' ideas, including extrapolation of Edwards' eschatological notions, in these directions, and for such purposes, Hall's approach charts a viable way forward.

If Hall formulates what might be considered an Edwardsean social philosophy, Gerald McDermott urges an Edwardsean public theology, by which he refers to "Edwards's conception of the civil community and the Christian's relation to it."[37] The latter's argument, however, is constructed from a close reading of the entirety of Edwards' corpus, including his unpublished writings. McDermott thus proceeds thematically, first unpacking the overall contours of Edwards' prophetic and overall largely pessimistic standpoint regarding and against New England's failure to live as the covenant people of God, thus precipitating the divine wrath on their sinful disobedience (in this reading, the glimmers of optimism are relatively fleeting in relationship to the waxing and waning of revival fervor, as I will explicate further below); second expositing Edwards' vision of the millennium as expanding inexorably, especially by the later 1740s, toward an international (rather than provincially American) horizon that nevertheless also provided the norms for

---

[35] Ibid., 58.
[36] Ibid., 309–10.
[37] Gerald R. McDermott, *One Holy and Happy Society: The Public Theology of Jonathan Edwards* (University Park, PA: Penn State University Press, 1992), 6–7. Although McDermott's doctoral thesis was written in the late 1980s and published in 1992 under the same title, he mentions neither Hall's or Bryant's dissertations. He would at least have been aware of the latter since he cites a Bryant essay that references the 1976 thesis, but perhaps did not feel the polemical character of that argument was relevant to his own reading of Edwards for public theological purposes.

Edwards the social critic; third delineating Edwards' social ethic in relationship to this philosophical theology as one that resisted any individualistic privatization of Christian faith;[38] and fourth explicating his theology of the magistracy, both in terms of the biblical (as opposed to medieval or emerging American nationalist renditions) purposes of government understood as public authority appointed by God to work out the divine history of redemption and its limitations. From these explorations, McDermott concludes toward a theology of citizenship that includes both privileges and duties, in which love for neighbor and even country are united and motivated first and foremost by love for God. On the one hand, Edwards' theology of civil society and the public domain remained hierarchically structured (with free men over women and slaves, for instance), a vision consistent with his Platonic idealism; on the other hand, such was also adapted and refracted into his theological distinction between regenerate and unregenerate humanity so that the former, given their teleological and theological reorientation toward the coming kingdom and vision of God, would manifest divine ideals as an egalitarianly constituted church in a fallen world.

Although consistent with Bryant's position that especially the later Edwards' transcendent eschatological horizon resourced his prophetic demeanor as sociopolitical critic, McDermott moves also toward a constructive reappropriation of such a deportment by observing how Edwards proffered an eschatologically inflected public theology. For instance, the Northampton minister's post-revival beliefs that his parishioners' way of life was subject imminently to divine judgment dampened his nationalism and ethnocentrism on the one hand, and nurtured his internationalism on the other hand. So although there is no doubt about the "intensity of Edwards's absorption with the millennium and its antecedent events" and that "the millennium was a continual obsession" in his thinking over the years,[39] these prodded his expectations that renewal and revival would be extended beyond the nation to human history as a whole. As the failure of ancient Israel made possible the grafting in of the Gentiles into the covenant, so also does America's disobedience make possible the eschatological redemption of the world in God's work of salvation.

Many tongues—many eschatological postures—many contextual public theologies: Pentecostal theology and Edwards in critical and constructive conversation

In this final and longest section of the chapter, I have two goals. First, I propose that pentecostal pneumatology can provide a pluralistic framework for appreciating

---

[38] On this point see also Gerald R. McDermott, "Jonathan Edwards and the Culture Wars: A New Resource for Public Theology and Philosophy," *Pro Ecclesia* 4, no. 3 (1995): 268–80, esp. 269–73; cf. the earlier argument of Paul J. Nagy, "The Beloved Community of Jonathan Edwards," *Transactions of the Charles S. Peirce Society* 7, no. 2 (1971): 93–105.

[39] McDermott, *One Holy and Happy Society*, 43, 44.

the full range of Edwards' eschatological and political theological ideas albeit while appreciating and augmenting the broad thrust of his teleological vision. Second, then, I suggest how what appears to be Edwards' shifting millennialism can also resource pentecostal thinking about eschatology toward a broader political theological platform. Attaining the former aim requires that we move swiftly across Edwards' writings and make some (hopefully) intuitive theological connections. Receive the following, then, as an imaginative dialogical exercise in political theology.

I embark on this thought experiment with Edwards not because I have a full grasp of his life work—an impossibility given the extensiveness of the Yale edition of his works—but in order to test two hypotheses: that there are discernible correlations between Edwards' historical settings, his fluid millennialism, and his social sensibilities, and that the full scope of his legacy in these areas might be more widely received if given further pneumatological assistance (our first objective for this final part of the chapter). We have already seen that there is a diversity of views regarding the relevance of Edwards as a social or public theologian. My hunch, to be outlined rather than argued at length, is that there is a way of reading and receiving the various strands of Edwards' eschatological and public theological thinking once we recognize that their diversity is related in part to the various social locations from out of which he theologized.[40] In brief, let me postulate that Edwards' social and public theological ideas can be variously categorized according to his writing as a revivalist, as a colonialist, and as a missionary, and each of these social identities, at once distinct and yet intertwined within their historical contexts, illuminates the alterations of his eschatological views and invites a corresponding set of attitudes, perspectives, and behaviors vis-à-vis the polis.[41] Let us tease out these correlations in order.

I suggest first that when considered in terms of Edwards' social location, we can tease out at least the following three contexts behind the millennialist ideas he variously defended: a Christendom context wherein he worked as a revivalist, a colonial context in which he was a (faithful) subject of the British empire, and a marginal context when he was a missionary. We have seen above that Edwards has been presented as inhabiting the full postmillennialist spectrum, believing in its imminent arrival on the one hand and then thinking it to be far off on the other hand. I propose the following: that his initial optimism regarding the revivals as impending and hastening the arrival of the millennial reign of God—what Edwards called "the glorious work of God" (I.366)[42]—including his belief that the latter would

---

[40] Here I follow the cue of Rachel Wheeler, whose social-contextual reading of Edwards' treatise on *Original Sin* highlights the importance of his role as missionary to the Indians; see Rachel Wheeler, "'Friends to Your Souls': Jonathan Edwards' Indian Pastorate and the Doctrine of Original Sin," *Church History* 72, no. 4 (2003): 736–65, at 761.

[41] I do not discuss Edwards' eschatology systematically here, only in relationship to how such has been understood by those attempting to explore his social and public theological ideas; for an overview of Edwards' eschatology, with which I would argue is consistent with the discussion that follows, see Michael J. McClymond and Gerald R. McDermott, *Theology of Jonathan Edwards* (Oxford: Oxford University Press, 2012), chapter 35.

[42] Unless otherwise noted, I will refer hereafter, by volume and page number, to this edition of Edwards' works: Edward Hickman, ed., *The Works of Jonathan Edwards*, 2 vols. (1834; reprint, Edinburgh and Carlisle, PA: The Banner of Truth Trust, 1990), with italics from the original also,

"probably . . . begin in America" (I.381), reflected Christendom assumptions related to America as one of the most important extensions of the British imperial reach and thus was consistent with the sense that revival in the New World would be a harbinger the world to come and that the American church would be a crucial, if not central, instrument of such divine work. More precisely, Edwards enthusiastically anticipated:

> If we may suppose that this glorious work of God shall begin in any part of *America*, I think, if we consider the circumstances of the settle of *New England*, it must needs appear the most likely, of all *American* colonies, to be the place whence this work shall principally take its rise. And, if these things be so, it gives us more abundant reason to hope that what is now seen in *America*, and especially in *New England*, may prove the dawn of that glorious day: and the very uncommon and wonderful circumstances and events of this work, seem to me strongly to argue that God intends it as the beginning or forerunner of something vastly great. (I.383)

Following from this, then, when the ardor of revival faded, Edwards as a (then) citizen of good standing under the English crown, presumed the international awareness shaped by British colonial activity and presence, and this not only tempered any enthusiasm and parochialism about the New England Church but also gave him a longer term and futurist perspective on the millennial advent. Thus, by the later 1740s, Edwards joined with Scottish ministers to publish *An Humble Attempt* which sought to herald, through fervent prayer, the *Advancement of Christ's Kingdom on Earth* (which is the end of the long title),[43] and in this context, adopted a less imminent stance regarding the millennium—since "many things which are spoken concerning a *glorious* time of the church's *enlargement* and *prosperity* in the *latter days*, have never yet been fulfilled" (II.285)—and proclaimed "that there should come a time, when *all nations*, throughout the whole habitable world, should embrace the true religion, and be brought into the church of God" (II.185). If in the revivalist context earlier in the decade Edwards found himself and the Northampton community at the center of what could only be

---

unless otherwise noted. In this case, I cite from Edwards' *Some Thoughts Concerning the Present Revival of Religion in New England*, written in the wake of the revivals of the early 1740s.

Permit a brief autobiographical digression: Although I am now aware that scholars much prefer reference to and use of the multivolume Yale critical edition of *The Works of Jonathan Edwards* (specific installations of which I also will refer to), I first read Edwards in the fall of 1991, when, as part of my Western Evangelical Seminary (changed at one point to George Fox Seminary and then again to, now, Portland Seminary) studies, I took a course (and transferred credit over) from Western Conservative Baptist Seminary (also in Portland, Oregon, now Western Seminary) through which John Gerstner, a conservative Reformed interpreter of Edwards, offered both Hickman volumes to students who would read them within a year, which I did. That fall I wrote a paper on Edwards's trinitarian theology—nothing like diving into the "deep end" of the Edwardsean and theological pool for a second year seminarian!—and I am thus taking up this opportunity to reopen the pages of this classic edition almost twenty-five years later to reconsider the relevance of his ideas for the global pentecostal ferment, particularly as pentecostal theologians think about making a viable public and political theological contribution for the twenty-first century.

[43] As Stephen Stein—in his "Editor's Introduction," *WJE* 5:34—notes, "Public prayer was a social action with religious and ecclesiastical implications;" hence, for us, the *Humble Attempt* emerges as a social and even political manifesto, with public implications.

deemed as the dawn of God's glorious work interpreted, understandably, according to the apocalyptic horizons that had long retained his interests, such expectations were quickly doused within a few years later, in the wake of post-revival "apostasy." In this situation, Edwards' lenses zoomed back out from his own immediate context and widened to engage the colonial frontiers, envisioning also their roles, however distant geographically and far-off temporally, in the millennial reign of God.

Yet there is a third social space that Edwards later inhabited, one that in many respects did not leave behind but transfigured his identity as a New England preacher and revivalist on the one hand and a citizen of the British crown on the other, and this was his role as a missionary to the Stockbridge Indians in the last seven years of his life. In this social milieu, Edwards found himself more often than not, for various reasons that we do not need to go into, on the side of the Indians against land grabbers, greedy traders, and exploitative colonizers,[44] all the while without taking off his etic perspective as an outsider to the Mahicans among whom he ministered. Hence Edwards was simultaneously at the center of the Christendom and imperial narratives and complicit with their agendas on the one hand, but also on their outer margins, with the "heathen" of Stockbridge no less than among other pagans on the outer edges of the colonial world, resisting injustice, on the other hand. I wonder how, as Edwards persisted in solidarity with and even "won the affection of his Indian parishioners,"[45] his perspective changed. My theory is that it is precisely from out of this ambivalence that Edwards' millennial and apocalyptic thinking was transformed into a more strictly teleological dimension, one that was less invested in how the kingdom of God would be materialized in human history and more inclined to consider the *End for Which God Created the World*, which was published preceding *The Nature of True Virtue* as one combined book, in transcendent terms, applicable as the divine norm of critique and judgment on human affairs.[46] Hence these last two of Edwards' works are his most

---

[44] There is a growing literature on Edwards' missionary efforts at Stockbridge, including Stephen J Nichols, "Last of the Mohican Missionaries: Jonathan Edwards at Stockbridge," in *The Legacy of Jonathan Edwards: American Religion and the Evangelical Tradition*, ed. D. G. Hart, Sean Michael Lucas, and Stephen J. Nichols (Grand Rapids, MI: Baker Academic, 2003), 47–63; April C. Armstrong, "Last Were the Mahicans: Jonathan Edwards, Stockbridge, and Native Americans," *Southwestern Journal of Theology* 48, no. 1 (2005): 19–31; and Ronald Edwin Davies, "Prepare Ye the Way of the Lord: The Missiological Thought and Practice of Jonathan Edwards (1703–1758)" (PhD diss., Fuller Theological Seminary, School of World Mission, 1988), chapter 6. See also Ian D. McFadden, "Amidst the Great Darkness: The Practical Missiology of Jonathan Edwards at Stockbridge, 1751–1758" (STM thesis, Yale Divinity School, 2008), who discusses Edwards as educator, preacher, and reformer; and cf. the editors' introductory comments on not only Edwards' letters, especially, but also sermons and other discourses, during the Stockbridge years in Edwards, "Editor's Introduction," *WJE* 16:17–25 and "Editor's Introduction," *WJE* 25:24–32.

[45] Gerald R. McDermott, "Missions and Native Americans," in *The Princeton Companion to Jonathan Edwards*, ed. Sang Hyun Lee (Princeton, NJ: Princeton University Press, 2005), 258–73, at 268.

[46] The tentativeness of this proposal cannot be underemphasized, particularly in light of the apt warning by Rachel Wheeler that "linking Edwards's theological and philosophical writings with his immediate social context is a tricky business [not least because] Edwards himself certainly did not consciously reflect on the implications of his encounter with the Stockbridge Indians for his theology." Yet Wheeler herself draws certain connections (see next note), so we proceed cautiously and provisionally here, along the path she opens up. See "Edwards as Missionary," in *The Cambridge Companion to Jonathan Edwards*, ed. Stephen J. Stein (Cambridge: Cambridge University Press, 2006), 196–214, at 207–8.

philosophical and abstract, honed, I believe, through these years of wrestling with human sinfulness that engulfed all people—British, American, and Indian similarly, himself included[47]—and finding that what fallen human creatures cannot accomplish has to be achieved by God. From this perspective, Edwards is less inclined to dwell on penultimate human efforts (in revivals or otherwise) in human history (even the arrival of the millennial glory) and more focused on ultimate divine ends, even on the trinitarian God's own self-knowledge, self-love, and self-enjoyment, and on true virtue for humans as their participation in these emanating realities of the divine being.[48]

I hazard to propose then, painting with an exceedingly broad brush, there is a correlation between nine different faces of Edwards across three registers. Edwards the revivalist, colonialist, and missionary is concurrently Edwards the imminent postmillennialist, futurist millennialist, and practical amillennialist, and thus also Edwards the social reformer, the internationalist, and the prophetic public theologian. Although the revivalist Edwards is clearly postmillennial according to the standard typology of that time, the post-revivalist Edwards is arguably either a millennialist of a general sort, to the point where pre- or post- is immaterial, or arguably a practical amillennialist in the sense that however and whenever the millennium turns out, for the present, human beings are under divine judgment even as they are oriented toward the glory that will be revealed. These millennial views have political theological implications consistent with Edwards' writings in the last decade of his life.

If we read Edwards first and foremost as revivalist (as did Heimert and others), then he appears as one interested in and committed to the social and political formation of New England and the colonies as instantiating the kingdom of God on earth. From this perspective, the Great Awakening revival and new births could be understood as ushering in a "new age" that would "abolish traditional political and social hierarchies and will establish universal equality and justice,"[49] precisely the line of thinking that has fed the Heimert thesis. But if we considered Edwards as theologian of Northampton more broadly (as did Hall) and took into account the full scope of his eschatological, millennial, and apocalyptic writings (as did McDermott), then his international horizons come more completely into view and his social theoretical and public theological insights can be deduced more readily from his extant writings.

---

[47] On the egalitarian nature of human depravity, forged in part from out of his work with the Indians, see Wheeler, "Friends to Your Souls"; cf. Rachel Wheeler, "Lessons from Stockbridge: Jonathan Edwards and the Stockbridge Indians," in *Jonathan Edwards at 300: Essays on the Tercentenary of His Birth*, ed. Harry S. Stout, Kenneth P. Minkema, and Caleb J. D. Maskell (Lanham, MD: University Press of America, 2005), 131–40.

[48] The issues are complex, but my goal here is to hypothesize about the relationship between Edwards' eschatological views and his public theological sensibilities; for supporting expositions of these last two Edwardsean dissertations that I have summarized here all too quickly, see Helen P. Westra, "Divinity's Design: Edwards and the History of the Work of Revival," in *Edwards in Our Time: Jonathan Edwards and the Shaping of American Religion*, ed. Sang Hyun Lee and Allen C. Guelzo (Grand Rapids, MI: Eerdmans, 1999), 131–57 and Walter J. Schultz, "Jonathan Edwards's Concept of an Original Ultimate End," *Journal of the Evangelical Theological Society* 56, no. 1 (2013): 107–22, among other interpreters.

[49] David L. Weddle, "The Democracy of Grace: Political Reflections on the Evangelical Theology of Jonathan Edwards," *Dialog* 15, no. 4 (1976): 248–52, at 250.

However, if we allowed the later Edwards of *The End for Which God Created the World* and *The Nature of True Virtue* to inform our thinking (as did Bryant) and if we were to situate these ideas in their social context of his mission to the Indians (as I am urging), then Edwards the prophet of Northampton for over two decades and Edwards the millennialist theologian is transmuted by the ambiguity of his personal, ecclesial, and political identity into Edwards the prophet of human society in general, on the one hand admonishing human sinners to turn toward the only one who can save them, and on the other hand inviting human creatures to behold the glory and beauty of God that makes it possible for them to experience true self-knowledge (in relationship to God), to experience genuine love (for others and God), and to enjoy authentic happiness. Thus in this framework, it is right to say that Edwards envisioned a Christian commonwealth, not a pluralistic state. His was a God-imbued (Augustinian) vision, with true virtue possible only as enabled by and directed toward God, and self-love as fulfilling only in the context of loving God first. Yet genuine conversion, true religious affections, for Edwards, involved fellowship not only with God but also with others, and in that sense, improved political relations.[50] For the later Edwards, then, there is no other discourse for political life except the theological, and ultimately, we can only gesture beyond history to the heavenly polis.[51]

I hope that Edwards' specialists can recognize at least the plausibility of the thesis sketched here. I am not arguing for any one-to-one correlation between Edwards' social circumstances, his eschatological views, and his public stances. Instead I am suggesting that these various strands of Edwards' thinking did not emerge *ex nihilo* but are socially situated, and, hence, the arguments for each one can be better appreciated within this framework. The larger point for our purposes, however, is that we can therefore also realize that there is no *one* civil, social, or public theological vision that can or ought to be induced from Edwards but that an Edwardsean political theology is inevitably multifaceted and informed also by eschatological and teleological responses to the variety of life situations in which humans find themselves.

It is therefore also along these lines that I propose a pentecostal or pneumatological assist to such an Edwardsean political theology, consistent with and complementary of his trinitarian vision of God. This builds on my own argument for a pluralistic political theology, one which correlates the redemption of the many tongues and languages of the Spirit's outpouring on all flesh (Acts 2:17) with the many political contexts that shape pentecostal social life, and is captured by the motto, "many tongues, many political practices."[52] Briefly stated, I suggest that the pentecostal—here I mean more so Day of Pentecost related, from Acts 2, than with regard to the modern movement under that name—gift of the Spirit not only inaugurated "the last days" (Acts 2:17a) but also invites thinking about pneumatology and eschatology together in relationship to the "all flesh" or political spheres of life. The short of it is that as Edwards is right to think

---

[50] See Frederick Guyette, "Jonathan Edwards, the Ethics of Virtue and Public Theology," *International Journal of Public Theology* 4, no. 2 (2010): 158–74.

[51] Thus, we might also engage with Edwards' lifelong fascination with the idea of heaven—summarized by Robert W. Caldwell III, "A Brief History of Heaven in the Writings of Jonathan Edwards," *Calvin Theological Journal* 46, no. 1 (2011): 48–71—from a political theological perspective.

[52] Unfolded over more than 350 pages in Yong, *In the Days of Caesar*.

about the political in penultimate terms, such a pentecostal and pneumatological assist insists that such penultimacy is not unimportant. Instead, there are pneumatological, and hence theological and trinitarian, reasons to think about political theology and praxis in relationship to the trinitarian life of God.

If Edwards' end-of-life focus was on the ultimate ends of creation, it is still possible for a more pneumatologically and trinitarianly robust Edwardsean political theology to be formulated, and this would be informed at least in part by thinking with Edwards through the civic, social, and public aspects of the Pentecost narrative.[53] What I mean is that when the revivalist Edwards of the so-called Heimert thesis, for instance, is refracted through the lens of both *The End for Which God Created the World* and the Pentecost narrative, then what emerges is not only *an* American theology but an expanded range of American political *theologies* with relevance for both the multiplicity of American social contexts and the plurality of American international relations; or that when the later Northampton (Hall) and international (McDermott) Edwards is reconsidered not only in view of Pentecost at and "to the ends of the earth" (Acts 1:8) but also as arriving at these ends (in Rome, Acts 28), then such a partially realized eschatological vision not only anticipates that which is teleologically ultimate but has present implications for Christian mission in a pluralistic global context; or that when the transcendent Edwards (Bryant) is brought into a pentecostal and pneumatological frame of reference, then his prophetic stance applies across multiple historical contexts, challenging both the political center and the margins, albeit variously. In other words, I am suggesting that a "pentecostalized" Edwards can sustain inquiry after a multiplicity of (international) political beliefs and practices not just because such pluralism is politically correct according to contemporary conventions but because they are warranted pneumatologically by an eschatological and trinitarian vision.[54]

Such a suggested "pentecostalization" of Edwards is but a short step, I would proffer, from Edwards' own thinking wherein pneumatology and eschatology were deeply interrelated. As John Bolt notes in his comparative study of the political theologies of Edwards and Abraham Kuyper, "The tie between eschatology and creation through the perfecting, beautifying work of the Holy Spirit is crucial to [Edwards]. . . . The Spirit which perfects and beautifies through love, which brings creation to its final glory, is the same Spirit directly and intimately involved with creation from the beginning."[55]

---

[53] The latter of which I do—engaging with the book of Acts and its predecessor, the Gospel of Luke—in my book, *Who Is the Holy Spirit: A Walk with the Apostles* (Brewster, MA: Paraclete, 2011).

[54] Here of course my work as a pentecostal theologian working with and through Pentecostalism as a global phenomenon—for example, Yong, *The Spirit Poured Out on All Flesh: Pentecostalism and the Possibility of Global Theology* (Grand Rapids, MI: Baker Academic, 2005)—interfaces with Edwards' internationalist horizons.

[55] Such a suggested "pentecostalization" of Edwards is but a short step, I would proffer, from Edwards' own thinking wherein pneumatology and eschatology were interrelated. As John Bolt notes in his comparative study of the political theologies of Edwards and Abraham Kuyper, "The tie between eschatology and creation through the perfecting, beautifying work of the Holy Spirit is crucial to [Edwards]. . . . The Spirit which perfects and beautifies through love, which brings creation to its final glory, is the same Spirit directly and intimately involved with creation from the beginning." See John Bolt, *A Free Church, a Holy Nation: Abraham Kuyper's American Public Theology* (Grand Rapids, MI: Eerdmans, 2001), 219; from chapter 4, "America as God's Kingdom: Abraham Kuyper and Jonathan Edwards."

The point is that pneumatological prioritization would not be alien to Edwards' deepest impulses, and that these connect not only with the expansive pneumatology in his revival writings but also with the overarching eschatological and teleological framework of his philosophical theology.[56]

I now turn briefly to the other goal of this final section: that of asking how the apparently unstable millennialism of Edwards' eschatology can in turn enrich pentecostal political theology. There are at least two related ways in which Edwards' millennialism has been received: on the one hand, observation is made about the development of his thinking from the imminent to the futurist millennialism across the 1740s and then toward a transcendent (heavenly) eschatological hope by the end of his life;[57] on the other hand, Edwards' terminal position is understood as his final, mature eschatological vision, one in which the prospect of heaven at least fulfills, if not displaces completely, whatever millennial ideas may have persisted through his thinking.[58] I would urge both that the heavenly hope does not dispense with millennial expectation and that the variety of millennial positions is due at least in part to the under-determination of biblical data and also in part to the hermeneutical horizons brought to the reading of Scripture, as evinced above regarding Edwards' social and political contexts. Put alternatively, the shifting nature of Edwards' millennial thinking ought not to be understood as due to the inability to make up his mind, but as appropriate efforts to understand and live into the biblical message amid the vicissitudes of life. In short, Edwards models how we might envision multiple millennial scenarios by paying close attention to Scripture and considering what the New Testament calls the "signs of the times" (Mt. 16:3).[59] Hence Edwards exemplifies both an apocalyptic mentality and an eschatological reserve: exemplifying how it is possible to adapt our millennial expectations in a responsible manner precisely by not holding dogmatic attitudes toward how the ends of God will come to pass.

I propose that such a flexible eschatological imagination is actually a theological strength rather than a weakness. More to the point, openness to eschatological reconsideration is not only biblically justifiable (note the diversity of views represented across the pages of the New Testament particularly as we can differentiate later from earlier material) but also can sustain the diversity of political theologies needed for Christian faithfulness in different and always changing places and times. If the viability

---

[56] See also Patricia Wilson-Kastner, *Coherence in a Fragmented World: Jonathan Edwards' Theology of the Holy Spirit* (Washington, DC: University Press of America, 1978) and, more recently, Robert W. Caldwell III, *Communion in the Spirit: The Holy Spirit as the Bond of Union in the Theology of Jonathan Edwards* (Milton Keynes; Waynesboro, GA: Paternoster, 2006).

[57] For example, Brandon G. Withrow, "A Future of Hope: Jonathan Edwards and Millennial Expectations," *Trinity Journal*, n.s., 22, no. 1 (2001): 75–98.

[58] This is at least how I read John F. Wilson, "History, Redemption, and the Millennium," in *Jonathan Edwards and the American Experience*, ed. Nathan O. Hatch and Harry S. Stout (New York: Oxford University Press, 1988), 131–41.

[59] Edwards' notes on the book of Revelation that he kept for decades reveal his historical reading of this biblical apocalypse, even to the point of considering how its various symbols and "events" were applicable to or coordinated with the times in which he and his fellow human beings lived; for more on Edwards' historicism on the *Apocalypse*, see further Stephen Stein's "Editor's Introduction," *WJE* 5: passim.

of a political theological platform depends at least in part on its capacity to sustain a variety of political practices, then Edwards' contextually delineated millennialism is capable of generating not a rigid but malleable theological modality for our political being-in-the-world. The preceding interpretation of Edwards is suggestive, I believe, for understanding how the many aspects of his millennial and eschatological commitments are related, at least loosely, to the variety of ways in which his social and public theology has been received.

Pentecostal theology can benefit from Edwards' millennial nimbleness, as it were, given the polarization that exists across the global pentecostal movement on these matters. There are rigid and unbending eschatological ideas across the pentecostal spectrum, from dispensationalists who have the rapture of the church woven into their doctrinal statements and thereby also presume that the world is getting increasingly worse on the one side to prosperity churches that have an overly realized eschatological dogmatism on the other side. There are certainly many aspects to this intransigence in the various camps that we cannot resolve here, but my point is that there are political inclinations that flow from these eschatological commitments and inflexibility on these latter matters leads also to political obstinacy if not arrogance.

I present Edwards' adaptive millennialism as exemplary for tempering the eschatological presumptiveness (on the "right" and "left") that otherwise permeates global Pentecostalisms. If indeed on things eschatological Jesus' words remain authoritative, that "it is not for you to know the times or periods that the Father has set by his own authority" (Acts 1:7), then the empowerment of the Spirit for witness (Acts 1:8) can also have political application in the here and now. Edwards' efforts to read history and the world in light of Scripture, and vice versa, serve as a model for how to be eschatologically supple and thereby be open also to considering political adjustment as the signs of the times are discerned. There may be occasions when revivalism empowers political witness, even as there may be times when millennial fervor ought to be checked and somberness about the political situation ought to prevail. In all cases, however, the already-but-not-yet reign of God will confront the polis in its many forms and multiple historical expressions with its shortcomings, and those who are people of the Spirit—pentecostal or not—can and should be the prophetic voices that challenge thereby the political status quo.[60]

Conclusion

This chapter proceeds from the assumption that Edwards' voice, ringing out as it were from the wilderness at Stockbridge no less than from the colonial outposts of

---

[60] For example, Kees J. Klop, "Equal Respect and the Holy Spirit: The Liberal Demand for Moral Neutrality in the Political Sphere and Christian Respect for the Creation," in *Public Theology for the 21st Century: Essays in Honour of Duncan B. Forrester*, ed. William F. Storrar and Andrew R. Morton (London and New York: T & T Clark, 2004), 96–106.

Northampton,⁶¹ has something to say to a global pentecostal movements that are located now primarily, although not exclusively, in twenty-first-century urban contexts. On the one hand, to the degree that the people of God are and remain aliens and strangers to this world, to that degree the "ends of God" will provide critical, even prophetic perspective on the ways in which the present world remains desolate in comparison to the city of God to come; on the other hand, to the degree that they are also *in*, even if not *of*, this world, and to the degree to which while *in* the world they are to "seek the welfare of the city where" (Jer. 29:7) they abide, to that same degree the call is to live fully in the Spirit amid the present polis in anticipation of the coming reign of God.⁶² And inasmuch as earthly cities come in many forms, multiple modalities of political life will need to be discerned and enacted that are faithful to the ends for which God created the world—so come Holy Spirit, renew the polis.

---

⁶¹ Perry Miller, *Errand into the Wilderness* (Cambridge, MA: Belknap, 1956); Miller devotes the sixth chapter to Edwards.

⁶² I wrote about such a theopolitics of the city, drawn from this Jeremiah text, a few years ago in conversation with Mennonite theologian John Howard Yoder: "The Church and Mission Theology in a Post-Constantinian Era: Soundings from the Anglo-American Frontier," in *A New Day: Essays on World Christianity in Honor of Lamin Sanneh*, ed. Akintunde E. Akinade (New York: Peter Lang, 2010), 49–61; cf. Yong, *In the Days of Caesar*, 182–86. More recently, Yoder's sexual abuse, under the scholarly radar when I did my research on political theology in 2007–08, has come into more prominent light—for example, Rachel Waltner Goossen, "'Defanging the Beast': Mennonite Responses to John Howard Yoder's Sexual Abuse," *Mennonite Quarterly Review* 89, no. 1 (2015): 7–80. This is not to say that his ideas are no longer worth consideration but that any deployment of Yoderian insights will need to be critically evaluated in light of his own connection between belief and practice. For a helpful assessment by Yoder's good friend (who attempted to urge him to repentance) and prominent theologian, see Stanley Hauerwas, *Hannah's Child: A Theologian's Memoir* (Grand Rapids, MI: Eerdmans, 2010), 242–47.

Part Five

Responses

15

The Promise of Edwardsean Theology

Oliver D. Crisp

Jonathan Edwards is an unusual theologian. He is unusual because he was a man of many parts, a pastor, a missionary, an evangelist, a college president, a theologian, a biographer, an apologist for the evangelical awakening—the list goes on. He was also unusual because of the influence that he has had, and continues to have today. How many theologians whose work is the subject of serious intellectual study can claim that it is read with equal interest by Harvard historians, Princeton theologians, and Brazilian pastors? In their recent magisterial account of Edwards' theology, Michael McClymond and Gerald McDermott suggest that Edwards may be the theologian for the twenty-first century because he has such wide appeal. He is, they maintain, a "global theologian for twenty-first century Christianity."[1] Mainline Protestants study Edwards for his theological subtlety or his philosophical originality. New Calvinists read Edwards as an intellectual forebear whose "Sinners in the Hands of an Angry God" is a sermon to be celebrated for its theological message, not just its literary form. Pentecostal and charismatic Christians hold up Edwards as a theologian of religious experience pointing to his significant body of work on the subject culminating in his *Religious Affections*, as well as his personal involvement in the Great Awakening, and his observations of the ecstatic experiences of his wife, Sarah. But is Edwards a theologian that *really* speaks to all these different contexts?

Like the other contributors to this volume, Christopher Stephenson's paper responds in the affirmative. Laying Edwards' work on the affections alongside Teresa of Avila's account of meditation and affective prayer, and the recent pentecostal and charismatic practice of "resting in the Spirit," he presents us with a theological bricolage of approaches to theologizing about encountering God. He makes "no attempt to reconcile points of tension among them." Instead, he hopes that "using the spiritual tradition as a bridge between Edwards and Pentecostals" will develop "Edwards' notion that immanent acts like contemplation tend to practice and shows that Pentecostals sometimes follow a form of prayer that is not far from meditation in soaking prayer (even if not usually discursive)." We might say that in Stephenson's estimation, Edwards is an interlocutor and friendly foil for the development of pentecostal and charismatic liturgical practices.

---

[1] Michael J. McClymond and Gerald R. McDermott, *Theology of Jonathan Edwards* (New York: Oxford University Press, 2012), 727.

L. William Oliverio, Jr. recommends Edwards' biblical hermeneutics as a resource for contemporary pentecostal and charismatic approaches to Scripture. There has been a lot of work done on Edwards' reading of Scripture. He was not a fan of the emerging historical-biblical critical approach to biblical texts. Oliverio is right to point to the importance of typology in Edwards' understanding of Scripture. In fact, he thought of Scripture as a world of signs that we must be immersed in so that we can fully understand the way in which Scripture mirrors reality. There is much here that may be of use to theologians today whose approach to Scripture is predicated on the notion that within its pages one finds revelation, or the record of, or witness to revelation, rather than merely historical curiosities or the relics of bygone ages. But I must say that I am less sanguine about some of the ways in which Edwards uses Scripture. For one thing, historical-biblical criticism has done a lot of good, and we ignore it at our peril. (One need not adopt foundationalism or Enlightenment approaches to these texts to find historical-biblical criticism useful—after all, many within the guild of biblical studies do the same.) For another thing, Edwards sometimes does have a decidedly premodern understanding of the biblical texts that sounds rather flat-footed to modern ears and for good reason. Plotting the unfolding of contemporary events in history as the fulfillment of biblical prophecy smacks more of enthusiasm (in the eighteenth-century sense of the term) than of careful, theological reasoning. Yet Edwards spent a lot of time doing just this, often with very peculiar results.[2]

Edmund J. Rybarczyk explores some of the aesthetic dimensions to Edwards' theology and suggests that it may be fruitfully applied to pentecostal thought. I am sure that is right, though I might add: Edwards has things to teach Christians of many different traditions on this particular topic! Rybarczyk refers to Edwards' notion of beauty as something like a fundamental way of thinking about the divine life since (as Edwards says) "one alone cannot be excellent"[3] and excellency, an aesthetic and ontological notion for Edwards, finds its apogee in the divine life. Yet there is a tension here in Edwards' thought. He also endorses the classical theistic tradition and its view of God as absolutely metaphysically simple. Can a simple God be beautiful if that beauty entails irreducible plurality within God? I have argued at length elsewhere that this is a fundamental tension in his doctrine of God that he never adequately resolves.[4] Rybarczyk also discusses the way in which Edwards links beauty and the aesthetic to the work of the Spirit in particular.[5] But to my mind what was missing here was a discussion of the way in which Edwards connects this secret spiritual work with the end for which God creates human beings, namely, union with the divine in theosis. Rybarczyk thinks Edwards maintains a clear Creator-creature

---

[2] The best treatment of Edwards' use of the Bible to date is Douglas A. Sweeney, *Edwards the Exegete: Biblical Interpretation and Anglo-Protestant Culture on the Edge of the Enlightenment* (New York: Oxford University Press, 2015).

[3] Edwards writes, "One alone cannot be excellent, inasmuch as, in such case, there can be no consent. Therefore, if God is excellent, there must be a plurality in God; otherwise, there can be no consent in him." Edwards, "Miscellany 117," *WJE* 13:284.

[4] See Oliver D. Crisp, *Jonathan Edwards on God and Creation* (New York: Oxford University Press, 2012).

[5] In this connection, see also W. Ross Hastings' work, *Jonathan Edwards and the Life of God: Toward an Evangelical Theology of Participation* (Minneapolis, MN: Fortress, 2015).

distinction, and (from one point of view) that is right. But not quite for the reasons he supposes. According to Edwards there is no material world, all that exists are minds and their ideas. We only exist as created minds projected, as it were, from God. But our existence is liminal. God is constantly recreating the world moment by moment, including us as well. So the beauty that Edward has in mind in the created order is both an ideal beauty and an ephemeral beauty—a fleeting, momentary beauty that is radically dependent upon the stable life of the one in whom we live and move and have our being. God alone is constant. We are shadows of the reality that is God, emanated and remanated back to him.

Turning to consider Edwards' doctrine of God more directly, in his chapter Steven Studebaker argues that Edwards' Trinitarianism is an amalgam of Augustinian and social elements that can be developed by pentecostal theologians. This is in keeping with Studebaker's earlier work on Edwards' Theology Proper.[6] Although I think it perfectly Edwardsean to develop the thought of the Northampton Sage in new directions (for surely Studebaker is right that Edwards himself does that in important respects with the Reformed tradition he received), I have rather different views than Studebaker about the shape of Edwards' doctrine of the Trinity.[7] I also have rather different views about Edwards' ontology (a recurring theme in the volume).[8] This is not a matter that Studebaker enters into in great detail, but it does seem that he is beholden to a way of conceiving Edwards' ontology that appears to me to be mistaken. Edwards does not articulate a "dispositional ontology." His account of the divine nature is rather more classical than this, and depends upon an essentialist metaphysics that carves up the world into substances and their properties. If Edwards' way of understanding metaphysics and the divine nature is rather more traditional than Studebaker implies, that does not prevent his thought from being developed by pentecostal theologians. In fact, for those pentecostal thinkers who are more classical in their conception of the divine nature, it may be a reason to turn to Edwards rather than looking elsewhere for inspiration.

One obvious place at which Edwards' thought may well be of use for charismatic and pentecostal theologians is in his Spirit Christology, which Gerald McDermott takes on in his chapter. Here Edwards really is involved in a more progressive theological enterprise, taking a cue from the Puritan John Owen[9] and thinking systematically about how Christ relied upon the work of the Spirit—including the controversial

---

[6] See Steven M. Studebaker, "Jonathan Edwards' Social Augustinian Trinitarianism: An Alternative to a Recent Trend," *Scottish Journal of Theology* 56, no. 3 (2003): 268–85; Studebaker, *Jonathan Edwards' Social Augustinian Trinitarianism in Historical and Contemporary Perspectives* (Piscataway, NJ: Gorgias Press, 2008); and Studebaker and Robert W. Caldwell III, *The Trinitarian Theology of Jonathan Edwards: Text, Context, and Application* (Burlington, VT: Ashgate, 2012).

[7] See Oliver D. Crisp, *Jonathan Edwards among the Theologians* (Grand Rapids, MI: Eerdmans, 2015), chapter 3 and Oliver D. Crisp and Kyle C. Strobel, *Jonathan Edwards: An Introduction to His Thought* (Grand Rapids, MI: Eerdmans, 2018), chapter 2.

[8] See Crisp, *Jonathan Edwards on God and Creation*.

[9] A standard account of Owen's Spirit Christology can be found in Alan Spence, *Incarnation and Inspiration: John Owen and the Coherence of Christology* (London: T&T Clark, 2007). I have tackled Edwards' Christology in "Jonathan Edwards, Idealism, and Christology," in *Idealism and Christian Theology: Idealism and Christianity*, vol. 1, ed. Joshua R. Farris, S. Mark Hamilton, and James S. Spiegel (London: Bloomsbury Academic, 2016), 145–75.

notion that the Spirit was the divine person who sustained the hypostatic union after the first moment of Incarnation, not God the Son. If Christ, like us, is dependent upon the Spirit's immediate sustaining work then (so the pentecostal and charismatic theologian might think) we have some Christological warrant for exploring how it is that the Spirit may work in and through Christians today.

This brings me to a wider matter, having to do with the different aspects of Edwards' thought. The contributors to this volume have highlighted a number of different aspects of Edwards' theological legacy as potentially fruitful theological topics for exploration by pentecostal and charismatic theologians—far more than I can usefully survey in a short response like this one.[10] Nevertheless, I want to suggest a further topic that unites them all together in some respects. Edwards' reflections upon the revivals and his *Religious Affections*, his work in biblical interpretation and typology, and his interest in theological aesthetics all intimate the fact that he was a wide-ranging thinker whose breadth of learning (and size of output) makes him difficult to categorize. That is no bad thing. But he was also interested in the fundamental fabric of creation and how it is that God relates to what he creates. It is his metaphysical worldview that underpins these different aspects of his thought. For Edwards was nothing if not a "God-intoxicated theist."[11] He bent everything to a theological theme from natural science to aesthetics and much more in between. His philosophical theology, which few outside the guild of Edwards scholars are familiar with, might prove to be a most fertile field for pentecostal and charismatic theologians to till. For, as with these other aspects of his thinking, Edwards was a thinker who bucks trends and arrives at conclusions that seem most unusual, even implausible, and yet thought-provoking and intellectually stimulating. But surely this is the mark of a superior interlocutor. In searching for resources to retrieve from historic thinkers we shouldn't pursue our interests with merely antiquarian ideas of cataloging and displaying ideas from the past. After all, contemporary systematic theology should not be the religious equivalent of Victorian lepidoptery—gathering butterflies to pin and label in display cases. Instead, we should be engaged in wrestling with thinkers of the past, receiving from them what is helpful, but always with a view to reshaping or retooling these ideas for our contemporary context. If we think of Edwards as such an interlocutor it seems to me that he may well turn out to be a global theologian for the twenty-first century, one that pentecostal and charismatic intellectuals may find very congenial for their own theological and philosophical projects. It is not incidental that this is just how Edwards' thought was received by the school of thought that developed out of his work in late-eighteenth- and nineteenth-century America, in the New Divinity and New England Theology. Perhaps the time has come to take up the task of retooling Edwardsean ways of thinking once

---

[10] Inevitably, I have had to cherry-pick some of the chapters and reflect on them. Naturally, this is not a reflection on the quality of the other contributions to this work, which also repay careful reading.

[11] See, for example, Michael J. McClymond, *Encounters with God: An Approach to the Theology of Jonathan Edwards* (New York: Oxford University Press, 1998), 29. The reference to being "God intoxicated" was originally made in reference to Spinoza by Novalis, but has been reapplied to Edwards on more than one occasion—and for similar reasons. See the editor's Introduction to Baruch Spinoza, *Ethics, Treatise on the Emendation of the Intellect, and Select Letters,* trans. Samuel Shirley, ed. Seymour Feldman (Indianapolis: Hackett, 1992), 10.

again, picking up where the last New England Theologians left off—a task not just for pentecostal and charismatic theologians, though it may include such thinkers.[12]

Well then, is Edwards a useful interlocutor for pentecostal and charismatic theology? My own answer to this question is both yes and no.[13] Yes, because he shares with pentecostal and charismatic Christians a serious interest in religious affections and in spiritual practices that foster the religion of the heart. His work in reporting and reflecting upon the Great Awakening, especially his *Religious Affections*, stand as a permanent testimony to this interest, and it is worth noting that *Religious Affections* has never been out of print since its publication. There are certainly deep affinities between Edwardsean spirituality and that of pentecostal and charismatic Christians today. However, there is a "no" that must qualify this "yes." Like many in the Reformed tradition Edwards was a cessationist when it came to the charismatic gifts. He did believe that God continues to work marvels in the hearts and minds of human beings that lead to saving affections, and he believed that startling religious experiences can accompany such change. However, he would not have endorsed the use of charismatic gifts in worship. More importantly, perhaps, he would have been surprised by the liturgies of pentecostal and charismatic churches. After all, he came from a time in which church worship involved the singing of unaccompanied psalms, Bible readings, and sermons of at least an hour in duration. However, let us not be too quick to make of this historical context a barrier to fruitful dialogue across traditions and times. It seems to me that the authors of the chapters in this volume are right in this regard: Edwardian theology has much that can be fruitfully retrieved for contemporary constructive theology, including pentecostal and charismatic theology (as I have tried to indicate above). Let me put it like this. It seems to me that a good argument can be made for the following conclusion. The cessationism in Edwards' thought coupled with his views on appropriate church worship are superficial differences. The deeper continuities between the affectional theology of Edwards (including what Perry Miller called the "rhetoric of sensation" in his sermons) and pentecostal and charismatic praxis are, it seems to me, much deeper.[14] One could benefit from Edwards' theological account of affections and of spiritual theology more generally, without worrying too much about his views regarding the exercise of spiritual gifts. He was, after all, a thinker whose location in time shaped him as it does us. As the chapters collected in this volume suggest, there are resources Edwards provides us that are still serviceable today, and would be of great value to pentecostal and charismatic theologians in particular. Perhaps Edwards may prove to be a global theologian for the twenty-first century, after all.

---

[12] For discussion of the reception of Edwards' ideas and the development of the New England Theology, see Oliver D. Crisp and Douglas A. Sweeney, eds., *After Jonathan Edwards: The Courses of the New England Theology* (New York: Oxford University Press, 2012) and Douglas A. Sweeney and Allen C. Guelzo, eds., *The New England Theology: From Jonathan Edwards to Edward Amasa Park* (Grand Rapids, MI: Baker Academic, 2006).

[13] See also the final chapter of Crisp and Strobel, *Jonathan Edwards: An Introduction to His Thought* for more on this issue.

[14] In this connection, see Michael J. McClymond's chapter in this volume.

16

The Surprising Work of God Continues

Amy Plantinga Pauw

When the Jonathan Edwards Center in São Paulo, Brazil, holds events at the Presbyterian-affiliated MacKenzie Institute, lots of pentecostal pastors show up. What is it about this eighteenth-century Calvinist that attracts contemporary Pentecostals? The chapters in this book teem with answers to that question, and in the process teach us a good deal about both Jonathan Edwards and the future of Pentecostalism.

This book marks the beginning of a new theological conversation. The interaction between Jonathan Edwards and Pentecostalism in this volume is unprecedented, and would not have been possible even a generation ago. Two relatively recent shifts have fueled this engagement. First, we now have easy access to much of the enormous corpus of Edwards' writing, thanks to the ongoing efforts of Yale University's Works of Jonathan Edwards office and its satellite institutions around the world. Second, starting in the 1990s, according to Amos Yong's chronology, a new generation of pentecostal theologians began exploring their own confessional resources and engaging with larger theological traditions.[1] This book is the fruit of this happy confluence of factors. It brings together two streams of Christian tradition that might at first seem unrelated or even opposed to each other.

Christian theology thrives when its important figures are rediscovered from time to time. These chapters help us rediscover Jonathan Edwards by bringing new questions and interests to bear on his life and writings. Dimensions of his work that were deemed marginal or even embarrassing to some of his earlier interpreters are now an impetus to new theological construction. This is especially true with respect to Edwards' intense interest in the Holy Spirit. Weaknesses and tensions in his thought also come into sharper relief. How, for example, is Edwards' cessationism compatible with his receptivity to the surprising newness of the Spirit's work? The results of this theological interaction are mutually beneficial. We see how pentecostal perspectives can challenge and broaden interpretations of Edwards, and also where Edwards' writings can critique and serve as a resource for pentecostal theology.

The fruitfulness of this engagement is made possible by the generosity of the authors' interactions with Edwards. While they do not hesitate to disagree with him or point out his theological limitations, they do not use him merely as a negative foil

---

[1] Amos Yong, "Pentecostalism and the Theological Academy," *Theology Today* 64, no. 2 (2007): 244–50.

for their own positions. Instead they seek to read him *in meliorem partem*, looking for openings in his theology that resonate with their own theological convictions and concerns. This generosity toward Edwards is accompanied by the authors' non-defensive willingness to acknowledge weak places in their own traditions where they think Edwards can be of help. The engagement with Edwards in this book is also enhanced by the theological diversity among the authors themselves: a dynamic movement like Pentecostalism has many voices, and the readings of Edwards in this book are enriched by the internal conversations that are already going on within pentecostal traditions.

Theological traditions signal their maturity when they have the confidence to work out their identities in public, entering the give and take of broader conversations, both to learn from others and to make their own contributions. This book is evidence of this maturity among pentecostal traditions, even though they are still relative newcomers on the theological scene. This dialogical character may be in Pentecostalism's DNA. As Steven Studebaker points out, Pentecostalism began as and remains a renewal movement. It has shown from the beginning its capacity to be a leavening agent within many different Christian traditions.

In the same way, the interpretation of Jonathan Edwards has to be broadly dialogical in order to reach its full theological potential: it is not enough for it to remain an intramural Reformed exercise. Reformed Christians have sometimes taken a proprietary attitude toward Edwards, with various factions laying claim to providing the authoritative interpretation of his work. While proprietary interpretations of Edwards remain perennially tempting, they do not do justice to the rich complexity of his thought. William Oliverio notes that the metaphor of a symphony has been used to describe Edwards' theology. Wide ecumenical engagements with Edwards' theological legacy are essential to keeping its many parts in play. Edwards' theological significance is not established by uncritical reverence for him or by attempts to repristinate his thought among a small circle of devotees, but only in broader public conversations of his work. Here Pentecostals have a vital role to play.

One of the contributions of this book is to make clear how Reformed interpretations of Edwards have systematically underplayed certain features of his theology. Nineteenth-century Old School Presbyterians at Princeton, for example, lauded what they regarded as Edwards' steadfast orthodoxy on original sin and double predestination, but were dismayed by Edwards' support for revivalism and dismissed his dissertation on *The Nature of True Virtue* as both wrong-headed and peripheral to his main theological concerns. Contemporary pentecostal theologians, by contrast, sidestep Edwards' Calvinist angularities and gravitate to precisely those parts of his thought that made his earlier Presbyterian champions nervous. Their approach accentuates neglected parts of Edwards' corpus and sheds new light on places where Edwards' thought could be developed. What emerges from these chapters is a broader appreciation of the capaciousness of Edwards' thought.

Constraints of space make it impossible to give adequate attention to each chapter. Instead, I will trace some key themes across them. These themes are the centrality of religious affections, bodily faith, and salvation in the Spirit. I conclude with reflections on the unfinished character of theological work.

The centrality of religious affections

Edwards liked to say that the devil went to the best divinity schools—a comment, I suppose, on the best divinity schools as well as on the devil. What he meant was that, on one level, the devil's intellectual grasp of the claims of Christian faith was excellent—but it was what Edwards called a speculative, notional knowledge. What was utterly missing were the affections, the love that would unleash the transformative power of that knowledge in life-changing ways. Edwards' emphasis on religious affections resonates with pentecostal accounts of the Spirit's presence and power. Orthodoxy—right doctrine—is not enough. A central theme across these chapters is the importance of orthopathy—right feeling. As Christopher Stephenson indicates, Edwards does not dismiss speculative theology. Yet he insists that true religion is centrally about the ordering of our affections: in the final analysis, we are what we love. It is our affections, rather than our reason, that drives our acting and knowing. Edwards and Pentecostals agree that there can be no true religion without affections.

Here is a place where pentecostal theology can be an important corrective to Reformed tendencies to allow a focus on the biblical Word and doctrinal truth to veer toward a rationalism that fears or denigrates religious affections. Reformed Christians have sometimes promulgated "logocentric" theologies in which Christian faith is primarily about receiving clear verbal communication and then articulating and defending the truth that has been received. On this subject, as on so many others, Edwards presents a mixed picture. He shared his era's quest for a "rational account" of Christian faith, and at times exhibited bracing confidence in the reach of human reason to understand the things of God. He could also promulgate distressingly bad apologetic arguments for the truth of Christianity. Yet other dimensions of Edwards' theology tempered these rationalist tendencies in important ways. He insisted that the exercise of God's intrinsically communicative nature is not confined to verbal expression. In fact, as William Oliverio notes, the entire creation preaches aloud about God's great work of redemption. What is finally of utmost importance in the Christian life for Edwards is not mastery of doctrinal truth, which even the devil has, but a responsiveness to God made possible by a "sense of the heart."

Clearly, Edwards thought doctrinal truth and genuine religious affections were connected. Those who have deficient understandings of God's great work of redemption, for example, will not love and praise God as they ought. But as Edwards matured as a pastor, he came to affirm the Spirit's gracious presence even in the midst of human error and confusion. The Spirit can be at work even where human reason falls short. "There may be true exercises of grace . . . that may be founded on an error, that which is not agreeable to the truth," Edwards declares, and "the erroneous practice founded on that error may be the occasion of those true and holy exercises which are from the Spirit of God."[2] As David Courey affirms, the Spirit's work freely transcends our rational definitions and boundaries. The heart has its own ways of knowing. Pentecostal readings of Edwards, with their emphasis on orthopathy, helpfully

---

[2] Edwards, "Miscellany 999," *WJE* 20:326.

move interpretations of his thought toward what James K. A. Smith has called "a more expansive, affective understanding of what counts as knowledge and a richer understanding of what we know."[3]

Yet if pentecostal emphases can nudge Edwards' affectional theology in the right direction, Edwards can also return the favor. In Edwards' view, not all religious affections are genuine, and Christopher Stephenson thinks Edwards can be helpful to Pentecostals in curbing "overly optimistic" and uncritical evaluations of human affections. As the colonial revivals wore on, Edwards became skeptical about emotional displays—whether they involved flailing bodies, "many tears," or "emphasis and pathos of expression"—as conclusive signs of the Spirit's presence.[4] He also witnessed the divisive effects that special gifts of the Spirit can have within Christian communities, something we see the Apostle Paul already wrestling with in first-century Corinth. Rather than attributing particular spiritual manifestations wholly to the Spirit or wholly to Satan, Edwards recognized the ambiguity of all Christian religious experience. This side of the eschaton, the presence of the Spirit in individuals and communities is incomplete and remains susceptible to corruption and sabotage. As Michael McClymond shows, Edwards advocates following a middle path regarding manifestations of the Spirit: Christians have to avoid a sinful slowness to recognize the Spirit's work on the one hand, while avoiding spiritual pride and a gullible acceptance of all spiritual claims on the other.

Bodily faith

Christian life is a material life, a way of conducting public, bodily life in community. Faith is embodied and communal to its core: it is not first and foremost about what is going on in the privacy of our individual subjectivities. Both Pentecostals and Edwards have theological contributions to make toward a material Christian spirituality, and both have theological weaknesses. One of the gifts of this volume is to show how pentecostal and Edwardsean perspectives on embodied faith can complement each other.

Pentecostal traditions have emphasized that outpourings of the Spirit engage our whole selves, including our bodies. Here Pentecostals can nudge Edwards toward his best theological instincts. Edwards acknowledged not only that all true religion involves affections but also that all spiritual affections have some bodily effects. We know that he witnessed people falling under the power of the Spirit, including his own wife, Sarah, and that he even yearned for that experience himself. He describes Sarah as enjoying "extraordinary views of divine things, and religious affections, being frequently attended with very great effects on the body, nature often sinking under the weight of divine discoveries." Edwards reports that she was filled with "a kind of

---

[3] James K. A. Smith, *Thinking in Tongues: Pentecostal Contributions to Christian Philosophy*, Pentecostal Manifestos (Grand Rapids, MI: Eerdmans, 2010), 59.
[4] Edwards, *Religious Affections*, WJE 2:407.

omnipotent joy" that caused her "to leap with all [her] might, with joy and mighty exultation of soul."⁵ Surely here is a picture of spiritual experience that accords well with Edwards' theology: the human subject defined by surrender to God's gracious sovereignty. Yet Edwards gave only grudging acknowledgment to the kinesthetics of the Spirit's work. This kind of bodily ecstasy was for Edwards only a "negative sign," neither proving nor disproving the presence and work of the Holy Spirit.

Edwards' reluctance to give theological significance to extraordinary bodily manifestations of the Spirit is surely in part due to his limited experience. We have no evidence that Edwards ever witnessed miraculous healing or heard glossolalia. What Michael McClymond calls Edwards' "soft cessationism" appears to be limited empirical observation masquerading as theological principle. Since extraordinary gifts appear to have ceased in the Christian experience he was acquainted with, he followed other Reformed theologians in providing a theological reason for why they *must* have ceased. The key concern seems to be to protect the sufficiency of Scripture: extraordinary gifts were only needed in the infancy of the church, before the canon of Scripture was completed. In Edwards' view, any extraordinary bodily manifestations of the Spirit since then are epiphenomenal. Edwards views these physical effects as "accidental" rather than transformational, and thus of no theological significance.

However, this constricted approach breaks with Edwards' own principle of not making one's own experience of the Spirit the rule for others.⁶ As Edwards acknowledged, the Holy Spirit uses a "great variety" of methods, and we cannot predict in advance how God will work. If all material reality functions as images and shadows of divine things, why should Edwards be hesitant to affirm our own bodies as conduits for knowing and loving God? Lisa Stephenson is right to observe that Edwards unnecessarily pits ordinary and extraordinary gifts of the Spirit against each other. Bodily signs and wonders can help sustain rather than detract from a love-centered discipleship. Stephenson cites the research of Margaret Poloma that shows links between extraordinary spiritual gifts and acts of benevolent service. Here pentecostal interpretations of Edwards can help him move him more decisively away from the Enlightenment's elevation of disembodied human reason toward a more full-orbed spirituality.

On the other hand, Edwards' emphasis on the ordinary, ongoing work of the Spirit can be of help to Pentecostals in developing a fuller material spirituality as well. According to Edwards, we have not fully accepted Christ until we have done it "practically," that is, "with the whole man: soul, spirit and body."⁷ For Edwards, embodied Christian practice is "the sign of signs" of the Spirit's presence. Practical Christian discipleship cannot avoid concerns for what Amos Yong calls "penultimate works of the Spirit." Spirit-filled Christians yearn to see the power of the Spirit manifested in suffering and disenfranchised bodies. This attention to longer-term moral and social transformation includes commitments to peacemaking and economic justice as well as to more culturally sensitive mission (as noted by Angela Tarango). A

---

5 Edwards, *Some Thoughts Concerning the Revival,* WJE 4:332.
6 Edwards, *A Faithful Narrative,* WJE 4:185.
7 Edwards, "Miscellany 996," WJE 20:324.

material spirituality attends to present political, economic, and cultural issues without letting go of its apocalyptic hope in God's promised future.

Edmund Rybarczyk wonders if more openness to aesthetic categories might have both theological and practical benefits for Pentecostals. God's beauty and loving practice go together for Edwards. Edwards' social imaginary was of Christians so swept up in the relational beauty of the triune God that they would become, by the power of the Spirit, one holy and happy society themselves. The Spirit who binds the Father and the Son together in beautiful harmony also binds believers together in community and empowers them for service. By the power of the Spirit, our experience of God's beauty is reflected in loving creaturely relations. This means for Edwards that "to speak of Christian experience and practice as if they were two things, properly and entirely distinct, is to make a distinction without consideration or reason."[8] The experience of God's beauty is intimately related to the development of loving dispositions and just patterns of communal life. The authors of these chapters agree with the theological proposals by Amos Yong and Frank Macchia to identify the Holy Spirit's presence with love, rather than with power in the abstract. As Andrew Gabriel observes, this Edwardsean move may help Pentecostalism move away from an overemphasis on signs and wonders toward more attention to the lasting fruits of the Spirit in community. In the words of Frank Macchia, "Love is the greatest miracle that all extraordinary signs of the Spirit serve."[9] Edwards provides theological impetus for this broader understanding of bodily faith.

Salvation in the Spirit

Edwards' account of the Spirit's presence in the colonial revivals was couched within a Calvinist framework, but the future of revivalism in North America belonged to Arminians, and Pentecostalism is heir to that trajectory. I could imagine another volume of chapters titled "From New York City to Azusa" that traced Charles Finney's connections with Pentecostalism. The gap between Calvinist and Arminian understandings of human salvation is lurking in the background in the present chapters but rarely engaged head on. It is worth exploring whether more attention to the Holy Spirit can be helpful in narrowing this gap. In the work of the Spirit the Pauline dynamic of "I but not I" (Gal. 2:20) is most tangible to Christian experience.

In different ways, both Edwards' theology and pentecostal theologies suffer from an underdeveloped pneumatology. Steven Studebaker notes that Pentecostalism's intense interest in the subsequent work of the Holy Spirit is bolted onto an account of salvation that has little role for the Spirit. Pentecostal attention to experience of the Spirit has not been accompanied by attention to a theology of the Spirit. The result can be accounts of salvation that, at least to Calvinist ears, sound very decisionist, as

---

[8] Edwards, *Religious Affections*, WJE 2:450.
[9] Frank D. Macchia, *Baptized in the Spirit: A Global Pentecostal Theology* (Grand Rapids, MI: Zondervan, 2006), 149.

if we were autonomous agents casting the deciding vote about our spiritual future. Likewise, Edwards recognized the inadequate role given to the Holy Spirit in standard Reformed accounts of salvation, and, as Gerald McDermott shows, developed a Spirit Christology that has some potential for addressing this problem. But it was not thoroughly integrated into Edwards' theology. It is easy to find in his writings overly forensic accounts of justification that make salvation seem like a divine transaction occurring over our heads, leaving humanity untransformed by grace. (James Henderson notes the growing recognition of this one-sidedness in sixteenth-century Protestant accounts of justification.) And perhaps not surprisingly, the Spirit whom Edwards identifies with God's love is absent in Edwards' reflections on hell torments. The God whose everlasting hatred burns there seems disconnected from the triune God Edwards affirms elsewhere. Both Reformed and pentecostal traditions have room to grow in incorporating the Holy Spirit more integrally into their theologies of salvation.

It is worth noting that soteriological differences between Calvinists and Arminians can seem to melt away in the heat of spiritual experience. In his famous "Sinners in the Hands of an Angry God" sermon, Edwards implores his hearers to respond to their present "opportunity to obtain salvation": "And now you have an extraordinary opportunity, a day wherein Christ has flung the door of mercy wide open, and stands in the door calling and crying with a loud voice to poor sinners."[10] Conversely, pentecostal accounts of being slain in the Spirit and soaking prayer emphasize being overcome by divine power and surrendering to divine love. Both Edwards and Pentecostals experience the Spirit as powerfully affecting and unpredictable, blowing where it will (Jn 3:8) and being poured out on both the unsuspecting and those actively seeking God's grace.

The Spirit is at once more intimate to us and more different from us than we can imagine. Despite their disagreements regarding salvation, both Arminians and Calvinists should retain this tension, avoiding zero-sum accounts of divine and human agency. That is, they should avoid the theological assumption that the more God does, the less there is for human beings to do, as if the two were acting on the same agential plane. Divine and human agency are not in competition; they do not operate in inverse proportion. God's immediate and universally extensive agency is the ground of all human agency, not an impediment to it. I remain unconvinced by panentheistic solutions to this issue of divine agency, as well as by accounts that locate divine presence primarily in interruptions or suspensions of the ordinary rules of the universe—though both find some support in Edwards. It is better to affirm that the triune God is both totally involved in and totally different from the universe. Within that framework, both Arminians and Calvinists can urge Christians to live in gratitude for the gift of salvation in Christ Jesus, and in open receptivity to the surprising work of the Spirit.

---

[10] Edwards, *God's Grace Carried on in Other Places*, WJE 22:103.

Conclusion

Edwards' theology was forged in Bible study, pastoral perplexities, and the heat of polemics. Respecting Edwards' context means keeping him to some degree strange and discomforting. Contemporary theologians should resist the temptation to tie up the loose ends and trim off the rough edges of his thought. It is better to acknowledge the parts that chafe and the places where Edwards pushes back against our own theological assumptions.

Edwards was a theological risk-taker, not a careful systematician. Push any of his provocative assertions too far and you end up in theological trouble. Edwards' example ought to inspire some risk-taking among contemporary theologians. According to Edwards, heaven is a progressive state: even there, our knowledge and love of God will continue to increase. With God, there is always more. By definition, then, all earthly theology is a work in progress. Instead of all trying to be the ear or eye, it is better for the members of Christ's body to accept their differences and commit to working together and learning from each other. No part of Christ's body can say to another, "I have no need of you" (1 Cor. 12:21). God has theological gifts for us that we can only receive from each other. This volume is a living example of this truth.

17

"Some Thoughts" on the Retrieval of Jonathan Edwards by Pentecostals

Robert W. Caldwell III

The more I study Jonathan Edwards, the more I am amazed at how appealing his work is to people from so many different backgrounds. Reformed Calvinists, Wesleyan Arminians, premillennial dispensationalists, analytic theologians, evangelical historians, progressive liberals, and theologians from Roman Catholic and Eastern Orthodox traditions have all found Edwards to be stimulating and fruitful to study. With this volume, I rejoice to find pentecostal theologians engaging in Edwards' work. What, theologically, can be more "American" than Pentecostals, that major branch of world-Protestantism birthed in the United States over a century ago, interacting with "America's theologian," Jonathan Edwards?

Undoubtedly, the Edwards that Pentecostals are drawn to is not the Calvinist predestinarian found in *Freedom of the Will* or "God Glorified in Man's Dependence," but rather the Edwards who was a master-observer of religious experience (*Religious Affections*), the Trinity (*Discourse on the Trinity*), and aesthetics. Some may balk at the idea of cherry-picking through the garden of a major theologian to choose only that which fits into one's own system. Yet this is essentially what theologians do all the time. Just look at the way the Reformers appropriated Augustine's anti-Pelagian writings while passing on his Catholic ecclesiology, or how contemporary evangelical apologists celebrate the towering accomplishments of Aquinas and other medieval schoolmen. The truth is that one can learn a great deal from the theological giants of the past even if it is only one facet of that theologian's entire system. These chapters demonstrate how Edwards' writings can generate hundreds of pages of provocative interaction by contemporary theologians who, at first glance, would not be thought of as having much affinity with the sage from Northampton.

In what follows, I offer several comments and observations about the articles contained in *Pentecostal Theology and Jonathan Edwards*. while making a few recommendations. First, on the devotional-theological front, I encourage greater exploration into Edwards' theology of religious experience, that doctrinal quadrant where Edwards was at his best, and where Pentecostals could camp out for a lifetime of fruitful pondering. Second, on the historical-theological front, I commend further digging into Edwards' own evangelical heritage for I believe that the dynamic, "dispositional" God we find in Edwards can be found elsewhere in his immediate context, a context that funds both evangelical and pentecostal traditions. Lastly, on the trinitarian front, I go old-school by commending Edwards' psychological analogy of the Trinity as a helpful way to balance the head and the heart in the Christian life.

In sum, if there's one big point of application that encapsulates all my comments below, it would probably echo what Congregationalist pastor Israel Holly wrote to a theological sparring partner in 1770: "Sir, if I was to engage with you in this [point of doctrine], I would say *Read Edwards!* And if you wrote again, I would tell you to *Read Edwards!* And if you wrote again, I would still tell you to *Read Edwards!*"[1] Translation: if you are a Christian, read Edwards! He seemingly has something to say to everybody!

Jonathan Edwards, Pentecostals, and the taxonomy of religious knowledge

If there's one thing that both Jonathan Edwards and Pentecostals have in common, it is that they share a robust fascination with authentic religious experience. Edwards made the identification and exploration of "religious affections" one of the central pursuits of his life, a point we can see in his journal. As a young man of twenty-one, he wrote there that "the very thing I now want, to give me a clearer and more immediate view of the perfections and glory of God, is *as clear a knowledge of the manner of God's exerting himself, with respect to spirits and mind*, as I have, of his operations concerning matter and bodies."[2] How does God "exert" himself in our spirits and minds? Given his lengthy resume on the subject—most prominently his revival treatises—we may confidently conclude that he made substantial progress toward fulfilling this goal.

Many of the scholars in this book have observed this similarity between Edwards and Pentecostals. Oliverio and Reichard note how Edwards' work on the affections and revivalism resonate strongly with pentecostal spirituality.[3] Henderson observes how "surprisingly Pentecostal" Edwards' doctrine of justification is with the way he emphasized it as the "living transformative presence of the Holy Spirit" in the believer.[4] And McClymond offers outstanding advice on how to be more Edwardsean in spiritual discernment: observe more closely, differentiate more accurately, and analyze more

---

[1] Israel Holly, *A Letter to the Reverent Mr. Bartholomew of Harwinton: Containing a Few Remarks upon Some of His Arguments and Divinity* (Hartford, CT: Green & Watson, 1770), 3–4.
[2] Edwards, "Personal Narrative," *WJE* 16:787 (emphasis added).
[3] See above L. William Oliverio Jr., "'True Religion, in Great Part, Consists of Holy Affections': A Critical Comparison of the Biblical Hermeneutics of Jonathan Edwards and Pentecostals," 24 and Joshua D. Reichard, "Divine Action and Divine Affection: Jonathan Edwards, the Pentecostal and Process Theologian," 62–63.
[4] See above, James M. Henderson, "Transformation by the Spirit in Justification and Sanctification," 146.

patiently.[5] As I worked through these chapters, it struck me that Pentecostals would benefit from further engagement on this topic for there is so much in Edwards that might be fruitfully appropriated.

The place to begin exploring would be Edwards' fascinating private notebook entry, "Miscellanies," no. 782, entitled a "Sense of the Heart."[6] There Edwards developed an elaborate taxonomy of religious knowledge, a sort of exploration of the different levels of how we know spiritual and divine objects. The entry provides an excellent example of how theological reflection can aid in the process of spiritual discernment and enhance our religious affections.

Edwards begins a "Sense of the Heart" by noting a fundamental distinction in the way the human mind handles information: the distinction between *mere cogitation* and having an *ideal apprehension* of an object of thought.[7] Much of our thinking consists of the former type, mere cogitation. This is basically where we employ a shorthand symbol in the flow of our reasoning to handle objects of thought. Thus, when thinking of God's attribute of "goodness," I do not muster the concept of goodness up in full view of my mind, a process that would take too long to accomplish in the course of reading or conversing. Rather, I utilize a symbol for it which has the benefit of speeding up the reasoning process but unfortunately yields only a vague, shadowy form of knowledge. Mere cogitation, Edwards concludes, is not what the Bible refers to when it speaks of knowing God.[8] Edwards identifies a higher form of knowing with the term "ideal apprehension." This occurs when we entertain the real ideal of the object of thought in the mind. When we "apprehend" an idea this way, that idea is actually "repeated" in the mind such that we can say a representation of divine "goodness" is *in* the mind when we reflect deeply on it. "Persons can't have actual ideas of mental things *without having those very things in the mind*."[9]

Knowing God, however, is not merely having an ideal apprehension of God because Edwards notes that there are two different forms of ideal apprehension: speculative and sensible. *Speculative* ideal apprehension is a fancy term for speculation or "head knowledge," where one's knowing does not incorporate the motions of the will. *Sensible* ideal apprehension moves beyond head knowledge to involve the will. The object apprehended by the mind is either beautiful, drawing us toward it in love or delight, or it is repulsive, leading us away from it out of distaste or hatred. Edwards termed this apprehension the "sense of the heart," a form of knowledge that involves the whole person: mind, understanding, and will.[10]

Interestingly, Edwards is not done at this point in his quest to identify the nature of true spiritual knowledge of God. Many religiously pious individuals, he maintained,

---

[5] See above, Michael J. McClymond, "Edwards Against Himself? Conflicting Appeals to the Writings of Jonathan Edwards During the 1990s Pentecostal-Charismatic Revivals in Toronto and Pensacola," 177–79.
[6] Edwards, "Miscellany 782," *WJE* 18:452–66. The full title of the entry is "Ideas. Sense of the Heart. Spiritual Knowledge or Conviction. Faith." Edwards composed this entry sometime in early 1739.
[7] Ibid., 458.
[8] Ibid., 452–57.
[9] Ibid., 459 (emphasis added).
[10] Ibid., 460.

can have authentic, "sense-of-the-heart" knowledge of God without truly knowing God in a Christian way. The natural moral sense that we are equipped with can foster a vast network of sensible knowledge of a religious nature. For instance, our natural sense of justice can lead us to fear divine punishment and live a moral life, or shout for joy when God moves to judge the oppressor and vindicate the oppressed. Similarly, our awareness of divine power when we ponder the Milky Way can generate deep feelings of awe and humility toward our Creator who sustains all things. Such sensible religious knowledge—knowledge that is a sense of the heart—is knowledge that is ultimately natural, accessible to nonbelievers, and possesses nothing of a saving nature in it. In fact, the religions of the world are filled with such knowledge.[11]

It is only when the mind possesses a sensible, ideal apprehension of "spiritual" objects—objects illuminated in the mind by the Holy Spirit himself—we have the basis for true, saving knowledge of God. The objects that Edwards speaks of here concern "divine things": the gospel, the condescension of God in giving his Son, Christ's work on the cross, the way of salvation via faith not works, the expansion of the gospel in the world through revival and missionary endeavors, and so on. When the saint knows, loves, and rejoices in these things, and when this knowledge overflows into a life of holiness and zealous fidelity to the triune God, then, according to Edwards, a person truly knows God in a saving way.[12]

This taxonomy of religious knowledge undergirds much of his public writings on the subject: his sermon on "A Divine and Supernatural Light" and sections of the *Religious Affections* draw from his meditations on the sense of the heart in "Miscellanies" no. 782. Now, certainly there are elements here that have the earmarks of eighteenth-century philosophy and theology. But is there anything that can be retrieved here to help Pentecostals today as they construct their theology of religious experience? It seems to me that a major task for Pentecostals, as for most evangelical theologians who appreciate "New Light" revivalism, concerns the way we articulate this distinction between the latter two forms of knowledge Edwards described above: affective knowledge of God's natural attributes (his greatness), which non-Christians can have, and affective knowledge of his moral attributes (his excellency), which is unique to Christians. Did Edwards overthink this distinction, arguing too many people out of the Kingdom of God? Or did he capture something of the way Scripture speaks of how Christians uniquely know God? I would be eager to see what pentecostal Edwards scholars have to say in answering questions like these for it seems that Edwards is a wonderful resource who can help inspire twenty-first-century Pentecostals in their theology, spirituality, and Christian practice.

---

[11] Edwards develops these ideas in several places in his writings. First, see the way he categorizes the divine attributes between God's natural attributes (attributes of power, omniscience, greatness, etc., which non-Christians can know sensibly) and his moral attributes (attributes related to holiness, moral excellency, love, and grace, which only Christians can sensibly know in a salvific way); Edwards, *Religious Affections*, WJE 2:256. Also, see Edwards' related discussions of secondary beauty, self-love, and natural conscience in Edwards, *Dissertation II. The Nature of True Virtue*, WJE 8:561–608.

[12] Edwards, "Miscellany 782," WJE 18:462–63.

Edwards' "dynamic" theism and pentecostal theology

Sang Hyun Lee's interpretation of Edwards' philosophical theology, known as "dispositional ontology," has exerted a profound influence on Edwards interpreters in the last generation. We see this fact in several of the chapters contained in this volume.[13] At the risk of oversimplification, Lee argued that Edwards developed a modern understanding of the divine being, one that pointed beyond classical theism with its emphasis on the infinite actualization of a static divine essence.[14] By contrast, Edwards, says Lee, noted how God's being was disposed to an infinite and eternal replication of a prior ontological fullness, a fact which is expressed by God in a twofold manner: first in God's trinitarian being (i.e., the Son is the infinite repetition/generation of the divine being's thinking of itself and the Spirit is the infinite repetition of the Father's and the Son's mutual love for each other) and second through God's decision to create the world. Divine being, in other words, is "dispositional," not static, for it necessarily seeks further repetition and communication of its inherent fullness within and beyond God's nature.

Dispositional ontology underscores the dynamism inherent in Edwards' portrait of the divine nature. God is not static. Dynamism and inter-relationality are necessary to his being in such a way that allows for a genuine relationship between Creator and creature. Scholars have employed Lee's insights to make several interesting suggestions, a few of which surface here in this volume. Joshua Reichard, for instance, notes how Edwards' metaphysics was a possible forerunner to a process-relational theology we see surfacing in the work of Charles Hartshorne and Alfred North Whitehead.[15] Tony Richie notes how scholars have observed how Edwards' dispositional metaphysic may suggest the possibility of salvation for the unevangelized and those who have never heard the gospel.[16]

Whether Edwards would have affirmed these suggestions or whether he would have recognized "dispositional ontology" as an accurate interpretation of his views are questions that are beyond the scope of this response chapter. I merely want to point out two simple facts. The first is that Edwards' reflections on divine ontology do indeed showcase a God who is fundamentally relational, deeply interactive, and powerfully dynamic in his engagement with his people. It is thus no surprise that Pentecostals have discovered in Edwards a kindred spirit and a fellow pilgrim for he gives voice to a vivid and powerful spirituality with which Pentecostals can readily identify.

---

[13] The essays by Joshua Reichard, David J. Courey, Gerald R. McDermott, and Edmund J. Rybarczyk all interact with Lee's work to varying degrees.

[14] For further study of Sang Hyun Lee's thesis, consult his magisterial monograph *The Philosophical Theology of Jonathan Edwards* (Princeton, NJ: Princeton University Press, 1988). For a more accessible summary of Lee's thesis, see Sang Hyun Lee, "Jonathan Edwards' Dispositional Conception of the Trinity: A Resource for Contemporary Reformed Theology," in *Toward the Future of Reformed Theology: Tasks, Topics, Traditions*, ed. David Willis and Michael Welker (Grand Rapids, MI: Eerdmans, 1999), 444–55.

[15] Reichard, "Divine Action and Divine Affections," 62.

[16] See above, Tony Richie, "'The Grand Design of God in All Divine Operations': Pentecostal Retrieval of Jonathan Edwards' Distinctive Contribution to the Positive Significance of Non-Christian Religions," 223–25.

Second, it is important to note that Edwards developed this view of God squarely within the confines of his tradition, however we identify it (Puritan, Reformed, early Evangelical, etc.). While he undoubtedly was a highly creative theologian, his positions were generally consistent with the wider vistas of his own thought and his evangelical tradition. This is important to note because the dynamic, relational God that Edwards describes is not one that he discovered by going outside his immediate tradition; he found it through a creative engagement from within it.

The upshot of this for the task of the historical theologian should be clear. While it might be informative to identify theological "echoes" that reverberate between Edwards' writings and more progressive theological positions (like process theism or wider-hope theories for the unevangelized), I would argue that it is perhaps more fruitful first to explore the immediate backgrounds to Edwards' dispositional ontology. His immediate theological predecessors, the evangelical revivals of the First Great Awakening, and his Puritan devotional heritage all created a rich context that informed the dynamic theological ontology Edwards articulated. That milieu shaped Edwards, and that milieu funded the later evangelical theological tradition of which Pentecostalism is a part. It is thus prudent and wise as a historical theologian to interpret Edwards with one eye squarely upon his immediate evangelical heritage, for my hunch is that his views, while creative, reveal more continuity with his immediate theological tradition than is sometimes acknowledged. Reichard's point is well said: "A creative reading of Edwards . . . can (and should) stay within the bounds of broad Christian orthodoxy."[17] With this in mind, I wholeheartedly encourage pentecostal philosophical theologians to continue to engage Edwards' rich theological ontology. There is so much there, and possibly much more to be mined!

Edwards, the Trinity, and pentecostal spirituality

Another topic of similar interest between Edwards and pentecostal scholars concerns the way both have tried to address a perceived deficit in pneumatology in the Christian tradition. For over a century Pentecostals have addressed this by directing attention to the extraordinary manifestations of Spirit's work in the Christian community and to its dramatic results: glossolalia, prophesy, healing, and other charismatic phenomena. Pentecostal scholars have tried to address this problem by countering cessationism and developing a robust theology of the Spirit's operations in the church. Some, like Studebaker and others in this volume, have dug deeper, identifying the problem with a defective understanding of the Trinity that downplays the role of the Holy Spirit both *ad intra* and *ad extra*.

Edwards similarly thought that part of this pneumatological deficit lay in a defective Trinitarianism and theology of sanctification. "If we suppose no more than used to be supposed about the Holy Ghost, the concern of the Holy Ghost in the work of redemption is not equal with the Father's and the Son's, nor is there an equal part of

---

[17] Reichard, "Divine Action and Divine Affections," 67.

the glory of this work belongs to him."[18] To understand the Holy Spirit as the one who merely applies the work of Christ's redemptive benefits to his people "is but a little thing" when compared with the grandeur of Christ's great sacrifice.

As several essays in *Pentecostal Theology and Jonathan Edwards* have noted, Edwards' solution to this theological imbalance was to re-envision the person of the Holy Spirit as *the* gift of God's love to the world—essentially, *the* communion of the triune fellowship sent to believers as an affective, holy relation who indwells the souls of the redeemed, inspiring holy affections for God and Christ. By making this point, Edwards was attempting to establish a theological equality between the persons of the Son and the Spirit: the *price paid* in human redemption (rendered by Christ in his sacrificial work) and *that "thing" purchased* in redemption (the Holy Spirit given to believers) are of equal value to the Christian. "To be the love of God to the world is as much as for the Father and the Son to do so much from love to the world; and to be [the] thing purchased was as much as to be the price: the price, and the thing bought with that price, are equal."[19] To be sure, the way Edwards re-envisioned the Spirit as the relational nexus between the Father and the Son might run the risk of depersonalizing the third person of the Trinity, but this need not be the case. Indeed, Amos Yong speaks of the Holy Spirit in a very Edwardsean way when he writes that "the Spirit is the 'between' which enables creaturely relationality and human interrelationality."[20] This language is vintage Edwardsean Trinitarianism!

One challenge Edwards might pose to Pentecostals, based upon the contributions in this book, lies in the function and status of the intellect in the pentecostal world. While he championed the necessity of religious affectivity, he did believe that the affections can become untethered from the intellect resulting in the eclipse of sound reason in the life of the church. This was precisely his issue with the radical revivalist James Davenport during the First Great Awakening.

Edwards believed that the doctrine of the Trinity has something vitally important to say to the question of the relationship between intellect and emotion in the Christian life. The key lies in the psychological analogy of the Trinity. While theologians today find inadequacies in the Augustinian psychological model, Edwards found it both serviceable and illuminative of his overall biblical theology. The triune God—understood as the divine *mind* and its two modes of operation, the *understanding* and the *affection* or will—is necessarily constituted in such a way that the three divine persons, equal in every way, form an eternal society that is nonetheless structured in an identifiable order. The divine mind (i.e., the Father) eternally reflects upon and rejoices in his own excellency, a process that yields two other divine persons in accordance with the two modes of operation inherent in the divine mind: (1) the subsistence of the *divine understanding* (i.e., the *Logos*, or Son) who is eternally generated through the Father's self-reflection and (2) the subsistence of the *divine will* (i.e., the *agape* of God,

---

[18] Edwards, *Discourse on the Trinity*, WJE 21:137.
[19] Ibid., 137–38.
[20] Amos Yong, *The Cosmic Breath: Spirit and Nature in the Christianity-Buddhism-Science Trialogue*, Philosophical Studies in Science and Religion 4 (Leiden: Brill, 2011), 191, as cited by Reichard, "Divine Action and Divine Affections," 66.

or the Holy Spirit) who is the personal love of the Godhead eternally breathed forth between Father and Son.[21]

While deity subsists fully and equally in each of the three, this does not eliminate the divine order that obtains among them. The Son, equal in glory and honor to the Father, is second in order to the Father since the understanding is a secondary operation of mind (both in God and in humanity). As the personalized divine understanding, the Son is thus uniquely suited to be the one who communicates knowledge of God to the world. The Spirit, also equal in glory and honor to both the Father and the Son, is third in order, since will is a tertiary operation of mind that presupposes both mind and its understanding. As the personalized divine affection, the Holy Spirit is uniquely suited to be the communication of divine love to the world.

The result of this is that, for Edwards, the Spirit performs a self-effacing ministry, highlighting the excellency, person, and work of the Son. This is because Edwards maintained that "affectivity"—emotion, will, love, and so on—is always meant to have an intellectual reference point. In other words, emotions "fire" only in respect to some object known to the understanding. "Such is the nature of man, that nothing can come at the heart but through the door of the understanding: and there can be no spiritual knowledge of that of which there is not first a rational knowledge."[22] Edwards affirmed this not because he was an intellectual imperialist who thought that the head should have dominance over the heart, but because the very structure of the Trinity led him to this conclusion. The understanding is prior to the affections in the psychological order because the Son (as the divine understanding) is prior to the Spirit (the divine affection) in the immanent Trinity. Or as he put it "the understanding must be considered as prior in the order of nature to the will or love or act, both in creature and in the Creator."[23]

As we apply these insights to the chapters in this volume, Edwards would no doubt be encouraged by the pentecostal emphasis on religious affectivity. Yet he probably would have had concerns about the way some statements call into the question the solid connection between pentecostal experience and theological reflection. Are spiritual experiences in the Spirit "ineffable?" Do "power encounters evade full rational disclosure"? Are they "better felt than telt?"[24] If so, then how can Christians test the spirits (1 Jn 4:1) or "weigh" and "pass judgment" on what is prophesied (1 Cor. 14:29)? To be sure, Edwards did struggle with finding language that articulates the subtleties of religious experience. But he nonetheless plowed forward to find such language out of a commitment to unite the head and the heart. Without that, Edwards feared that the church could be lost in the "enthusiasm" he identified among some of the radical revivalists of his day.

To avoid this potential pitfall Edwards believed that we must honor the ontological order inherent in the Trinity. This essentially consists in affirming the priority of

---

[21] Edwards, *Discourse on the Trinity*, WJE 21:113–22.
[22] Edwards, *The Importance and Advantage of a Thorough Knowledge of Divine Truth*, WJE 22:88.
[23] Edwards, *Discourse on the Trinity*, WJE 21:134; see also Edwards, *Religious Affections*, WJE 2:266 and McClymond's quote above (p. 247).
[24] See Courey's excellent essay, "Discerning the Signs of the Spirit: Pentecostal Experience Engages Edwardsian Religious Affections," 75–76, where he cites several authors who note the ineffability of pentecostal religious experience.

the understanding to the will, love, or act in the order of nature. Such would keep a knowledge of Christ the Son in constant view, a knowledge that, if "affected" by the Spirit, would envelope the redeemed soul in joy and love, just as it does *ad intra* within the Godhead.

Conclusion

Before working through *Pentecostal Theology and Jonathan Edwards*, I had not previously come across the name of Daniel Warren Kerr and his fitting phrase—"facts on fire"—meant to encapsulate a particular attitude toward knowledge of the Bible, knowledge that is not merely intellectual but ablaze with the life of the Holy Spirit.[25] It seems that if there was a theologian whose writings embodied this ideal, it would be Edwards. The Northampton pastor spent the greater portion of his life trying to set the facts of Scripture on fire in his preaching and writing not only because he believed them to be true but also because he encountered them in the Spirit, and experienced their divinity and excellency. As pentecostal theology continues to mature, I would only expect its theologians to engage more and more with a broader range of voices from across the spectrum of church history. Yet I would not be surprised to find them coming back to Edwards time and again for fresh insight, challenge, and inspiration. After all, you never really graduate from Edwards; no one ever does!

---

[25] Oliverio, "True Religion, in Great Part, Consists of Holy Affections," 35.

Contributors

Robert W. Caldwell III (PhD, Trinity Evangelical Divinity School) is Associate Professor of Church History at Southwestern Baptist Theological Seminary, Fort Worth, Texas, and has published a number of books, including two on Jonathan Edwards.

David J. Courey (PhD, McMaster Divinity College) is Lecturer at Continental Theological Seminary, Brussels, Belgium, and at Evangelische Theologische Faculteit, Leuven, Belgium, as well as Adjunct Faculty at McMaster Divinity College, Hamilton, Ontario, and is the author of *What Has Wittenberg to do with Azusa? Luther's Theology of the Cross and Pentecostal Triumphalism*.

Oliver D. Crisp (PhD, University of London; DLitt, University of Aberdeen) is Professor of Analytic Theology in the Logos Institute, School of Divinity, University of St Andrews. He has authored or edited over two dozen theological texts, including many on Jonathan Edwards.

Andrew K. Gabriel (PhD, McMaster Divinity College) is Vice President of Academics and Associate Professor of Theology at Horizon College and Seminary, an affiliated college of the University of Saskatchewan, Canada, and the author of *The Lord Is the Spirit* and *Barth's Doctrine of Creation*, among other books.

James M. Henderson (PhD, Regent University) is Assistant Professor of Biblical Studies and Christian Ministry at Regent University, Virginia Beach, Virginia, has published articles on the work of the Holy Spirit in justification and sanctification, and regularly presents papers at meetings of the Society for Pentecostal Studies.

Michael J. McClymond (PhD, University of Chicago) is Professor of Modern Christianity at Saint Louis University, and is the author or editor of many books, including *Encyclopedia of Religious Revivals in America*, 2 vols., *Theology of Jonathan Edwards* (which won the 2012 *Christianity Today* Book of the Year in Theology/Ethics), *The Wiley-Blackwell Companion to World Christianity* (2016), and *The Devil's Redemption: A New History and Interpretation of Christian Universalism*, 2 vols.

Gerald R. McDermott (PhD, University of Iowa) is Anglican Chair of Divinity at Beeson Divinity School, Birmingham, Alabama, and has written, coauthored, and edited at least six books and scores of articles on Jonathan Edwards, among many of his other publications.

L. William Oliverio, Jr. (PhD, Marquette University) is Associate Academic Dean at SUM Bible College and Theological Seminary, El Dorado Hills, California, the author of *Theological Hermeneutics in the Classical Pentecostal Tradition: A Typological Account* along with other articles and reviews, and has served as Philosophy Interest Group Leader of the Society for Pentecostal Studies since 2008.

Amy Plantinga Pauw (PhD, Yale University) is Henry P. Mobley Jr. Professor of Doctrinal Theology at Louisville Presbyterian Theological Seminary, Louisville, Kentucky, has served on the editorial board for the Yale University Works of Jonathan Edwards series, and has published many books on Jonathan Edwards and other topics.

Joshua D. Reichard (PhD, University of the Western Cape) is the Vice-President of Academic Affairs at Valley Christian Schools, Youngstown, Ohio, with interdisciplinary scholarship in a wide range of journals, including the *American Journal of Theology and Philosophy*, *Zygon: Journal of Religion and Science*, *Journal of Interdisciplinary Studies*, *Journal of Pentecostal Theology*, *Journal of Education & Christian Belief*, *Wesleyan Theological Journal*, *Religious Education*, and *Process Studies*, among others.

Tony Richie (PhD, London School of Theology/Middlesex University; DMin, Asbury Theological Seminary) is Adjunct Professor of Historical and Systematic Theology, Pentecostal Theological Seminary, Cleveland, Tennessee, and the author of many articles and several books, including *Toward a Pentecostal Theology of Religions: Encountering Cornelius Today* and *Speaking by the Spirit: A Pentecostal Model of Interreligious Dialogue*.

Edmund J. Rybarczyk (PhD, Fuller Theological Seminary) is a Christian podcaster and the author of several journal articles and a number of books including *Beyond Salvation: Eastern Orthodoxy and Classical Pentecostalism on Becoming Like Christ*, *The Spirit Unfettered: Protestant Views on the Holy Spirit*, and *For Him Who Has Eyes to See: Beauty in the History of Theology*.

Christopher A. Stephenson (PhD, Marquette University) is Assistant Professor of Systematic Theology at Lee University, Cleveland, Tennessee, the author of *Types of Pentecostal Theology: Method, System, Spirit* and articles in *Journal of Ecumenical Studies*, *Journal of Pentecostal Theology*, *Religion Compass*, and *Istina*, and is writing another monograph for OUP tentatively titled *Redeeming Rituals*, which explores the intersections among systematic, spiritual, liturgical, and ecumenical theology.

Lisa P. Stephenson (PhD, Marquette University) is Associate Professor of Systematic Theology at Lee University, Cleveland, Tennessee, with articles published in various journals including *Pneuma*, *Journal of Church and State*, *Scottish Journal of Theology*, and *Religions*, and other edited volumes, and the author of *Dismantling the Dualisms for American Pentecostal Women in Ministry*.

Steven M. Studebaker (PhD, Marquette University) is Professor of Historical and Systematic Theology, Howard and Shirley Bentall Chair in Evangelical Thought at McMaster Divinity College, McMaster University, Hamilton, Ontario, and the author and editor of several books, including *From Pentecost to the Triune God* and *The Trinitarian Theology of Jonathan Edwards*.

Angela Tarango (PhD, Duke University) is Associate Professor of Religion at Trinity University, San Antonio, Texas, and has published *Choosing the Jesus Way: American Indian Pentecostals and the Fight for the Indigenous Principle*.

Amos Yong (PhD, Boston University) is Professor of Theology and Mission and Director of the Center for Missiological Research at Fuller Theological Seminary, Pasadena, California, and has authored or edited over four dozen volumes.

Index

action, divine   51, 54–62
aesthetics   81, 103–4, 252
affections   16–17, 31–2, 36–7, 269
   divine   62–7
   holy   71–2, 74
   religious   11, 13, 241, 256–7, 263, 268
Albrecht, Daniel   78
Alexander, Corky   208
Alexander, Estrelda   38
Allen, R. Michael   129 n.16, 131 n.31, 135 n.65
Allen, Roland   206
Althouse, Peter   47
amillennialism   240
analogia agapē   36
analogia entis   37
analogia fidei   37
analogy   116–17
   psychological   88, 91, 263
Anderson, Allan   206
anthropology, philosophical   233
apocalypticism   79–81, 239, 243
apologetics   113, 215
apophatic tradition   76
apostasy   239
Aquinas, Thomas   44, 91, 158 n.25, 189 n.44
Argue, A. H.   80
Arianism   107
Arminianism   7, 14, 28, 107, 112, 127, 137, 212, 220, 224, 259–60, 262
Arnott, John   47
Athanasius   100
atonement   103–7
attributes
   communication of   105
   divine   116, 125–6
Augustine   18, 72, 85–93, 100, 104, 116, 120, 139, 158 n.25, 192, 241, 251, 262, 268
Augustine, Daniela C.   13 n.55
Azusa Street Revival   8, 24–5, 157

Ball, Henry   206
Balthasar, Hans Urs von   104
Barth, Karl   91, 106–7, 121
beatific vision   72–4, 79–80
beauty   114, 181–7, 191–4, 251
Bell, E. N.   157
Berkeley, George   75
Berkhofer, Robert J.   207 n.53
Bezzant, Rhys   152
Bolt, John   242
Bombaro, John   54, 61
Bonaventure   88, 190 n.49
bond of love   100, 116, 122, *see also* mutual love
book of nature   29
Borg, Marcus   192 n.53
Bracken, Joseph   65–6
Brainerd, David   15, *see also Life of David Brainerd*
Bray, Gerald   214
Brown, Peter   223 n.100
Brown, Robert   29
Bryant, M. Darrol   232–4, 236, 241–2
Bush, Michael   109

Caldwell III, Robert W.   7, 102, 117, 122, 188 n.35
Calvin, John   128, 131, 145, 189 n.44
Calvinism   1, 6, 28, 54, 204, 211–12, 260
   New   249
Catch the Fire   48
certainty, epistemic   5
cessationism   81, 160 n.34, 172, 174, 253–4, 258
Chai, Leon   5
Chan, Simon   37, 63
charismatics   44
Charity and Its Fruit   152–4, 173
Chauncy, Charles   68–9
Cherry, Conrad   4
Chevreau, Guy   68–70, 81, 165–6
Christendom   237, 239

Christianity, global 6
citizenship, theology of 236
civil society, theology of 236
Cobb, John 53, 61 n.42, 63
colonialism 237, 240
community, philosophy of 234
complexity 65
Confucius 215
Congar, Yves 121 n.29
Conkin, Paul K. 231 n.20
Constantinianism 28
constitutionalism 23 n.2
conviction, spiritual 42
Courey, David 256
Craig, Phillip A. 70
creatio ex nihilo 51, 57
creation 54, 59, 252
    continuous 62, 64
Crisp, Oliver D. 4–6, 36 n.74, 52, 61–2, 67, 125, 212, 227–45
Crocco, Stephen D. 2

Danaher, William J. 4
Daniel, Steven H. 5
Davenport, James 69, 268
DeArteaga, William 69
decisionism 259–60
Deism 215 n.39
deists 28
de Lubac, Henri 140, 145
demonization 226
depravity, human 240 n.47
determinism 29, 51, 62
devil 170–1, 202, 256
Dewey, John 187
dialogue, interreligious 224, 226
dipolarism 55
discernment, spiritual 18, 112–14, 166–7, 175–6, 178, 263–4
Discourse on the Trinity 88–9 nn.9–11, 262
dispensationalism 80, 228–30, 244, 262
dispositions 23, 262
Distinguishing Marks of a Work of the Spirit of God 1, 32 n.55, 70, 112, 165, 167, 173
"Divine and Supernatural Light, A" 26, 29, 265
Duffield, Guy P. 136–7, 142–4, 146

Dunn, James D. G. 140 n.114
Dyrness, William A. 182 n.8

Easton, Richard 165
Ecclesiastical Writings 152
Edwards, Sarah 249, 257
egalitarianism 209, 236
election, divine 14
Elwood, Douglas 182
emanation 190, 192
embodiment 73, 78–9, 81, 105, 257–9
emotions 73, 78, 138, 169, 257, 269
empiricism, radical 64
End for Which God Created the World, The 53, 55, 239, 241–2
Enlightenment 5, 29, 77, 191 n.51, 250, 258
enthusiasm 63, 66, 160, 200, 238, 250, 269
epistemology 25
Epperly, Bruce 63
Erdt, Terrence 3
Ervin, Howard 121
eschatology 79–81, 227, 229–30, 233, 243
essentialism 61
ethnocentrism 202–4, 208–9, 236
evangelicals 7
evangelism 113, 226
evangelization 209
excellency, divine 27, 42
experience
    psychology of religious 73
    religious 262–3
    of the Spirit 15, 34
    spiritual 10, 35
experientialism 63–4

Faithful Narrative of the Surprising Work of God, A 1, 31, 112, 167, 174–5, 177
Farewell Sermon 235
fellowship 93, 268
filioque 88, 90, 110, 120–3
Finished Work Pentecostalism 119, 136–7, 143–6
Finney, Charles G. 14, 112, 259
Fischer, Linford 202
Fivefold Gospel 230
forensic declaration 130–3

forensics 127–9, 260
foundationalism 25, 250
freedom 56
Freedom of the Will 1, 3, 262
free will 14, 29, 51, 126, 144
Full Gospel 135
fundamentalism 10, 215
futurism 243

Gabriel, Andrew 259
Gadamer, Hans-Georg 31, 34
Gause, R. Hollis 137–9, 142, 144
Gelpi, Donald L. 65
Gerstner, John 7, 238 n.42
gifts 18, 95–6, 100, 114, 159, 192, 205, 257
  charismatic 162, 172–7, 253
  extraordinary 154–5, 160–2, 173, 258
  miraculous 67, 154, 156
globalization 10
glossolalia 34, 47, 50, 78, 97, 161, 204, 258, 267
God Glorified in Man's Dependence 1, 262
"God is Infinitely Strong" 203
goodness, divine 87
grace
  experience of 99
  prevenient 60, 137, 224
  theology of 93–6
Great Awakening, First 13, 69, 167–8, 176, 208, 211, 232, 240, 249, 267
Great Commandment 160
Great Commission 79, 193
Gregory of Nazianzus 107
Guelzo, Allen C. 3–4

habits 23
habitus 147
Hall, Richard A. S. 232, 234–5, 240, 242
Hanegraaff, Hank 174–5
Hansen, Colin 6
happiness 87
  divine 7
Hart, D. G. 7
Hart, Larry D. 124
Hartshorne, Charles 54, 56 n.17, 57, 266
Hastings, W. Ross 6–7, 102, 106–7

Hatch, Nathan O. 4
Hauerwas, Stanley 245 n.62
Hawkins, Larycia 221 n.90
Haykin, Michael A. G. 7, 69
Heimert, Alan 232–3, 235, 240, 242
hell 260
Helm, Paul 6–7, 62
Henderson, James M. 263
Henry, Matthew 28 n.28
hermeneutics 30
  pentecostal 32–8
  spiritual 34
hesychasm 142 n.124
heterodoxy 54
historical criticism 250
history
  intellectual 4
  philosophical 103
  redemptive 23 n.2
History of the Work of Redemption, A 28, 80, 199, 211, 217, 226, 233
Hodge, Charles 11
Hodges, Melvin 207
Holifield, E. Books 28 n.28
holiness 124–6
Hollenweger, Walter J. 98, 205
Holm, Randall 77
Holmes, Stephen R. 4, 6, 52, 103–4, 125
Holy Spirit 118, 249, 254, 265, 269
  baptism in the 119, 137, 140, 145–6, 157, 230
  and beauty 188–91
  indwelling 133–5, 139, 189
hope 243
Humble Attempt 112, 234–5, 238
Humble Inquiry 234–5
hypostatic union 102, 105

idealism 29, 61, 111, 117, 128
  Platonic 236
imaginary, social 259
imagination 27, 37, 169, 190, 191, 243
  pneumatological 193
immanence 77
imputation 127–8, 145
incarnation 18, 77, 91–2, 96, 102–7, 109, 114, 187, 216–17, 252
ineffability 269 n.24

infusion   134
internationalism   234, 236, 238, 240, 242
intersubjectivity   65
Islam   220-3

Jacobsen, Douglas G.   76, 98 n.40
James, Henry   178
James, William   174
Jenkins, Philip   10
Jenson, Robert W.   4, 105, 127
John of Damascus   107
Jonathan Edwards Center   8
Judaism   222-3
Julian of Norwich   45-6
justice   114
  social   229
justification   93-4, 100

Kärkkäinen, Veli-Matti   98 n.40, 120, 135, 145
Keating, Thomas   50
kenosis   59
Kerr, Daniel Warren   17, 35-6, 270
kingdom of God   24, 233, 239, 265
knowledge
  affective   265
  rational   128
  religious   263-7
  speculative   264
koinonia   122
Kristeller, Paul Oskar   182 n.8
Küng, Hans   140
Kuyper, Abraham   181, 242

Land, Steven J.   13, 24, 36, 75, 211
Lane, Belden C.   57, 65
Latter Rain   79
Lee, Sang Hyun   4-5, 52-4, 59-63, 67, 72, 79, 110, 189, 214, 266
liberalism   3, 10
libertarianism   212
liberty, human   212
Life of David Brainerd, The   15, 74, 198 n.6, 233-5
literal sense   31
Locke, John   29, 75
Lombard, Peter   49-50
Lossky, Vladimir   140
Louie, Kin Yip   182

love   23, 43, 117-18, 122-4, 152-7, 159
  baptism of   161
  divine   87
  principle of   90
Lovelace, Richard   7, 169, 178
Lucas, Sean Michael   213
Luce, Alice   206
Luther, Martin   140, 189 n.44

MacArthur, John   69, 166, 172, 174-5
Macchia, Frank D.   14, 66, 96, 98-101, 116, 120-2, 135, 139, 142-3, 145-7, 158, 160, 205, 259
McClymond, Michael   5-6, 23, 26, 28, 32 n.55, 35, 67, 77, 102, 115, 183 n.14, 188 n.35, 237 n.41, 249, 252 n.11, 257-8, 263
McDermott, Gerald R.   5-7, 23, 26, 28, 32 n.55, 35, 67, 72, 77, 115, 182, 183 n.14, 185 n.28, 188 n.35, 199, 213-15, 217, 232, 235-6, 237 n.41, 240, 242, 249, 251, 260
McGee, Gary B.   205
McHale, Gary W.   69
McPherson, Amy Semple   80
Maddox, Randy   65
Mannermaa, Tuomo   145
Marsden, George M.   6, 28-9, 214-15
Martin, Lee Roy   37-9
Mason, Charles Harrison   34, 36
materialism   25, 61
meditation   44-6
Mencius   215
Menzies, Robert P.   36, 97, 119
Menzies, William W.   119
messages, prophetic   173
metaphysics   61
  dispositional   223 n.97
  essentialist   251
  substance   61
method, analogical   58
millennialism   28, 235-8, 240-1, 243-4
Miller, Perry   2-4, 6-7, 231-2
missiology   193
missionary   237, 240
missions   113, 201-2, 206-8
  history of   108
Mitchell, Louis   183, 188

models of Trinity
  mutual love   88
  psychological   89
  social   89
modernism   3
modernity, late   76
monergism   52, 56
monotheism   220–1
Moody, Josh   6–7, 128 n.7, 131 n.32
Morimoto, Anri   4, 132, 213–14
Mozart, Wolfgang Amadeus   114
mutual love   117, 122, 192, *see also* bond of love
mysticism   128–9

narrative   224
nationalism   234, 236
naturalism   25
nature, book of   29
nature, theology of   193 n.57
Nature of True Grace, The   1, 233
Nature of True Virtue, The   235, 239, 241, 255
Needham, Nick   69
Neumann, Peter D.   76
New Divinity   252
New Lights   31, 69, 265
Nichols, Stephen J.   7, 239 n.44
Niebuhr, H. Richard   2–3

objectivity   75–7
occasionalism   60, 62
Old Lights   31, 68–9, 265
Oliverio Jr., L. William   250, 255–6, 263
ontology   251
  dispositional   51–2, 54, 58–60, 63, 72, 213, 251, 266
  dynamic   214
  relational   86–8
Oord, Thomas J.   59–60
open theism   54
orality   224
ordo salutis   97
"Original Sin"   237 n.40
Orthodoxy, Eastern   262
orthodoxy   7, 13, 15, 53–4, 60–2, 67, 69, 75, 93, 120, 255–6, 267
orthopathy   13, 33, 36, 75, 256
orthopraxy   13, 33, 75

Ortlund, Dane C.   133, 142
Owen, John   86 n.1, 106–7, 251

panentheism   6, 53, 56–7, 60–1, 215, 260
  pneumatological   192 n.53
Pannenberg, Wolfhart   92 n.22
Parrington, Vernon Louis   2
paternalism   207, 209
Pauw, Amy Plantinga   4, 89, 116, 188 n.35
peacemaking   229
Pearlman, Myer   36
Pentateuch   29–30, 35
Pentecost
  Day of   229–30, 241–2
  Spirit of   91–2
pentecostalization   242
perfection, divine   57
perichoresis   37, 107, 123
persuasion   66
Pinnock, Clark   76–7
Piper, John   7
pluralism   16, 215, 229, 230, 236, 242
Poloma, Margaret M.   161, 165 n.2, 176, 177 n.36, 258
Poole, Matthew   28 n.28
postmillennialism   28, 79, 237, 240
postmodernism   15
power   124
power encounter   82
practices, liturgical   249
praeparatio evangelica   216
pragmatism   202–4, 208–9
prayer   44–6
  soaking   46–8
predestination, double   255
premillennialism   36, 262
Presbyterians, Old School   255
pride, spiritual   171, 257
prisca theologia   30, 213
privatization   236
prophecy   241, 244–5
prosperity   244
Pseudo-Dionysius   190
Puritanism   12, 20, 28, 31, 57, 85–6, 89, 130, 181, 199, 267

Rahner, Karl   91
Ramabai, Pandita   9

Ramsey, Paul 4
rationalism 5, 24, 33, 256
reason 185
redemption 107–8
  economy of 91, 96, 153
  history of 109, 198
reform, social 240
Reformed tradition 117
regeneration 129, 136, 141, 146, 160
Reichard, Joshua D. 263, 266–7
relationships 187
relativism 215
religion 185 n.29
  false 219
  theology of 5, 218, 224–5
  true 29, 32, 218–19
Religious Affections 1, 3, 13, 24, 31–2, 34, 38, 40–4, 49 n.30, 69, 95, 112–13, 141, 165, 167, 169, 176, 235, 249, 252–3, 262
repentance 138
restorationism 174
revelation, typological 216
revival 14, 199, 209
  theology of 112
revivalism 12, 15, 63, 237–8, 240, 244, 259, 263
Richard of St. Victor 88
Richie, Tony 266
righteousness 130, 134
Robeck Jr., Cecil M. 33 n.57
Roman Catholicism 262
Rybarczyk, Edmund 259

Satan 170, 221–21, 223, 228, 257
satisfaction 103
science 61
self-communication 87
self-sufficiency, divine 55
"sense of the heart" 264
Seymour, William J. 8, 32, 36, 119, 157
Sherry, Patrick 104, 190
signs, negative 258
Silverman, David 201–2
Simonson, Harold P. 3
simplicity, divine 250
sin, original 29, 62, 255
"Sinners in the Hands of an Angry God" 89, 204, 249, 260

skeptics 28
slavery 48, 236
Smith, James K. A. 12 n.55, 33, 77–8, 257
Snyder, Howard 214
Society for Pentecostal Studies 11 n.55
Some Thoughts Concerning the Revival 32 n.55, 69, 112, 165, 167–8, 176, 238 n.42
soteriology 94
sovereignty, divine 212, 233
Spinoza, Baruch 252 n.11
Spirit baptism 13–14, 96–9, 159–60
spirituality 1, 7, 9, 13, 17, 19–20, 129
  pentecostal 17, 24, 33, 63, 75, 78–9, 161, 227–9, 263, 267–70
spiritual sense 31, 35
Spittler, Russ 180
Stein, Stephen J. 232 n.21, 238 n.43, 243 n.59
Stephens, Bruce M. 4
Stephenson, Christopher A. 249, 257
Stephenson, Lisa P. 258
Stockbridge 19, 197–204, 209, 213–14, 234, 239, 244
Storms, Sam 7, 64–5
Story, J. Lyle 139 n.100, 144 n.139, 146
Story, Ronald 5
Stout, Harry S. 4
Strobel, Kyle C. 7
Stronstad, Roger 36
Studebaker, Steven M. 102, 105, 111, 117, 133 n.46, 134, 140 n.110, 144 n.138, 177 n.35, 183 n.13, 184 n.20, 189, 251, 255, 259
subjectivism 5
subjectivity 75–7, 81
suffering 60
Supreme Harmony of All, The 89
Sweeney, Douglas A. 7

Tarango, Angela 258–9
taste 41, 128–9, 142, 181 n.2
teleology 79–81, 129, 218, 236–7, 239, 241–3
Teresa of Avila 45, 249
testimony 224
theologian
  analytic 262

liberal 262
New England 253
political 227
prophetic 240
public 231
of religious experience 249
theology
constructive 95
liberation 229
logocentric 256
natural 224
New England 252
philosophical 52, 65, 236, 243, 252, 266
political 228–31
progressive 15
Reformed 128
relational 52–62
spiritual 211
systematic 11, 16–17, 35, 120, 252, 260
theopolitics 245 n.62
theosis 140, 145, 250
Third Wave 8–9
Thomas, John Christopher 159 n.30
Tillich, Paul 158 n.25
Toronto Blessing 68, 70, 76
traditionalism 29, 35–6
traditioning 37
transcendence 77–9
transcendentalism 234
Treatise on Grace 110
Trinity 72, 117, 267–70
economic 85, 92
immanent 85, 92, 118, 269
typology 28, 250, 252

unevangelized 213, 266–7
unions 118
Unitarianism 107
unregenerate 26, 73, 134 n.62, 182, 189–90, 236

voluntarism 23 n.2
Vondey, Wolfgang 13 n.55, 33

Wagner, C. Peter 9
warfare, spiritual 112
Welker, Michael 63
Wesley, John 60, 64, 75, 135, 179, 223 n.101
Wesleyanism 210–12
Westphal, Merold 25
Wheeler, Rachel 197, 202, 237 n.40, 239 n.46, 240 n.47
Whitefield, George 1, 69, 184
Whitehead, Alfred North 54–5, 65, 266
Wilkinson, Michael 47
will, freedom of the 29
Wilson-Kastner, Patricia 116
Wimber, John 9, 68
Winiarski, Douglas 200
Winslow, Ola 2
Wolf, Matthew 77
worship 9, 66–7, 77–8, 81, 100, 157, 165, 187, 216, 221, 223, 253

Yoder, John Howard 245 n.62
Yong, Amos 12 n.55, 14, 36, 65–6, 96, 98–101, 116, 119–22, 124, 137, 140 n.114, 158, 160, 190 n.50, 192 n.53, 193, 225, 254, 258–9, 268

Zylla, Phil C. 5

www.ingramcontent.com/pod-product-compliance
Lightning Source LLC
Chambersburg PA
CBHW070020010526
44117CB00011B/1657